RUSSIAN PEASANT WOMEN WHO REFUSED TO MARRY

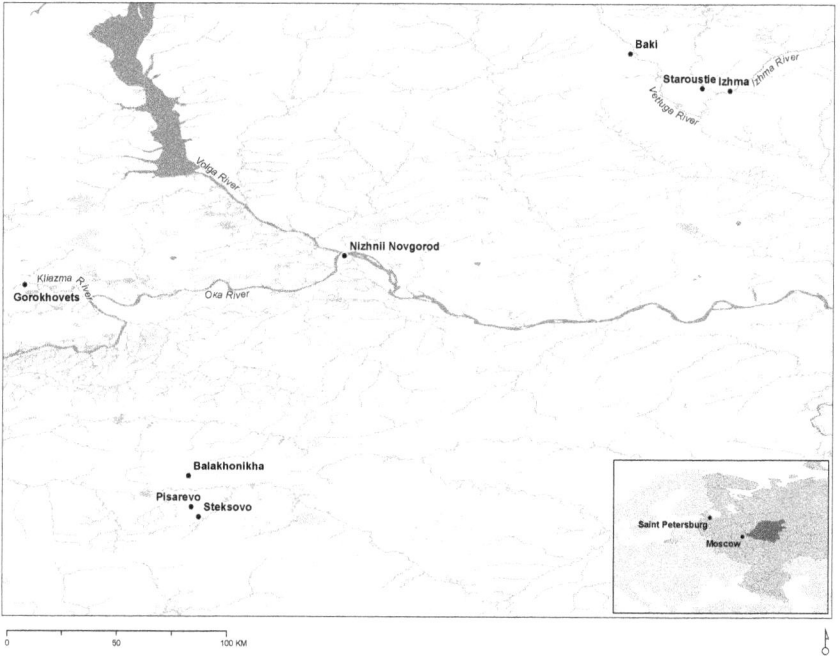

Map 0.1 North-Central European Russia, Case Study Sites.
Contains information from OpenStreetMap, which is made available at
https://www.openstreetmap.org under the Open Database License (ODbL).
Modified by Kelsey Rydland, licensed under CC BY-SA 2.0.

RUSSIAN PEASANT WOMEN WHO REFUSED TO MARRY

SPASOVITE OLD BELIEVERS IN THE EIGHTEENTH AND NINETEENTH CENTURIES

JOHN BUSHNELL

Indiana University Press

This book is a publication of

Indiana University Press
Office of Scholarly Publishing
Herman B Wells Library 350
1320 East 10th Street
Bloomington, Indiana 47405 USA

iupress.indiana.edu

Manufactured in the United States of America

Cataloging information is available from the Library of Congress.

ISBN 978-0-253-02965-2 (cloth)
ISBN 978-0-253-02996-6 (paperback)
ISBN 978-0-253-03013-9 (ebook)

1 2 3 4 5 22 21 20 19 18 17

CONTENTS

ABBREVIATIONS

GAIaO	Gosudarstvennyi arkhiv Iaroslavskoi oblasti
GAKO	Gosudarstvennyi arkhiv Kostromskoi oblasti
GANO No. 3	Gosudarstvennyi arkhiv Nizhegorodskoi oblasti No. 3
GARO	Gosudarstvennyi arkhiv Riazanskoi oblasti
GAVO	Gosudarstvennyi arkhiv Vladimirskoi oblasti
GIM OPI	Gosudarstvennyi Istoricheskii muzei, Otdel pis'mennykh istochnikov
IaGIAM	Iaroslavskii gosudarstvennyi istoriko-arkhitekturnyi muzei
LP	Lieven Papers, British Library
PSS	Polnoe sobranie sochinenii
PSZ	Polnoe sobranie zakonov
RGB OR	Rossiiskaia gosudarstvennaia biblioteka, Otdel rukopisei
RGADA	Rossiiskii gosudarstvennyi arkhiv drevnikh aktov
TsANO	Tsentral'nyi arkhiv Nizhegorodskoi oblasti
TsIAM	Tsentral'nyi istoricheskii arkhiv Moskvy

RUSSIAN PEASANT WOMEN WHO REFUSED TO MARRY

Introduction: What Is the Opposite of Eureka?

This study of Russian peasant women who would not marry emerged from two simultaneous, wholly unanticipated discoveries that raised a tangle of questions I could not answer. The discoveries came in a set of confession registers—household lists of parishioners who had and had not made the annual confession required of all Orthodox Russians. These particular registers were from Kuplia parish, a cluster of villages near the very small city of Gorokhovets in eastern Vladimir province. One discovery was demographic: in some of those villages in the late eighteenth century, a very high proportion of adult women never married. It is not uncommon to find one or two unmarried adult women in an eighteenth- or nineteenth-century Russian village, but it is just as likely that every single adult woman had married. The consensus among Russian historians and ethnographers is that Russian peasants practiced close to universal marriage. In Kuplia parish that was extravagantly not so. As of 1795, 44 percent of women twenty-five and over in the village of Sluchkovo had never married. Even that figure grossly understates the resistance of Sluchkovo women to marriage; tax census returns reveal that, of all the women born in the village who turned twenty-five between 1763 and 1795, fully 70 percent never married. The overwhelming majority of Sluchkovo wives had been imported from other villages by Sluchkovo men, almost all of whom married. Further investigation revealed that while Sluchkovo women almost certainly refused to marry at a higher rate than women in other villages in the area, a 20 to 40 percent rate of abstention among women native to their villages was common in that part of the Gorokhovets district in the late eighteenth century. Nothing that I had ever learned about Russian peasant marriage, or Russian peasant culture, anticipated or explained what I had discovered about marriage in Kuplia parish.

1

The same confession registers told me who the non-marrying women were: members of the Old Believer Spasovite covenant. That was a surprise on two counts. In the first place, Spasovites did not forbid marriage; indeed, they were notorious among Old Believers for marrying in Orthodox churches. In the second place, I had never before seen a confession register in which the priest identified the Old Believers in his parish by covenant. Many confession registers identify Old Believers (or, as the Orthodox Church called them, schismatics) generically. Priests provided that identification to explain why particular parishioners had skipped confession. In Kuplia parish, priests named Old Believer covenants from sometime before 1830 down to at least 1850. They were not required to do so, but the example of the first priest who named covenants was taken up by his successors. The Kuplia confession registers may not be unique in that way, but then again, they may be. That I had ordered volumes of confession registers that contained the Kuplia registers rather than confession registers from another section of the Gorokhovets district was a stroke of luck. Spasovites were notoriously difficult to identify, even at the time, because they masqueraded as Orthodox. They were baptized in the church, married in the church, and, before marrying, they confessed and took communion in the church. Parish priests generally listed them among the Orthodox. In Kuplia parish, however, Spasovites revealed their confessional identity to the local priest.

That the Old Believer women in Sluchkovo who did not marry were Spasovites added to the mystery rather than solving it. Spasovites were among the many Russians who rejected the textual and ritual reforms introduced by Patriarch Nikon (elevated 1652, abandoned office 1658, deposed 1667) and formally endorsed by a church council in Moscow in 1666. Those reforms caused turmoil in the Russian church. Opponents considered each and every one of them a heresy, the post-Nikonian Orthodox Church heretical, and in consequence the end times under way and the Antichrist perhaps already stalking the world. Unfortunately for the anti-reformists, while priests and monks were among their most important early leaders, no bishop joined. Because only bishops could ordain priests, when the last priest who had been ordained prior to Nikon's patriarchy died, the world would be— according to the most stringent, or logically consistent, Old Believers— bereft of priesthood, hence also without anyone to perform most of the sacraments. The exceptions were baptism and confession, both of which could, according to old rules of the Orthodox Church, be administered by laymen in an emergency, for instance, when no priest was available. These priestless Old Believers, as they were called, explicitly rejected marriage, there being no non-heretical priests to officiate. More pragmatic Old Believers accepted runaway Orthodox priests who abjured the Nikonian heresy and were ritually redeemed by anointment with myrrh. They came to be known as priested Old Believers, and they play almost no part in this story.

Spasovites had emerged as a distinct priestless covenant in the late seventeenth century and in some ways were more radical than other priestless covenants. They asserted that without priests, none of the sacraments, not even baptism and confession, could be administered; that God had withdrawn his grace from the world; and that there was no longer anything Christians could to do to work toward their own salvation. Down to at least 1730, they explicitly banned marriage. By the late eighteenth century, however, they had sharply revised their teaching on marriage: Spasovites could marry in Orthodox churches, and Orthodox priests could baptize their children. Because the Orthodox Church required a couple who were to be married to confess and take communion, Spasovite couples acted out those sacraments, too.[1] Spasovites continued to deny that Orthodox marriage, baptism, confession, and communion were actually sacraments, but evidently they did not believe—as most other Old Believers did—that they endangered their immortal souls when they accepted these non-sacraments from heretical (i.e., Orthodox) priests. Since priests considered anyone who accepted Orthodox sacraments to be Orthodox, they routinely recorded undeclared Spasovites as Orthodox in the confession registers.

There are very few sources on eighteenth-century Spasovites, and none of them (none from the nineteenth century, either) explain why Spasovites decided to permit marriage in Orthodox churches. Yet in this respect, Spasovites did not differ greatly from most other priestless covenants, which likewise gradually made their peace with marriage during the eighteenth and nineteenth centuries because they could not retain a large lay following if they rigorously enforced a ban. Priestless covenants that continued to reject marriage lost members to marrying covenants, and in both the eighteenth and nineteenth centuries, some covenants splintered over the issue of marriage. The Spasovites' acceptance of marriage during the eighteenth century, in other words, was part of a broader trend among the priestless. They alone, however, condoned the use of Orthodox priests to perform the marriage ceremony.

More puzzling is the fact that even as Spasovites accepted marriage by Orthodox priests, more and more Spasovite peasant women avoided marriage, and not just in Kuplia parish. Doctrine moved toward marriage; female practice moved away. Yet few nineteenth-century commentators on the Spasovites were even aware that large numbers of Spasovite women avoided marriage. In fact, I have found only one such source: an observant government official who noted that in one region there was an unusually large number of single Spasovite women. But that observation came without an explanation. In chapter 5, I offer what I think is a plausible interpretation of Spasovite women's choice not to marry: they did so out of despair at living in a world to which God was utterly indifferent. The evidence on that critical point is at best indirect and contextual. I admit, with regret, that I still cannot offer definitive answers to some of the questions that tumbled from the pages of the Kuplia confession registers.

Even in the absence of an explanation of Spasovite nuptial behavior, even if my own suppositions should prove to be erroneous, the demographic and social ramifications of exceptionally elevated abstention from marriage are clear. Spasovite households left a distinctive footprint in demographic sources. Theirs were women-accumulating households—unmarried sisters and daughters of the head, the wives of the head and his sons, sometimes the head's unmarried granddaughters, sometimes other female relatives who moved in after their own households collapsed. Many Russian peasant households disintegrated because of random demographic misfortune; Spasovite households with unmarried adult women courted collapse, and every collapsed household increased the demographic pressure on other households within which survivors took refuge. Spasovite marriage practice produced households and communities structured in a way that violated traditional Russian peasant survival strategies.

Spasovite nuptial behavior also produced tension in the surrounding peasant community. Given widespread resistance to marriage among Spasovite peasant women and almost universal marriage among Spasovite peasant men, where did the men get their wives? Except in the largest Russian villages, many or even most peasant men found their brides in other villages, within a search radius of around ten kilometers. That was the normal search radius for Kuplia parish men in the 1760s, just as large numbers of Spasovite women began to withdraw from the marriage market. By the late eighteenth century, they were searching farther than that—within a standard radius of fifteen kilometers and in individual cases considerably beyond—and they were often forced to buy serf women as brides, which they had rarely done before (Sluchkovo peasants themselves were not serfs). Since there were substantial numbers of Spasovite households (identifiable by the distinctive Spasovite household structure) in many of the villages close to Kuplia parish, we might conclude that in a district thick with Spasovites, the greater distance traveled to find brides, and the expense of purchasing serf brides, were problems the Spasovites had brought on themselves. We might even marvel at the success Spasovite men had in securing brides.

However, the Spasovites' nuptial conundrum was larger than the local imbalance between men and women willing to marry. They lived alongside peasants who were not Spasovites and who assumed that all peasants, men and women both, married. Peasants did recognize exceptions: a few women who suffered from physical and mental disabilities so severe that they could not carry out the household chores incumbent on a wife, a few women (Orthodox and Old Believers both) who did not marry because they felt they had a religious vocation. But most of the Spasovites' neighbors assumed that, with only rare exceptions, all peasants married. They also assumed, indeed insisted, that all young peasant women should be available for marriage. Russian peasants understood—some of their petitions reveal—that universal marriage required multilateral exchange of daughters among all households in the neighborhood. They understood that if an appreciable number of young women did not marry, there would be a local shortfall of brides and their sons might have difficulty obtaining wives. Households that sought wives for sons but withheld their own daughters provoked anger among neighboring peasants, and Spasovites, because so many of their daughters did not marry, were unusually dependent on peasants not of their community to provide brides.

There is indirect evidence that some villages that had exchanged daughters with Sluchkovo in the 1760s were refusing to allow their daughters to marry into Sluchkovo by the 1780s. There is a great deal of quite explicit evidence of the anger that female refusal to marry generated on serf estates: serfs complained to their owners that because women were refusing to marry, their sons could not find wives. They asked their masters to compel fathers to surrender their daughters in marriage. I present that evidence in chapter 2. Serf-owners in the second half of the eighteenth century were the first Russians, aside from peasants themselves, to learn about widespread resistance to marriage because their male serfs reported it to them, and I will argue that male serf complaints about women who refused to marry was what provoked routine intervention by serf-owners into their serfs' marital affairs.

I also advance an argument, which my choice of verbs has already telegraphed, that within the Spasovite covenant the choice to marry or not was indeed made by women. In Kuplia parish, in the first quarter of the nineteenth century, all or almost all women born into Spasovite households shunned marriage, but that was not true in all Spasovite communities. Nor was it true in Kuplia parish prior to the late eighteenth century. What the demographic records show is that in some Spasovite communities, at some times, some daughters in a household married while others did not. If we were not dealing with peasants, the obvious implication would be that daughters were probably making their own decisions about marriage. For Russia, however, the strongly held conventional wisdom is that peasant parents made all of the decisions about their sons' and daughters' marriages. Conventional wisdom holds true in some, but not all, Russian regions throughout the eighteenth and early nineteenth centuries. When a few peasant girls married at the minimum legal marriage age of twelve (early eighteenth century) or thirteen (late eighteenth century) and most girls married by age fifteen or sixteen (most boys by age sixteen or seventeen), children could not have had much say about whom they married. As marriage age rose and children spent an increasing number of years as unmarried adolescents and young adults engaged in courtship games and actual courtship, the conventional wisdom no longer holds—at least not so obviously.

To stick with Kuplia parish, we do not know what the average age at marriage was in the eighteenth century. In the Vladimir Diocese, very few priests recorded age at marriage even in the late eighteenth century. All that we know is that in some households, some daughters married and some did not. Were Spasovite fathers and mothers deciding which daughters were to marry and which were to stay home? It seems much more likely that, in a religious community in which, for whatever reason, there was mounting resistance to female marriage, parents may have discouraged their daughters from marrying but—on the evidence of tax census returns—permitted them to do so or perhaps simply could not prevent some daughters from marrying. To put that another way, in a very sharp departure from peasant tradition, young Spasovite women appear to have had agency, to have made their own decisions about whether to marry or not. If that basic choice was theirs, then surely they must also have had considerable opportunity to choose their own grooms. Or so I will argue over the course of the case studies of Kuplia parish (chapters 3 and 4), Baki in southeastern Kostroma province (chapter 6), and Steksovo in southern Nizhnii Novgorod province (chapter 7).

Women who would not marry were a disruptive force in peasant society in many ways. When large numbers of peasant women refused to marry, scarcely any facet of peasant culture was left undisturbed. When, as I will argue, young women in Spasovite communities, as early as the third quarter of the eighteenth century, acquired the right to decide whether they would wed or not, and by extension whom they wed, they struck a blow against traditional peasant culture. But that was only part of a larger—albeit, not necessarily conscious—assault on some of the principal structures of traditional Russian peasant society. The crumbling of the larger cultural matrix must in turn have eased the way for, or even required, young women to take control of nuptial decisions.

I do not claim that only Spasovite women chose not to marry. In Kuplia parish, for example, in the first half of the nineteenth century Spasovite women's refusal to marry spread to women in the priestless Pomorsk covenant at a time when Pomorsk leaders promoted marriage. Elsewhere, where priests labeled all Old Believers generic schismatics, it is sometimes difficult to identify the covenant to which marriage-averse women belonged. Nevertheless, the Spasovite covenant does seem to have been the principal site of female refusal to marry and a source of contagion, or inspiration, for others. How significant this was in Russian peasant society at large depends on how many Spasovites there were.

When the Ministry of Internal Affairs produced a statistical analysis of the Old Believer population as of 1859, the anonymous author could say of the Spasovites only that "the majority of the Spasovite covenant, very numerous along the Volga," could not be distinguished from the Orthodox because they, along with some other dissident sects, faithfully fulfilled the annual requirement to confess and take communion.[2] (The author ought to have substituted "sometimes" for "faithfully.") Spasovites could not be counted because, in their outward religious behavior, they were difficult to distinguish from the Orthodox.

It was difficult enough to estimate how many Old Believers of all sorts there were. The ministry did, however, work hard to come up with a more or less reliable estimate. Beginning in 1844, it sent officials to provinces where Old Believers were most numerous, and they developed a method for estimating schismatic numbers based on information priests reported in their annual confession registers. In addition to the openly declared Old Believers, they also counted those reported not to have confessed because they were "inclined to the schism," those who had not made their annual confession because (as priests characterized this omission) they were negligent or forgetful, those who had confessed but had not taken communion, and a portion of those who had given plausible reasons for not confessing (most often, absence from the parish during Lenten confession season).[3] While there might seem to have been no evident reason to assume that all peasants unwilling to take communion or who claimed to have forgotten to go to confession were actually Old Believers, ministry officials—after consulting with priests and others who had close knowledge of Old Believers—concluded that such was the case. Examination of the annual confession registers revealed, for example, that the forgetful forgot to confess year after year.

The results of these official investigations were stunning. In Iaroslavl province, for example, officials calculated that there were thirty-seven times more Old Believers than officially reported: in 1859, 278,417 against 7,454. That was an extreme case; the ministry concluded that, overall, there were roughly ten times as many Old Believers officially registered (875,382), approximately 8 million in 1859, or about one-sixth of the nominally Orthodox (that is, largely Russian) population.[4]

In 1868, Pavel Melnikov, who had studied and persecuted Old Believers in Nizhnii Novgorod province for years as a Ministry of Internal Affairs official (and later, under the pseudonym Andrei Pecherskii, wrote novels about the province's Old Believers), published an article on "Calculating [the Number of] Schismatics" ("*Schislenie raskol'nikov*"). He discussed the many reasons why local government officials and priests deliberately underreported the number of Old Believers; for the most part, these were variations on bribery, extortion, and fear of reporting disagreeable information. He then recomputed the ministry's numbers to arrive at a total of 8,584,494 Old Believers. To that figure, he added 110,000 to cover a variety of secretive small sects generally not classified as schismatic (Khlysty, Skoptsy, and others) because they did not claim to be within the Orthodox tradition and an estimated 700,000 Spasovites, who "perform the rites in Orthodox churches, that is they baptize their children, take communion (especially prior to a wedding), and are wed. They are all recorded in confession registers as present at confession and communion."[5] Melnikov's estimate for all Old Believers came to 9.3 million as of 1859. But he added that, given what was thought to be Russia's 1.3 percent annual population growth rate, the total had reached 10,295,000 as of 1868 (Melnikov neglected to compound growth annually).

Melnikov did not explain how he arrived at his estimate of 700,000 Spasovites. However, he pointed out that the Ministry of Internal Affairs count (that is, his own) for Old Believers in Nizhnii Novgorod province, 170,506, was much lower than a figure subsequently provided by Bishop Ieremiia of Nizhnii Novgorod—283,323—and suggested that Spasovites, whose strength in the province he now put at 60,000, probably accounted for much of the difference.[6] Bishop Ieremiia and his Nizhnii Novgorod consistory had themselves decided to concede to reality by including in their Old Believer totals those who had skipped confession for a number of years, probably because they knew Melnikov was providing a much higher count of the province's Old Believers to the Ministry of Interior. Applying that rule in 1855, they apparently added to the 23,323 self-admitted Old Believers about 85 percent of the 286,639 who had skipped confession out of "forgetfulness" to arrive at the 283,000 figure. The Holy Synod promptly reprimanded Ieremiia for the huge increase in reported Old Believers—explain the disparity between Melnikov's and your numbers, he was told—and Ieremiia just as promptly decided that only those who had avoided confession for fifteen to twenty years or who claimed they had confessed only because of compulsion should be classified as schismatic. The stubborn unwillingness of the Orthodox hierarchy to admit that Old Believers were Old Believers was the single most important source of the gross misrepresentation of Old Believer numbers.[7]

Melnikov's years of discussion with Old Believers and priests probably underlay his estimate of 700,000 Spasovites. Presumably he extrapolated from what he knew of Nizhnii Novgorod province to Russia as a whole. Serge Zenkovsky, accepting Melnikov's estimate for 1859, estimated in turn that by the early twentieth century, there were 1.5 to 2 million Spasovites, a figure presumably based on an assumption that Spasovite numbers increased at roughly the same rate as the empire's Orthodox population.[8]

Melnikov almost certainly underestimated both total Old Believer and Spasovite numbers. For one thing, beyond the Old Believers who pretended to be Orthodox (including most Spasovites), there was a penumbra of men and women who went to confession and communion who were not adherents of any particular covenant but thought of themselves as Old Believers and abandoned the church for an Old Believer covenant in old age or when they sensed death looming. Others freely mixed Orthodox and Old Believer practices, yet others told their priests they were Orthodox but preferred the old books and old rituals. For present purposes, however, we can accept Melnikov's estimate of those who were practicing (even if concealed) Old Believers as a reasonable baseline. At the overlapping margins, Orthodox and Old Believer were indistinguishable. Even if we could calculate with certainty the number of those who pretended to be Orthodox but whose private religious identity was firmly Old Believer, there would still be millions more with shifting or indeterminate religious inclinations.

We should take Melnikov's estimate of 60,000 Spasovites in Nizhnii Novgorod province as of the 1850s as expert testimony. His book-length 1854 report to the Ministry of Internal Affairs on the Old Believers of the province demonstrated a deep familiarity with local Old Believer history as they themselves told it, local government and diocesan documents bearing on that history, the geographical distribution of the various covenants within the province, the Old Believer role in the province's economy, their practices and beliefs, and even the differences among the icons that the various covenants favored.[9] And he provided considerable information about the province's Spasovites. Nevertheless, as conscientiously as he labored to calculate the true number of Old Believers and Spasovites in the province, he almost certainly fell short.

Melnikov estimated that in the serf village of Steksovo (the subject of chapter 7), 60 percent of parishioners in the early 1850s were in fact Old Believers. He further estimated that in the cluster of sixteen parishes of which Steksovo was a part, 50 percent of the population adhered to one or another Old Believer covenant.[10] His estimate for the village of Steksovo was much higher than could be computed using the methodology of the Ministry of Internal Affairs. In 1826, for instance, of the 1,164 Steksovo parishioners age seven and above, 218 (18.7 percent) failed to confess because they were declared Old Believers, inclined to the Old Belief, forgetful, or absent.[11] However, the volume of discussion of Old Believers in the manorial correspondence and the frequency of diocesan investigations (as discussed in chapter 7) provide strong support for Melnikov's estimate that 60 percent were Old Believers. Yet the 1861 confession register for the parish (configured differently than in 1826) contains a surprise. That year, during the Lenten confession season, only 28 of 723 serf parishioners confessed. The other 695 (96 percent) did not and were recorded as being either declared Old Believers or "inclined to the schism."[12] It is not a coincidence that 1861 was the year in which serfs were emancipated. In Nizhnii Novgorod province, priests read the Emancipation Manifesto to their peasant parishioners between March 12 and March 20, during Lent.[13] In the context of the rumors about emancipation that were already circulating broadly and the wildly exaggerated expectations that the manifesto triggered, Steksovo serfs must have believed that the tsar had liberated them not just from bondage but also from the need to pretend to be Orthodox. As an Old Believer peasant from Kostroma province said later, "I remember and honor one date above all others, 19 February, 1861 [the official date of the Manifesto]. . . . I haven't been to church since that day, for I no longer had anything to fear."[14]

Diocesan documents leave no doubt that the majority of Steksovo Old Believers were Spasovites. Probably it was precisely because Spasovites were so difficult to identify that Melnikov and his local informants underestimated Steksovo Old Believers by 36 percent (or to calculate the mistake another way, the number of Old Believers in Steksovo was 60 percent larger than Melnikov thought). That one documented case of significant underestimation precisely where Old Believers were predominantly Spasovite is of uncertain evidentiary weight.[15] Nevertheless, it at least suggests that the number of Spasovites in Nizhnii Novgorod province in the 1850s was closer to 100,000 than to 60,000.

While we should assume that Melnikov's estimate of 700,000 Spasovites in the empire as a whole was well grounded in what he knew about Spasovites in other provinces, it does seem to be the case that he misunderstood the geographical distribution of sizeable Spasovite populations. He believed Spasovites were most numerous in the Volga provinces, from Nizhnii Novgorod south to Astrakhan, as well as in Penza, Tambov, and Voronezh provinces.[16] He was apparently unaware of the sizeable concentration of Spasovites in the Gorokhovets district and likely in eastern Vladimir province in general. That he apparently did not know that there were large numbers of Spasovites in Kostroma and Iaroslavl provinces as well, possibly more than in Nizhnii Novgorod province, is somewhat more surprising. Keeping in mind that even the very conscientious Melnikov considerably underestimated the number of Spasovites in the province for which he was responsible, that estimates from other provinces were likely also low, and that he either ignored or minimized the number of Spasovites in Vladimir, Iaroslavl, and Kostroma provinces, I think it reasonable to estimate that there were at least one million Spasovites in the middle of the nineteenth century—but possibly as many as one and a half to two million (3 to 4 percent of all the nominally Orthodox in the Russian Empire)—and on the order of three million in the first decade of the twentieth century. Those numbers do lend significance to Spasovite marital practices. Since Spasovites were concentrated in provinces along the Volga River, from Iaroslavl down to Astrakhan, they made up a particularly numerous component of the populations of those provinces. Since they were not distributed evenly in those provinces, their weight locally could be enormous and, therefore, enormously disruptive, as in Kuplia parish and its vicinity.

I did not immediately grasp the implications of the nuptial behavior of Kuplia parish Spasovites, which differed from almost everything I thought I knew about Russian peasant marriage, and so did not then and there begin to write the present book. Indeed, I had to return to the Vladimir archive several more times before I had a reasonably good understanding of resistance to marriage among the Spasovite women of Kuplia parish, and in the surrounding Gorokhovets district, from the early eighteenth to the mid-nineteenth century. Nevertheless, that first reading of the confession registers did precipitate a gradual reassessment of scattered evidence of resistance to marriage among Old Believer peasant women that I had encountered earlier. For instance, an 1845 household inventory from Sergei Mikhailovich Golitsyn's Steksovo estate had revealed that among women twenty-five and over, 17.6 percent in Steksovo village and 14.1 percent on the entire estate never married. From the estate papers, it was reasonably clear that those resisting marriage were Old Believers of some sort and that Sergei Golitsyn and his estate managers had struggled for many years, without much success, to compel all serf women to marry.

But even within an Old Believer context, Steksovo had seemed anomalous; most peasant Old Believers, after all, did marry, in one way or another. Kuplia pointed me toward Spasovites, and diocesan documents in the Nizhnii Novgorod historical archive provided evidence of the Spasovite presence in Steksovo. Very few confession registers survived from Steksovo parish, and none of those identified Old Believers by covenant. But I could piece together a run of tax and manorial censuses that spanned the mid-eighteenth to mid-nineteenth centuries. The demographic history of Golitsyn's Steksovo estate is an interesting variation on Kuplia parish's.

I had also encountered evidence of Old Believer resistance to marriage very early in my research into peasant marriage in the form of complaints from serf men about serf women who wouldn't marry. I had even written about them in an article on Vladimir Orlov's regulation of serf marriage on his many estates. But I had concluded that "nothing in the manorial papers suggests that there were ever very many" serf women who refused to marry.[17] That conclusion referred to the totality of Orlov's many estates and is more or less true as to what those papers actually reveal. If I had paid attention to the geographical distribution of serf complaints about marriage-averse women, and if I had followed leads and examined relevant demographic documents located in provincial archives, I might have reached a different conclusion or at least have offered some geographical qualification. By the time I had worked through the documentation from Kuplia and Steksovo, I had a much different understanding of the non-quantitative evidence of Old Believer serf women who resisted marriage—whom I now understood to be not simply Old Believers but most likely Spasovites—or other participants in widespread female rejection of marriage among priestless Old Believer peasants in areas north of Moscow and along the course of the Volga River.

When I began to tell historians, both in and outside of Russia, what I thought I had found—a very high level of refusal to marry among Spasovite women from at least the middle of the eighteenth century to the middle of the nineteenth century—they were interested, but many were understandably skeptical. What I was telling them could not be squared with what everyone knew, what I myself had known before stumbling onto the Kuplia confession registers: that with only scattered exceptions, Russian peasants married universally. A few asked whether I was sure that I had properly understood the documents. One accepted my facts but suggested that the Kuplia case was surely anomalous and must have been a response to some local economic exigency. Others suggested that what I had probably found was not an excess of unmarried women but a deficit of marriageable men, likely an effect of locally excessive conscription: so many men taken by the army that there weren't enough potential husbands for the available women. I can rebut all of those objections, but the questions certainly helped me formulate my argument.

I reacted to the initial skepticism in two ways. First, I concluded that I needed even more evidence to bludgeon my point home. I decided to look at the Baki estate papers in the British Library because Edgar Melton's publications on the Baki estate suggested that there was a strong Old Believer presence there.[18] The estate's copy of the 1795 tax census for Baki and surrounding villages did indeed reveal considerable female marriage resistance. Continuing my research in the Kostroma historical archive, I found that no confession registers from Baki parish had survived, but that there were enough tax census returns from Baki to reconstruct the estate's demographic history. And every census volume for Kostroma province that I opened held returns from village after village in which numerous adult women had never married.

My second reaction to the skepticism I encountered, and to the pile of evidence I had accumulated, was to decide that in order to be persuasive, the evidence had to be presented extensively rather than in summary form. There is, in fact, a great deal that needs explaining. The story of Spasovite resistance to marriage could not be just one chapter in a history of Russian peasant marriage; it required, and merited, a book of its own.

I get to the history of Spasovite female marriage resistance, somewhat circuitously, only in chapter 3. I discuss serf-owners' confrontation with marriage resistance in the second half of the eighteenth century in chapter 2 because the bits and pieces of information found in manorial archives make it possible to sketch the geographical range of marriage resistance. Moreover, the way serf-owners reacted to what their male serfs reported to them is also a part of this story. Spasovite nuptial practices provoked a harsh response from many proprietors, who thought female resistance to marriage threatened their own interests. Some owners sought to compel every last serf woman to marry and to marry on their natal estates rather than across estate boundaries. Spasovite nuptial behavior, in other words, is part of the history of serfdom.

However, that argument contradicts a widely shared belief that serf-owners sought to control their serfs' marriages virtually from the onset of serfdom in the seventeenth century or that at least from the early eighteenth century regulating serf marriage was understood to be an element of good estate management. Thus, in chapter 1, I demonstrate that in the seventeenth century, owners almost never attempted to control or intervene in their serfs' marriages and that in the first half of the eighteenth century, most serf-owners continued to allow their serfs to marry as they would. This argument has, admittedly, nothing to do with Spasovite marriage resistance, but it is a necessary preliminary to chapter 2. It is also an introduction to normal Russian peasant nuptial behavior, from which Spasovites practices were a radical departure.

The study more or less ends with the 1850 and 1858 tax censuses, the last censuses in which the local returns, recorded household by household, are available. With rare exceptions, only the summary returns have survived from the 1897 census. Confession registers from the early 1860s are very scarce and then disappear entirely. A ruling by the Soviet archival administration in the 1920s that confession registers dating from after 1865 could be destroyed seems to have been interpreted everywhere as a command.[19] I have found no comparable documents later than the early 1860s from the localities on which I have focused. Still, there is reason to believe that the rate of female marriage resistance among Spasovites did decline, possibly substantially, after the 1850s. I make that tentative case in chapter 5 (on the Spasovite covenant) and in the conclusion.

NOTES

1. Everyone, priests included, believed this was the rule, but as the Holy Synod pointed out in 1839, there was no provision in Orthodox canon law that required a couple to confess and take communion before the wedding ceremony; *Sobranie postanovlenii po chasti raskola*, book 2, pp. 359–61. The synod ruled that priests should continue to tell the couple to take the sacraments, but as advice rather than command. In practice, the misunderstanding retained the force of law.

2. Bushen, *Statisticheskie tablitsy*, vol. 2, p. 235. This formulation suggests that the information came from Pavel Melnikov, the ministry official in charge of investigating Old Believers in Nizhnii Novgorod province in the late 1840s and early 1850s. See the sources that follow.

3. These figures can be found in the printed summaries of the Holy Synod's annual reports in the 1850s, e.g., *Izvlechenie iz otcheta . . . za 1859 god*, p. 21.

4. Bushen, *Statisticheskie tablitsy*, vol. 2, pp. 210–12, 216–17, 234–35. The ministry's figure also included a proportionate number of children under seven, who were excused from confession, and an estimated one million "secret schismatics" among those who both confessed and communed. Two reports to the ministry—from 1852 and 1853, both from Iaroslavl province—are in *Sbornik pravitel'stvennykh svedenii*, vol. 4, pp. 1–187. The report for 1852 justifies the counting rules at length and, in my view, persuasively. Irina Paert provides, in "'Two or Twenty Million?'," pp. 75–98, a useful discussion of the various estimates of Old Believer numbers. However, I believe she

is mistakenly dismissive of the calculations by Minister of Interior officials. Marsden, *Crisis of Religious Toleration*, pp. 112–13, follows Paert in suggesting that ministry officials' Old Believer totals were arbitrary and exaggerated. As will be evident below, there is evidence that the ministry count was, if anything, low.

5. Mel'nikov, "Schislenie raskol'nikov," *PSS*, 2-oe izd., t. 7, pp. 384–409 (the quotation is from p. 408).

6. Ibid., pp. 404, 409. Melnikov reported 170,506 Old Believers in the province in 1853 (Mel'nikov, "Otchet," p. 3). He must have reported the higher number that appears in the ministry analysis a year or two later.

7. "O merakh, predpriniatykh v 50-60 godakh," no. 1, pp. 24–29. The figure reported by Metropolitan Ieremiia is in a long list of instructions from the Holy Synod from 1856 on measures to be taken against the schism in his diocese (*Sobranie postanovlenii po chasti raskola*, book 2, pp. 672–82). In the various sources, Ieremiia is also mistakenly referred to as Gerontii and Antonii. I have assumed that the consistory used the 1855 figures because the 1856 figures could not have been compiled as of April 1856, when Ieremiia abruptly tightened the requirements for being recognized as an Old Believer.

8. Zenkovskii, *Russkoe staroobriadchestvo*, p. 472. Orthodox and Old Believers together numbered 54,628,083 in 1859 and 89,328,200 in 1897, a 70 percent increase in less than forty years (Bushen, *Statisticheskie tablitsy*, vol. 2, pp. 233–34; *Pervaia vseobshchaia perepis'*, vol. 1, p. 248). By contrast, the Ministry of Interior's Department of Religious Affairs put the total number of Old Believers in the Russian Empire at 2,206,621 as of January 1, 1912 (*Statisticheskie svedeniia o staroobriadtsakh*, p. 3). Peter Waldron trusts the British Foreign Office estimate of 11 million Old Believers as of 1907 (Waldron, "Religious Reform," p. 115).

9. Mel'nikov, "Otchet."

10. Ibid., pp. 33, 40, 44.

11. TsANO, f. 570, op. 559a, d. 966, ll. 449–66.

12. Ibid., d. 1502, ll. 100–107, 123–320b (as of 1861, the parish had two priests, each with his own congregation).

13. Zvezdin, "K 50 letiiu," pp. 66–67.

14. Prokof'eva and Nagradov, "Istoriia staroobriadchestva v Verkhnem Povolzh'e," p. 51.

15. The last volume of the Holy Synod's annual report to include statistics on the number of nominally Orthodox who had skipped confession was for 1860: *Izvlechenie iz otcheta po vedomstvu dukhovnykh del . . . za 1860 god*, p. 24. Apparently the report for 1861 was never published, and subsequent volumes from the 1860s provide no similar statistics.

16. Mel'nikov, "Schislenie," p. 408.

17. Bushnell, "Did Serf Owners Control Serf Marriage?," pp. 427–433. The quotation is from p. 433.

18. In particular, Melton, "Household Economies," pp. 559–85.

19. "O rabote mestnykh Razborochnykh komissii," p. 7.

CHAPTER 1

THE MORAL ECONOMY OF RUSSIAN SERF MARRIAGE,
1580s–1750s: SERF MARRIAGE UNREGULATED

In the first half of the eighteenth century, Russian serfs' marriages were embedded in a moral economy. For example, in 1706, Peter the Great granted his field marshal Boris Sheremetev (1652–1719) a crown estate centered on Voshchazhnikovo, in the Rostov district, roughly two hundred kilometers north of Moscow. As crown peasants, the villagers had paid dues supporting the ruler, his kin, and his government. Among the occasional charges levied was a ten- or twenty-five-kopek bridal departure fee (*vyvodnye den'gi*, or *vyvod*) when their daughters married peasants not subject to the crown administration, such as serfs owned by nobles or monasteries.[1] Generally, the groom's family was responsible for the payment. Sheremetev continued to collect the departure fee, probably at roughly the crown administration rate. In January 1712, he sent management rules to Voshchazhnikovo, perhaps for the first time; they included no directive on the departure fee or on any other aspect of his serfs' marriages.[2]

Probably in late 1717, however, he announced that henceforth, the bridal departure fee would be five rubles. His peasants protested against that increase as well as against an increase in quitrent and other imposts. About the departure fee specifically, they claimed that neighboring peasants refused to pay so much, that they themselves didn't have the money, "and among us orphans, those maidens, because of so great a departure fee, have increased in no small number and can't make matches on our estate."[3] They asked that the departure fee be levied at the same rate local nobles charged. On May 4, 1718, Sheremetev responded that he had bought the estate with his blood, that it had been given to him to enjoy as he saw fit, that his serfs would do as they were told, and they would submit no more petitions. Nevertheless, he immediately agreed to reduce the bridal departure fee to whatever the local customary rate was.[4]

Neither Sheremetev nor any Russian noble would have believed that what his serfs told him was literally true, yet he conceded that he was wrong to impose what was, as of that date, an exceptionally high charge for women marrying away from the estate (at the time, five rubles was likely twice or more the market price of a marriageable serf woman in the Voshchazhnikovo area) and that he really did not know what a reasonable departure fee in that district might be. His immediate and complete capitulation on that point suggests that he understood he had crossed a moral line. His sons Petr and Sergei followed his example. In 1733, they charged a woman who married off the estate a fifteen-kopek departure fee, which was close to the average charge in the Rostov district that year.[5] At least down to 1772, Petr occasionally collected a one-ruble departure fee but more often let women from Voshchazhnikovo marry away without collecting any fee at all.[6]

His serfs' successful remonstrance demonstrates that, in the matter of serf marriage if on nothing else, Sheremetev and his serfs were in agreement: a serf-owner should place no financial impediment in the way of his serf women marrying. As E. P. Thompson has shown in "The Moral Economy of the English Crowd in the Eighteenth Century," a similar consensus shared by the poor and the local political and social elite in eighteenth-century Great Britain—that high bread prices should not deny the laboring poor access to food—was why in years of dearth laborers could often compel farmers, millers, and bakers to reduce the prices of grain, flour, and bread to customary levels.[7] The Voshchazhnikovo incident is not the only basis for my assertion that serf marriage was embedded in a moral economy until roughly the middle of the eighteenth century. There were strikingly similar conflicts over the departure fee elsewhere in the early eighteenth century, with identical outcomes, and I take them up at the end of this chapter.

However, I want to introduce at the outset the idea that there was a moral economy to serf marriage that persisted to the 1760s or thereabouts, when a good part of the nobility rejected the consensus. The evidence from the seventeenth century only hints at the moral economy illuminated by Field Marshall Sheremetev's surrender at Voshchazhnikovo, but the hints are clear enough. I am going to demonstrate that between the 1580s, when the Russian government began to ban peasant movement, and the 1750s, serf-owners seldom intervened in or sought to control serf marriage.

Since over the course of the seventeenth and first half of the eighteenth centuries serf-owners' coercion and intrusions into serf lives steadily increased, why did they *not* try, at the very least, to profit from serf marriage? Why did they ignore the obvious opportunity to turn the nominal bridal departure fee into something like a sale, as Sheremetev must have meant to do in 1717? If seventeenth-century nobles had been asked to explain themselves, they would probably have said they were observing tradition. Probably few of them gave any thought to their serfs' marriages and simply allowed serfs to follow local custom. Peasants themselves articulated their understanding of the moral economy of marriage only when custom was attacked. I use the concept of moral economy here to emphasize that for a long time, Russian serf-owners acknowledged their serfs' right to marry as they wished and the wrong that they themselves would do if they tried to control or profit from serf marriage.

I do not use "economy" as a metaphor. Russian peasant marriage in the eighteenth century, as in earlier and later centuries, involved a set of economic transactions. The groom's family paid a bride price. Groom and bride families negotiated how much would be spent on meals, drink, and gifts during the celebratory feast. A marriage license had to be bought from the bishop, and the priest had to be paid for celebrating the marriage. Into the first half of the eighteenth century, most marriages involved payment of a small fee, or comestibles, to whomever managed the village, be it a noble, his steward, a monastery's village manager, or the local government official in charge of peasants who weren't serfs. The additional fee paid when a bride moved from one jurisdiction to another ordinarily accounted for only a small portion of wedding expenditures. Sheremetev's serfs did not protest the departure fee itself, only the sudden twenty-fold increase from twenty-five kopeks to five rubles. Like eighteenth-century British laborers during years of dearth, they asked only that the price be reduced to what they were used to paying.

SERF WOMEN'S MOBILITY IN MARRIAGE

Setting aside the web of rules imposed by the Orthodox Church, serf marriage in Russia was taxed but almost entirely unregulated prior to the second half of the eighteenth century. In the conventional story, with the definitive imposition of serfdom in 1649, peasants who lived on noble estates—serfs—lost the right to move away from those estates. In fact, only male serfs lost the right to move; women could leave through marriage. According to chapter 11, article 19, of the Law Code of 1649, "should a *votchinik* or *pomeshchik* (proprietor of a hereditary estate or of property held on service tenure, respectively) or his stewards or elders, undertake to release maiden daughters of peasants, or widows, in marriage to others' slaves or peasants," the women were to be given manumission papers, signed by their owners or priests. These documents were to be kept on hand in the event of a dispute over who actually owned the women. An agreed upon bridal departure fee was to be collected, and the amount was to be recorded in the manumission document.[8] This provision not only afforded women mobility denied men; it was also in principle at variance with a number of provisions in the code that were meant to prevent the depopulation of service estates, such as a ban on manumitting (male) serfs from those estates.[9] The 1649 Law Code presumed that women moved about freely through marriage and endorsed the practice.

Of course, serfdom was merely codified, not instituted, in 1649. Beginning in 1582 intermittently and then continuously from 1603, Russian rulers had decreed "forbidden years" during which peasants were not allowed to leave the property on which they were living. During those years, peasant women crossed property lines when they married. They were taxed when they left—a bridal departure fee was paid—but forbidden year or not, they did leave.

The departure fee itself predated serfdom; it was a tax collected by grand and lesser princes from at least the mid-fifteenth century and is sometimes mentioned in immunity charters that exempted the inhabitants of properties from taxes of various sorts. What may be the earliest of the surviving immunity charters mentioning the departure fee—a five-year exemption from that and other taxes granted by Prince Iurii Vasilevich of Iaroslavl to the Novinsk Monastery—dates from 1464; the departure fee must have been in effect for some time before that.[10] Not surprisingly, most of the charters that have survived were granted to monasteries and other ecclesiastical domains, but immunities were, at least on some occasions, granted to lay proprietors. For example, in 1487, Ivan III exempted half of the village of Gliadiashchii (and extensive land and lakes around it) in the Murom district from that fee and other minor levies when he deeded it as hereditary estate to Ivashka Gliadiashchii.[11]

Although these charters did not usually say so, in most cases the grantees must have continued to collect the departure fee for their own benefit. When Ivan IV gave property in the Rzhev area to Metropolitan Afanasii in 1564, he explicitly assigned Afanasii the right to collect the departure fee.[12] In 1590, when Patriarch Iov transferred patriarchal land to the Novinsk Monastery, he specified that the departure tax previously paid to the patriarch was henceforth to be paid to the father superior of the monastery.[13] Since the grand prince must have granted both land and immunity to the patriarch (or before him, the metropolitan), the right to collect the fee had arrived at the Novinsk Monastery through secondary reassignment. More generally, when the tsar began to grant land as service estates in the late fifteenth century, the holder of the estate received the right "to collect the grain and income"—apparently including the bridal exit fee, which would have been included in the "petty income" (*mel'kii dokhod*) sometimes included in the grant formula—that had previously gone to the tsar, to his local administrator, or to the former owner of a confiscated estate.[14] By the seventeenth century, owners of both hereditary and service estates, as well as clerical proprietors, collected what was by then a private tax for off-estate marriages. On large estates, the departure tax was generally assigned as income to the steward.

The evidence that even during the forbidden years serf women married away from the estates on which they lived is robust, if not plentiful. While there is no evidence at all that serf women were prevented from marrying away, it must have been the case sometimes. In 1591, the Iosifo-Volokolamsk Monastery instructed one of its stewards to collect six kopeks (up from the four kopeks charged earlier) when a father gave his daughter in marriage off the estate.[15] In 1607, Patriarch Germogen ordered peasants belonging to the Annunciation Monastery in Nizhnii Novgorod to pay their stewards ten kopeks when they married away from the monastery's properties.[16] In 1619, Tsar Mikhail Fedorovich reconfirmed to the patriarch a grant of land in the Rzhev district that had originally been deeded to the metropolitan of Moscow in 1564 and that explicitly gave the right to the metropolitan, and now the patriarch, to collect the bridal departure fee, among others.[17] In 1620 and 1621, he conferred the same privilege on other patriarchal properties.[18] Sometime around 1620, Tsar Mikhail decreed that those who lived at state postal settlements (*iamskie slobody*) and in the surrounding territory, thus including peasants, must pay the tsar three kopeks when daughters married into other jurisdictions. In the 1620s and the 1630s, the archbishop of Riazan and the Intercession Nunnery in Suzdal set departure fees on their properties at ten to twenty kopeks.[19]

Evidence from the first half of the seventeenth century that lay proprietors released their serf women for marriage is scant, but in 1631, Voin Karsakov ordered the elder on his Vysheslavskoe estate in the Suzdal district to collect a departure fee when women married away.[20] In 1643, the steward of an estate owned by the widow Feodosiia Volynskaia in what would later be Vologda province charged a bridal departure fee of two rubles for a woman who turned out to be already married and ordered the local priest to celebrate the wedding. The steward no doubt demanded an exorbitant two rubles for facilitating an illegal marriage.[21]

In any case, the abundant evidence from the second half of the seventeenth century is decisive. The reason we have little evidence of how nobles dealt with serf marriage in the first half of the century is that few private documents of any sort have survived from that era. The practice of releasing women from estates was so broadly assumed at the beginning of the seventeenth century that in 1607, in a decree on the forbidden years, Tsar Vasilii Shuiskii declared that the freedom to move for purposes of marriage extended even to slaves: if the slave's master had not arranged for a woman's marriage by her eighteenth year, or for a man's by age twenty, then a government official would issue manumission papers so they could seek spouses on their own.[22]

The wording of chapter 11, article 19, of the 1649 Law Code—"should" a noble decide to release a peasant woman in marriage—suggests release was optional, and Vasilii Semevskii postulated that the formal requirement that nobles had to provide a manumission document must have encouraged them to refuse to do so, thereby preventing serf women from marrying away from their estates.[23] However, I have found only one bit of evidence that confirms that a few proprietors balked at releasing serf women: sometime in the second half of the seventeenth century, the Resurrection Monastery in Cherepovets forbade widows and maidens on its Belozersk district properties to marry anyone who didn't inhabit a village belonging to the monastery.[24] Aleksei Novoselskii has argued that Andrei Bezobrazov (1621–1690, executed for employing sorcerers to win the favor of the young Peter I) intervened energetically in his serfs' marriages, paving the way for full serf-owner control of marriage in the eighteenth century.[25] Novoselskii's assumption that such must have been the case led him to misread the evidence. One of Bezobrazov's stewards did report that some serf women had married off the estate without asking Bezobrazov's permission, as required, but there is no evidence in the correspondence that Bezobrazov ever refused permission (he may only have been trying to ensure that the required manumission documents were provided) and much evidence his serf women married away from his estates without hindrance. Bezobrazov did respond to serfs' pleas that they were so poor that no one would accept their sons' suits by ordering stewards to find brides for the unfortunate lads, using compulsion if necessary (but was sometimes unavailing). From a groom's point of view, at least, Bezobrazov thus rendered a marital service.[26]

All the other evidence points to a conclusion that almost universally, proprietors permitted their serf women to marry across estate boundaries. The Pafnutev-Borovsk, Spaso-Prilutsk, Kirillo-Belozersk, and Trinity–St. Sergius Monasteries and the Nizhnii Novgorod Bishopric permitted marriage off the estate in the second half of the seventeenth century, for example.[27] The thousands of marital manumission papers that have survived from the second half of the seventeenth century are prima facie evidence that property boundaries were not marital boundaries. And while the 1649 Law Code appeared to apply only to serf women marrying serf (or slave) men—in which case their freedom was fleeting, ending when they married and reverted to serfdom—in fact, serf women sometimes married peasants who were not serfs, or townsmen, and upon marriage they, too, assumed their husbands' legal statuses.

The overwhelming majority of the surviving seventeenth-century manumission papers failed to meet the 1649 Law Code's requirement that they state the amount of the bridal departure fee. Some say nothing at all about the fee, which may mean that in fact no money was collected when the girl left the estate; some manumission papers state explicitly that no departure fee was taken (*bezvyvodno*).[28] Some say the fee was collected "by agreement," others that it was collected "according to the [owner's] instructions," yet others that the fee had been "paid in full." Manumission papers that specify the charge suggest that departure fees were low at mid-century, rose slowly into the 1680s, and then in the late 1680s and 1690s rose on some but not all properties by an order of magnitude or more.

In the mid-seventeenth century, most departure fees were ten to twenty kopeks. Ten kopeks was the fee crown estate administrators levied on departing brides as of 1647.[29] In the 1650s, manumission papers brought to Suzdal's Nativity Cathedral properties by girls from noble, monastic, patriarchal, and crown estates recorded fees in the range of twelve and a half to twenty kopeks; a serf who wrote the manumission paper for his own daughter charged a serf of the Suzdal Archbishopric twenty-five kopeks.[30] Around the same time, Boris Morozov, the most powerful figure at the court of Tsar Aleksei Mikhailovich, levied a departure fee of either thirteen kopeks or whatever neighboring lords charged if his own serfs had to pay more.[31] In the 1650s, lesser nobles, monasteries, and the Cathedral of the Dormition in the Kremlin charged seven to twenty-five kopeks to release serf women for marriage.[32] In 1658, the archimandrite of Nizhnii Novgorod's Caves Monastery ordered that ten kopeks be collected for a maiden and twenty for a widow or that the fee match whatever neighbors were charging the monastery's serfs if that were more.[33]

Departure fees rose only slightly from the 1660s to the late 1680s. In the 1660s, a government official charged twenty-five kopeks (he probably estimated what the local custom was) for a girl marrying away from a confiscated estate in the Kazan region, while in the Belozersk district, two nobles charged one and two rubles (these were outliers).[34] In the 1670s–90s, monasteries in Pereslavl-Zalesskii, Suzdal, and Vladimir issued and received manumission papers with recorded departure charges of thirteen to forty kopeks.[35]

In the late 1680s and 1690s, a number of proprietors raised the fees they charged sharply and, apparently, abruptly. In 1681, for instance, the Savvo-Starozhevsk Monastery instructed its subordinate Spaso-Zaretsk Monastery to impose departure fees equal to those on neighboring properties, so we can assume that in that year, the Savvo-Starozhevsk monks followed the custom of the country on their own properties.[36] Then in 1689, the Savvo-Starozhevsk Monastery instructed its subordinate Purdyshev Monastery that the departure fee for women marrying away from its villages should be two rubles, twenty kopeks, which surely indicates that the Savvo-Starozhevsk Monastery had decided to charge the same.[37] In 1691, Ivan Semenov in the Rzhev district collected five rubles for a widow who married a serf belonging to the Iosifo-Volokolamsk Monastery; she took three unmarried daughters with her, and Semenov was to receive three rubles when each of them married.[38]

On the other hand, the Bishopric of Nizhnii Novgorod in the 1690s collected only fifteen kopeks for women marrying away from its properties.[39]

Individual departure fees were two rubles in 1690 in the Kashin district, five rubles in 1690 in the Staritskoe district, six rubles in 1693 around Moscow, thirty kopeks in 1695 in the Suzdal district, and two rubles in 1696 in the Kurmish district.[40] Most monasteries charged from twenty to fifty kopeks.[41] There is no reason to think that a majority of serf-owners charged above two rubles when women married off their estates, since (as I will show shortly) two rubles was exceptional even in the early eighteenth century. Nevertheless, we can say that in the 1690s, some serf-owners did begin to think of the departure fee not as a relatively low, customary fee but as a sale of property.

This emergent understanding of the departure fee coincided with the development of a market in serfs. With perhaps a few exceptions, the sale and purchase of individual serfs (that is, detached from land) only began in the second half of the seventeenth century, at first in roundabout ways: payment of money to the former owner of fugitive serfs now living on your estate or using a serf as security for a loan never repaid. It wasn't until 1675 that deeds of purchase of landless serfs could be officially registered with the government, and it was only in 1688 that a separate register for sales both direct and indirect was established. It was just at that point that sales of all kinds seem to have expanded dramatically. Apparently the only statistical measure available comes from the number of indirect sales registered in Novgorod: 4 in 1667–76, 7 in 1677–86, and 124 in 1687–99.[42] It is impossible to establish what the going rate for a marriage-age serf girl might have been because most serfs were sold in family groups. However, in one 1689 transaction, a marriage-age girl sold for ten rubles. That was a substantial sum, much higher than the two- to four-ruble cost of unmarried serf women in the 1740s.

Almost all of the known prices for groups of serfs in the late seventeenth century were higher than they were for similar groups in the first half of the eighteenth century.[43] Probably it is characteristic that when a market emerges for a new commodity—in this case, serfs separate from land— prices begin high but then fall as volume expands and sellers and purchasers work out a market-clearing price. The spike in bridal departure fees in the 1690s was almost certainly a reflection of the high prices charged for landless serfs when they first became available on the market in something like substantial numbers.

The formulaic manumission documents—woman's and husband's names, departure fee (when specified), proprietors releasing and receiving the bride—conceal the human drama that must sometimes have preceded their composition, but there are occasional hints. The manumission paper that recorded the 1691 agreement by the Rzhev noble to release a widow for five rubles, with the promise of future three-ruble payments when each of her three daughters married, is more than just an example of the spike in departure charges in the 1690s. What was it about the widow and daughters that made them so attractive to the Iosifo-Volokolamsk Monastery serf who was willing to pay the price, and where did he get the money? And what about the serf father who issued the manumission paper for his daughter and collected the departure fee for himself? Was he defrauding his owner, and might that have been a common practice in areas where serfs lived in small settlements distant from their masters' eyes?

Fraud perpetrated by stewards must have been common on remote properties, as a case involving Andrei Bezobrazov's serfs illustrates. On March 9, 1670, the steward at Ivashkova village in Vladimir province wrote Bezobrazov that he had collected a fifty-kopek departure charge for each of three girls manumitted for marriage. On March 13, serfs from the same village sent a petition begging for relief from their many hardships, charging that the steward had in fact collected sixty kopeks for each of the three girls released, and had released three others for two and a quarter rubles each while reporting to Bezobrazov that he had collected no departure fees for them because they had been exchanged for incoming women. The Ivashkova serfs also complained that they had to pay one and a half rubles and more for the release of girls from neighboring villages and, in the next sentence, asked that their haulage duties be reduced.[44] The serfs were attempting to wrest some advantage for themselves from the differential in local bride release fees and the information about the steward's malfeasance.

Petitions that Bezobrazov received (coincidentally, also in March 1670) from a village in the Suzdal district suggest that the peasant community was at least as likely to obstruct marriage as any noble of that time. Artem Semenov complained that his neighbors refused to give their daughters in marriage to his son Frolka because they believed Artem and his wife had beaten Frolka's first wife to death. Artem swore that wasn't true. Bezobrazov received a separate report from local serfs that Frolka was a wife beater. Frolka complained in his petition that no one in his village would give him a daughter, nor would anyone from surrounding villages; they demanded five rubles and more in bride price, which he could not pay. That must have been their polite way to refuse his suit.[45]

If, understandably, a five-ruble bride price was an insurmountable obstacle to marriage around Frolka's village, at what level did a departure fee become a serious impediment to a peasant's pursuit of a bride? Day labor of the sort performed by many peasants earned on average three kopeks, masons averaged eight kopeks per day. The median price of an ordinary stove of the type a peasant might pay to have built was one ruble, seventy kopeks, the price of the bucket of vodka the groom's family brought to a wedding averaged fifty-five kopeks.[46] In the late seventeenth century, a fifty-kopek fee was probably within reach of most peasant households. Any departure fee of two rubles or more probably discouraged many potential suitors, but the surviving manumission papers recording those charges are proof that some peasants could pay fees in that range. Standard fees were often less than fifty kopeks at the very beginning of the eighteenth century but were rising toward the one- or, in some districts, two-ruble level.[47] The standard seventeenth-century fee would not have discouraged many serfs from looking for brides on neighboring estates or peasants who weren't serfs from marrying serf women.

In any case, the bride price that a groom's father paid to the bride's father probably had a greater influence on the selection of spouses than the departure fee. Evidence on what seventeenth-century peasants actually charged each other when they released their daughters in marriage is available only from a single group of properties owned by the Solotchinsk Monastery in the Riazan district and dates from the late 1680s and 1690s. In those years, most fathers of grooms on Solotchinsk properties paid a bride price of three to four rubles. In one case, a father demanded six rubles for his daughter; in another, a father reduced the charge to two rubles, presumably because his son-in-law was moving into his household rather than taking his daughter away.[48]

As the Solotchinsk serfs complained in petitions to the archimandrite, the peasants' own demand for a substantial bride price was the real impediment to securing a bride.[49] By comparison, the departure fee for Solotchisnk brides until 1696 was modest: twenty-five kopeks. In November 1696, the monastery attempted to raise that fee, at least at one of its properties, to three rubles. Serfs protested, and the fee was reduced to two rubles or to whatever the monk administering the village thought proper.[50] When a girl married away from another village in 1708, the monastery collected only a one-ruble departure fee.[51] The monks in 1696 probably attempted to capture for themselves as much money in departure payments as peasants received in bride price. Like Sheremetev, they retreated.

It should be clear that seventeenth-century nobles allowed serf women to depart through marriage because they understood that the traffic in brides flowed in both directions: their women left, but their men brought women in and would continue to do so as long as all serf-owners in the neighborhood followed the same rule. Peasants themselves understood that marriage involved multilateral exchange of daughters, as the Solotchinsk serfs explained in petitions to the archimandrite. Twelve of the eighteen fathers who asked for his assistance in securing wives for their sons during the September 1693–February 1694 wedding cycle reminded him that they had given away their daughters at his behest and therefore expected compensation in kind. The January 1694 petition from Vaska Klimentev was typical: "In October you ordered me to give my daughter to Leontii Podshivalov's son, my son Timoshka has come of age, my wife is infirm, Zakhar Afanasev has a daughter of marriageable age, please order him to hand her over so my household doesn't collapse."[52] What the peasants could understand as exchange among, rather than between, households on a single estate, seventeenth-century nobles must have understood as exchange among multiple estates.

SERFS' VIEWS ON THE MORAL ECONOMY OF MARRIAGE PREVAIL, MORE OR LESS, 1700–1750s

Over the course of the eighteenth century, nobles increasingly compiled detailed rules for managing their estates, and there is something like a historiographical consensus that from early in the century nobles intervened forcefully in their serfs' marriages, in particular forbidding serf women to marry off the estate and compelling all of their serfs to marry, and to marry young.[53] However, evidence from the first half of the eighteenth century is clear: in the matter of serf marriage, most nobles remained noninterventionists. The managerial instructions that we know about—surely only a random sample of those issued—were mostly compiled by great magnates and are probably representative of the thinking of that class. Up to 1750, they gave little thought to serf marriage. We have very few comparable sources from lesser nobles, the great majority. Few of them, probably, bothered to elaborate management codes, but other sources give us access to their actual practices.

It is true that at least two magnates included in their estate codes rules that forbade maidens and widows to marry off the estate. In 1718, Dmitrii Andreevich Shepelev (1681–1759), a favorite of Peter the Great, sent instructions to his Glinka property in the Mikhailov district and, with minor variations, to his properties in Uglich, Lukhovsk, and Riazhsk districts (all of them properties that Peter the Great's wife, Catherine, had recently given Shepelev's wife as dowry, apparently) that women not marry away from the estate and to collect fifty kopeks from both bride and groom when serfs married.[54] Prince Aleksei Mikhailovich Cherkasskii (1680–1742) drew up instructions for his Markovo estate near Moscow in January 1719, perhaps in anticipation of his appointment in May as governor of Siberia. He, too, proscribed marriage on the side and for good measure banned marriage to hired hands working on his estate.[55] Neither Shepelev nor Cherkasskii explained the reasons for these interdictions, but we can assume they thought they suffered property loss when women married away. In 1742, in an unpublished essay, Vasilii Tatishchev (1686–1750, then governor of Astrakhan, better known as a historian and forger of historical evidence) recommended that maidens and widows be barred from leaving their estates in marriage because what they took with them in dowry drained wealth from the estate.[56]

By contrast, Artemii Volynskii (1689–1740, executed on the charge of conspiring to overthrow Empress Anna) did not forbid his serf women to leave the estate through marriage, but he may have been the first to require serfs to marry by a fixed age. In 1724, perhaps because he had been appointed governor of Kazan in 1723, he compiled a lengthy set of rules for his property manager, Ivan Nemchinov. Among other things, he ordered Nemchinov to see to it that men marry by age twenty because, Volynskii supposed, they delayed marriage to avoid being assigned to a *tiaglo*—that is, to a corvée labor and dues-paying unit. He also ordered that they be assigned to a labor unit at age twenty even if they weren't married; the imperative to marry by age twenty was soft rather than hard.

At the same time, Volynskii ordered that assistance be provided to help poor orphan girls marry. They were to be given one to two rubles when there was not much money available or five rubles when there was more, but they were to receive that money only when marrying peasants on their own estate, not when they married away. He ordered that fatherless girls be put to work in the estates' manor houses and that they be married to estate peasants when they came of age. If there happened to be no potential grooms on the estate at that moment, they could marry off the estate, but with a bridal departure fee (amount not specified) taken from the groom.[57]

Shepelev, Cherkasskii, and Volynskii were certainly not the only nobles who attempted in the first half of the eighteenth century to exercise control over where and at what age their serfs married, but there are more surviving sets of manorial rules—compiled by proprietors just as eminent (Stroganovs, Sheremetevs, Saltykovs, Golovkins, the patriarchy, the Kirillo-Belozersk Monastery)—that commanded, at most, that a bridal departure fee be collected, that women marrying onto the estate have manumission papers, or that manumission papers be properly issued to serf women departing the estate.[58] The Buturlins issued only the most general guidance to the stewards managing their Palekh estate (in what later became Vladimir province). From time to time they issued brief rules on marriage: women could marry off the estate so long as a departure fee was paid, and women could be taken from the side only if they had manumission papers.[59] Mikhail Golovkin was vice-chancellor under the regent Anna Leopoldovna when he drew up a "Contract" with his Kimry estate serfs (in the Kashin district of what later became Tver province) in 1740. That document ended up among the papers of the crown's properties administration when Golovkin was arrested and exiled to Siberia and his properties confiscated by the newly installed empress Elizabeth in 1741. Golovkin allowed peasant women to leave the estate through marriage without collecting a departure fee and displayed no interest in the age at which his serfs married. The only instruction he gave concerning marriage was that every groom on the estate had to pay forty-five kopeks.[60]

Clerical owners were equally latitudinarian. In 1726 instructions to managers of properties that supported the archbishopric, Archbishop Pitirim of Nizhnii Novgorod made an ineffectual gesture at restricting women's movement. When both an estate peasant and an outsider courted an estate woman, Pitirim wrote, she should marry the local man. Women without local suitors could marry outsiders, so long as a departure fee was paid. Any self-respecting peasant could exploit so capacious a loophole, and it is hard to believe Pitirim failed to understand that.[61] In the 1720s, the

Trinity Gledensk monastery in Velikii Ustiug ordered its estate manager to ensure that women marrying onto monastery properties have manumission papers and pay exit fees equal to what nobles in the area charged when they married away from monastery properties.[62]

When they mentioned marriage in their instructions, most proprietors in the first half of the eighteenth century did no more than tell managers to collect a departure fee when women married off the estate and, much less often, to collect a small fee when marriages were celebrated on the estate and to verify that manumission papers were in order. Most nobles assumed that serf women would both marry away from and onto their estates. They did nothing to interfere with the traditional peasant practice of arranging marriage across property boundaries, and they paid no attention to the age at which their serfs wed.

When they thought at all about compelling their serfs to marry, nobles around the middle of the eighteenth century seem to have focused on men and the creation of *tiagla*—labor and dues-paying units—just as Artemii Volynskii had in 1724. One such example is Aleksandr Zhukov, who was born around 1700 into a poor provincial family and is so obscure that his biographer could not determine his date of death. He began military service in the ranks but in the 1730s became an adjutant to General Aleksandr Rumiantsev. In 1744 (presumably through Rumiantsev's influence), he was appointed governor of Penza, in which post he was arrested for brutality and corruption in 1752. He owned no estates when he married, but his wife brought two properties in dowry, for which he composed managerial instructions in 1743. With his ill-gotten gains, he purchased another estate in 1751. For all three estates, he repeated verbatim a directive that he labeled "On Increasing the Number of *Tiagla*" in the 1743 instructions to his Troetskoe estate in the Elets district (subsequently in Orel province). It read in part: "If a peasant has sons or nephews fit for marriage, compel them to marry and impose half a *taiglo* each on husband and wife, and if anyone thinks of not marrying so that a *tiaglo* not be added, then no matter what impose half a *tiaglo* on him."[63] Like Artemii Volynskii, Zhukov on the one hand seemed to want to make marriage compulsory but was, on the other, satisfied to impose a labor obligation even on young men who didn't marry. We do not know which part of that directive his managers applied.

Other nobles, although they also linked imposition of labor and money dues to marriage, assumed that all of their peasants married willingly. For example, Timofei Tekutev, a guards officer who was also propertyless until his wife brought a small estate into the marriage, composed an extraordinarily detailed management code—69 manuscript pages (138 if we count both sides)—between 1754 and 1757, in which he mentioned marriage only once, like Zhukov, in connection with his serfs' dues: "When they are 18 and married and take on a *tiaglo*, they should pay three rubles."[64] He did not imply that men had to be forced to marry.

If they are at all representative, the management rules that nobles sent to their scattered estates tell us what they were thinking—and that only a small minority sought to regulate serf marriage—but not what actually happened in their or anyone else's serf villages. On the other hand, registry of deeds (*krepostnye kontory*) files, in which property transactions (manumissions included) had to be recorded if they were to have legal standing, suggest that in the first half of the eighteenth century serf women routinely married away from the estates on which they had been born, at least north of the Oka River (Moscow and most of Vladimir provinces to the north, Tula and most of Riazan provinces to the south), and that departure fees were modest.[65]

In 1725 in the Serpukhov district, just north of the Oka, the average departure fee for seventy-three women manumitted for marriage was only 1.43 rubles if we include the sixteen cases in which no charge at all was levied and 1.82 rubles if we count only the fifty-seven cases in which a fee was paid. Between May and December 1739 (the records for January–April are missing), eighteen women were manumitted for marriage in the district, with an average departure fee of 1.42 rubles. The average charge for twenty-two manumissions in 1741 was 1.73 rubles and 2.03 rubles in 1744 for thirty departures. By the 1760s, the average charge had risen to around 2.50 rubles.[66] The departure fee did increase between the 1720s and the 1760s, but very slowly.

In at least one large portion of Iaroslavl province in the first half of the eighteenth century, the majority of serf-owners demanded no payment of a departure fee at all when their serf women married onto other estates. Four manumission documents that arrived at Iusupov properties in the Romanovo district in the early 1700s mentioned no departure fee, though another set the fee at 1.2 rubles.[67] Meanwhile, the Shcherbatov family archive contains a file with a sample of thirty-five manumission papers distributed rather evenly over the years 1719–62.[68] One is a copy of the manumission document for a Shcherbatov serf released to another estate in marriage;

the rest ended up in the file because they accompanied serf women who married onto Shcherbatov properties in the contiguous Iaroslavl, Rostov, and Romanovo districts. Of the first eight in the file, dating from 1719 to 1735, only one mentions a departure fee: 1 ruble, in 1730. Many of the others record 9- or 10-kopek fees for writing and recording the documents at district registries of deeds. This gives us reason to think that, at least in the eighteenth century, when manumission papers failed to mention a departure fee, it was not an oversight but an indication that none had been collected. Beginning in 1736, some of the manumission documents specify that the women were released "without a departure fee"—so state four of the seventeen issued between 1736 and 1750—while over the same years, eight others mentioned no fees but those associated with the production and registration of the documents themselves. Only five of the seventeen recorded a departure charge: 1 ruble four times, 2 rubles once. Another manumission document, not in the Shcherbatov file but given in 1739 to a woman marrying onto an estate close to a cluster of Shcherbatov villages, recorded a departure fee of 1 ruble.[69]

Down to 1750, in other words, when a departure fee was demanded for the women they were taking back to their village in marriage, Shcherbatov serfs almost never paid more than one ruble. Most of the time they paid no departure fee at all. That was not because they returned again and again to a few estates where brides were free. Most of the brides' natal estates appear in the file only once, and their owners ranged from great magnates like the Saltykovs, Sheremetevs, and Golitsyns to nobles likely unknown beyond their own districts. Presumably nobles in this region of predominantly miniscule estates understood that the serfs belonging to all of them would have to find wives beyond their own estates and that, over the long term, the trade would balance.[70]

Manumission papers issued for marriage in the Rostov district, which overlapped geographically with the Shcherbatov estates, confirm that the documents in the Shcherbatov file faithfully represent practice in that area. In 1733, no departure fees were charged for thirty-eight of eighty-three serf women recorded in the district registry as manumitted for marriage; in the first half of 1750, no fee was paid for thirty-one of sixty-eight women marrying off their estates; in 1751, forty-six of ninety-seven paid no departure fee; and in 1771 and 1772, a majority of women released for marriage—thirty-two of fifty-seven and forty-one of eighty-one, respectively—were charged no departure fee. The departure fee, when levied, was minimal: an average of 23 kopeks in 1733, 94 kopeks in 1750, and 75 kopeks in 1751. In 1771 and 1772, men taking women from properties that had formerly belonged to monasteries or other church institutions—they were now classified as "economic peasants"—were charged 10 to 11 rubles (whereas they had often paid nothing prior to the secularization of church properties in the early 1760s). In those years, noble proprietors charged on average 3.13 and 3.88 rubles.[71] That was a reflection of a countrywide increase of the departure fee toward the market price of a marriageable serf woman.

In the first half of the eighteenth century, however, Rostov district departure fees had no relationship at all to the market price for marriageable serf women. In 1733, when no departure fee was paid for thirty-eight women manumitted for marriage and the average charge for the other forty-five was a very modest 23 kopeks, eleven marriageable serf women in the district were sold at an average price of 5.09 rubles. If we exclude the two women sold for 15.00 and 10.00 rubles as likely special cases, we get what was probably a more accurate approximation of the average price, 3.44 rubles.[72] Around Rostov, it wasn't until the 1770s that the departure fee began to close on the market price for serf maidens.

The Rostov district was certainly at the low end of the departure fee scale, but it shared that space with other districts. In the Poshekhonie district, then in Novgorod but subsequently in northwestern Iaroslavl province, between 1709 and 1715 the average departure fee was under a ruble; in 1749, it was slightly more than a ruble.[73] In a set of thirty-three manumission papers accumulated in the 1720s–50s by monasteries in the Pereslavl-Zalesskii district, midway between Moscow and Rostov, eight provide no information about the departure fee, thirteen specify that none was collected, eight report a one-ruble fee, and one a fee of three and a half rubles. Three mention that there was a fee but not what it was.[74] In a set of eight manumission papers brought to a Shuvalov property in the Vladimir area between 1735 and 1754, seven carried a departure fee of one ruble; the other (from 1754), a fee of two rubles.[75]

Fees elsewhere, even bordering on Iaroslavl province, were not always so low. A file of thirty-eight manumission papers brought to Glebov-Shtreshnev properties in the Novotorzhok district, just to the west of the Iaroslavl district, shows that prices could be highly variable even in a single district. The five letters of manumission dating from 1708 to 1718 recorded departure fees averaging 2.40 rubles, twenty-one from the 1720s average 2.93 rubles, and eleven dated 1730–50 average 1.31 rubles. One dated 1764 recorded a ten-ruble fee. Here, unlike in the nearby Iaroslavl and Rostov districts, there was no widespread waving of the departure fee. Moreover, the average fee for the 1720s is the highest I have found for the first half of the eighteenth century. On the other hand, the eleven manumission papers from 1730–50, while an unsatisfactory sample, make it almost certain that the departure fees really did decline in the 1730s–40s, perhaps by something like 50 percent. The properties the women arrived from belonged to the Dolgorukovs, Ladyzhenskies, Buturlins, and Musin-Pushkins, as well as to many lesser nobles.[76]

In the Riazan district, most of which lay south of the Oka River, departure fees in the 1720s–30s were also relatively high and then fell. In 1726–27, the average of twenty-seven departure fees paid in the district was 2.07 rubles. The lowest was 50 kopecks; the highest, 4 rubles.[77] In 1737, ninety-three manumissions for marriage were registered in the district, and the average departure fee was 2.17 rubles; in 1738, the average fell to 2.02 rubles (ninety-two manumissions) in 1739 to 1.67 rubles (thirty-six manumissions), but in 1754 rose to 2.42 rubles (ninety manumissions).[78] The fees here fluctuated, as they did in the Novotorzhok district.

In the Riazan district, as elsewhere, few marriageable serf women were sold individually, so it is difficult to compare departure fee to purchase price. Only one such sale was registered in the Riazan district in my 1738 sample, but in 1739, there were four more: the price was 3 rubles twice, and 2 rubles thrice. The average selling price of ten maiden house serfs in those years was 4.3 rubles.[79] Some may have had skills that increased their value, but in the first half of the eighteenth century, maiden house serfs sometimes cost less, sometimes more, than maiden field serfs. A reasonable conclusion is that, in the Riazan district, the average departure fee was closer to the market price of a marriageable woman than in the Rostov district but still only about half the local price of a serf girl.

For Nizhnii Novgorod province to the east, we have a file containing the manumission documents of twenty-four women who married onto the Iusopov estate of Bezvodnoe (twenty-five kilometers east of Nizhnii Novgorod) between 1732 and 1754. In fourteen cases, the women's owners charged one to one and a half rubles, in five cases two rubles, and in five cases three to four rubles. There was a clear tick upward after 1750: owners charged two to four rubles for the four women who married into Bezvodnoe in those years. Again, the significance is not just the relatively low average departure charge but also the owners who released the girls in marriage, among them Golitsyns, Volkonskies, Musin-Pushkins, Lunins, Shereme-tevs, and Apraksins, as well as the Nizhnii Novgorod Bishopric.[80] In the first half of the eighteenth century, the overwhelming majority of the great noble families released their serf women for marriage.

The departure fees I have taken from notarial records and manumission papers, which did have a tendency to rise, have to be corrected for inflation. From 1701 to 1730, average market prices for grain and manufactured goods doubled. Prices in the 1730s and the 1750s were almost identical, although they had risen a bit and then declined a bit in the intervening years.[81] In other words, departure fees that were one or two rubles in the 1720s would have had to rise to one and a half to three rubles by the 1750s to keep pace with inflation. In some districts they did; in others they did not, and the real cost of taking a girl away from her natal estate in marriage fell. Given the quite different price dynamics in different districts, probably the safest con-clusion to draw is that, overall, there was either no change in the inflation-adjusted departure fee or a slight decline from the early to mid-eighteenth century.

While I assume that some nobles refused to allow young serf women to leave their property in districts north of the Oka River, I have encoun-tered no evidence they actually did so, aside from the Shepelev and Cher-kasskii estate instructions of 1718 and 1719. In the Riazan district, on the other hand, while many women were manumitted for marriage, the owners of some large estates would not let their women marry away. The evidence comes not from estate instructions but from the 1762–63 tax census returns. This was the first census to list women, and census takers were instructed to record their ages as well as their native villages and, if serfs, their former owners, in order to track the chain of ownership.

At Konstantinovo, on the south bank of the Oka River, where ownership was divided among a number of families, the largest share in 1762 belonged to Semen Naryshkin. Of the ninety-nine married and widowed Naryshkin serf women, ninety-seven had been born not just in Konstantinovo but in the Naryshkin portion of the village; the other two had been imported from distant Naryshkin properties. Only a single woman over twenty had never married, probably because she was severely handicapped.[82] Almost all had married before 1762; Naryshkin women at Konstantinovo had probably been compelled to marry on the estate since the 1720s. I suspect compulsion because, left to themselves, some Naryshkin women would have married men from other portions of Konstantinovo and from other villages in the area. If that had been the case, some Naryshkin men would have had to have found wives on other properties; they, too, must have been compelled to marry on the estate if marriageable women were available.

The same situation prevailed on a large Volynskii estate that overlapped Semen Naryshkin's. In Egor Volynskii's share of Konstantinovo, twenty-three of twenty-four wives were born on Volynskii properties; only one wife had been imported from a different nobleman's property. Remarkably, in the four villages (or portions thereof) that made up the Volynskii estate, there were 128 married or widowed men, and only one, age twenty-four, who was single; he may have married subsequently. All 137 women twenty and over were married or widowed, and only four had not been born on Volynskii properties; a few had been imported from Volynskii estates beyond the Riazan district.[83]

There is no reason to believe that when the Naryshkins and Volynskies banned off-estate marriage they also compelled every serf on their estate to marry; universal marriage was the rule among all peasants in the area. In 1762, the peasants in the large village of Novoselki and the moderately sized village of Cheshuevo were shifting from ownership by the Solotchinsk Monastery to their secularized status as "economic peasants." Their monastic proprietor had permitted women to marry off the estate and had used no compulsion to force marriage, yet in Cheshuevo in 1762, all forty-nine men twenty and over were married or widowed, and only two of the fifty-three women twenty and over had never married; twenty-four women had arrived in Cheshuevo through marriage. The two unmarried women were both twenty and almost certain to marry.[84] If we measure from the age beyond which marriage was highly unlikely—twenty-five—then the propensity to marry among Cheshuevo men and women was 100 percent. In Novoselki in the same year, all but one of the 261 men twenty-five and over were married or widowed, as were all but one of the 307 women twenty-five and over.[85]

In this part of the Riazan district, seigniorial and monastery serfs both married universally. They also married at identical ages. In a sample of seven economic peasant villages (including Cheshuevo and Novoselki) and five serf villages (including Konstantinovo and Fediakino, which is about to become part of this story), the mean ages at marriage in the 1780s were virtually identical: 17.5 and 17.6 years for male serfs and economic peasants, respectively, and 15.7 and 15.5 years for female serfs and economic peasants.[86] Universal and relatively early marriage among Riazan serfs should not be taken as evidence of aggressively promarital policies among serf-owners; it was rather what all local peasants worked hard at to achieve on their own.

It was possible to sustain a regime both of universal marriage (the peasant practice around Riazan) and demographic autarky (the ideal of some nobles) on relatively large estates, at least if the owner could, if necessary, import brides from other family properties. That was not true on smaller estates. The large serf village of Fediakino, immediately adjacent to Konstantinovo, had multiple owners, one of them the Volynskii family; those serfs exchanged daughters only with other portions of the Volynskii estate. The other fourteen owners with small shares—as small as a single household—owned no large properties nearby. They could not be demographically self-sufficient, try as they might. Of the 145 wives they collectively owned, fifty-two married within the mini-portions of Fediakino in which they had been born, owners imported fifteen others from their distant properties; the other seventy-eight were women from other nobles' estates or (a few) non-serf women. All women twenty and over had married. Among men twenty and over, 126 were married and eight were single. Six of those were between twenty and twenty-seven and had some chance of marrying, but in a district where universal marriage predominated, those eight unmarried adult males were likely an index of demographic distress in Fediakino.[87] With the women of the large neighboring Volynskii and Naryshkin properties unavailable to them, Fediakino men had to cross many boundaries to acquire their wives. Even the Volynskies recognized the futility of pursuing demographic autarky at Dubrovichi, about twenty kilometers east of their main holdings, where they owned only forty-six serfs and a small portion of the village. There they permitted the exchange of brides with serfs belonging to other nobles.[88]

It is possible that the Oka River border—to the north, very little evidence that owners tried to control their serfs' marriage; to the south, evidence that owners did in fact ban off-estate marriage, at least on some large estates—was ecological in origin. In the Riazan area, the Oka corresponds roughly to the boundary between infertile northern and fertile southern soils. Perhaps the increasing aspiration of eighteenth-century nobles with sizeable estates in the south to grow grain for the market and their consequent introduction of corvée labor regimes led them to focus on maximizing the number of labor units by making sure that women were locally available for their men.

On the other hand, demographically autarkic Naryshkin and Volynskii estates may have been atypical even for the Riazan district. Located on or close to the Oka River, they were exceptionally well placed to ship grain to the Moscow market, which was quite close. The relatively high bridal departure fee in the Riazan district may not have been typical of all areas south of the Oka, either. The Iusopov file of manumission papers includes one from a Prince Repin, who released a girl in marriage for no given departure fee in what would later be Tula province; another in which a Tula girl was released for three rubles; and a final in which a girl was released for two rubles in what would become Orel province. Three departure fees in the Briansk district from the 1720s to the 1750s point to roughly one ruble as the standard charge.[89]

While there was considerable local and individual variation in the way nobles dealt with their serfs' marriages in the first half of the eighteenth century, the great majority allowed women to marry away and levied relatively low departure fees or, in a surprisingly large number of cases, no fee at all. There was, in other words, continuity with seventeenth-century practices. The Kirillo-Belozersk monks deliberately decided to follow precedent. When they issued instructions to a steward being dispatched to manage properties in the Nizhnii Novgorod and Arzamas districts in 1735, he was told to collect bridal departure fees as specified in the previous instruction for those same estates in 1653.[90] In 1726, the Nizhnii Novgorod Archbishopric raised its departure fee from the fifteen kopeks of the late seventeenth century, but only to thirty-one kopeks.[91] And it was not just in the Iaroslavl and Rostov districts that large numbers of women were assessed no departure fee. When managers appointed by the Aleksandr Nevskii Lavra, founded in St. Petersburg in 1713, set out in 1714 to take over properties in the Bezhetsk, Uglich, Iaroslavl, Tver, and Kashin districts that had been transferred from the Trinity–St. Sergius Monastery and Novgorod's Monastery of the Holy Spirit, they reported that in the recent past serf women on some of the properties had married away without paying departure fees.[92] The implication of these reports was not necessarily that the former estate managers weren't supposed to collect departure fees; their oversight may have been so lax that peasants routinely circumvented the rules.

Monastery and other church proprietors may have clung to past practices longer than nobles, but for the first half of the eighteenth century there is far more evidence of nobles' traditional nonintervention in serf marriage than there is of a desire to compel women to marry on their natal estates, to command marriage by a certain age, or to levy departure fees equivalent to market prices. When Prince Petr Aleksandrovich Rumiantsev in 1751 instructed the manager of his Nizhnii Novgorod properties, "Do not intervene in weddings among peasants in any way or under any pretext, do not use force to compel anyone to take a husband. . . . Let them celebrate their own weddings according to their own wishes and agreements," he was simply making explicit the hands-off practice of the great majority of nobles at the time.[93] Surely one reason why few nobles banned off-estate marriage was that they were not aware of any problem such a measure would solve. For owners of small estates, on which the Orthodox Church's elaborate consanguinity rules (which encompassed in-laws and spiritual kin through god parenthood) would have ruled out almost any same-estate marriage, multilateral exchange of women among estates was the only way, short of purchase, to ensure that all men found wives.

Into the 1750s and 1760s, serfs and other peasants encountered no, or only minimal, impediments to marriage across estate boundaries in much of Iaroslavl province in the Serpukhov, Pereiaslavl, Novotorzhok, and Nizhnii Novgorod districts; and no doubt elsewhere as well. The Riazan district was a partial exception to that rule, though surely not the only one. Those exceptions are, at the very least, curious: allowing serfs to sort out their marriages by themselves worked so well that there is no self-evident reason why, in the first half of the eighteenth century, the Naryshkins and Volynskies forbade their Konstantinovo serf women to marry away from their estates.

It is not obvious, either, why in the first half of the century, nobles continued to collect either no departure fee at all or fees well below the market price of marriageable serf women, but I think the moral economy—let custom prevail—is the overarching explanation. Moral economy comes into view only when custom is challenged, and I have already introduced two instances (the Solotchinsk Monastery in 1696 and Sheremetev in 1717) when proprietors backed down after their serfs protested sharp increases.

Sometimes conflicts between serfs and their owners over the amount of the bridal departure fee erupted when new owners replaced old and raised the fee. The Aleksandr Nevskii Lavra instructed its local administrators, sent to take over the monastery's new properties in 1714–16, to impose departure fees of five rubles or not less than two rubles.[94] This caused consternation in the villages. At Priseki in the Bezhetsk district, for instance, peasants in late 1716 or early 1717 complained that "there is no one to give our daughters to" because local peasants wouldn't pay that much and the nearest property belonging to the Lavra was fifty kilometers away. They begged the archimandrite to have mercy so that their women would "not go forever without marrying, not grow old" unmarried. In February 1717, the archimandrite told the Priseki administrator to stick to the five- or two-ruble rule.[95] Peasants from the village of Kunganovo, Novotorzhok district, also protested the new fee early in 1717, reporting that they had previously exchanged daughters with their neighbors without either side paying departure fees and suggesting that the archimandrite recall the Kunganovo women to the village, which was—so they said—increasingly deserted.[96] In July 1717, the Lavra began to reverse course, following another complaint from a property in the Olonets district that the five-ruble fee was preventing their women from marrying. The archimandrite decided that the exchange of daughters, at the customary local charge, was permitted with peasants on the properties of other monasteries and the Archbishopric of Novgorod. Shortly thereafter, the archimandrite decided that the exchange of marriageable women with noble estates that did not levy departure fees was also permissible. In September 1718, the archimandrite folded; he instructed all of his property managers to collect whatever neighboring serf-owners charged for women released to marry.[97]

It is surely significant that in two of the three known protests, the Lavra's serfs emphasized the harm the five-ruble fee did to women by preventing them from marrying (what exactly the Kunganovo serfs claimed was the problem is not entirely clear) rather than the fact that the fee caused neighbors to retaliate—as surely they must have—either by charging the Lavra's men five rubles for wives or by refusing to release their own women to Lavra properties. Sheremetev's Voshchazhnikovo serfs, too, emphasized the harm that Sheremetev's five-ruble departure fee inflicted on their daughters. Perhaps peasants believed the harm to women was in fact the greater or, more likely, the strongest argument they could make. Perhaps the archimandrite himself understood (as the Kunganovo peasants may have been implying) that the Lavra's own men were having trouble securing wives. Perhaps the monks came to understand that there was a genuine market in brides and that they simply could not charge whatever they wanted. Or perhaps they conceded that it was simply wrong to impede women's marriages.

The argument that serf women had the right to marry, even if that meant marrying away from the estate, proved powerful. If we can understand why, that should help us understand how Russian peasants and nobles understood peasant marriage as of the early eighteenth century. The serfs who advanced the argument certainly did not mean that their daughters should have the right to choose husbands for themselves. The conventional understanding that peasant patriarchs and matriarchs chose their children's marriage partners without much deference to their children's own opinions is certainly exaggerated. Nevertheless, as of the early eighteenth century, when peasant marriages really were between children—girls and boys often no older than fifteen—parental opinion must ordinarily have been decisive.[98] Nor did serfs believe that young women had the right to choose whether to marry. As we will see in chapter 2, serfs in search of brides for their sons often demanded that their owners compel other fathers to hand over their marriage-resistant daughters. In the peasant view, daughters had either the right or the duty to marry, depending on circumstances.

The harm that peasants pointed to, and that Sheremetev and the Aleksandr Nevskii monks understood, was almost certainly moral: girls "would go forever unmarried." Spinsterhood itself was the harm; all women (as all men) must marry. Peasant sayings and proverbs, collected mostly in the nineteenth century but certainly not much changed from 1700, characterize the spinster as an embittered old woman—in fact not fully a woman at all, because she had never been a wife or mother. Ethnographic accounts from the nineteenth century describe the treatment of old maids as useless mouths (consuming food, producing nothing), as women with no established role in the household and so deserving no respect, and indeed as outcasts, unless they had deliberately chosen spinsterhood as a religious vocation or plausibly simulated such a choice.[99] It must have seemed to early eighteenth-century peasants so utterly wrong to turn women into unnatural creatures that they made that the basis of their appeal to Sheremetev, who immediately conceded, and to the Aleksandr Nevskii monks, who, perhaps because of their own religious vocation, at first rejected the appeal but did in the end relent. The moral appeal worked because nobles shared their serfs' view of the unnaturalness of single adult women. They were, after all, anxious to find suitable matches for their own daughters.

The peasant view that the spinster was not just unfortunate but unnatural made sense in a society in which single adult women were indeed rare and, if not living an unworldly religious life, were either mentally or physically crippled. In fact, in the many large villages in which every single adult man and woman was married, severely impaired men and women must have been among them. Universal marriage and dread at the prospect that daughters might go unwed were mutually reinforcing.

The serfs' moral appeals to their owners to rescind departure fees that threatened to turn young women into spinsters were so compelling that they worked even without the disquieting threat of violence that added force to the demands eighteenth-century British laborers made for relief when bread prices shot up. The moral appeal had so much force, in fact, that it worked even when the claim of harm was implausible. When the Voshchazhnikovo serfs told Boris Sheremetev that some of their daughters were unable to make matches on the estate, they almost certainly stretched the truth. Voshchazhnikovo was a huge property, with a population in 1765 of 1,910 male and 1,911 female serfs—and so probably around 2,500 to 3,000 serfs in the early eighteenth century—in villages spread out over 130 square kilometers.[100] Because the estate was physically so large, it surely was more convenient for many of its serfs to make matches with neighbors on the other side of the property line than to search for brides in distant villages on the estate. But with a population of that size, demographic autarky was feasible. The field marshal declined to argue the point.

NOTES

1. *Materialy po istorii sel'skogo khoziaistva i kres'tianstva Rossii. Sel'skokhoziastvennye instruktsii (pervaia polovina XVIII v.)*, pp. 12, 147. The ten-kopek charge is in instructions sent in 1703 to the crown property manager at Voshchazhnikovo; the twenty-five-kopek charge is in a 1705 instruction to crown properties generally.

2. Ibid., pp. 24–25.

3. *Arkhiv sela Voshchazhnikova*, p. 98. "Orphans" was a standard expression of obeisant dependence.

4. Ibid., p. 99.

5. RGADA, f. 615, op. 1, d. 9159, 1733, l. 44.

6. Ibid., d. 9177, ll. 7, 23; d. 9180, ll. 40b–50b, 12–120b, 150b; d. 9205, ll. 100b–11, 16–160b, 220b–23; d. 9207, ll. 9–90b, 28–290b, 39–390b, 70–700b.

7. Thompson, "Moral Economy of the English Crowd," pp. 76–136; Thompson, "Moral Economy Reviewed," pp. 259–351.

8. Hellie, *Muscovite Law Code (Ulozhenie) of 1649*, part 1, p. 90. The Russian and English are on facing pages. My translation differs slightly from Hellie's. That the ban on movement applied only to men is obvious in the seventeenth-century Russian, in which *krest'ianin* always referred to a man while women were called peasant wives or daughters.

9. Ibid., p. 101.

10. *Akty feodal'nogo zemlevladeniia*, part 1, p. 68. In 1471, Prince Iurii also exempted property belonging to the Trinity St. Sergius Monastery; *Akty sotsial'no-ekonomicheskoi istorii*, vol. 1, p. 292. These are the first references to the *vyvodnaia kunitsa* that I have found. There are earlier references to a *novozhennaia kunitsa*, which was likely a different and lower tax on all marriages in the realm, a tax subsequently, or interchangeably, called the *ubrus*. It may be that the term *novozhennaia kunitsa* sometimes included the extra fee collected for leaving a particular jurisdiction.

11. *Akty sotsial'no-ekonomicheskoi istorii*, vol. 3, p.146–47.

12. *Akty feodal'nogo zemlevladeniia*, part 3, pp. 98–99. This is in a 1619 reconfirmation of possession of the land and the right to collect the marriage tax to Patriach Filaret.

13. Ibid., part 1, p. 45. There are other patriarchal grants similar to this one.

14. *Arkhivnyi material: novootkrytye dokumenty*, pp. 124–28 and passim. See also "'Se az pozhaloval esmi," pp. 187–89; Korbin, *Vlast' i sobstvennost*, p. 107; Hellie, *Enserfment*, pp. 27–28.

15. *Kniga kliuchei*, pp. 161–62; Shchepetov, "Sel'skoe khoziaistvo," p. 116.

16. *Akty feodal'nogo zemlevladeniia*, part 3, pp. 85–86.

17. Ibid., p. 98.

18. Ibid., pp. 107, 115.

19. Vozdvizhenskii, *Istoricheskoe obozrenie*, p. 75; *Materialy dlia istorii Vladimirskoi*, vol. 3, p. 329; GIM OPI, f. 17, op. 2, d. 2a, d. 302, l. 1.

20. *Materialy dlia istorii Vladimirskoi*, vol. 3, p. 333. The text breaks off a line before Karsakov set the amount of the fee.

21. *Sbornik starinnykh bumag*, part 3, p. 79. The peasant denied knowledge of his wife's bigamy, but he probably lied.

22. *Pamiatniki istorii krest'ian*, p. 49. The 1607 decree did not say that serf women had the right to leave through marriage, probably because everyone already knew that. The text of the decree is, unfortunately, unreliable, fabricated in part by Vasilii Tatishchev on the basis of later seventeenth-century documents. There is a very careful analysis by Arakcheev, "Sobornoe ulozhenie," pp. 98–114. He concludes that this provision was in the surviving fragment of the original because it was not included in later laws and decrees from which Tatishchev borrowed.

23. Semevskii, *Krest'iane*, t. 2, p. 302.

24. GIM OPI, f. 229, op. 1, d. 46, ll. 12–120b. The document is undated but is written in what an archivist's notation identifies as a mid- to late seventeenth-century hand.

25. Novosel'skii, *Votchinik*, pp. 73, 78, and passim.

26. For Bezobrazov's correspondence on serf marriage, see RGADA, f. 1257, op. 1, d. 1, l. 401–30b; d. 3, l. 271–710b; d. 4, l. 317, 403–30b, 463–640b; RGB OR, f. 29, d. 135, ll. 92–93. Three of the documents have been published in *Arkhiv stol'nika*, part 1, pp. 442, 658–61. For additional reports from stewards on departure fees forwarded to Bezobrazov or on girls released from estates through marriage, see *Arkhiv stol'nika*, part 1, pp. 441, 458, 500, 638, 646.

27. Bulygin, *Monastyrskie krest'iane*, p. 258, 300–1; RGADA, f. 1441, op. 2, ch. 1, d. 2285, l. 2; Shchepetov, "Sel'skoe khoziaistvo," p. 116; TsANO, f. 570, op. 552, 1726 d. 42, l. 11.

28. GIM OPI, f. 17, op. 2 Kollektsiia, ed. khr. 13, delo 1363, ll. 2, 5 (ll. 1, 5, Murom posad; these are for townswomen marrying into serf villages); Shumakov, *Obzor "Gramot Kollegii Ekonomii,"* vol. 4, pp. 415–16.

29. Gnevushev, *Novgorodskii*, pp. ix–x.

30. *Opisanie aktov sobraniia Grafa A. S. Uvarova*, pp. 129, 131–32.

31. *Akty khoziaistva*, p. 152; Zabelin, "Bol'shoi boiarin," no. 1, pp. 22–23; Petrikeev, *Krupnoe krepostnoe khoziaistvo*, p. 71.

32. GIM OPI, f. 17, op. 2, dd. 1a, 2a, 3, 136, 152, 296c, 428; Dmitrieva, "Ustavnye gramoty," pp. 266–67.

33. *Dopolneniia k Aktam istoricheskim*, vol. 4, p. 98.

34. Shumakov, *Obzor gramot "Kollegii ekonomii,"* vol. 2, p. 30 (Belozersk); *Akty, otnosiashchiesia do iuridicheskogo byta*, vol. 2, col. 582 (confiscated estate); GIM OR, f. 229, op. 1, d. 46, l. 19 (Belozersk).

35. Shumakov, *Obzor "Gramot Kollegii ekonomii,"* vol. 2, p. 238; ibid., vol., 4, p. 415; *Materialy dlia istorii Vladimirskoi gubernii*, vol. 3, pp. 281–82; GIM OPI, f. 17, op. 2, d. 1, d. 102; op. 2a, d. 251, 252; op. 4, d. 550.

36. *Akty istoricheskie*, vol. 5, p. 96.

37. Ibid., p. 333.

38. RGADA, f. 1192, op. 1, d. 1148.

39. TsANO, f. 570, op. 552, 1726 d. 42, l. 51. This information comes in the form of notes made in 1725 about what departure fees had been in the past in preparation for compiling a new set of instructions for estate managers.

40. *Akty, otnosiashchiesia do iuridicheskogo byta*, vol. 2, cols. 650–52 (the cases from 1690, 1693, and 1696); GIM OPI, f. 17, op. 2, ed. kh. 4, d. 563 (1695).

41. GIM OPI, f. 17, op. 2, d. 1, d. 115, 119; d. 3B, d. 461, 465, 473.

42. Man'kov, *Razvitie*, pp. 193–217. The statistics are on p. 205. For an apparently well-founded assertion that Boris Morozov purchased serfs without land prior to 1650, see Petrikeev, *Krupnoe krepostnoe khoziaistvo*, pp. 156–57. References to "purchased peasants" occasionally show up in Andrei Bezobrazov's correspondence. See *Arkhiv stol'nika*, pp. 230–31 (1671), 650 (1681).

43. Man'kov, *Razvitie*, pp. 210–11; Borisov, "Pomeshchich'e khoziaistvo," pp. 22–24.

44. *Arkhiv stol'nika*, pp. 441–42.

45. RGADA, f. 1257, op. 1, d. 3, ll. 402–30b.

46. Hellie, *Economy and Material Culture*, pp. 419, 450–51, 139, 105.

47. GIM OPI, f. 17, op. 2, dd. 1a, 148; f. 229, op. 1, d. 4, l. 79; RGADA, f. 615, op. 1, d. 8526; op. 1, d. 8529. The Riazan district, discussed below, was one of the first in which a two-ruble departure fee became standard.

48. RGADA, f. 1202, op. 1, dd. 265, 324, 451, 502; Dobroklonskii, "Solotchinskii monastyr'," p. 72.

49. For a full exploration of marriage among Solotcha serfs in the 1690s, see Bushnell, "Bor'ba za nevestu," pp. 81–98.

50. The petition's formulation, which appeared to make Solotchinsk fathers responsible for paying the bride price, was misleading.

51. RGADA, f. 1202, op. 1, dd. 499, 502.

52. Ibid., d. 324, l. 29. The other petitions are ibid., ll. 4, 5, 8, 13, 14, 18, 19, 25, 26, 27, 28. I deal with the practice by which peasants on the Solotcha properties required that the archimandrite order them to hand over their daughters in marriage in Bushnell, "Bor'ba za nevestu." In brief, this was the way they avoided what they took to be the dishonorable act of giving their daughters away voluntarily.

53. To cite only the most serious historians: Semevskii, *Krest'iane*, vol. 1, pp. 302–24 and passim; Aleksandrov, *Sel'skaia obshchina*, pp. 303–9; Pushkareva, *Chastnaia zhizn'*, pp. 152–53; Mironov, *Sotsial'naia istoriia Rossii*, vol. 1, pp. 167–68. They have read evidence from the second half of the eighteenth century as representing developments over the entire century. An exception to the consensus is David Moon, *Russian Peasantry*, p. 168. On noble estate instructions in general, see Aleksandrov, *Sel'skaia obshchina*, pp. 47–116; Tikhonov, *Dvorianskaia usad'ba*, pp. 337–413; Rubinshtein, *Sel'skoe khoziaistvo Rossii*, pp. 132–148.

54. Petrovskaia, "Nakazy votchinnym prikazchikam," pp. 224, 234–35; *Russkii biograficheskii slovar'*, vol. 23, pp. 96–97. The fifty-kopek charge was a relic of the *ubrus*, the princely tax on every marriage that, like the *vyvodnaia kunitsa*, had been privatized.

55. Petrovskaia, "Nakazy," pp. 250–53; *Russkii biograficheskii slovar'*, vol. 22, pp. 183–94.

56. Tatishchev, *Izbrannye proizvedeniia*, p. 409.

57. *Instruktsiia dvoretskomu Ivanu Nemchinovu*, pp. 14, 16–19; Anisimov, *Five Empresses*, pp. 78, 100, 121–23.

58. Andreev, "Nakaz votchnnika," p. 271 (Andrei Vinius, 1709); Ustiugov, "Instruktsiia votchinnomu prikazchiku," pp. 160–61 (Stroganovs, 1725); Shcheptov, *Krepostnoe pravo*, p. 267 (Anna Sheremeteva, 1727); Riazanovskii, *Krest'iane Galichskoi votchiny*, pp. 39–40 (Vladimir Saltykov, 1732); RGADA f. 1441, op. 2, ch. 1, d. 2285, l. 2 (1735); Gorchakov, *O zemel'nykh vladeniiakh*, Prilozhenie, pp. 168–69 (1714). In his 1724 decree forbidding parents to compel brides and grooms to marry, Peter the Great also said in passing that masters must not compel their slaves (*rab, rabynia*) to marry against their will (*PSZ*, vol. 7, pp. 197–98). Peter had abolished slavery in 1723, but the decree had been drafted in 1722. Probably Peter meant the decree to apply only

to actual slaves. The decree says nothing about serfs; Peter most likely assumed that serf-owners were not compelling serfs to marry.

59. RGADA, f. 1365, op. 1, d. 20, ll. 6 (1717), 18–19 (1719); d. 36, l. 3–4 (1720), l. 5 (1721); d. 36, l. 8–80b (1721), l. 26–20b (1728).

60. Tikhonov, "Dogovor (Kontrakt) 1740 goda," pp. 146–51.

61. TsANO, f. 570, op. 552, 1726 d. 42, l. 11. The Holy Synod had ordered Pitirim to issue manorial instructions, and he reported that he had done as told (ibid., ll. 20–210b). The original directive from the synod is not in the file; possibly the synod provided guidelines. Neither the synod nor Pitirim could suggest that actual compulsion be applied to peasants because that would have violated the church's rule that those being wed must consent to the match.

62. RGADA, f. 1187, op. 1, d. 2366, l. 109–1090b.

63. RGADA, f. 196, op. 1, d. 1618, l. 7–70b, 36–360b, 480b–49; Zaozerskaia, "Pomeshchik Zhukov i ego khoziaistvo," pp. 213–26; Neelov, "Sledstvennaia kommissiia," pp. 1–40.

64. Smilianskaia, *Dvorianskoe gnezdo*, pp. 58–59. The entire code covers pp. 32–145.

65. There were seventeenth-century predecessors, but Peter the Great regularized these offices; *krepostnaia kontora* was the name employed from 1719. See Kapustina, "Zapisnye knigi Moskovskoi krepostnoi kontory," pp. 216–73.

66. RGADA, f. 615, dd. 10197, 10206, 10207, 10231, 10266, 10269.

67. RGADA, f. 1290, op. 1, d. 193, ll. 2–6.

68. RGADA, f. 1289, op. 1, d. 149. A draft 1762 census return for the large Mikhailovskoe and Kozmodemianskoe estates in the Iaroslavl district identifies a number of women who married onto the estate; none of their manumission documents are in the file.

69. GIM OPI, f. 182, op. 1, d. 13, l. 45.

70. A volume of the tax census conducted in 1762–64 in Igretsk *volost'* and in Zakotorozhsk and Verkhovsk *stany* in the Iaroslaval district—three precincts that supplied wives for Shcherbatov serfs—has census returns for sixty-five noble estates, not one of which had even 50 male serfs; most had 10 or fewer (RGADA, f. 350, op. 2, d. 4301, ch. 1). In a set of forty returns from gentry and church estates from the same census in Zakotorozhsk stan alone, ten had more than 100 male serfs (the largest, a monastery estate, had 1,438 male serfs), while sixteen dwarf estates had 10 or fewer male serfs, which is to say that they usually consisted of only two or three serf households (ibid., d. 4301, ch. 2).

71. RGADA, f. 615, op. 1, d. 9159 (1733), 9177 (1750), 9180 (1751), 9205 (1771), 9207 (1772).

72. Ibid., d. 9159. ll. 127–182. The women included six single women: four house serfs (whose average price was lower than that of the others), and two widows.

73. RGADA, f. 615, op. 1, d. 8526, 8528, 8529, 8531, 8594.

74. Shumakov, *Obzor "Gramot Kollegii Ekonomii,"* vol. 4, pp. 414–22.

75. RGADA, f. 1288, op. 1, d. 7.

76. TsIAM, f. 1614, op. 1, d. 118.

77. GIM OPI, f. 229, op. 1, d. 91, ll. 128–218.

78. RGADA, f. 615, op. 1, d. 8509 (1737), 8510 (1738), 8511 (1739), 8512 (1754). The last file has been misdated "1751" in the archival inventory list and on the front cover; the document begins with the notation "In 1754. . . ." Most of the manumissions for marriage involved single peasant women, a few involved widows and female house serfs, whose departure fees were in the same range as for single women from farming families. In every year, a few of the women paid no departure fee, which slightly reduces the average. In every year but one, the modal fee was two rubles; in 1739, it was one ruble.

79. Ibid., d. 8510, ll. 60b–70b, 14, 18, 190b, 220b; d. 8511, ll. 2–40b, 50b–6, 7, 8, 12, 130b, 17, 18, 20, 24.

80. RGADA, f. 1290, op. 1, d. 193, ll. 9–11, 13–14, 17, 19–25, 27–31, 34–40.

81. Mironov, "Consequences of the Price Revolution," pp. 457–59.

82. RGADA, f. 350, op. 2, ch. 2, d. 2616, ll. 485–574. I have not counted house serfs or a group of mostly single men at the end of the census return; the latter appear to be either additional house serfs or men recently moved to Konstantinovo from some other Naryshkin estate. In 1792, of the 150 adult women in that portion of Konstantinovo (then owned by the Golitsyns) only 2, ages twenty-six and twenty-eight, were unmarried, and they were both cripples (GIM OPI, f. 17, op. 1, d. 2503, ll. 16–28).

83. RGADA, f. 350, op. 2, d. 2616, ll. 187–212. I have not included the serfs in the village of Volyn, all of whom appear to have been house serfs. The difference in the number of ever-married men and women is accounted for largely by the fact that widows outnumbered widowers.

84. RGADA, f. 350. op. 2, d. 2616, ll. 295–3040b.

85. Ibid., ll. 305–50. I have excluded a group of *pribyli*—men and women who had moved to Novoselki after the preceding census in 1744—because they had likely married prior to their arrival.

86. GARO, f. 627, op. 249. The parish registers were from 1781, 1785, 1786, and 1787. In the 1760s, most priests did not record the ages of brides and grooms. The 1762 census returns might be used to calculate the singulate mean age of marriage for men, but in that year, women's ages suffered from extreme heaping.

87. Ibid., ll. 141–860b.

88. Ibid., ll. 210–12.

89. RGADA, f. 1290, op. 1, d. 193, ll. 6, 12, 16; ibid., l. 1, dated 1700, from what would be Tula province, had a five-ruble departure fee, clearly not representative of the period; RGADA, f. 1200, op. 1, dd. 157, 201, 616.

90. RGADA, f. 1441, op. 2, ch. 1, d. 2285, l. 2.

91. TsANO, f. 570, op. 552, 1726 d. 42, l. 460b.

92. *Opisanie arkhiva Aleksandro-Nevskoi lavry*, vol. 1, cols. 485, 623, 651, 704; vol. 3, col. 412.

93. Dovnar-Zapol'skii, "Materialy dlia istorii votchinnogo upravleniia v Rossii," no. 12 (1903), p. 7. Others have described Rumiantsev's instruction as a singular exception to noble intervention in serf marriage. However, a draft law code from the second

half of the 1750s recognized that off-estate marriage was a common practice, as it gave nobles the right to manumit widows and maidens for marriage. Since the draft code simultaneously gave nobles the unrestricted right to do with their serfs what they would (save murder, torture, or knouting), the fact that nobles also had the right to ban off-estate marriage needed no specification (Latkin, *Proekt novogo ulozheniia*, pp. 119–20, 131). This third and final version of part 3 was completed as of 1762 and deals with the rights of clergy and factory owners as well as nobles, while the earlier versions from the 1750s dealt only with noble rights. For what little is known about the drafting of this section, see Latkin, *Zakonodatel'nye komissii*, pp. 90–91, 136, 140, and passim. For a brief account of the draft code, see Anisimov, *Rossiia v seredine*, pp. 64–68.

94. *Opisanie arkhiva Aleksandro-Nevskoi Lavry*, vol. 2, col. 256, 609–11, 807, 839–40.

95. Ibid., col. 10.

96. Ibid., col. 69.

97. Ibid., col. 209, 332, 585.

98. The actual evidence on peasant marriage age in the first half of the eighteenth century is scant, because age at marriage was not recorded in the parish registers in most dioceses until the nineteenth century (not until the 1830s in many). I agree with Daniel Kaiser (Kaizer, "Vozrast pri brake," pp. 225–36) that while some peasants may have married at the legal minimum age (twelve for girls, fifteen for boys), most girls probably married later than that. According to what Solotchinsk serf fathers said in petitions when they opposed the marriage of their daughters, the standard marriage age of young women there in the late seventeenth century was fourteen or fifteen (Bushnell, "Bor'ba za nevestu," p. 92). As we know from Bestuzhev-Riumin's 1737 description of his Poshekhonie estate (see the next chapter), many girls there married at twenty and later.

99. Tul'tseva, "Chernichki," pp. 80–82; Gromyko, *Traditsionnye normy*, pp. 103–4; Mironov, *Sotsial'naia istoriia Rossii*, vol. 1, p. 161; Worobec, *Peasant Russia*, pp. 4, 264; Zimin and Spirin, *Poslovitsy i pogovorki*, pp. 264–65. Mukhina, "Starye devy," provides a concise summary of the ethnographic evidence.

100. Shchepetov, *Krepostnoe pravo*, p. 326; Dennison, *Institutional Framework*, p. 32.

CHAPTER 2

Nobles Discover Peasant Women's Marriage Aversion

Up to the 1750s, few nobles cared that their serf women married off the estate or paid attention to the age at which their serfs married. After 1750, many nobles—at least those with large holdings who drew up detailed management instructions—intervened directly in their serfs' marriages, both in their general rules and in individual cases. They may have worried that their serf women weren't marrying or weren't marrying early enough, thus impeding the formation of the basic labor and dues-paying unit, the *tiaglo*, which on most estates was the married couple. Serf-owners did not imagine the problem; their discovery that on some of their properties women really were reluctant to marry prompted many to impose *terminus ante quem* rules. These rules sometimes set a ceiling marriage age for men, too, but most men were eager to marry. When their female neighbors turned marriage-averse, they asked their owners for help. Those appeals were often how nobles learned that there was a marriage problem in the first place. Perhaps it was worry that men were having trouble finding brides that prompted other nobles to require as well that their serf women marry on the estate. They may have imagined that women marrying away could only increase the bride deficit.

Combatting Fornication: Petr Bestuzhev-Riumin Demands Women Marry by Twenty

The only noble known to have adopted a rule on female marriage age in the first half of the eighteenth century is Petr Bestuzhev-Riumin (1664–1743). The problem he thought he was addressing was not serf women's reluctance to marry but their premarital fornication. Bestuzhev discovered this problem only because he fell into disfavor at court. In 1712, Peter the Great appointed him chamberlain to his niece, the widowed duchess Anna Ioannovna of Courland.[1] Bestuzhev managed Anna's finances, looked out for Russia's interests in the duchy, and at some point became Anna's lover. In 1727, he was recalled to St. Petersburg to answer charges that he had enriched himself at Anna's expense. When he returned, Ernst Biron (Büren) had replaced him in Anna's bed. In 1728, Bestuzhev was arrested after Anna denounced him for robbery (at the very least, she exaggerated) and because of palace intrigue involving his daughter. After Anna, with Biron in tow, took the throne in 1730, she exiled the sixty-six-year-old Bestuzhev to "distant villages," which turned out to be his estate in the Poshekhonie district, then in northern Novgorod province, later in northern Iaroslavl province. Bestuzhev's holdings there were extensive. Two villages had parish churches, and he resided in each of them in turn: Lukovesi, ten kilometers west, and Gorodishche, eight kilometers south of the small city of Cherepovets, both on the banks of the Sheksna River. Smaller villages were scattered in the dense forest in between and even deeper in the woods.[2]

Bestuzhev had probably never set foot on the estate before and apparently knew little of his serfs' lives when he arrived. He had served for at least three decades without, apparently, any extended leave except when under investigation; what time he had away from political affairs he was likely to have spent on his estate near Moscow. When in 1731 he issued instructions to his Poshekhonie steward, the only rule concerning marriage was contradictory: "Peasant maidens should not be given [in marriage] on the side, and if a manumission paper is written for anyone, collect a 5-ruble departure fee in advance (or 3 rubles, depending on the place)." He added that no money was to be collected for marriage within the estate.[3] We might interpret this rule to mean, if possible, don't let women marry away from the estate, collect 5 rubles if you do, but I'll accept 3.

In August 1737, Anna forgave Bestuzhev his transgressions and permitted him to live in Moscow or on any other of his estates, and he probably wrote his 1737 "Instruction" before or immediately after he left Poshekhonie. He described not only the steward's duties but also "what you should know about the serfs paying quitrent."[4] He produced, in fact, a partial ethnography of his serfs' lives. They were practicing slash-burn agriculture ("They should also work in the clearings and prepare them year round"), and they were scattered widely in the tiny homesteads characteristic of peasants who had to clear suitable patches of forest every few years. They should keep more horses and livestock and use the manure for fertilizer. They should be fined one kopek when they failed to attend church or make their annual confession. They should celebrate for no more than two or three days the holy days for which they brewed beer.[5] These were all additions to his 1731 "Instruction."

He also made two changes to his directive on marriage. First, he added "without asking" to his rule that women not marry away.[6] Perhaps he was clarifying his contradictory 1731 rule; perhaps he had learned that for some of his far-flung serf households, the exchange of daughters with peasants not his own was unavoidable. Second, he said that young women should marry by age twenty. He prefaced that requirement with an explanation: young men and maidens who had come of age did whatever they liked, which was to consort with each other. Their parents didn't force them to work,

> and from this willfulness and fearlessness young men take up thievery, while maidens fall into fornication . . . and women big with child have been given in marriage, and others have given birth as maidens, and they have been punished in front of all the people with the cat. . . . And therefore peasants should hold their children close and in fear and in punishment, and therefore fathers and mothers should not keep their daughters as maidens above 20, but give them in marriage, and if prior to age 20 they fall into fornication because they fear not their fathers and their mothers be not watchful, for that father and mother and maiden, and the fornicator who fornicates with her, are to be punished with the cat before an assembly of the people.[7]

Bestuzhev also asserted that his Poshekhonie serfs married their boys to older maidens but that others married at equal ages, that spouses came to hate each other, lived apart, and committed adultery.[8] It isn't clear whether he thought that boys marrying older women, or age parity, or either or neither was responsible for adultery.

These provisions of the 1737 instruction grew directly from Bestuzhev's observations during his exile. They raise questions to which there are no certain answers. He framed his requirement that young women marry by age twenty as an effort to deal with rampant sexual immorality fostered by parental indifference. Parents would naturally have been indifferent if premarital sex and marital separation had been the norm in the area for some time. Indeed, such may have been the case—this part of Poshekhonie was within the area Archbishop Markell of Vologda and Belozersk had identified in 1658 as thoroughly infected with irregular marriage and unmarried cohabitation.[9] Given the dense forest, low population density, and the distance between many forest peasants and their priests, that is not surprising. In the late nineteenth century, peasants remembered a time when, they said, Poshekhonie youngsters engaged in group sex parties.[10] But the behavior Bestuzhev observed may have been a byproduct of the schism. The forests of Poshekhonie were then and later thick with priestless Old Believers, and suspicion of the institution of marriage may well have worked itself out among peasants in the way Bestuzhev described.[11] Nowhere in his 1737 instruction did he refer to the Old Belief, but the very first article dealt with irregular church attendance. While we cannot say how widespread the practices Bestuzhev described were, or what explains them, we can certainly say that had he not spent time at his Poshekhonie estate, he would have known nothing about them.

MIKHAIL SHCHERBATOV DISCOVERS, AND MISUNDERSTANDS, PEASANT WOMEN'S MARRIAGE AVERSION

Prince Mikhail Mikhailovich Shcherbatov (1733–1790) was among the first—perhaps the very first—to establish an age *ante quem* for his female serfs' marriage because he believed many would not marry except under compulsion. Shcherbatov owned several thousand serfs. He gained fame for passionate speeches at Catherine the Great's Legislative Commission in 1767–68, defending the privileges of the nobility and calling for their extension, attacking the merchantry, and denouncing any suggestion of easing the lot of the serfs as ruinous for Russia and the serfs themselves. He held a number of leading positions in the government, including senator; was appointed Russia's official historian and authored a five-volume history of Russia; and wrote a famous critique of social and political mores during Catherine's reign, as well as a utopian novel in which a monarch reigns while virtuous aristocrats rule.

In his 1758 "General Instruction" to the steward of his Mikhailovskoe and neighboring Kuzmodemianskoe estates in the Iaroslavl district, he ordered that serf women marry by seventeen, men by twenty. This was his explanation: "Since it is seen in many villages that many peasants remain bachelors until old age and don't marry, likewise maidens grow old unmarried, wherefore: 1. Homes are empty, 2, and there are fewer souls and in consequence all collections, both by the state and by the master, are more burdensome for the peasants. So see to it that maidens sit no more than 17 years as maidens, and that whatever peasant needs a worker can take in a son-in-law, and that men marry at 20."[12] Shcherbatov had spent part of his youth at Mikhailovskoe, the family's seat. After two years serving in the Semenovsk Guards regiment in St. Petersburg, 1755–56, he returned to Mikhailovskoe with his newly wedded wife and infant daughter but was shortly recalled to duty because of the Seven Years' War. He composed the General Instruction in July 1758 while serving in St. Petersburg, adding amendments through 1762.[13] He took advantage of the 1762 liberation of nobles from obligatory service to retire from the army, spent much of his time between 1762 and 1767 at Mikhailovskoe, and did so again after he retired in the mid-1780s. Shcherbatov knew his Mikhailovskoe serfs well, as his abundant correspondence with the stewards shows.

One might expect that, like Bestuzhev-Riumin, Shcherbatov's rule on marriage derived from observation of his own serfs' habits, but that was not the case; the "many villages" in which young men and women weren't marrying weren't his. According to the draft return for the 1762 tax census, there were more than 1,200 serfs, male and female, on his neighboring Mikhailovskoe and Kuzmodemianskoe properties.[14] Almost all men and women were married by age twenty. Only five women over twenty had not married. Their ages were forty, forty-five, fifty, fifty (*beznogaia*, missing a foot or a leg, thus probably not marriageable), and sixty.[15] There were somewhat more never-married adult men: five between twenty and twenty-four and quite likely to marry and eight ages twenty-seven to fifty-seven. The extensive correspondence between Shcherbatov and his Iaroslavl stewards in the years shortly before and after 1758 offers not a trace of evidence that his female serfs were resisting marriage, that his male serfs had difficulty obtaining brides, or that he devised his marriage rule because of the handful of unmarried men and women on his Iaroslavl estates. The correspondence does show that serfs from time to time asked permission to bring in brides from one or another of his properties and that he always gave permission (formulated as an order) for them to do so.[16]

As the ages of the never-married women in 1762 show, if it had ever been difficult to persuade women on the estates to marry, the problem had been resolved twenty years earlier, but such other evidence as there is indicates that Shcherbatov men never found it difficult to secure wives.[17] Some may have had difficulty finding brides on the estate, but they could obtain brides from neighboring properties inexpensively, as the sample of thirty-five manumission papers from 1719 to 1762 (discussed in chapter 1) shows and as the 1762 census returns confirm. The manorial correspondence that has survived from the first half of the eighteenth century represents only a fraction of all the orders sent to Mikhailovskoe, yet it is indicative that marriage comes up only once, in 1741. After one of their serfs claimed to have married a manumitted woman who turned out to be a soldier's wife, Princess Irina and Prince Petr Shcherbatov (Mikhail's mother and older brother) ordered that the marrying priests verify the manumission papers of all incoming women.[18]

The peasants among whom women failed to marry belonged to Shcherbatov's neighbors. The 1762 census returns demonstrate that there were growing numbers of unmarried adult women on nearby estates. For instance, in the village of Zhabino, property of the Monastery of Our Savior in Iaroslavl, nine of the fifty-three women twenty-five and older (17 percent) had never married, and six of the forty-four women thirty and over (14 percent) had never married. Among the thirty-seven men ages thirty and above, only one had never married. Two of the eight men ages twenty-five to twenty-nine had never married but were likely to do so. The same cannot be said about the women over twenty-five.[19]

Zhabino was not the only village in the area that accumulated unmarried women. According to the 1762 return from Kuzminskoe, owned by Lieutenant General Vasilii Naryshkin, eleven of sixty-nine women twenty-five and older (16 percent) and seven of fifty-five women thirty and above (13 percent) had never married, proportions almost identical to those in Zhabino. However, in Kuzminskoe, unlike Zhabino, four of sixty-four men over twenty-five (6 percent), all of whom were over thirty, had never married.[20] Shcherbatov would undoubtedly have asserted that those men had failed to marry because local women weren't marrying, and there is a small possibility that he would have been right. However, the 1762 census return for Kuzminskoe recorded where every wife had come from, and 58 percent had married onto the estate. Presumably the unmarried men could have found wives in the neighborhood if they had wanted to.

Zhabino had 8.4 percent more women of all ages than men of all ages; Kuzminskoe, 13 percent more. In a sample of eleven other estates in the area, with total populations (men and women both) ranging from 182 to 2,843 serfs (thus not likely to be subject to sharp random variations in sex ratios), five had between 10 and 19 percent more women than men and so were likely home to substantial numbers of never-married women. Three of the five estates were owned by monasteries, one was a state peasant settlement, one a seigneurial estate.[21] That does not mean that properties belonging to monasteries were the most likely to have gender imbalances. Most of the properties owned by nobles in that part of the Iaroslavl district were dwarf estates, consisting of no more than two or three households, the result of many generations of subdivision through inheritance and dowry.[22] In any event, as of 1762 probably half of the medium-size and large estates within the vicinity of Shcherbatov's Mikhailovskoe were accumulating unmarried adult women. Like Bestuzhev, Shcherbatov probably did report what he had seen and perhaps talked about with his neighbors.

Shcherbatov's conviction, expressed in 1758, that many serfs had to be compelled to marry—and that doing so was beneficial both for the serfs themselves and for their owners and the state—held firm to the end of his life. He spent his last five or so years ruminating, writing, and managing Mikhailovskoe, where there was demonstrably no marriage problem at all: the returns for the 1782 tax census list only one never-married adult woman, age thirty-four, at Mikhailovskoe and Kuzmodemianskoe, and one adult man, twenty-nine, and the voluminous manorial correspondence from preceding years never mentions serf resistance to marriage.[23]

It was only in retirement that Shcherbatov offered, in any of his extant writings, any explanation of peasants' alleged reluctance to marry. In general, however, Shcherbatov consistently argued that serfs would not do what was in their own best interest unless they were ordered to do so by their owners; that conviction was widely shared among Russian nobles of the time. In his unpublished "Reflections on Egoism," apparently written in the latter half of the 1780s, Shcherbatov argued that peasants' laziness and compulsive self-gratification, if unchecked, inexorably produced poverty, which together with their excessive desire for copulation led them to deceit and crime. Thus, "they often take from their sons what their sons need, and avoid giving their daughters in marriage so as not to deprive themselves of workers."[24] What is interesting about that statement is that, when asked why they hadn't yet given daughters in marriage, peasant fathers often did say that the women's labor was indispensable to the household. Sometimes they were lying.[25] Sometimes they were telling the truth.[26] Shcherbatov may have heard peasants explain themselves that way and then interpreted the answer within the framework of his assumptions about serf indolence, deceit, and copulation.

At about the same time that he wrote "On Egoism," Shcherbatov expanded on the problems posed by the reluctance of serf women to marry in another unpublished essay, "Reflections on the Disadvantages of Giving Freedom to Peasants and Servants in Russia":

> *All those who assiduously observe good order on their estates have frequently noted that fathers give away their daughters unwillingly, retaining them as workers for their own profit, and only the masters' compulsion constrains them to hand over their daughters, a compulsion that inclines toward the general welfare of the state. Without this compulsion how many maidens and young widows not marrying there would be in every village, and single men and unmarried widowers, and how much reduction of the population would result therefrom. Crown and economic peasants present a clear example. Among them one can find in almost every village a multitude of single men and unmarried widowers, and also maidens and young widows, not marrying and not fulfilling the duty of humanity to multiply the nation.*[27]

It is remarkable how much in that passage is wrong. Tax census returns, the annual parish censuses that priests compiled in the form of confession registers, and household inventories from serf estates all demonstrate conclusively that in most of Russia, peasants of all varieties married almost universally, without the least compulsion from owners or the officials in charge of non-seigneurial peasants. While it is certainly true that some households needed to retain female labor, at least temporarily, peasant fathers generally had an economic incentive to give their daughters in marriage. Married sons were a necessity for household survival and a tolerable parental old age. Peasant fathers all over Russia had to pay a bride price, which often fluctuated according to market pressures, in order to obtain wives for their sons, and only by giving their daughters in marriage could they collect a compensatory bride price. Even though Shcherbatov had discovered that, at least in his area, female serfs on some properties really were resisting marriage, he completely misunderstood the source of the problem. Russian peasants' supposed sloth and cupidity had nothing to do with it.

VLADIMIR ORLOV LEARNS TO PROFIT FROM HIS SERFS' NUPTIAL BEHAVIOR

Vladimir Orlov (1743–1831), many of whose serf women really did reject marriage, also misidentified the cause before learning the truth from his serfs themselves. Vladimir was the youngest and best educated of the five Orlov brothers who shot to the heights of Russian politics and society after

Catherine the Great's coup in 1762. His brother Grigorii was, at the time, Catherine's lover and an organizer of the coup, and Grigorii and brother Aleksei immediately assumed commanding positions in political and military affairs. Catherine made all five brothers counts and enriched them with grants of estates; as of the early 1770s, they owned collectively at least twenty-seven thousand male and a roughly equal number of female serfs, most of them on properties received from Catherine.[28]

Vladimir himself, only nineteen in 1762, played no part in the coup. In 1763, his brothers sent him to Leipzig University where he studied for three years. When he returned in 1766, Catherine appointed him director of the Academy of Sciences or, in effect, acting president. The nominal president, Kirill Razumovskii, never took an active part in academy affairs. Vladimir did interest himself in the academy—for instance, reaching an agreement with the mostly German membership to change the academy's language of record from Latin to German (although he proposed Russian)—and organized academy exploratory expeditions. One, led by Peter Pallas, passed through Simbirsk province and sent Orlov a report on the soil quality and natural resources of an estate Orlov had recently acquired there. As the years passed, he spent less time in St. Petersburg, and after Grigorii (who fell from Catherine's favor in 1772) retired in 1774, Vladimir did, too, and spent much of the rest of his life managing his estates.[29]

With intermittent exceptions, Orlov abided by noble tradition and allowed women to marry away from his properties. One exception was his first known rule on marriage, a 1767 ban on off-estate marriage at Porechie-Rybnoe, in the Rostov district.[30] That was probably the instinctive decision of a young and inexperienced property owner who assumed that the loss of a woman through marriage was an obvious loss of property. Vladimir's major involvement in estate administration began in 1773, when his brothers entrusted to his management all the properties they then owned jointly. He immediately asked bailiffs how quitrent was assessed, how frequently village assemblies met and what issues they discussed, how conscription was handled, and about many other issues on which a diligent manager would have to rule.[31] He did not ask about serf marriage. However, when the bailiff at Sidorovskoe (Nerekhta district, Kostroma province) asked in 1773 what to do about a peasant who wanted to import a bride for his son and also marry his daughter off the estate, Orlov ruled (only with respect to Sidorovskoe, apparently) that in the case of exchanges like that, no departure fee need be levied on the daughter.[32] In 1774, his first comprehensive set of management rules permitted single women to leave through marriage if they were not the sole heirs in their natal households. Subsequent correspondence added that childless widows could also marry away from the estate but not widows with children.[33]

Yet Orlov remained of two minds about serf girls who married away from his estates. He gave blanket permission for his women to marry onto his brothers' estates (many of which bordered his own) without paying a departure fee, so long as there was a rough balance in the inter-estate bride trade. He also permitted women on a property in Orel province to marry away at no charge if neighboring estates followed the same rule.[34] On the other hand, he banned marriage off his Bezhetsk district estate in 1779. In 1790, when he bought the Simbilei estate (Nizhnii Novgorod province) from the Princes Prozorovskii, who had permitted women to marry away, he ordered: "Do not let women out for marriage onto other people's estates as occurred in the past!"[35] Orlov's periodic prohibitions of off-estate marriage after 1773 may have been responses to his discovery, or fear, that neighbors did not always reciprocate.

However, when he composed a "Law Code" (*Ulozhenie*) for all of his properties in 1796, he permitted single women and widows without sons to marry outside the estate on payment of an (unspecified) departure fee. There was only one exception: women without brothers could not leave the estate through marriage "so that property not pass into an outsider's hands."[36] He probably had in mind the household goods they might eventually inherit. That remained the law on Vladimir Orlov's estates down to his death in 1831 and, in some cases, even beyond.

While Orlov's tolerance of off-estate marriage was in keeping with long-standing noble practice, the amount of money he extracted when women exercised that right was not; rather than the nominal charge of the past, he treated the release of a serf woman through marriage as a sale. The single surviving reference to the bridal departure charge Orlov imposed in the 1770s is from his Bezhetsk estate, where it was fifteen rubles in 1776. That was what Vladimir's oldest brother, Ivan, had set at Sidorovskoe in 1773.[37] Vladimir apparently copied his brother. That was much more than other nobles charged at the time. Around Sidorovskoe, they took one to two rubles; in the Rostov district, not far from Bezhetsk, nobles charged two to five rubles in the early 1770s.[38] Ivan and then Vladimir Orlov set their departure fee above the roughly ten-ruble market price of a marriageable serf woman in the 1770s.[39] By 1783, Orlov had raised the departure fee at Sidorovskoe and probably elsewhere to thirty rubles, while other nobles around Sidorovskoe were charging around ten rubles in 1780.[40] Departure charges were rising everywhere, but Orlov's rose faster than most.

The reason Orlov's 1796 "Law Code" did not specify the amount of the departure fee was that by then it varied according to the wealth of the departing bride's household. Orlov may have understood that a wealthy household would give a daughter only to another wealthy household, but I don't think he reasoned so subtly. If the daughter of a wealthy father were to marry off estate, the fee would be large, and he didn't care who paid. Because the market price of marriageable serf girls (as for serfs generally) rose over time, Orlov's average departure fee also rose.[41] In 1792, Orlov set the minimum exit fee for his Gorodets estate at 50 rubles; at Sidorovskoe in the 1790s, the departure fees ranged from 30 to 100 rubles.[42] In the first quarter of the nineteenth century, the charge for most girls marrying away from Orlov's estates ranged from 100 to 150 rubles, although it sometimes dipped to 60 rubles and occasionally rose much higher—420 rubles for a girl from Gorodets in 1821, for instance.[43] From 1799 to 1825, most of the marriageable serf girls Orlov himself purchased for men for whom no brides were available locally cost 100 to 150 rubles.[44] If women marrying away were replaced by their cash equivalent, there was no reason to worry about property loss. Orlov's understanding of that equation explains why his 1796 "Law Code" permitted women from all of his estates to marry away. He may have decided that the marriage of serf women off the estate was an additional source of revenue.

In real terms, Orlov's departure charge did not rise by the six to seven multiple indicated by the difference between the 15 rubles of the 1770s and the 100-ruble average charge around 1800. Correcting for inflation and assuming that, after 1789, the default currency (almost never specified) was the paper *assignat* rather than the silver ruble, the real average departure charge levied on women marrying away from Sidorovskoe doubled between 1773 and 1800.[45] Starting from the 1760s, however, when the crown estate manager at Sidorovskoe probably levied a 2-ruble fee on departing girls, by 1800, the real exit charge there had increased thirteen-fold.[46] Since around 1760 serf-owners normally levied a 2- to 4-ruble fee and, like Orlov, were charging around 100 rubles by 1800, the real price of the standard departure fee increased by a multiple of between six and a half and thirteen in the last third of the eighteenth century.

In 1777, apparently for the first time, Orlov turned his attention to serf women who refused to marry. He commanded that women at Sidorovskoe do so by age twenty; if unmarried women of that age were discovered in the future, the bailiff would be fined, and the women would be given in marriage to serfs on other Orlov properties.[47] That new rule caused consternation. The Sidorovskoe bailiff, Ivan Ratkov, reported that there were too many women over twenty to arrange marriages for all of them immediately. Orlov relented, so long as the women married "in a timely fashion."[48] Nothing in the surviving Orlov or Sidorovskoe papers explains exactly what prompted Orlov to order women to marry by age twenty or suffer draconian punishment, but most likely he learned only in 1777 that some women at Sidorovskoe refused to marry, probably from a Sidorovskoe serf who asked his assistance in obtaining a wife. There is no such document in the surviving records, but when brides were in short supply, male serfs routinely appealed to their owners.

At the time of the 1763 tax census, the Sidorovskoe estate, just south of the Volga, had a population of 1,208 men and 1,277 women; Sidorovskoe village, 234 men and 281 women.[49] It had been a crown estate before being given to the Orlovs in 1773, and while many of the peasants farmed, its economy was based on fishing, commerce, and increasingly on crafts, production of jewelry in particular.[50]

The estate also had a substantial Old Believer population. Documents from 1764 listed 34 male and 64 female Old Believers ages twenty-five and over. In Sidorovskoe village alone, 17 of 116 men (14.7 percent) and 32 of 141 women (22.7 percent) in that age group were registered Old Believers.[51] There is no reason to think that all the Old Believers in the village as of 1764 had registered (that is, reported themselves). Men who registered had to pay double the annual capitation tax, registered female Old Believers paid at the Orthodox male rate, and Orthodox women paid no tax at all.[52] Furthermore, registration lists called them schismatics (*raskol'niki*). They themselves believed that it was the official Orthodox Church that was schismatic or worse, and there were Old Believers who refused to register because they believed doing so amounted to an admission of schism and therefore a renunciation of the true faith. The one gain from registering was that they would not be hounded by church and state to accept Orthodox sacraments or suffer a fine.

Much larger numbers of self-reported Old Believers appear on a list from 1800—twenty-five men and seventy-five women in Sidorovskoe village and twelve men and forty-nine women on the rest of the estate—no doubt because Empress Catherine had repealed many of the laws discriminating against them.[53] The 1800 list provides male and female numbers by village, not names or ages, but since children almost never appeared on such lists, we can assume that almost all of the Sidorovskoe Old Believers of 1800 were adults. We can assume, in other words, that in Sidorovskoe village almost half of all adult women, and probably 20 percent of all adult men, were registered as Old Believers in 1800. We should also assume that some other Old Believers remained unregistered.

Old Believers came in many varieties, but it is almost certain that almost all of those registered in 1763 were members of priestless covenants, those who believed that the Nikonian reforms of the mid-seventeenth century had extinguished the priesthood and, with it, the sacrament of marriage. In 1763, in the village as a whole, 25 of 141 women twenty-five and over (17.7 percent) had never married, while 18 of the 25 never-married adult women were registered Old Believers. The other 7 were likely unregistered Old Believers. Among the Old Believer men in the village who were at least twenty-five, only 2 had never married (they were thirty-eight and fifty-four), while 15 had married. The 1764 lists do not distinguish between priestless and priested Old Believers (those who employed priests who had deserted from the Orthodox Church and who strongly favored marriage), but the 1800 list does. In that year, 55 women in Sidorovskoe village were priested, while 20 were priestless, a number that very nearly coincides with the single adult women as of 1763. The priestless women belonged to two different covenants: 17 Spasovites and 3 Pomorsk. The rest of this book is, in effect, an extended explanation of those statistics on married and unmarried adult women at Sidorovskoe and their religious identities. For Vladimir Orlov, all that mattered was that many of his Sidorovskoe women shunned marriage.

Before 1777, Orlov probably knew little about the Old Believers, and at first he seems not to have understood that they were the women who refused to marry at Sidorovskoe. After commanding that the unmarried marry, his second step was to forbid parents of potential Sidorovskoe brides to demand a bride price for their daughters and to refund it if already collected (in one case from that year, the bride price was seven rubles).[54] Probably his first thought was that bride price deterred marriage at Sidorovskoe. He soon knew better.

Later in 1777, he referred to the marriage-averse maidens and widows as "being in illegal conversions"—that is, he had learned they were Old Believers.[55] The quoted phrase is from the introductory sentence to his order to send women to his Moscow office to be given in marriage in his other villages if it turned out that there were canonical impediments (blood or spiritual kinship, for example) to the marriages being arranged. In June 1779, bailiff Ratkov wrote that widowers had been unable to persuade any women to marry them, so Orlov ordered the bailiff and village assembly to make the matches themselves: "Order them to marry without fail, any excuses from the women notwithstanding."[56] Then, in July, he sent a decree that began: "It has come to my attention that many peasant women live unmarried until they are quite old, as a result of which fornication and other disorders must occur"—the conventional charge made by the Orthodox against priestless Old Believers. The assembly was to select grooms for them, making certain only that the match be between equivalent individuals (*chtoby chelovek cheloveka stoil*). If the women continued to resist marriage, they were to be married even against their will.[57] The Sidorovskoe assembly immediately compelled three women to marry widowers and continued to force matches in later years.[58]

What he had learned about Sidorovskoe prompted Orlov to look for evidence of female refusal to marry on his other estates. In October 1779, when asking the bailiff at Gorodets (Nizhnii Novgorod province) to provide information about the number of prosperous peasants and how they made their money, he also asked who had single daughters who ought to have married already and whether there were any young widows. When in December 1779 a Gorodets widower asked Orlov to compel a young widow to marry him, Orlov ordered that she be sent to his Moscow residence if she continued to refuse—obviously as punishment, probably to be forced to marry elsewhere.[59] There were many Old Believers at Gorodets, but they were mostly priested. There was a priested Old Believer chapel at Gorodets, and Orlov's priested Old Believers married there. It would be very surprising if refusal to marry at his Gorodets property was more than minimal.[60]

Orlov included many rules to combat refusal to marry in his 1791 Simbilei "Instruction." He repeated the prohibition of bride price: "Fathers are not to take money for their daughters under threat of harsh punishment!"[61] But he was unable to root out that custom—collection of bride price was reported from Simbilei in 1821, for instance—so he gave up the effort. Subsequently, he did no more than express the wish that bride price be moderate.[62] He reaffirmed the rule first issued for Sidorovskoe that remained in effect for the rest of his life: if women had not married by age twenty, fathers should find grooms within six months. If they failed, families of the unwilling brides would be fined: ten rubles for the average household, fifteen rubles for the prosperous. If a household were so poor that it could not pay the fine, the young woman's father was to be caned in the presence of assembled villagers. Should fine and caning have no effect, bailiff and elders were to select a bride themselves, taking care that bride and groom were of roughly equal age and household (*chtoby drug drugu i dom domu stoili*).[63] Orlov immediately applied those rules. The "Instruction" was dated September 26, 1790. On October 8, he told his Simbilei bailiff to send lists of bachelors and the marriageable but unmarried women assigned to them and ordered that they be married forthwith.[64]

Orlov retained all but one of those rules (caning) in his 1796 "Law Code" and added others—for example, that bachelors and widowers of twenty-five years or older be treated in the same way as single women and widows (but there is no evidence in the voluminous manorial correspondence that this rule had any practical consequences). Fines on the unmarried were raised to twenty-five and fifty rubles; the very poor were to be fined at the discretion of the bailiff. Orlov added that men and women genuinely unfit to marry should not be compelled to do so. Lists of those who were supposed to marry should be sent to his Moscow office with notations of what estate authorities intended to do in each instance.[65] While caning was abandoned, the Orlov papers show that in the years after 1796, village assemblies did force some recalcitrant women to marry (but occasionally ran into problems with priests who enforced the church rule that parties to a marriage had to give their consent); Orlov and his Moscow office also sold or threatened to sell others or exiled them to Siberia.[66]

Orlov's rules on serf marriage illuminate both the issues that arose and how he wrestled with them. He went back and forth on women marrying off the estate until he arrived at the understanding that in allowing women to marry away at the market price, he suffered no loss of wealth; sometimes he charged far more than the market price. While from beginning to end he was willing to order (and authorize village bailiffs and elders to impose) harsh sanctions on unmarried adult women, his resort to fines allowed for some moderation and produced another new stream of revenue. His not quite relentless efforts to compel women to marry were without question heartless, although not exceptionally so, given the mores of his age. He abandoned public caning (although there were instances of whipping after 1796), and he gave up the attempt to root out bride price.

In addition, he was willing to purchase serf girls for marriage when his male serfs could find no brides locally—a cruelty toward young women certainly, but a tremendous boon to the men who received the purchased wives. He instructed his bailiffs that when serfs bought their own serf women and then gave them in marriage, the departure fees went to his serfs, not to him.[67] Furthermore, on many of his estates all of the time and on most of them much of the time, his marriage regulations were simply irrelevant: girls married of their own accord, mostly before they turned twenty, young men mostly married by their early twenties, and they or their parents made the matches themselves with no interference from Orlov.[68]

Orlov's rule on universal marriage, and his persistent effort to enforce it, was just what his male serfs wanted. Universal marriage was a long-standing custom; Orlov commanded women to behave like the Russian peasants they were. Male serfs routinely (widows who headed households occasionally) asked Orlov to compel marriage, and village assemblies were often willing accomplices. At an estate in the Romanovo district, Iaroslavl province, serf authorities in 1801 failed to compel a twenty-seven-year-old Old Believer woman to marry; as the bailiff reported, "Out of obstinacy she told the priest she wouldn't marry anyone at all." The community proposed to banish her from the estate; Orlov's Moscow office ordered that she be sold or sent to one of his factories if there were no purchaser. Meanwhile, she was held in irons for three months. In June 1802, after the bailiff and elders, with the concurrence of the Moscow office, prepared to send her to the Iaroslavl jail, she agreed to marry. The bailiff thereupon suggested that all marriage-averse women be sent to jail since fines had no effect. The home office told him to abide by Orlov's 1796 "Law Code," which had no such provision.[69]

The Romanovo elders were outraged because a woman's refusal to marry threatened not just one frustrated bachelor but the entire community. They viewed women as a community resource. Coincidentally, the Romanovo serfs had occasion in 1802 to make their communal claim on women explicit. A young, childless widow who had married onto the estate asked to be allowed to return to her father's household. Her father-in-law consented, because he was eager to get back the 100-ruble bride price he had paid, but the bailiff and elders thought otherwise. The widow was young and healthy; she should be kept on the estate and fined 25 rubles for refusing to marry. Vladimir Orlov himself decided that the widow could return to her father.[70]

Male serfs explained in their petitions what was at stake in marriage: household survival. They spelled out why they desperately needed women: "I've been widowed for two years, I have five small children, I can't get along without a wife to raise them and preserve their health, so make the thirty-year old woman in Sokhtonka who lives dissolutely marry me"; "I'm thirty-seven, I have two young children and a sixty-one-year old father, without a wife I can't manage my dues."[71] These and many other petitions are so similar one to another that there is reason to think that the petitioners all made the argument they thought most likely to persuade their owner to intervene: household collapse, or impoverishment, did threaten his interests. Yet they were likely telling the truth; many households did suffer from the demographic misfortunates the petitioners described, and many of their households really would sink into destitution, incapable of fulfilling their duties to their master, if wives weren't found. On matters of marriage, Orlov's and his male serfs' interests coincided.[72] That was fortunate for Orlov because he was more dependent on his serfs for enforcement of his rules than most serf-owners; he hired a steward to manage only the one estate that imposed corvée labor almost exclusively, while serf bailiffs managed estates—all of the others in the late eighteenth century—on which his serfs paid quitrent.[73]

Nevertheless, where bailiffs were themselves Old Believers, they sometimes deceived. Gavriil Palkin, bailiff at an estate in the Liubim district, northern Iaroslavl province, reported in December 1805 that because men on the estate imported brides, some women were left without husbands. He would have fined them according to the rules of the 1796 "Law Code," he said, but the women's parents protested that would be unfair. They asked instead to be allowed to pay 100 rubles each for manumission papers so their daughters could marry off the estate. In April 1806, Orlov's Moscow office issued eleven manumission documents. Four years later, in March 1810, bachelors from the Liubim estate sent an anonymous denunciation: there was a shortage of brides, and local fathers demanded 300 rubles in bride price, which the petitioners could not pay. A bride price so high was obviously meant to put daughters beyond reach. Moreover, avowedly Old Believer fathers refused to give their daughters in marriage on any terms.[74] Bailiff Palkin, almost certainly an Old Believer himself, had perpetrated a hoax; the girls had been manumitted to avoid marriage, not to marry. Both the temporarily successful fraud and its ultimate exposure are indicative: Orlov could not know what his serfs did not tell him, but men desperate to marry might turn even on powerful bailiffs when they tried to protect marriage-averse women. In this case, however, the men who had denounced Palkin were so fearful of him that they would not reveal themselves even when Orlov sent an agent to investigate the case.[75]

Palkin erred in perpetrating fraud on a large scale. Manorial correspondence concerning two small estates in Kostroma province—Bolotnikovo and Matveikha, both in the Kineshma district, both reporting to the Sidorovskoe bailiff rather than directly to Orlov and his Moscow office—suggest that it was often possible to protect marriage-averse women one at a time, if the effort had community support. At Bolotnikovo in 1805, twelve of the approximately sixty-five women twenty-five and over (18 percent) had never married. Ten of them were concentrated in three households, a certain sign that they had avoided married for religious reasons. Seven were reportedly physically or mentally disabled and thus unfit for marriage, which at least in the case of three sisters is highly improbable. Three other sisters had neither been fined nor forced to marry because of the merits of their deceased father, probably a former bailiff and priestless Old Believer. In three smaller villages on the estate—in all twenty-nine men—three of the probably thirty-three women adult women were single and, according to the bailiff's account, disabled.[76]

Later in the same year, the bailiff, Vasilii Fedorov, was replaced for drunkenness and general misconduct, including taking bribes rather than forcing single women to marry. We can detect in Fedorov's reports from 1798 how he deflected the pressure to compel marriage: he reported chiefly on couples who had married of their own free will while gesturing at forthcoming or future matches. When ordered to do so, however, he fined and whipped fathers of single women.[77] In 1820, the Sidorovskoe bailiff visited Bolotnikovo and reported to Moscow that the serfs complained that the nine single women and the one bachelor whom the current bailiff, Efim Balakirev (appointed in 1805), had fined were actually disabled and therefore exempt from the fine.[78] But apparently Balakirev had not attempted to compel them to marry. In fact, in 1818, Balakirev himself had an unmarried granddaughter and an unmarried grandniece, both twenty-four, both with illegitimate infants. That information came in a protest from a peasant whom Balakirev had "advised" (the peasant's word, meaning Balakirev had not given him an order) to yield his own daughter in marriage to a local bachelor.[79]

At Matveikha, too, a suspiciously large number of women were reported in February 1804 to be incapable of marriage.[80] And, apparently, more kept turning up. In February 1804, Stepan Ivanov from the village of Dubanki said that his son needed a wife and requested that Maksim Nikitin in Matveikha be forced to yield his daughter. The Sidorovskoe bailiff, Ivan Retnev, ordered the Matveikha elders to investigate; they reported that while the girl was of age, she was sickly and unfit for marriage. They rejected a similar request from Timofei Sergeev, claiming that they had found the woman he wanted to be too old and lame for marriage.[81] The elders lied, unless we are to believe that Stepan and Timofei had picked brides who actually were unfit rather than women capable of marriage. But they knew who the girls were and where they lived and must have seen them. If no healthy women were available, they could have appealed to Orlov to provide wives; he responded favorably to such requests from Matveikha.[82]

The Matveikha bailiff and elders also rejected requests for specific women on the grounds that the households of bride and groom were not of equal standing—like physical incapacity, a loophole provided by the 1796 "Law Code" itself—and they found other excuses to turn down persistent requests to marry single women.[83] In more than one instance, families refused to accept a girl whom the village elders had chosen for them.[84] Were those families part of a communal conspiracy? Were the elders suggesting matches they knew would be rejected? Since we cannot ourselves assess the women's health, we cannot sort out the conflicting claims, but the available documentation leaves the strong impression that the male serfs entrusted with administering the estate were determined to protect marriage-averse women. To a considerable extent, they seem to have succeeded.

And what of Sidorovskoe village? At the time of the 1834 tax census, it had been Orlov property for fifty-four of the fifty-seven years since Orlov had ordered all single women there to marry, yet 12.7 percent of women twenty-five and over had never married, as opposed to 17.7 percent in 1763.[85]

That was not a signal success. More impressive is the number of women who—surely with the connivance of bailiffs—had defied Orlov. In 1858, 13.8 percent of adult women in the village had never married, despite the fact that its Panin owners continued to apply Orlov's managerial "Law Code."[86] We should assume that at Sidorovskoe, too, Old Believers were the serfs in charge and that they managed to protect many women who shrank from marriage. When in 1821 two Bolotnikovo fathers asked that they be allowed to purchase the manumission of their daughters, ages eighteen and thirty-nine, for 200 rubles each, the Sidorovskoe bailiff passed the request along to Orlov with the recommendation that it be granted.[87] Even without direct evidence, we may suspect that the bailiffs at Sidorovskoe, Bolotnikovo, and Matveikha worked together to deflect, whenever possible, Orlov's attempts to compel women to marry.

Orlov manorial correspondence tells us much about the alliance of interest between Orlov and young men wishing to marry and about how presumably Old Believer bailiffs deflected Orlov's orders. It also goes a long way toward delineating the geographical distribution of female marriage aversion. There were significant numbers of unmarried women on Orlov estates in the contiguous provinces of Iaroslavl, Kostroma, and Nizhnii Novgorod, and there is unmistakable evidence that the women who resisted marriage were Old Believers. Vladimir's older brother Aleksei Orlov (and subsequently Aleksei's daughter) also owned estates in Iaroslavl province on which there were many priestless Old Believers, of the Fedoseev covenant, who wouldn't marry.[88] By contrast, on Vladimir Orlov's large estates in Moscow province (Kolomna and Serpukhov districts) and Orel province (Epifan and Bolkhov districts), marriage aversion was either absent or insignificant, as evidenced by the silence on the issue in the abundant manorial correspondence.

It is true that for a few estates, the volume of correspondence that has survived is so small, or Orlov's management so short-lived, that no judgment is possible. Nevertheless, there is only a single identifiable geographical outlier: the Usolie estate at the Samara Bend (where the Volga makes a hairpin turn) in Simbirsk province. On that estate, fathers of an appreciable number of unmarried women paid fines.[89] However, we will see later that Usolie was not an outlier at all but part of a geographical belt of female marriage resistance along the southward run of the Volga River.

Nobles at Large: Banning Marriage Off the Estate or Profiting from Manumission?

Other nobles focused on the same issues on which Vladimir Orlov legislated: whether to allow serf women to leave the estate through marriage, what the bridal departure fee should be, what to do about women who refused to marry, and the bride price peasants charged each other. Like Orlov, some changed their minds from time to time, and their rules—like Orlov's—were either unexplained or obvious reactions to their peasants' nuptial practices.

One measure on which nobles clearly took the initiative was the reversal of their previous indifference toward off-estate marriage. From the 1750s onward, more and more nobles forbade women to marry away. Prior to 1759, for example, the Buturlins made no objection to their Palekh women departing through marriage and, as of the 1750s, charged only two rubles for the privilege. Then, in 1759, Ivan Buturlin ordered his Palekh bailiff to read an order to the estate's serfs: henceforth, fathers could give their daughters in marriage only to estate men. Buturlin also ordered that his serfs pay him two rubles for every wedding celebrated, obviously to compensate (and more) for the lost bridal departure fees. The rule remained in effect at least until the late 1780s.[90] In 1785, the Princes Gruzinskii banned off-estate marriage at a property in Nizhnii Novgorod province.[91] Neither the Buturlins nor the Gruzinskies bothered to explain their orders.

In a surprisingly large number of cases, nobles' management codes from the late eighteenth and early nineteenth centuries say nothing about serf marriage, while noble interventions often reveal policy.[92] If Russia's greatest eighteenth-century general, Aleksandr Suvorov (1730–1800), ever composed detailed management instructions, they haven't survived. During the few years he was not entirely absorbed in military affairs, he frequently intervened in serf marriage, personally choosing which single men should marry which single women when they wouldn't make matches themselves. He also purchased women for men who needed wives and contributed ten rubles toward the departure fee his male serfs had to pay when they sought brides on other properties. Otherwise, bridal departure fees never come up in his correspondence. Together with the other evidence, that suggests brides didn't depart.[93]

In the abundant correspondence between Aleksandr Mikhailovich Golitsyn (1723–1807, inter alia, vice-chancellor of the College of Foreign

Affairs, 1762–1775) and his Konstantinovo estate in the Riazan district, there is not a single mention of departure fees and many other indications that Golitsyn would not let women leave in marriage.[94] When the bailiff at his small Karlovka estate (1782: seventy-five men) in the Belev district reported in 1780 that the households were all related to each other and so brides would have to be exchanged with neighboring estates, he reacted skeptically: details about each particular case were to be submitted to him, and he would decide what to do.[95]

At the Gagarins' Petrovskoe estate (Tambov province), where peasant women married young and universally in the first half of the nineteenth century, there is no evidence in the extensive manorial correspondence that management either ever intervened in the first marriages of field serfs or permitted young women to marry away, only that they occasionally allowed widows to do so.[96]

As Suvorov's example suggests, some nobles exercised very close control over their serfs' marriages. Two Kovrov district (Vladimir province) nobles exemplified that tendency in the first half of the nineteenth century. Aleksei Chikhachev summoned prospective serf couples from his scattered estates to his residence in order to rule on the suitability of their matches.[97] In 1834, A. M. Cheremisinov instructed an elder to draw up lists of marriageable men and women and, if they did not reach agreements with each other, matched couples himself. However, he also allowed his serfs to make marital exchanges with neighboring proprietors.[98]

The noble who took micromanagement of serf marriage to the extreme was Aleksei Arakcheev (1769–1834), principal minister during the second half of the reign of Alexander I. He said nothing about off-estate marriage in the twenty-four "Rules on Weddings" he issued in 1805 for his Gruzino estate in Novgorod province, apparently because he thought it inconceivable. Unlike almost all other marriage regulations, his rules focused almost entirely on men. Women figured only in the injunction that girls of bad conducted were not to marry unless a wealthy family wanted one of them. Arakcheev's regulations were unusual, too, in shifting the wedding season from the customary pre-Lenten weeks in January and early February to the period between Easter Week and Trinity Sunday: lists of marriageable men were to be compiled in January; during Lent, Arakcheev tested them for knowledge of the Lord's Prayer and the Ten Commandments; during Easter Week, he inspected all the couples; and after inspection, those permitted to marry would do so. Like some other nobles, he also tried to limit wedding expenses and, uniquely I think, banned the consumption of vodka during wedding celebrations.[99]

Parish marriage registers sometimes identify nobles who proscribed or permitted marriage off the estate. In six small villages around Nikolskoe in the Riazan district in 1781, for example, there were two marriages between Veliaminov serfs, four between Okorokov serfs, and one each between Khludnev and Levonov serfs. No marriage at the Nikolskoe church mixed property that year.[100] That cannot have been an accident—those serf-owners required their male and female serfs to marry each other. Similarly, in the parish church at Talezh, in the Serpukhov district (Moscow province), in 1803 and between 1805 and 1817, serfs from the village of Bershovo, then owned by Fedor Koltovskii celebrated only eight marriages; three joined brides and grooms from Bershovo. In the other five, Bershovo grooms married brides from other Koltovskii estates in other districts. Koltovskii went to great lengths to ensure that his serf men and women married only each other.[101] But if some owners of small properties clutched their serf women tight, others trusted to the circulation of brides in a market. In the second half of the 1850s, Bershovo was owned by Andrei Boborykin, and the Talezh parish register for that period shows that his male serfs brought in brides from outside, which almost necessarily means that some of his own women left through marriage.[102]

Probably just as many serf-owners raised customary departure fees to uncustomary levels. On Kurakin properties, the departure fee was fifteen rubles in the 1770s, the same level as on Orlov properties in those years; the Kurakins designated ten rubles for the communal treasury and five for themselves.[103] In 1767, General Mikhail Golitsyn, brother of Vice-Chancellor Aleksandr Golitsyn, issued an "Instruction" to his Troitskoe estate in Perm province that allowed women to marry away (unless they stood to be the heir to the household), so long as an unspecified (thus probably locally customary) departure fee was collected.[104] In 1789, he collected a ten-ruble and a fifteen-ruble fee for girls marrying away from his Sulost estate in the Rostov district and directed that the money go to the parish church. In 1794, he collected fifty rubles for each of two girls who married away from Sulost and kept the money for himself. In all four cases, according to the bailiffs, the girls were so poor that no one on the estate would marry them.[105] Probably Mikhail Mikhailovich preferred to keep serf women on the estate but was willing to make exceptions and, by 1794, to profit from them.

One hundred rubles was the normal departure fee around 1800, as can be seen at Princess Dashkova's Korotovo estate in the Cherepovets district (Novgorod province) and at Shishkin as well as at Orlov properties.[106] The fee continued to rise. Vladimir Orlov-Davydov (1809–1882), grandson of Vladimir Orlov, inherited some Orlov properties in 1831 and retained the family "Law Code": he allowed women to marry away for a departure fee that was higher and more standardized than Vladimir Orlov's.[107] Nikita Panin (1801–1879), minister of justice under both Alexander I and Nicholas I, who through his wife acquired other Orlov properties—including Sidoro-vskoe and at Gorodets—permitted bridal exchange without fees, released others for fees in excess of 200 rubles, and fined unmarried adult women.[108]

Abundant Glebov-Streshnev documentation shows that from 1815 down to emancipation women married away from their many properties in Iaroslavl, Kostroma, Tver, Vladimir, Pskov, Moscow, Tula, Orel, and Simbirsk provinces (and had obviously done so before 1815), and their neighbors reciprocated. Correspondence from the estates occasionally mentions that Sidor asks to give his daughter off the estate and wants to remind the owners that he earlier acquired a bride for his son from a neighboring property. From 1815 on, the Glebov-Streshnevs levied a departure fee of 250 or 350 rubles, the higher figure applying to wealthier households, with only an occasional reduced charge (225 rubles, for example) for women from poor households.[109] Many serf-owners understood, as had Vladimir Orlov, that when they set departure fees at or above the rising market price for marriageable serf women, they suffered no loss when women married away.

By 1800, many serf-owners aimed at maximizing profit from off-estate marriage, none more nakedly than the Sheremetevs. Evidence from the first half of the eighteenth century is that Petr Borisovich Sheremetev (1713–1788) then charged either a nominal departure fee or none at all, but instructions he issued to his many estates in 1764 set the fee at 10, 20, or 30 rubles, depending on household wealth; the 20- and 30-ruble fees were far above what was then the market price of a marriageable serf girl. Moreover, if a daughter's father conducted business that brought in more than 500 rubles per year, she could not leave without his personal permission.[110] In such cases, obviously, he determined how much to exact.

Nikolai Petrovich Sheremetev (1751–1809), who inherited in 1788, increased the standard fees to 40, 80, or 120 rubles in 1789 and then to 100, 150, or 200 rubles in 1790, at least for his north-central estates, where many of his serfs engaged in manufacture and commerce rather than agriculture. In 1796, he decreed that he personally would determine the departure fees for households with capital over 1,000 rubles. On the other hand, in 1796, he set a lower rate for his farming peasants—40, 80, or 120 rubles—and in the same year, at least for poor households on his Voshchazhnikovo estate in the Rostov district (Iaroslavl province) who pleaded the burden of other exactions, he permitted payment in yarn and linen. In 1800, he canceled in-kind payments and, at least in the commercial villages, reduced the cash fee for poor households to 50 rubles while raising the fee for middling households with a capital of between 500 and 1,000 rubles to 200 rubles; he himself would continue to determine the fee for wealthy households. In 1803, he raised the rate for farming peasants to 100, 150, and 200 rubles; if poor households could not raise the minimum charge, they might nevertheless marry their daughters off the estate on an exchange basis, but only if he personally approved.[111] At least occasionally, he charged thousands of rubles when the most prosperous households married their daughters away from the estate. After he inherited in 1809, Dmitrii Nikolaevich Sheremetev (1803–1871) retained the same scale of charges and the same prerogative to determine the charge for the very wealthy.[112]

The Sheremetevs had deliberately turned their serfs' off-estate marriages into a substantial revenue stream.[113] On the other hand, both in the eighteenth and nineteenth centuries, they also allowed girls from destitute households (as certified by serf elders and bailiffs) to marry away at no charge.[114] Only rarely did they forbid women to marry way—for instance, in 1834, in the case of a Voshchazhnikovo household whose quitrent arrears were greater than the 100-ruble minimum departure fee. The money would be better spent, ruled the Sheremetev home office, to pay down the debt. That was a stunning misunderstanding of who actually paid for the bride's departure—not the bride's household, but the groom's.[115]

WHEN SERF WOMEN REFUSED TO MARRY

There is considerable evidence from the late 1750s onward, and none from before that date, of nobles' reactions to their discovery that some of their serf women wouldn't marry at all. That is not because the survival rate of manorial papers increases after 1750 (it does) but because that was when serf-owners first learned of the abnormality. They learned from male serfs who reported the women's refusals and from tax census returns that beginning in 1763, listed women as well as men. Serf-owners responded in one or a mix of four ways: imposing a marry-by age, resolute compulsion, fines on single women, and the sale of manumission papers. On most estates where women avoided marriage, nobles were no more able than Vladimir Orlov to bring them to heel, but also like Orlov, they learned to profit from marriage aversion.

Nobles probably learned that their serf women weren't marrying only after spinsters had begun to accumulate. In 1764, a noble with an estate in the Rostov district, a certain Karnovich, learned that women in their twenties, and one at age thirty, were single and that they were Old Believers. He ordered that Old Believers be shunned—not admitted to meetings of estate peasants, not visited by other peasants—but to do nothing else until he arrived.[116] There is no further information on the case, but the timing of the report and the implication of Old Believers are indicative. In 1777, former vice-chancellor Alexandr Golitsyn began to collect a three-ruble fine on unmarried women ages eighteen to thirty-five and threatened to match single men and women by lot; he had discovered their existence in the 1762 tax census returns, which he must have looked at only after he retired as vice-chancellor in 1775. He later claimed that his orders had prompted four hundred women to marry, surely an exaggeration.[117]

Sometime in the 1770s, the Kurakins ordered their estate managers to see that men married by age twenty and women by eighteen; men who failed to marry were to be sent to the army, and women were to pay a two- to three-ruble fine into the community treasury. If no bride were available for a man in need, the community should buy one.[118] Possibly it was the discovery in 1770 that on a large Kurakin estate (1,271 men, 1,407 women) in the Rostov district, 11.5 percent of women twenty-five and over had never married (fully 26.9 percent in the estate seat, Rozhdestvenskoe village) that triggered the order. In the same year, the household inventory for the fourteen villages on the Kurakins' Petrovskoe estate, Suzdal district, revealed that 35 of 281 women twenty-five and over (12.5 percent) had never married. The Kurakins would not have been prompted to establish a *terminus ante quem* for marriage by the nuptial behavior at their properties far to the south in the Orel district (829 men, 801 women), where among women twenty and over only 11 had never married in 1763; of those, at least 6 were blind or crippled, and 3 others were in their early twenties and likely to marry.[119] But once the rule had been established, the Kurakins seem to have included it in instructions to all their estates, as shown by a 1775 instruction for an estate in Penza province.[120]

Countess Irina Vorontsova learned in 1796 that there were unmarried adult women at her estate in the Murom district, Vladimir province. She ordered that they marry voluntarily or be fined and sent to her Mozhaisk district estate, where they would be given in marriage.[121] Also in the 1790s, Count Ivan Shuvalov ordered that girls at his Myt estate in the Gorokhovets district (immediately north of the Murom district) marry by age twenty. If they didn't, they would be married even against their fathers' will.[122] The orders to these estates may have been singular, elicited only by the discovery of accumulations of unmarried women on particular estates, or they may have reflected policies on all of the Vorontsova and Shuvalov properties. In 1796, the bailiff at a Shishkin property in Kostroma province reported that there were grooms looking for brides and far more potential brides than needed to satisfy the grooms but that fathers wouldn't release their daughters. Male peasants on the estate claimed fathers demanded bride prices far higher than they could pay; the bailiff passed along their request that Sergei Petrovich Shishkin order the bride price be reduced to its previous five rubles.[123] From time to time, Vasilii Ivanovich Suvorov (not a close relative of the great general), who owned an estate in the Unzha region of Kostroma province from 1766 to his death in 1790, occasionally ordered peasant elders to match unmarried men and women or to force a father to yield a particular daughter. It is not clear that compulsion was actually required. At least, his Unzha serfs complained in 1782 that their previous owners had allowed them to marry as they wished and that everyone had married of their own free will. They may have lied. This Suvorov also allowed his serfs to find brides and marry men on neighboring estates.[124]

General Mikhail Mikhailovich Golitsyn learned in 1770 that some fathers of women on his Voskresenskii estate, Suzdal district, refused to give their daughters in marriage, with false claims that their households depended on their daughters or that they were sickly. He ordered the elders to compel marriage. That order persuaded some households to release their daughters but not others, so the community leaders themselves chose brides for waiting grooms. Mikhail Mikhailovich's comment was that "although it is not without sin to force a girl to marry against her will, on the other hand I would commit no less a sin if I left them in such a dissolute life," and he ordered that the priests who had objected to the forced marriages be told to mind their own business.[125] At his brother Aleksandr Mikhailovich's Puzhbol estate, Rostov district, probably around the same time, there were reported to be many unmarried adult women, but the surviving correspondence doesn't reveal what he did about it.[126] Perhaps this was the estate that prompted him to threaten matchmaking by lot.

As of 1815, the Glebov-Streshnevs received lists of unmarried women fifteen and up and imposed fines on them from age twenty. The bailiff of an estate in the Nerekhta district, Kostroma province, reported in 1815 that he had collected 6.50 rubles per maiden. However, fines may sometimes have varied with age or means; fines from that estate averaged 5.93 rubles in 1817 and 6.84 rubles in 1819.[127] As the estate correspondence makes clear, fines had little effect. The Nerekhta bailiff observed in 1815 that it was more difficult to force fathers to yield daughters for marriage than sons for conscription.[128] There was considerable resistance to marriage as well at Glebvov-Streshnev properties in the Soligalich and Kologriv districts (Kostroma province) and in the Romanovo district (Iaroslavl province). Fathers at those estates were permitted to purchase their daughters' manumission for 350 rubles, sometimes with—sometimes without—the bailiffs' assurance that they were unfit for marriage.[129] Fathers would not likely have wasted 350 rubles purchasing the freedom of incapacitated daughters. Reports on fines collected from, or manumission of, marriage-averse women come only from Glebov-Streshnev estates in Iaroslavl and Kostroma provinces, not from the family's many properties elsewhere.

The Iusupovs, with many estates in many provinces, seem to have ignored, were perhaps even ignorant of, their serfs' marriage practices as late as the 1830s. We can only tentatively infer from the available evidence that Prince Nikolai Borisovich Iusupov (1751–1831) probably forbade marriage off his estates. When he altered the labor units (*tiagla*) on his corvée estates from two married couples to one in 1780, he seems to have assumed it required compulsion to produce married couples and so imposed a ten-ruble fine on single women. The records don't indicate how old (or young) women were when they became subject to the fine, let alone whether there was any need to force them to marry.[130] Whatever the rule, it almost certainly fell quickly into desuetude; nothing like it recurs in the management rules that Nikolai and his son, Boris Nikolaevich (1794–1849), subsequently issued.[131] The 1825, 1831, and 1844 management rules for the Iusupov "steppe estates," where serfs performed corvée labor, were quite detailed but included no provisions of any sort on marriage.[132] It probably didn't matter what Nikolai thought about serf marriage, because—distracted by government duties, foreign travel, and art collecting—he was a negligent owner. As his son, Boris, wrote about the work of the Iusupovs' Moscow chancellery in his father's time, the chancellery "avoided the labor of verifying detailed reports, and if it received any, as if fearing their enormity, noted their receipt, wrapped them in cloth, and deposited them in the archive for eternal decay, for which reason affairs on all properties proceeded so badly that, to this day, even with my best efforts, I can barely set them right."[133]

From 1780 into the 1830s, the Iusupov papers that survived decay seem to have been silent on the matter of women who never married, at least insofar as the "steppe" and Little Russian estates are concerned. The subject not only never comes up in the instructions sent to managers, but it may also have been absent from the correspondence between estates and the Moscow chancellery.[134] The absence of evidence may be taken as evidence of absence, as suggested by a three-cornered exchange among the bailiff at a small property in Kostroma province, the Moscow chancellery, and Boris Iusupov in 1843. The bailiff reported that male serfs brought state peasant women home as wives and asked whether that meant that the estate's women could marry state peasant men. No, it didn't, responded the chancellery, and asked Boris Nikolaevich what his pleasure might be. Boris responded that if the women could not find husbands he had plenty of grooms for them on his other estates and concluded: "I have no rules on manumission, and I forbid it."[135] He meant that since there was no rule permitting manumission for marriage, then it was forbidden. Yet he did occasionally allow exceptions. In 1848, he agreed to manumit a serf maiden from another Kostroma estate, if the prospective groom delivered an exorbitant 525 rubles.[136]

The earliest surviving reference to marriage aversion on Iusupov estates, perhaps a response to an inquiry, may be an 1834 report from the supervisor of all the Iusupov "steppe estates" that "widowers demand brides, but maidens don't want to marry them; and on the other hand, there are marriageable girls who disdain marriage, many peasants in general don't surrender their daughters without compulsion."[137] He did not identify any particular estate as the locus of marriage resistance or who might have done the compelling. One possibility is the Tula province village of Spasskoe. In 1825, serfs there and in its satellite village, Prilepy, claimed that the estate clerk was in league with the local priest, who overcharged them for weddings and other sacraments. The priest denied the charge and presented a list of 173 men and 164 women from the two villages who had not made their required annual confession.[138] The implication was that they were schismatics.

Perhaps they were resisting the priest's efforts to draw them into the official church. Since there were 609 men and 647 women in those villages in 1834 (including children six and under, who were not required to confess), probably Old Believers of one kind or another made up a quarter of the villages' adult population. Old Believers or not, however, Spasskoe and Prilepy peasants married universally and as of 1834 had done so at least since the 1790s (shown by those in their fifties and sixties in 1834). In fact, all of the Iusupov serfs in Tula province practiced universal marriage.[139] Perhaps Old Believer fathers were unwilling to send their daughters to Orthodox households.

The Iusupov serf women who wouldn't marry anyone at all lived in Iaroslavl and Kostroma provinces (as Boris Iusupov knew), as well as in Nizhnii Novgorod province.[140] According to the 1834 census returns, at an estate in the Romanovo district, 841 male and 1,071 female serfs resided in forty-nine small villages. Women outnumbered men by 27.3 percent, an almost certain indication that many adult women never married. In a sample of those villages (493 men, 646 women), about 14 percent of the adult women had never married.[141]

That many of his serfs were Old Believers disturbed Boris Nikolaevich. In 1832 and 1833, shortly after he inherited the family estates, he sent one directive after another urging managers to promote church attendance and morality (he, too, associated the schism with fornication). But he also believed that Old Believers were his most trustworthy serfs (most likely to pay their dues in full, he probably meant) and worried they might not remain so if they became Orthodox. Rather than pressing them hard, he attempted mild persuasion. In 1846, his Moscow chancery convened a meeting of his Iaroslavl serfs then doing business in Moscow, and a priest sermonized on the benefits of joining the one true church. The Old Believers could only have concluded that there was no earthly reason to do so.[142]

Boris's son Nikolai, who inherited in 1849, in 1852 compiled "Rules on levying dues (*obrok*) on peasant maidens":

In former times there was a custom on the estate: a peasant girl whose parents ignored her moral education and who grew up without fear, led a depraved life without punishment, bore children, abandoned them, shunned honorable marriage, and then, when she grew old, joined a schismatic sect that indulges and encourages debauchery. To forestall this, dues were imposed on all spinsters

*without exception. After some changes, at present this impost is levied in the fol-
lowing fashion: from a maiden of 17, 1 ruble 50 kopeks; of 18, 1 ruble 75 kopeks;
of 19, 2 rubles; of 20 and older, 3 rubles.*[143]

Charges so low were not even a nuisance. Nikolai's reference to earlier rates
suggests that his father, Boris—who wished his Old Believers to be Orthodox but shied away from compulsion—had introduced the levy. Boris (or
just possibly Nikolai himself) apparently decided to turn his Old Believer
women's aversion to marriage into another, albeit not particularly large,
source of income. It had taken the Iusupovs an unusually long time, no doubt
because of the first Nikolai Borisovich's inattention to what was transpiring
on his estates, to respond to the widespread marriage aversion on their Iaroslavl and other northern properties, and the response was ineffectual.

The first Iusupov known to have turned a tax on single women into regular income, on an estate where marriage was close to universal, was Princess Tatiana Vasilievna Iusupova, the young widow of Catherine the Great's
one-time favorite Potemkin and then wife of Nikolai Borisovich Iusupov
and mother of Boris. In 1816, she sent letter after letter to her Buturlino estate
in western Kaluga province, demanding to know why she received only
1,179 rubles in charges on unmarried maidens and young widows in 1815.
That was far less, she said, than the 2,000 and more rubles she had received
the previous year or the more than 3,000 rubles received before that. She
demanded an investigation and a complete register of single women.[144]

In the 1816 census year, there were 5,272 men on the estate and approximately that many women. The register Iusupova received listed 418 single
girls and women of an age to be fined: fifteen to forty-one. Fully 138 were
fifteen years old; their fathers paid tribute just because they had fifteen-
year-old daughters. Only 38 were ages twenty-one to forty-one; at most,
1.5 percent of adult women twenty-one and over were single. The fines their
fathers paid were five rubles at age fifteen, an additional ruble for very year
up to age twenty, and ten and a half rubles at twenty and older.[145] These fines
were larger than those her son, Boris, later collected, but there is no evidence
that they encouraged young women to marry earlier than they would otherwise have done. Indeed, Princess Iusopova would have been disappointed
if they had because she clearly craved the income. She rejected a suggestion
by an agent sent to investigate that fines be abolished and all girls be forced
to marry by age eighteen.[146] It is tempting to suppose, in fact, that she fined
fifteen-year olds because there were so few single women in their twenties

to fine. In 1836, she again complained of a shortfall in income from fines on marriageable women.[147]

However, the men on the estate misunderstood Iusupova's purpose. When they discovered in 1816 that her agent was compiling a list of single women, forty asked for wives for themselves or their sons. Again, that was a miniscule portion of the adult men on the estate, but probably they really had found it difficult to make matches. One case the correspondence describes in some detail involved a retired soldier with two unmarried sons. He claimed that his household would collapse if his sons didn't marry, but he turned down a match with an orphan girl because she was too stupid. Furthermore, the household was not in danger of collapse; the soldier's wife was still alive, and a widowed sister or sister-in-law was living with them. The reason no young women would marry his sons was that the household was squalid.[148] Even in a peasant community that practiced universal marriage, there were households of such ill repute that fathers would not give their daughters to them. Serf men in that situation could only hope their masters would take their side.

The Sheremetevs, who in the late eighteenth century owned more serfs than any other family, learned of their female serfs' marriage aversion much earlier than the Iusupovs. Petr Borisovich Sheremetev first imposed fines on single women in 1768. His 1764 management instructions had not mentioned fines. The information about the 1768 order comes from a diary kept by a manufacturer in the Sheremetev's industrializing serf village of Ivanovo, in the Shui district, Vladimir province. At the time, most serfs in Ivanovo were Old Believers, many of them priestless Spasovites and Fedoseevites, whose women were the most likely to shun marriage. The fine was in yarn—two pounds from single women eighteen to twenty, three from those twenty to twenty-five, and ten from those twenty-five to thirty—or in cash at twenty kopeks per pound. That fine may have applied only in Ivanovo.[149] However, fines in yarn surface again in the 1790s on other estates, so there was at least an institutional memory of them.

Petr's son, Nikolai, appears to have learned that significant numbers of women on his estates were refusing to marry only when he (or his estate managers) looked at returns from the 1795 tax census. That census immediately followed a significant jump in female marriage aversion at his Voshchazhnikovo property, Rostov district. In Voshchazhnikovo village, population around one thousand (both sexes), marriage aversion reached almost 10 percent among women who turned twenty-five between 1791 and 1795, up from less than 5 percent among those who turned twenty-five between 1781 and 1790.[150] Of course, Sheremetev would have considered the much larger number of unmarried women under twenty-five part of the problem. In 1796, he wrote to the Voshchazhnikovo management that there were many unmarried and therefore useless women on the estate and also too many bachelors, widows, and widowers (young ones, presumably). He introduced fines for unmarried women, bachelors, and the widowed, ages twenty to forty, of two, four, or six rubles, depending on household well-being; he later added that the fine could be paid in yarn equivalent. And he ordered that management send him a list of all Voshchazhnikovo bachelors, maidens, widows, and widowers ages seventeen and above.[151]

Sheremetev sent virtually identical observations and orders to his Ivanovo estate in 1796. The figures he extracted from the 1795 census there were 550 bachelors and widowers ages eighteen to forty and 869 maidens and widows from fifteen to forty. Those were impressive numbers, though inflated because the count began at ages eighteen and fifteen. The figures also need to be considered in the context of the estate's total population, 3,357 men and 3,267 women, a generation earlier, in 1774.[152] Nevertheless, the proportion of never-married adult men and women in 1795 was probably substantial. Also in 1796, Sheremetev sent an order to his Serebrianye Prudy estate in the Vinevskii district (Tula province) to punish unmarried women. Unmarried women were detailed to work, or they could pay twenty pounds of yarn or six rubles.[153]

Surprisingly, perhaps, Nikolai Sheremetev initially misunderstood why women weren't marrying. Like Vladimir Orlov, his first thought seems to have been that excessively high bride prices prevented some men from marrying. When instituting fines for unmarried women at the Serebrianye Prudy estate in 1796, for instance, Sheremetev also commanded that "payment for the bride is to be completely abolished"; to encourage wealthy fathers to give their daughters to poor households, he said that in return, they would be forgiven all services to the estate.[154]

Sheremetev probably sent inquiries about bride price to many or all of his estates in 1802 because he received at least three reports about the local charge from three different estates that year. He had probably learned that peasants continued to demand bride price of each other even after he had ordered them to desist. The bride price at Borisovka, Belgorod province, was 100 rubles; and at the Sergeevsk estate, 20 to 30 rubles or more. At the Khvoshchevka estate in the Gorbatov district, Nizhnii Novgorod province, peasants complained that fathers deliberately demanded more than they could afford in order to turn suitors away. Local management ordered that the serfs report such cases—guilty fathers fit for military conscription would be sent to the army; those unfit would be sent to eternal hard labor.[155] It is quite possible that fathers at Khvoshchevka—we know that priestless Fedoseevites lived in that area—were indeed protecting their marriage-averse daughters in that way, just as fathers at the Orlov estate in the Liubim district were at the same time.[156]

But bride price was not the problem; that was Russian peasant custom, and while it no doubt complicated marriage for men from poor households, it was just as common among universally marrying peasants as among those with elevated levels of female resistance to marriage.[157] In any case, in 1804 Nikolai Sheremetev yielded; he ordered that henceforth poor peasants should pay no more than 20 to 30 rubles for the bride and middling peasants no more than 50 rubles. In 1815, his son and heir, Dmitrii (or managers acting in his name—Dmitrii was only twelve at the time), issued updated management rules that again banned bride price, but his serfs surely ignored that order just as they had ignored Nikolai's in 1796.[158]

Priestless Old Believers must have been the reason why so many women on the Sheremetev estates never married, just as it was wherever we have more than a smattering of information about Old Believers locally. At the Voshchazhnikovo estate (Rostov district), there is just enough evidence to postulate the connection. It is true that there is only bare mention of Old Believers in the very extensive records from Voshchazhnikovo.[159] One small set of documents even suggests that they were few. In 1847, estate management inquired of at least two priests—not in Voshchazhnikovo, but in other villages on the estate—whether there were any schismatics in their parishes. One responded that there were none; the other, that there were only three Old Believer couples.[160] The inquiry itself, perhaps, indicates that management had an inkling that there might be Old Believers about, but the replies were reassuring.

The annual confession register for 1843 from the Church of the Blessed Virgin—one of three churches in Voshchazhnikovo—tells a different story. Among its parishioners were 652 from the village. Thirty-five of the 207 women twenty-five and over (16.9 percent) had never married.[161]

That roughly coincides with the proportion of unmarried adult women as reported in tax censuses and estate household inventories from 1832 to 1858.[162] There was only a single declared Old Believer in the congregation, a thirty-nine-year-old married woman. However, an additional 30 women and 21 men had missed confession because of "forgetfulness," the explanation Ministry of Internal Affairs specialists considered an almost invariable indication of adherence to the Old Belief. Others—132 men, 42 women— had missed confession because they were away, and the same specialists thought absence was frequently timed to coincide with confession season (see the introduction). However, since large numbers of Voshchazhnikovo serfs did leave the estate on business or to find work, I will assume their absence was entirely innocent.[163]

Only four of the thirty-five women ages twenty-five or older absent from confession were single, but another ten single adult women lived in households in which one or more men twenty-five or older had supposedly forgotten to confess. Most of those households probably held secretive Old Believers. By themselves, neither singleness in women nor failure to confess were absolutely certain signs of religious dissent, but it is unlikely that two such predictors in the same household would mislead. That accounts for fourteen of the thirty-five single women over the age of twenty-five.

Of the twenty-one others, who lived in households in which everyone either confessed or was away working, three unmarried sisters ages fifty-three to fifty-six made up a household of their own; three unmarried women ages fifty-four to sixty-two, not sisters, also lived together by themselves; and a widower and his single sister and single adult daughter made up a final household. As will become clear from analysis in subsequent chapters, these were surely remnant households of priestless Old Believers, what was left after the households had committed themselves to celibacy or had taken a terrible demographic risk by failing to stock an adequate number of reproducing males. Probably the same was true of the two households that consisted of a single unmarried woman each, ages thirty-seven and forty-two.

The remaining ten single adult women lived in larger households than that. Perhaps some of them remained single because of physical or mental disability, but most were probably single for religious reasons. The Voshchazhnikovo women who were single in 1843, mostly by religious design, were the problem the Sheremetevs had been trying but failing to solve since 1796.

Much the same could be said of other serf-owners. The brothers Aleksandr and Mikhail Mikhailovich Golitsyn, esteemed Suvorov, reviled Arakcheev, Irina Vorontsova, Vladimir Orlov sometimes, and others did use brute compulsion to compel reluctant serf women to marry. But probably more—Orlov most of the time, the Iusupovs, Sheremetevs, Glebov-Streshnevs, Kurakins, Panins, Orlov-Davydovs, and others—resorted to fines and other punishments, stopping short of brute force, at least according to the evidence available. Fines, as everyone quickly discovered, were unavailing, but serf-owners continued to collect them as income. The fine on singleness was in the same class as the chickens, nuts, or half a sheep's carcass that many serfs had to provide annually for the master's table and often no more burdensome. The ever-rising fee that nobles extracted when women left the estate in marriage must certainly have prevented some women from marrying away, but the Sheremetevs and other nobles seem to have set their fees at what they judged to be an income-maximizing level rather than a level that would actually prevent women from leaving their estates. The sale of manumission papers that allowed unmarried women to remain single had the same purpose. That the charge was generally scaled to household wealth also reveals income maximizing intent.

While historians have almost universally characterized these policies as measures to regulate or control serf marriage, and in origin they may have been, most of the time they were not. While high departure fees had an effect on the marital choices of men from poorer households—but from households *outside* the estates with those rules, who might otherwise have sought brides there—the various taxes serf-owners levied on off-estate marriage and singleness yielded considerable income but scant change in serf women's nuptial behavior. Or, at least, that is what the demographic histories of the Orlov Sidorovskoe estate and the Sheremetev Voshchazhnikovo estate suggest.

Almost always, serf-owners' rules on marriage were prompted by misplaced fear of property loss (either in the form of the woman herself or in the form of a labor-dues unit that wouldn't be formed for lack of her) when women married away or their discovery that others remained on their estates unmarried. In other words, the behavior of their serfs largely determined the choices owners made. While the marriage regimes they devised varied considerably from noble to noble, serf-owners really had only two decisions to make: to end serf women's customary right to marry away from their natal estate or extract profit from marital mobility, and to force women to marry no matter how merciless the compulsion or turn female marriage aversion into cash income. It is not surprising that many nobles chose to profit from their serfs' nuptial behavior.

However we draw the balance between cruelty and avarice in nobles' intervention in serf marriage, their manorial correspondence helps us to reconstruct the history and geography of female marriage aversion. Nobles learned that serf women were avoiding marriage only in the second half of the eighteenth century. Nobles' responses to that development identify at least one region in which marriage aversion was concentrated: Iaroslavl, Kostroma, Nizhnii Novgorod, and Vladimir provinces—a belt of territory along the upper and middle course of the Volga River. Their manorial correspondence, and eighteenth-century tax census returns, suggest that female aversion to marriage, if it existed at all, was imperceptible in Moscow, Kaluga, Tula, Riazan, Orel, and other provinces south and west of Moscow, even though the noble families who have figured in this chapter owned many estates there.

NOTES

1. The biographical details are from "Petr Mikhailovich Bestuzhev-Riumin," pp. 14–21 (his own autobiographical chronicle); Solov'ev, *Istoriia Rossii*, book 9, pp. 418–21, 538; book 10, pp. 39–41, 89–92, 132–37, 178–79, 217, 259, 319; Anisimov, *Five Empresses*, pp. 72–74.

2. "Petr Mikhailovich Bestuzhev-Riumin," p. 5. Lukovesi now lies under the Rybinsk Reservoir. The character of the landscape emerges from Bestuzhev's 1737 instruction and is also described in a 1680 document reaffirming the rights of the Trinity Filipp Hermitage to land in the same area (Shumakov, *Obzor "Gramot Kollegii ekonomii,"* vol. 2, pp. 170–74).

3. *Materialy po istorii sel'skogo khoziaistva i krest'ianstva Rossii. Sel'skokhoziastvennye instruktsii (pervaia polovina XVIII v.)*, p. 182.

4. Ibid., p. 189.

5. Ibid., pp. 189, 195.

6. Ibid., p. 199.

7. Ibid., p. 201.

8. Ibid.

9. *Akty, sobrannye v bibliotekakh i arkhivakh Rossiiskoi Imperii*, vol. 4, pp. 145–46. According to the 1858 tax census, fully 6.31 percent of unmarried young women of marriageable age in Poshekhonie district had illegitimate children ("Obshchie svedeniia," in *Iaroslavskaia guberniia. Spiski naselennykh mest*, p. xlv).

10. *Russkie krest'iane. Zhizn'. Byt. Nravy*, vol. 2, part 1, p. 408.

11. On Old Believer self-immolation in the Cherepovets area and in Poshekhonie more broadly in the late seventeenth century, see Evfrosin, *Otrazitel'noe pisanie*, pp. 17, 70–71; Dmitrii, Metropolitan of Rostov and Iaroslavl', *Rozysk o Raskol'nicheskoi Brynskoi Vere*, pp. 585–87; *Staraia Vologda*, p. 153. On Old Believers seeking refuge in the forests of Poshekhonie in the nineteenth century, see GAIaO, f. 150, op. 1, d. 4354 ll. 7–100b, 160b–17, 96–980b, 212–15, 225–260b, 233–360b, 256–63 ; op. 1, d. 6068, l. 22–260b, 49–570b, 104–70b. These cases from 1843 and 1852 were typical of cases in many other years.

12. Indova, "Instruktsiia," p. 460.

13. Ibid., pp. 432–69. For biographical details, I have followed S. G. Kalinina's introduction to *Perepiska kniazia M. M. Shcherbatova*, pp. 3–42; Antony Lentin's introduction to Shcherbatov, *On the Corruption of Morals*, p. 21 and passim; and V. Fursenko, "Kn. Mikhail Mikhailovich Shcherbatov," in *Russkii biograficheskii slovar'*, vol. 24, pp. 104–24, which says little about his official career but provides good summaries of his speeches at the Legislative Commission and his writings. Fedosov, *Iz istorii russkoi obshchestvennoi mysli*, pp. 132–58, provides a workmanlike summary of Shcherbatov's views on serfdom. Sretenskii, "Pomeshchich'ia instruktsiia," pp. 197–211, provides a good analysis of the 1758 "General Instruction," while Daniel, "Conflict between Economic Vision and Economic Reality," pp. 42–67, compares the "General Instruction" to Shcherbatov's management practice. None of these studies mention the 1758 marriage rule. For a review of the literature on Shcherbatov, see Lentin, "A la recherche du Prince méconnu" pp. 361–98.

14. RGADA, f. 1289, op. 2, d. 84. This is a very rough draft of the return for the two estates, with so many emendations and excisions that only approximate statistics can be computed.

15. As these ages illustrate, there was extreme female age heaping in the 1762 tax census at ages twenty and above because this was the first census in which women were listed. There is little to no age heaping among the teenagers listed.

16. RGADA, f. 1289., op. 1, dd. 281, 306, 323, 326, 335, 356, 359: correspondence 1753 (from and to his mother) and 1757–61 (from and to Shcherbatov).

17. The 1745 tax census return lists only men but suggests households in which all the adult men, at least, were married (ibid., op. 4, d. 55).

18. Ibid., op. 1, d. 236. For other correspondence and orders from the first half of the eighteenth century, see ibid., dd. 113, 121, 144, 165, 169, 176, 183, 209, 214, 223, 225, 228, 237.

19. RGADA, f. 350, op. 2, d. 4302, ch. 2., ll. 29–38. I have excluded one *devka*—that is, a marriage-age woman—from the count, because discoloring has obscured her age.

20. Ibid., ll. 491–505.

21. Ibid., ll. 4–90b, 49–165, 176–401, 416–29, 439–60, 513–523. The fact that there were 8 to 13 percent more women than men is not in itself a guarantee that there was a cluster of unmarried female adults.

22. Ten noble estates described in RGADA, f. 350, op. 2, d. 4302, ch. 2, fit that description. In a set of sixty-five returns from the 1762 tax census from Igretskaia

volost' and the abutting Zakotorzhskii and Verkhovskii stans, close to or containing Shcherbatov properties, not one reported as many as fifty male serfs, and most reported fewer than ten (RGADA, f. 350, op. 2, d. 4301 ch. 2).

23. RGADA, f. 1289, op. 4, d. 162. The two were from the same household, which does usually indicate religious resistance to marriage. The relevant correspondence can be found in ibid., op. 1, dd. 484, 493, 508, 510, 519, 523, 525, 550.

24. Shcherbatov, *Sochineniia*, vol. 2, col. 429.

25. As at Charlotte Lieven's Baki estate in 1800. See chapter 6.

26. E.g., on a Shishkin estate in Vologda province, when a father asked that he be allowed to keep his daughter at home until winter because he needed her labor, while her prospective groom's household did not. But he also asked that his household be allowed to select the groom (GIM OPI, f. 182, op. 1, d. 8, ll. 203–40b). A professional estate manager with thirty years' experience also cited the need to retain labor as a reason why fathers sometimes kept daughters at home (Karpovich, *Khoziaistvennye opyty*, p. 275).

27. Shcherbatov, *Izbrannye trudy*, p. 154.

28. The brothers inherited 2,000 (male) serfs when their father died in 1746 (Polushkin, *Briat'ia Orlovy*, p. 10). Semevskii counted 27,000 male serfs on Orlov properties recorded in the General Survey (Semevskii, *Krest'iane*, vol. 1, p. 34). Galina Taseva counted 23,083 male serfs in the senate decrees conveying properties to the Orlovs up to 1774 (Taseva, "Organizatsiia upravleniia krupnoi pomeshchich'ei votchiny," p. 310).

29. There is a brief biography of Vladimir Orlov in *Russkii biograficheskii slovar'*, vol. 12, pp. 347–348, and a two-volume biography by his son-in-law and heir, Vladimir Orlov-Davydov, *Biograficheskii ocherk*. His life is also covered in Polushkin, *Briat'ia Orlovy*, pp. 385–432.

30. *Sbornik starinnykh bumag*, part 3, p. 338.

31. Orlov-Davydov, *Biograficheskii ocherk*, vol. 1, pp. 280–81.

32. RGADA, f. 1454, op. 1, d. 343, l. 25. This is a 1785 order from Orlov canceling the 1773 ruling and imposing departure fees on every girl who married away.

33. RGADA, f. 1273, op. 1, d. 510, ll. 70b, 107–1070b, 112–1120b, 114–1140b. These rules applied to at least three estates in Iaroslavl province, at least one in Nizhnii Novgorod province, and probably to all other Orlov estates as well. The log of orders for 1774 has been lost, but Orlov's 1774 rules were cited in the correspondence from 1776. A copy of the 1774 instructions sent to Sidorovskoe can be found in RGADA, f. 1454, op. 2, d. 92, ll. 1–5.

34. RGADA, f.1273, op. 1, d. 516, l. 60, 800b; d. 662, ll. 77–770b, 113–1130b, 1140b–115. The management instructions for his Semenovskoe estate (where he resided when not in Moscow) in Serpukhov district in 1776 contained no provisions at all on marriage, but that was probably because almost every village for miles around belonged to other members of the family (ibid., d. 510, ll. 520b–56).

35. Ibid., d. 516, l. 800b; d. 2763, l. 290b.

36. RGADA, f. 1384, op. 1, d. 1484, ll. 170b–19. There are no variations more significant than scribal errors in any of the other manuscript copies I have seen. For a

published copy, see Dovnar-Zapol'skii, "Materialy dlia istorii votchinnogo upravleniia v Rossii," no. 11, pp. 253–88.

37. RGADA, f. 1273, op. 1, d. 510, l. 10; f. 1454, op. 1, d. 344, l. 4. Up to 1789, when paper currency (*assignaty*) was first issued, prices are in silver rubles. From that year on, prices should be understood as paper currency (which fluctuated in value versus silver) unless otherwise specified. The Orlov papers seldom note whether charges were in silver or paper, but for most purposes, paper was the default currency.

38. RGADA, f. 1454, op. 1, d. 164, ll. 1, 2, 9, 10, 12–13; d. 41; d. 58; d. 115; GAKO, f. 228, op. 1, d. 6, ll. 1–20b; dd. 34, 41, 58; RGADA, f. 615, op. 1, dd. 9205, 9207 (Rostov district).

39. Semevskii, *Krest'iane*, vol. 1, p. 174. His sample is small, and there was much regional variation. In 1774, a Iaroslavl province official may have estimated the market price when he set the departure fee for a woman marrying away from a confiscated estate at ten rubles (RGADA, f. 1289, op. 1, d. 149, l. 57).

40. RGADA, f. 1454, op. 1, d. 308, l. 1. As of 1780, it was still fifteen rubles (ibid., d. 238, ll. 7, 9, 20, 22, 26). For the ten-ruble fee taken by nobles whose women married onto the estate in 1780, see ibid., d. 253, ll. 1–2.

41. For somewhat contradictory late eighteenth-century prices of serfs purchased for conscription and of males purchased by the estate full, see Mironov, *Blagosostoianie*, p. 257; Kahan, *The Plow*, pp. 64, 348.

42. RGADA, f. 1273, op. 1, d. 516, l. 790b; f. 1454, op. 1, d. 419, l. 1–10b; d. 446, ll. 1–2; Taseva, "Organizatsiia upravleniia," p. 329.

43. RGADA, f. 1273, op. 1, d. 705 l. 1030b, d. 562 l. 50, d. 661 l. 86, d. 662 l. 128, d. 707 ll. 260b–27, 580b; d. 742, ll. 60b, 167; d. 937, l. 590b; d. 1000 l. 500b, d. 936, l. 8 ob (Gorodets, 1821).

44. RGADA, f. 1273, op. 1, d. 533, ll. 430b–44, 61, 890b–90; d. 531, l. 162–1620b; d. 564, l. 1000b, d. 662, ll. 760b, 860b–87; d. 707, ll. 99, 161; d. 742, l. 20b; d. 937, ll. 1010b–102; d. 973, l. 1.; RGADA, f. 1454, op. 1, d. 1154, l. 2. In 1784, General Aleksandr Suvorov left 150 rubles in Moscow to purchase three girls for marriage; an estate official told him that wasn't enough. For 50 rubles, he could purchase only a maid who could do nothing at all, or for 80 rubles, he could purchase a skilled young woman. In 1785, Suvorov asked an agent to purchase four women to marry house serfs for 50 rubles each in Novgorod province, where they were less expensive (Rybkin, *Generalissimus*, pp. 23, 25).

45. I have used Mironov's measure of inflation in "'Revoloiutsiia tsen,'" pp. 49–61, and his "Consequences of the Price Revolution," pp. 457–78. Mironov gives all prices in silver rubles, so for the period after 1769, I have used the silver-to-*assignat* conversion rates in Owen, "Standard Ruble of Account," pp. 703–4. When the departure fee was only a few rubles, peasants probably paid in copper coins, of variable weight and value; see Iukht, *Russkie den'gi*.

46. A lengthy 1777 memorandum reviewing the history of the charges for leaving crown properties in marriage reported that the charge varied from place to place, from twenty-five kopeks to two rubles or sometimes up to five rubles (RGADA, f. 1239, op. 3, d. 49409–49420, ll. 432–350b).

47. RGADA, f. 1454, op. 1, d. 145, l. 2–20b.

48. Ibid., l. 20b; d. 181, l. 11–110b.

49. Ibid., d. 46, ll. 17–138ob.

50. Taseva, "Organizatsiia upravleniia," pp. 315–16.

51. RGADA, f. 1454, d. 46, ll. 1–100b. I have divided the population at age twenty-five because as of 1763 that seems to have been the ceiling age for female marriage. In 1763, ten of the thirty-seven women ages twenty to twenty-four were unmarried, while for those ages twenty-five to twenty-nine, six of twenty-one were unmarried, as were six of the twenty-one women aged thirty to thirty-four. The male ceiling age for marriage appears to have been thirty.

52. See, for instance, the report on Sidorovskoe's payment of the capitation tax for half of 1772 in RGADA, f. 1454, op. 1, d. 38, l. 26.

53. GAKO, f. 228, op. 1, l. 70b–8.

54. RGADA, f. 1454, op. 1, d. 145, l. 2–20b; d. 166, ll. 260b–270b.

55. Ibid., op. 166, l. 530b.

56. RGADA, f. 1273, op. 1, d. 516, l. 500b.

57. Ibid., l. 57.

58. RGADA, f. 1454, op. 1, d. 238, l. 101; d. 345, l. 22

59. RGADA, f. 1273, op. 1, d. 516, ll. 660b, 950b.

60. On Old Believers on the Gorodets estate, see RGADA, f. 1273, op. 1, d. 1000, ll. 230b, 240b. On Orlov serfs marrying in the Old Believer chapel, see TsANO, f. 570, op. 557, 1830, d. 46, ll. 2–3. A particularly valuable source on the priested at Gorodets is Mel'nikov, "Otchet," pp. 166–78.

61. RGADA, f. 1273, op. 1, d. 2763, l. 290b.

62. Ibid., d. 561, l. 270b; d. 936, l. 1430b.

63. Ibid., d. 2763, ll. 290b, 30.

64. Arkhangel'skii, "Simbileiskaia votchina," p. 181.

65. RGADA, f. 1384, op. 1, d. 1484, ll. 170b–19.

66. RGADA, f. 1273, op. 1, d. 561, l. 260b; d. 2830, ll. 1–20b; d. 936, l. 1430b; d. 661, l. 66–670b; d. 937, ll. 410b–42; d. 705, l. 78.

67. RGADA, f. 1384, op. 1, d. 113, l. 12.

68. Bushnell, "Did Serf Owners Control Serf Marriage?," pp. 437–45.

69. RGADA, f. 1273, op. 1, d. 561, ll. 60b–8, 330b, 37–370b, 580b.

70. Ibid.

71. Ibid., d. 756, ll. 1–2; d. 533, l. 61.

72. This confirms, once again, the argument made in Hoch, *Serfdom and Social Control*, pp. 91–132 and passim.

73. Taseva, "Organizatsiia upravleniia," p. 312.

74. RGADA, f. 1273, op. 1, d. 2772, ll. 1–11; d. 632, l. 250b, d. 731, ll. 1–50b.

75. Ibid., d. 731, ll. 1–50b. And so the Moscow office apparently took no action. The estate belonged to one of Orlov's daughters, Ektaterina Novosiltseva. Orlov managed it, but it was Novosiltseva who made the decision on manumission.

76. RGADA, f. 1454, op. 1, d. 3057, ll. 1–2, provides the census populations in 1812, when women were not counted, so I have added a few to the male total to approximate

the female total and counted half of those as aged twenty-five and older. Ibid., d. 2994, l. 5–50b, lists the women and their disabilities.

77. Ibid., d. 2971, ll. 7–70b, 8–80b, 10–100b, 120b, 14–140b, 26-260b; d. 2993, l. 9.

78. Ibid., d. 3131, ll. 20b–3.

79. Ibid., d. 3113.

80. Ibid., d. 3178, ll. 1–3.

81. Ibid., d. 3172, ll. 5–50b, 7–70b; d. 3176, l. 4.

82. Ibid., d. 3195. The order came formally from the owner, Prince Ivan Obolenskii, whose wife was a relative of Orlov's, whose office managed the estate (ibid., d. 3167, l. 3–4).

83. Ibid., d. 3163, ll. 5–50b, 10, 25–250b, 27–270b; d. 3193, ll. 1–2; d. 3197, ll. 1–20b.

84. Ibid., d. 3187, l. 2–20b.

85. Ibid., d. 2075, ll. 40b–59.

86. GAKO, f. 200, op. 13, d. 400, ll. 165–240.

87. RGADA, f. 1454, op. 1, d. 3137, l. 10.

88. RGADA, f. 1384, op. 1, dd. 44, 145, 163, 782, 1059, 1060.

89. Kataev, *Na beregakh Volgi*, pp. 42–45.

90. RGADA, f. 1365, op. 1, d. 120, ll. 26, 38; d. 202, ll. 20, 38, 40, 47, 84, 1260b, 145–146.

91. "Instruktsiia kniazei Gruzinskikh," pp. 49–57.

92. The Saltykovs issued many sets of instructions to their estates in the second half of the eighteenth century but apparently none on marriage (Kondrashova, "Maloizvestnye pomeshchich'i nakazy," pp. 237–38). Instructions issued to a Naryshkin estate in the Serpukhov district of Moscow province, undated but probably from the late eighteenth century, say nothing about marriage (RGADA, f. 1272, op. 2, d. 28, l. 29–290b). Samarin estate instructions to a Tula province property in 1778 and to estates in Simbirsk, Tula, Tver, and Vladimir provinces in 1788 say nothing about marriage (*Materialy po istorii sel'skogo khoziaistva i krest'ianstva Rossii. Sel'skokhoziaistvennye instruktsii (seredina XVIII v.)*, pp. 251–55; RGADA, f. 1277, op. 1, d. 665, ll. 1–68). Instructions issued to their estates in 1817 say only that when they come of age, young men and women should marry and form a labor-dues unit (*tiaglo*), but in a way that suggests that they did so naturally rather than that they married because compelled to do so (RGADA, f. 1277, op. 1, d. 223, ll. 1–26).

93. Petrushevskii, *Generalisimus*, vol. 1, pp. 272–75; Rybkin, *Generalissimus*, pp. 22–24, 66–67, 76; Semevskii, *Krest'iane*, vol. 1, pp. 309–10, 313, 317.

94. GIM OPI, f. 14, op. 1, dd. 2483, 2484, 2489, 2490, 2503. He issued management rules in 1785, but they do not mention marriage; ibid., d. 2484, ll. 51–620b.

95. "Pis'ma kniazia Alesandra Mikhailovich Golitsyna," pp. 7, 25.

96. Hoch, *Serfdom and Social Control*, pp. 119–22. House serfs did have to ask the Moscow office's permission when arranging marriages of sons and daughters.

97. Antonova, *Ordinary Marriage*, p. 58.

98. "Prikaz pomeshchika A. M. Cheremisinova," pp. 19–20, 28–29.

99. "Rasporiazheniia Grafa Arakcheeva," pp. 271–79.

100. GARO, f. 627, op. 249, d. 55, kn. 27.

101. TsIAM, f. 737, op. 1, t. 3, d. 3745. The records from 1804 are missing.

102. Ibid., d. 3752.

103. Semevskii, *Krest'iane*, vol. 1, p. 316; Kogan, "Volneniia krest'ian," p. 124.

104. *Sbornik starinnykh bumag*, part 3, pp. 337–38.

105. GIM OPI, f. 14, op. 1, d. 3097, ll. 5, 14–140b; d. 3101, ll. 1, 4, 8.

106. "Cherty iz zhizni kn. E. R. Dashkovoi," col. 584; GIM OPI, f. 182, op. 1, d. 8, l. 202.

107. Taseva, "Organizatsiia upravleniia," pp. 312, 330. Taseva does not report the amount of the new fee.

108. RGADA, f. 1274, op. 1, d. 1268, ll. 170b, 280b–30, 35–360b.

109. TsIAM, f. 1614, op. 1, d. 278, ll. 1, 28–280b; d. 279, ll. 35–350b, 46–460b, 48–49, 54–55; d. 281, l. 2–20b; d. 283, l. 14–140b, 55–56; d. 288, l. 4; d. 288, ll. 75–760b.; d. 290, ll. 1–52; d. 297, ll. 1–41; d. 302, ll. 6–9.

110. Shchepetov, *Krepostnoe pravo*, pp. 272, 274, 281–82. Identical rules were sent the same year to a Sheremetev property in the Murom district: Dovnar-Zapol'skii, "Materialy dlia istorii votchinnogo upravleniia v Rossii," no. 7 (1904), pp. 79–96; no. 8, pp. 97–103. For earlier years, see the *Krepostnye knigi* (Registers of deeds). For the Rostov district, see RGADA, f. 615, op. 1, d. 9159, l. 44 (1733); d. 9177, ll. 17, 21, 230b (1750); d. 9180, ll. 40b–50b, 12–120b, 150b (1751).

111. RGADA, f. 1287, op. 3, d. 555, ll. 9, 11, 21, 49–50; Shchepetov, *Krepostnoe pravo*, p. 78; Rubinshtein, *Sel'skoe khoziaistvo Rossii*, p. 140; Prokof'eva, *Krest'ianskaia obshchina*, pp. 48–49.

112. On the very high departure charges, see Garelin, *Gorod Ivanovo-Voznesensk*, ch. 1, p. 111; Rubinshtein, *Sel'skoe khoziaistvo Rossii*, p. 140; Prokof'eva, *Krest'ianskaia obshchina*, p. 49. On Dmitrii Nikolaevich's charges, see RGADA, f. 1287, op. 3, d. 791, ll. 1–8 (1821); d. 1217, l. 18 (1834); d. 1837, ll. 1–4 (1848); Dennison, *Institutional Framework*, p. 74.

113. Shchepetov, *Krepostnoe pravo*, p. 210, claims the total amount of departure fees Dmitrii Sheremetev collected in 1814 was 7,800 rubles (less in three other years), but that is surely an underestimate. Shchepetov counted only twenty-five women marrying away from Sheremetev estates between 1818 and 1850. Yet in 1834, eight or nine women were released for marriage from Voshchazhnikovo alone (RGADA, f. 1287, op. 3, d. 1217, ll. 1–68). In 1840, at least ten women were released for marriage from Voshchazhnikovo (others may have been released for other reasons) (ibid., d. 1837, ll. 1–62).

114. In 1771–72, no departure fee was collected for at least nine girls who married off the Voshchazhnikovo estate (RGADA, f. 615, op. 1, d. 9205, ll. 100b–11, 16–160b, 220b–23; d. 9207, ll. 9–90b, 28–290b, 39–390b, 70–700b). In 1837, four women were released from Voshchazhnikovo at no charge (ibid., f. 1287, op. 3, d. 1217, ll. 4–12, 21–280b, 44–48, 57–63). In 1848, at least five women were released from Voshchazhnikovo at no charge (ibid., d. 1837, ll. 5–9, 21–25, 28–30, 31–35, 36–38).

115. RGADA, f. 1287 op. 3, d. 1217, ll. 49–56. In exceptional cases, the bride's household might pay. The father of a groom courting a bride from a first-category household from the Iukhotsk estate was willing to pay 1,000 rubles but not the 2,000 rubles Nikolai Sheremetev demanded; in this case, the girl's grandfather paid the fee (Prokof'eva, *Krest'ianskaia obshchina*, p. 49). Prokof'eva's assertion that the Sheremetevs charged very high departure fees in order to obstruct off-estate marriage is obviously mistaken.

116. "Prikaz iaroslavskogo pomeshchika Karnovicha," pp. 365–68.

117. Semevskii, *Krest'iane*, vol. 1, pp. 311–12.

118. Ibid., p. 312.

119. RGB OR, f. 586, karton 2, d. 1, ll. 1–139; karton 1, d. 1, ll. 81–1610b. The 1770 document is an estate household inventory; the 1763 document is based on the tax census of that year, but with added information on economic resources. Titov, *Kurakovshchina*, pp. 1–10, provides a useful description of life on what had been the Rostov estate but says nothing about religious propensities and on pp. 11–26 reproduces management instructions sent in 1794, with no provisions on serf marriage. In 1770, Petrovskoe was actually in Suzdal *guberniia*, a part of the Vladimir *namestnichestvo*. It is now in the Kovrov district, not the Suzdal district.

120. Kogan, "Volneniia krest'ian penzenskoi votchiny," p. 124. Since the Penza estate was at the time in trusteeship—the heirs were minors— the trustees made the decision, at least in practice.

121. "Povelenie, podpisannoe grafinoi Irinoi Vorontsovoi," p. 144.

122. M. V. Dovnar-Zapol'skii, "Materialy dlia istorii votchinnogo upravleniia v Rossii," no. 7 (1909), p. 231.

123. GIM OPI, f. 182, op. 1, d. 8, l. 219–2190b.

124. "Iz perepiski pomeshchika s krest'ianami," pp. 3–4, 15–16, 26–27, 36, 49, 59, 92–93. The editor calls this Suvorov the general's father, but he was not.

125. GIM OPI, f. 14, op. 1, d. 1754, l. 43–430b.

126. Ibid., d. 3082, ll. 16–17. This report comes without a date and is misfiled in a set of documents labeled 1814–55; it is addressed to Aleksandr Mikhailovich, who died in 1807. It probably dates from the 1770s or 1780s.

127. TsIAM, f. 1614, op. 1, d. 283, l. 68; d. 288, ll. 10, 58, 590b.

128. Ibid., d. 278, l. 20.

129. Ibid., d. 278, ll. 48, 49; d. 279, ll. 23, 46–460b; d. 283, l. 13; d. 281, ll. 2–20b, 4–40b; d. 288, ll. 100b, 75–760b.

130. Sivkov, *Ocherki*, p. 157; Ivanov, *Drugoi Iusupov*, p. 21. Ivanov's *Drugoi Iusupov* is a semi-scholarly biography of Nikolai Borisovich, carelessly sourced and somewhat confused about his management practices.

131. In 1832–33, there was a similar switch from quitrent to corvée on what the Iusupovs called their Little Russian properties. Again there was an effort to increase the number of married couples, not by fining single women, but by giving maiden house serfs ten rubles and a cow to attract peasant grooms Nasonov, "Iz istorii krepostnoi votchiny," p. 518; Nasonov, "Khoziaistvo krupnoi votchiny," pp. 347–48.

132. RGADA, f. 1290, op. 3, d. 6732, ll. 18–23 (the 1825 rules); Sivkov, *Ocherki*, pp. 38–46, 50–52.

133. Nasonov, "Iz istorii krepostnoi votchiny," p. 501.

134. Here I am largely dependent on the work of Sivkov and Nasonov, cited earlier, both of whom were alert to issues of serf marriage but report nothing on exit fees or marriage off the estate.

135. RGADA, f. 1290, op. 3, d. 4731, ll. 22, 25, 35.

136. Ibid., d. 4736, l. 55. See also ll. 8–9, 147.

137. Sivkov, *Ocherki*, p. 177.

138. Ibid., p. 160.

139. Spasskoe and Prilepy were among the four largest Iusopov villages in Tula province. In those four villages, there were 400 married men twenty-five and older, only 2 who may never have married; among women of those ages, 418 married, 1 did not, 2 others may not have (RGADA, f. 1290, op. 3, d. 6783, ll. 220b–51, 530b–67, 950b–120, 1620b–171).

140. On Old Believers on the Nizhnii Novgorod estates, see RGADA, f. 1290, op. 3, d. 4352 (1830), ll. 55, 64–66, 75, 115–170b. For Kostroma province see ibid., d. 4715, a set of Kostroma province tax census returns for 1834; there is much other evidence as well.

141. Ibid., d. 4322, ll. 1820b–264.

142. Nasonov, "Iz istorii krepostnoi votchiny," pp. 514–15.

143. Ibid., p. 514.

144. RGADA, f. 1290, op. 2, d. 330, ll. 11, 120b, 34–35, 41; d. 331, ll. 37–38. The Iusupovs called this their Smolensk estate, probably because most of its small villages were in Smolensk province. Probably the previous owner, a Countess Musina-Pushkina, had initiated the practice of fining single women. Iusupova cited her on the income they generated.

145. Ibid., d. 331, l. 600b, 73, 108, 1430b, 145–66. Women obviously incapable of marriage were not to be fined and so were likely not in the register.

146. Ibid., d. 331, ll. 1430b., 143A.

147. Ibid., d. 480, ll. 9, 13, 21, 25, 31–340b, 38–380b, 40–400b, 44–450b. In 1836, fines began at age seventeen because, by then, the legal minimum female marriage age was sixteen.

148. Ibid., d. 330, ll. 34, 35, 37; d. 331, ll. 143, 143A.

149. Polushin, "Vypiski iz pamiatnoi knigi," pp. 179, 190; Garelin, *Gorod Ivanovo-Voznesensk*, pp. 42, 163–64. The historians who have worked through the Sheremetev archives—Shchepetov, Prokof'eva, and Dennison—apparently found nothing about this order to Ivanovo or elsewhere.

150. Dennison, *Institutional Framework*, p. 75. The evidence is in the 1816 tax census return for Voshchazhnikovo village: 9.6 percent of the women in the forty to forty-four cohort had never married. In the two preceding five-year cohorts, ages forty-five to fifty-four in 1816, only 3.2 and 4.8 percent of the women had never married.

151. RGADA, f. 1287, op. 3, d. 555, ll. 21, 26–260b, 49. Dennison, *Institutional Framework*, p. 74, incorrectly dates the 1800 cancellation of the yarn substitute to 1796; that was the year when the penalty was first imposed, or perhaps revived, at Voshchazhnikovo and Serebrianye Prudy.

152. Semevskii, *Krest'iane*, vol. 1, p. 312. Semevskii does not date the message to Ivanovo, but the identity of the language points to 1796. The population is from Shchepetov, *Krepostnoe pravo*, p. 310.

153. Shchepetov, *Krepostnoe pravo*, p. 116. The location of the estate is noted on p. 440.

154. Ibid., p. 116.

155. Ibid., p. 117.

156. Gritsevskaia, "Istoriia i sovremennost'."

157. Hoch, *Serfdom and Social Control*, pp. 95–102, summarizes much of the published information on bride price and offers an analysis of its function in Russian peasant communities.

158. Shchepetov, *Krepostnoe pravo*, p. 207.

159. Tracy Dennison read through those papers much more thoroughly than I have and found literally nothing worth saying about Old Believers in her study of the estate. Hers is a fine analysis, except in the chapter on the estate's abnormal demographic structure (Dennison, *Institutional Framework*, pp. 50–76). She attempted to locate the cause of the large number of never-married adult women in the marriage policies the Sheremetevs adopted. Those policies were either irrelevant or a response to rather than a cause of the serfs' marriage practices. Nor did Shchepetov or Prokof'eva, both of whom worked through the Sheremetev papers, mention Old Believers at Voshchazhnikovo.

160. RGADA, f. 1287, op. 3, d.1759, ll. 6–90b.

161. GAIaO, f. 230, op. 3, d. 47, ll. 1–110b; Titov, *S. Voshchazhnikovo*, pp. 2–3.

162. Dennison, *Institutional Framework*, p. 75.

163. Ibid., pp.171–72 and passim.

CHAPTER 3

THE OUTER LIMITS OF FEMALE MARRIAGE AVERSION:
KUPLIA PARISH IN THE EIGHTEENTH CENTURY

K uplia parish, in the Gorokhovets district, eastern Vladimir province,
is a particularly good place to begin a close examination of peasant
women's rejection of marriage. The parish seems to have been close to the
epicenter of marriage aversion, and we can watch aversion mount from the
beginning to the end of the eighteenth century. By 1795, so many women
shunned marriage that in some villages, they threatened community survival. One reason why marriage aversion developed unchecked in Kuplia
parish is that it was, in fact, unchecked. The main participants in Kuplia
parish, and in the entire Gorokhovets area, were crown (in the nineteenth
century, appanage) peasants rather than serfs. There were crown administrators in the village of Krasnoe Selo only seven kilometers distant, but
they seem to have been utterly feckless; there is no evidence that they ever
reacted to, or even noticed, the steadily mounting number of crown peasant women who would not marry. They thus enabled something like a natural experiment: how far would peasants in the grip of an anti-marriage
creed go?

The priests of Kuplia parish also contributed crucially to this study, by
identifying the religious community that was the principle carrier, the Old
Believer Spasovite covenant. That evidence dates from the first half of the
nineteenth century, but we can read it back easily into the eighteenth, as
I will show in chapter 4. On the debit side, we have none of the testimony
of manorial correspondence that sometimes illuminates resistance to marriage on large serf estates. We have not much more to work with than the
census returns that let us measure the incidence of refusal to marry in the

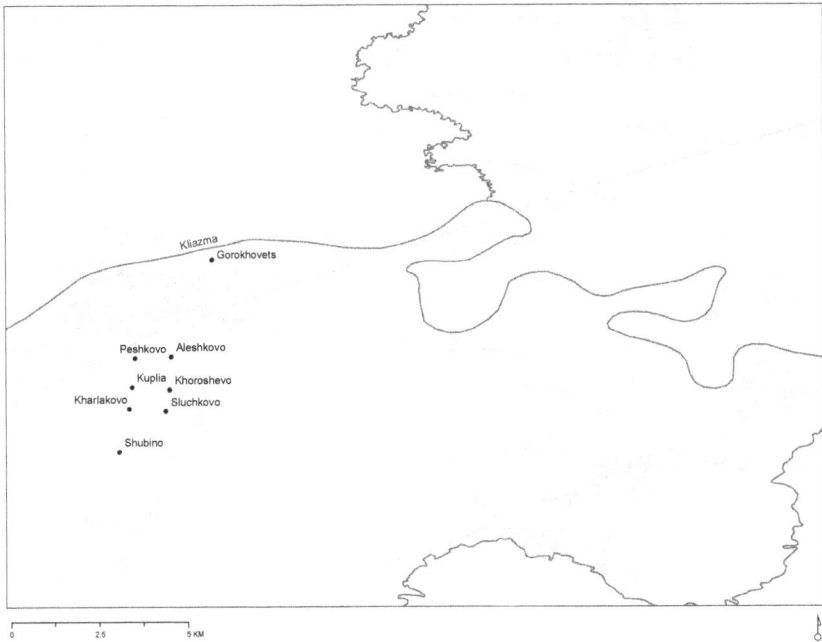

Map 3.1 Kuplia Parish and Shubino. Contains information from OpenStreetMap, which is made available at https://www.openstreetmap.org under the Open Database License (ODbL). Modified by Kelsey Rydland, licensed under CC BY-SA 2.0.

first place. But, in the second half of the eighteenth century, censuses documented much more than name, age, and marital status.

From the mid-eighteenth to the mid-nineteenth centuries, Kuplia parish, just south of the tiny city of Gorokhovets (population around 1,300 in the late eighteenth century, 2,555 in 1859[1]) on the Kliazma River, consisted of a core of six villages, three inhabited by serfs (Kuplia, Khoroshevo, and Kharlakovo), and three by crown peasants (Peshkovo, Aleshkovo, and Sluchkovo). These were small villages. According to the 1782 tax census, the crown villages had total populations (men and women, infants to elderly) of 157, 156, and 151, while the parish census conducted by the priest in 1777 put the population of the serf villages at 68, 89, and 113.[2]

Topography dictated village size. Kuplia parish was part of a twenty-five-kilometer-long wedge of human habitation, eight to twelve kilometers wide, south of the Kliazma River. The wedge was bounded to the south by an equally broad swath of uninhabitable marsh and forest. Immediately across the Kliazma from Gorokhovets, uninhabited and largely impassable marsh and forest stretched northward for forty kilometers and more. The peasants south of the Kliazma were themselves mostly surrounded by wetlands; their villages and fields sat on land that rose above the marsh. As a mid-nineteenth-century description of the district (not of Kuplia parish in particular) put it, what was a five- to ten-kilometer journey from one village to another during the winter freeze could turn into a fifteen- to thirty-kilometer trudge between April, when marshland thawed, and mid-November, when it froze anew.[3] Even in the early twenty-first century, not all villages in what had been Kuplia parish were accessible after a heavy summer rain, and those that were could only be reached by deeply rutted tracks whose thick sand-and-clay soil, viscous when waterlogged, could trap an incautious car and driver.[4]

Such land could not support the peasants who lived on it. Meadowland was inadequate for cattle; grain yielded as little as two and a half seeds for every seed sown. After setting aside seed grain for the next planting, peasants had only one and a half sacks of grain for consumption for every sack sown. Even in the eighteenth century, the Gorokhovets district imported grain from southern provinces. Although the soil was suitable for gardening along some portions of the Kliazma's south bank, peasants had no choice but to seek off-farm income. In the eighteenth century, they were deeply involved in craft production of various sorts, migrant labor, and commerce.[5] In their submission to Catherine II's Legislative Commission in 1767, the merchants of Gorokhovets described local peasants as building the boats on which merchants shipped wares downriver, hauling boats upstream, working as carpenters, producing leather for St. Petersburg, carting, and "performing other work, without which those peasants simply can't exist." The merchants complained that local peasants were trading as far south as Astrakhan, where they bought fish and brought it up the Volga for sale at Saratov and also returned with grain and other comestibles for sale in Gorokhovets, thus circumventing the merchantry's supposed monopoly on such commerce.[6]

As early as the seventeenth century, peasants quarried limestone from outcroppings just south of the Kliazma. In the seventeenth century, too, crown peasants of the district (including the ancestors of the eighteenth-century crown peasants of Kuplia parish) were put to work as distillers, working with grain from the south. That trade took them across much of central Russia even in the nineteenth century and, in the eighteenth century helped spawn a numerous class of migrant boilermakers (men specializing in the production of metal containers of various sorts). As of the late nineteenth century, the Gorokhovets district was the principal supplier of migrant boilermakers to Russian industry.[7]

The trackless marsh and forest north of the Kliazma blocked agricultural settlement but attracted religious dissidents even before the schism in the second half of the seventeenth century. The one-time, possibly self-tonsured, monk Kapiton—who preached extreme asceticism and practiced mortification of the flesh during the first half of the century and from the 1630s on was hunted by church and state for violating Orthodox liturgical practices and dispensing with clergy—took refuge in the trans-Kliazma forest in the 1650s and died there, probably in 1662–63. After his death, his followers continued to proselytize and contributed intellectually to the foundation of the Old Believer priestless covenants at the end of the seventeenth century.[8] Indeed, early priestless Old Believers were often called Kapitonites.

As tensions over the Nikonian church reforms grew and as the government imprisoned and executed Old Believer zealots, increasing numbers fled to the deep woods, including north of Gorokhovets. In 1662, the government sent soldiers to Viazniki, twenty-eight kilometers upriver from Gorokhovets, to hunt them down, but the documents generated by that search have been lost.[9] Documents from late 1665 and early 1666, when the government again sent soldiers to Viazniki to root schismatics out of the forest, have survived: By the time the operation concluded in 1666, the government had hauled out one hundred or so religious dissidents, most of them local crown peasants and serfs from Russia's central provinces. Hundreds of others, forewarned, escaped the dragnet. In 1673, officials turned their attention from the forest to villages where peasants supported the Old Belief. That produced an episode of group self-immolation in Shubino, immediately southwest of Kuplia parish.[10] Both the distillers and boilermakers of the district were reputed to be Old Believers, and in the eighteenth century, the Orthodox Church declared Florovo parish, not far from Kuplia, an anti–Old Believer missionizing center.[11]

EIGHTEENTH-CENTURY CENSUS DOCUMENTS AND WHAT THEY TELL US ABOUT PEASANT MARRIAGE

The only direct evidence we have about marriage practices and beliefs among the largely Old Believer peasants of Kuplia parish is what can be extracted from irregular tax census returns and from what amounted to annual parish censuses. Those are not promising sources on such matters as religious belief, but sometimes they tell revealing stories. The history of one serf family from the village of Malinovo, as related in successive confession registers (in effect, annual household censuses) for Florovo parish, neighbor to Kuplia parish, is at least fascinating and probably also offers a peek into the minds of marriage-averse peasants. The 1779 register listed as officially Orthodox Andrei Iakovlev, age thirty-nine; his wife, Matrena, age thirty-two; and their sons, Grigorii and Aleksei, eight and four. The 1800 register lists the widow Matrena (that year given a patronymic, Gerasimova), now said to be sixty-two, with her son Aleksei Gerasimov, forty-two; his wife, Katerina; his son, Grigorii, twenty-three; and his daughters, Ekaterina and Vassa, twenty-one and nineteen. Neither those nor subsequent ages should be considered accurate.

As of 1800, Aleksei had changed his patronymic from Andreev to Gerasimov, the same as his mother's. While the 1800 register still identified Aleksei as Matrena's son, the 1815 confession register recorded the widow Matrena Gerasimova, seventy-two, living with her bachelor *brother* Aleksei Gerasimov, fifty-eight; her maiden *sister* Vassa Gerasimova, fifty-six; and an *unrelated male*, Grigorii Konstantinov, thirty-nine and married with three young children. Son Aleksei had become brother, granddaughter Vassa had become sister. Grandson Grigorii had changed his patronymic, from Alekseev to Konstantinov, thus concealing his kinship.[12] Aleksei's wife must have died sometime between 1800 and 1815; his older daughter, Ekaterina, either died or married away from the family. Their disappearance, and probably also the arrival of a new and gullible parish priest, may have precipitated the reinvention of the family.

Yet the fact that Aleksei had become a Gerasimov by 1800 suggests that the family had plotted this transformation for years. It was certainly not the result of a series of errors by a succession of careless priests. Matrena and her descendants deliberately erased their history as a normally procreating household and reinscribed themselves in the confession registers as a celibate family who just happened to be sharing quarters with a younger, unrelated, sexually active family. Matrena never shed her title of widow, but since she had hidden every trace of her offspring, she could claim (if she wished; if anyone asked) that she, like other women who adopted an anti-marriage creed shortly after marriage, had lived a celibate life. We know from census returns that such things happened. The point of the Gerasimov (to use their chosen patronymic) family's fabrication was to become collectively celibate. Matrena, Aleksei, and Vassa must have believed that this was a claim worth making: three celibate siblings were better than a mother, son, and celibate granddaughter. Within their religious community (I assume, from everything that follows), celibacy was righteous, and sex was wicked. Why else would they have gone to such lengths to conceal that both Matrena and Aleksei had children? The Gerasimovs had to know that their neighbors and the members of their community of worship would not just forget the family's true history, but within their community, a transparently false claim to virtue was apparently more respectable than the sinful truth. We should keep the story of Matrena and her family in mind as we work through the evidence of increasing levels of marriage aversion among the women of nearby Kuplia parish.

The first tax census (*reviziia*), conducted in the early 1720s, and the second, dating from 1744, listed only males because their purpose was to produce a register of everyone subject to the newly instituted head tax—basically all males, infants included, who were neither nobles nor priests (later in the century, nor merchants)—and to conscription. Beginning in 1763, tax censuses listed women as well. Eighteenth-century censuses, after the first, grouped villagers not by household but by lineage. In 1744, for example, a father and his three sons were listed together whether they shared a household or not. If still alive in 1763, father and sons were again grouped together, with their wives and all of their descendants following below. If the sons' demographic fortunes were very good, they and scores of their descendants occupied several pages of the 1782 and 1795 tax returns, their household arrangements completely opaque. On the other hand, in an age when most peasants had only given names and patronymics and when many boys and girls had the same first names, only the tax census and its organization by lineage is a reliable guide to who beyond the household was related to whom.

The tax census also provides generally useful information on age. Every tax census after the first accounted for all males listed in the preceding census—living, dead, runaway, conscripted, or for some other reason no longer part of the tax-paying population—and added those born in the interim.[13] Thus, the returns from 1744, 1763, 1782, and 1795 have a left-hand column listing men from the preceding census and a right-hand column listing the current male population. The need for side-by-side comparison of current and preceding censuses—to ensure that no tax-paying male was inadvertently omitted—accounts for the enumeration of the population in lineages.

One benefit of that procedure is that it gradually reduced age heaping. There was considerable age heaping, of course, both during and after the first tax census. During the 1763 census, for instance, enumerators simply added nineteen years to the age of everyone listed in the 1744 tax census. In 1782, they added another nineteen years. This caused what we might call secondary age heaping, carried forward from one census to the next. On the other hand, children and teens were added to the lists at every census, and age heaping among the young was much less pronounced, presumably because adults in a household (or whomever the enumerator relied on for the information) actually knew, at least approximately, how old the children were. By the 1782 and 1795 censuses, when most living men had been born after 1744, age heaping was much diminished, except in the very oldest cohorts. Exactly the same thing happened with women, only later: considerable age heaping among them when first listed in 1763 that declined over time. There is no reason to think that the ages of children added to the census rolls were stated with precision, but the ages assigned were probably accurate within a year or two either way. The late eighteenth-century tax census returns provide data that are adequately reliable if we wish to use them to analyze demographic behavior—proportion married, for example—by five-year cohorts.[14]

Beginning with the 1763 returns, eighteenth-century censuses provide other valuable information as well. From 1763, they identified wives' villages of origin; from 1782, where daughters went in marriage. This information was recorded in order to document the chain of ownership, and it allows us to measure a number of marriage-related behaviors, such as the proportion of women who married away from their native villages and the distance men traveled to find wives.[15] Only a small minority of women married within their native villages. In 1763, of the eighty-four wives of known origin in the three crown villages of Kuplia parish, only fifteen (18 percent) were natives. Another thirteen (15 percent) came from other villages in Kuplia parish, and fifty-six (67 percent) had arrived from elsewhere. In the fifty-two marriages between 1763 and 1782, nine wives (17 percent) remained in their native villages, nine more (17 percent) were from the parish, and thirty-five (65 percent) came from other villages. Since these were small villages, it is not surprising that men so frequently sought wives at a distance. Just as most wives married into the parish, so most crown peasant daughters married away: 58 percent between 1763 and 1782 and 73 percent between 1782 and 1795.[16] The villages and parish were anything but demographically self-contained; the marriage market was the region.

Most of the villages around Kuplia parish were crown properties, and the crown peasants took most of their wives from other crown villages and from a scattering of serf and "economic" villages (monastery and other church properties secularized in 1763) within a five- to seven-kilometer radius. However, it was not unusual for them to take wives from villages ten or so kilometers away; there were over forty small villages within ten kilometers of at least one of the parish villages. Occasionally Kuplia parish peasants traveled considerably farther than that in search of wives. While the normal search radius of ten kilometers was in part dictated by the eight- to twelve-kilometer width of settlement south of the Kliazma, that was also the normal bride-search radius in the Riazan district in the late eighteenth century and in the Serpukhov district of Moscow province in the first half of the nineteenth century.[17] Ten kilometers may have been the natural radius of Russian peasants' social world. On the other hand, the distances I have just cited are in crow-flies kilometers, not peasant-walks kilometers. Particularly around Kuplia parish, they seriously understate the actual distance peasants traveled in their search for brides, especially during spring and summer months.

While the tax census had a financial purpose, the annual parish census emerged from measures to seek out and fine or otherwise punish Old Believers who avoided the annual Lenten confession required of the Orthodox and to impose a double head tax on those who chose to register as schismatics. In 1690, Metropolitan Kornilii of Novgorod ordered priests in his jurisdiction to submit lists of parishioners who had and had not confessed. In 1697, Patriarch Adrian required all priests to submit "denunciation registers" (*izvetnye imennye rospisi*) of parishioners who failed to confess. In 1714, 1716, and 1718, Tsar Peter I issued edicts commanding priests to provide lists of those who had and had not confessed, establishing a schedule of fines for those who had not and ordering that those who declared themselves Old Believers be registered with civil authorities and that they pay twice the tax paid by the Orthodox. I will call these documents confession registers. In Russian, their name varied: *dukhovnye rospisi, dukhovnye vedomosti, ispovednye rospisi,* and *ispovednye vedomosti,* among others. A standardized reporting form was distributed in 1737, a somewhat less cumbersome one in 1741. The rules on registering and taxing Old Believers and fining non-confessants were periodically reiterated because priests were slow to take up the task. It wasn't until roughly the middle of the eighteenth century that they submitted annual confession registers as a matter of routine.[18] By then, the registers resembled census returns: priests listed all of the members of their parishes by household and village and provided age and relationship to the head of the household, with additional columns for recording presence at confession and communion and brief explanations for noncompliance, most commonly that non-confessants were schismatic, absent, or forgetful.

The ages given in eighteenth-century confession registers, at least from Kuplia and other nearby parishes, cannot be trusted. If the 1777 register from Kuplia were to be believed, for example, between 48 and 69 percent of all peasants twenty and over in the seven villages then in the parish had decennial ages (twenty, thirty, forty, et cetera).[19] The priest did not even pretend to get the ages right. Ages in the registers also fluctuated, sometimes rising, sometimes falling from year to year. Even when ages seem to be distributed in a more or less normal manner, they almost never coincide with ages given in the tax censuses; differences in age as recorded in tax censuses and confession registers are especially large among the elderly. Occasionally households that appear in a village's tax census return are missing from a proximate confession register and vice versa. As the story of Matrena Gerasimova and her family illustrates, confession registers can be unreliable in many ways. Yet despite their limitations as demographic sources, confession registers are key to much of the analysis that follows because they group parishioners by household and because—in accordance with their original purpose—they provide information about villagers' declared religious affiliations.

They also provide information on the three serf villages of Kuplia parish. I have been unable to retrieve the tax census returns for the serf villages, perhaps because they have been lost, perhaps because of the way in which they were originally archived: grouped by administrative district (from 1782, the district), bound together in volumes organized alphabetically by the first letter of the owner's family name—but miscellaneously within each volume—with late returns bound together with mixed returns from non-serf villages. Since ownership often changed between censuses and the owner in a given census year is not always easily identified (because

ownership even of small villages was often divided among multiple proprietors), it is difficult to retrieve census returns from small estates or to piece
returns together to cover an entire village, even if the records have survived.
The analysis that follows therefore focuses disproportionately on the crown
peasant villages. The confession registers do, however, provide a basis for
comparison of crown peasant and serf villages.

AGE AT MARRIAGE AND UNITS OF ANALYSIS

Very few eighteenth-century parish registers have survived from the
Gorokhovets district, and apparently none remain from Kuplia parish.
More broadly, the parish registers that have survived from Vladimir province (Vladimir diocese) seldom give age at marriage before the 1830s. Whatever we can know about marriage age in Kuplia parish has to be gleaned
from tax census returns. There is a technique for calculating what is called
the singulate mean age of marriage from a nominal list such as a census
return; singulate mean age is a good approximation of mean age at marriage
and is commonly employed in demographic analysis.[20] However, the technique does not seem to me to be suitable for populations as small as those
in the Kuplia parish villages, with very large proportions of women who
never married and from which over 20 percent of every generation of men
was conscripted (see the following section). Upon their husbands' conscription, wives also disappeared from the village census roll, or they may never
have appeared if the conscript both married and was conscripted between
censuses. Nevertheless, the tax census returns do tell us quite clearly when
crown peasant women began to marry in Kuplia parish and when they
ceased to marry.

The legal minimum age at marriage—thirteen for girls and fifteen for
boys in the second half of the eighteenth century—had no bearing at all
on nuptial decisions. According to the census returns in the three crown
peasant villages between 1763 and 1795, teenage marriage was uncommon as
of 1763 and had declined almost to nothing by 1795. In 1763 in the fifteen to
nineteen age cohort, only two (at sixteen and seventeen) out of twenty-six
men and one (at nineteen) of sixteen women were married; in 1795, none of
the twenty-five men and only one of the twenty-five women (at age nineteen) were married.[21] The data for serf villages from the 1777 and 1800 confession registers are at least compatible with the same conclusion: marriage
commenced around age twenty.[22] Women in Kuplia parish ceased to marry

by age twenty-five. The fourteen crown peasant women in the twenty-five to twenty-nine cohort who were single in 1763 never married, nor did any of the thirty-four single crown peasant women in the twenty-five to twenty-nine cohort in 1782. Almost all crown peasant women who married in Kuplia parish did so between the ages of twenty and twenty-four, or—to allow for imprecision in the ages recorded—they almost all married between their late teens and mid-twenties. I will use the proportion of women twenty-five and over who were unmarried in a census year as the measure of resistance, or aversion, to marriage.[23] I will use the proportion of men twenty-five and over who hadn't married as an index of their resistance to marriage as well, even though their situation is slightly ambiguous: one of the three unmarried males in the twenty-five to twenty-nine cohort in 1763 did marry subsequently, perhaps (the census returns suggest) in a failed last-minute attempt to avert conscription. Only one of the twelve unmarried men in that cohort as of 1782 subsequently married.

THE SCALE OF MARRIAGE AVERSION AND CONSCRIPTION IN KUPLIA PARISH, 1763–95

Tables 3.1 and 3.2 present the numbers and proportions of crown peasant men and women twenty-five and over in Kuplia parish who had never married in the census years 1763, 1782, and 1795.

The tables show that the demographic histories of the three villages were different, the contrast between Peshkovo and Sluchkovo being especially striking. From 1763 to 1795, Peshkovo was in a demographic steady state, with marriage almost universal. The percentage of men and women who never married in Peshkovo was higher than the 1 percent that Boris Mironov has estimated was characteristic for the entire Russian population in the late eighteenth and first half of the nineteenth centuries. We would ordinarily assume that the small departure from universality was due to random fluctuations within a very small population: in Peshkovo, the failure of a single man or woman to marry reduced nuptiality by 3 percent.[24] The crown peasants of Sluchkovo seem to have lived in a different world altogether; 27 percent of adult women in the village in 1763 never married, while a stunning 44 percent who were twenty-five and older as of 1795 never married. Since most men in Sluchkovo continued to marry, they could do so only by bringing wives into the village. Sluchkovo accumulated women;

Table 3.1 Marriage Aversion in Kuplia Parish among Crown Peasant Men Twenty-Five and Older, 1763–95.

		Peshkovo	Aleshkovo	Sluchkovo
1763	Married	29	29	23
1763	Never married	1 (3.3%)	2 (6.5%)	0 (0%)
1782	Married	35	32	32
1782	Never married	2 (5.4%)	2 (5.9%)	8 (20%)
1795	Married	31	30	34
1795	Never married	1 (3.1%)	2 (6.3%)	3 (8.1%)

Table 3.2 Marriage Aversion in Kuplia Parish among Crown Peasant Women Twenty-Five and Older, 1763–95.

		Peshkovo	Aleshkovo	Sluchkovo
1763	Married	28	31	24
1763	Never Married	2 (6.7%)	6 (16.2%)	9 (27.3%)
1782	Married	33	34	33
1782	Never Married	4 (10.8%)	8 (19.0%)	22 (40.0%)
1795	Married	31	27	34
1795	Never Married	2 (6.0%)	12 (30.8%)	27 (44.3%)

Sources, tables 3.1 and 3.2: RGADA, f. 350, op. 2, d. 824, ll. 128–137, 176–970b; GAVO, f. 301, op. 5, d. 120, ll. 68–730b, 164–720b, 1820b–91; d. 202, ll. 58–630b, 153–600b, 165–700b.

by 1795, women twenty-five and over outnumbered men over twenty-five by sixty-one to thirty-seven. Random variation cannot be the explanation.

The titles I have given to tables 3.1 and 3.2 signal my own explanation. In large numbers, women born in Sluchkovo would not marry; a somewhat smaller but by Russian standards very unusual percentage of women in Aleshkovo also refused to marry. That is a more complicated assertion than it may seem at first glance, because it includes the claim that women themselves chose not to marry rather than their fathers and mothers making that choice for them. I will make that case later. Here I consider, in order to reject, other possible explanations for the unbalanced sex ratio.

Widows may have significantly outnumbered widowers, as was the case in villages we will encounter in later chapters. When that was so, widows numbered among the ever-married could unbalance the sex ratio even when peasants practiced universal marriage. But that was not the case in the three crown peasant villages. In 1795, widowers outnumbered widows six to four in Peshkovo and four to two in Aleshkovo; in Sluchkovo, there were five of each.

A possible explanation for the gender imbalance that cannot be so easily dismissed is conscription, which did have a major impact on the male population of Kuplia parish, as everywhere else in Russia. Between 1763 and 1795, conscription took twenty-nine crown peasant men from Kuplia parish for life or until incapacity. The tax census preceding their conscription provides their ages; the census following gives the year they were conscripted. We can compute their ages when conscripted: thirteen were teenagers, from fifteen to nineteen; nine were ages twenty to twenty-four; three were twenty-five to twenty-nine; and four were in their thirties, the oldest thirty-nine. The censuses names four wives left behind—their husbands were twenty-two, twenty-five, thirty-three, and thirty-four when conscripted—but they were not counted in the population because they were no longer legally bound to the village. It is certain that other conscripts had wives who left no traces in the census returns.[25]

Conscripts were levied steadily but irregularly, according to when the army needed to raise men. The army decided how many men were required; the government then calculated how many conscripts per one hundred or one thousand men in the most recent tax census were needed to reach the target. Quotas were assigned to territorial administrative units based on their populations.[26] The administrators of the Krasnoe Selo crown peasant precinct (*volost'*) would have decided how many conscripts the crown villages of Kuplia parish had to furnish. During the years 1763 to 1782, the base male population—the total from the 1763 census—was 203. The 16 men conscripted represented 7.9 percent of the male population as of 1763; the 13 men conscripted between 1782 and 1795 represented 5.9 percent of the 1782 male population of 220. That was just slightly higher than the average levy imposed on other crown peasants of the district.[27]

A far better measure of the impact of conscription is the rate by ten-year cohort. The army took ten of the forty-nine crown peasant men (20.4 percent) who turned fifteen (the age at which they entered the conscription pool in this period) between 1763 and 1772. Twelve of the forty-one men (29.3 percent) who turned fifteen between 1773 and 1782 were conscripted. Of the forty men who turned fifteen between 1783 and 1792, only three (7.5 percent) had been conscripted by 1795, but conscription would fall on them with particular force during the wars of the 1790s and the early nineteenth century. Over the entire period from 1763 to 1795, Kuplia's crown peasant villages surrendered to the army 26 of the 137 men (18.9 percent) who turned fifteen after 1763 (as well as 3 others who turned fifteen before but were drafted after 1763). That is a crude measure of conscription's impact on the availability of marriage-age men as of 1795. It disregards the men in their teens and early twenties who were conscripted after 1795, and it ignores the gradual shrinkage of each conscript cohort because of mortality. We can say confidently, however, that in Kuplia parish in the last third of the eighteenth century, the army consumed more than 20 percent of every generation of crown peasant men who lived to fifteen. Conscription decimated, twice over, the male crown peasants of Kuplia parish. That must, we might think, have been the reason why so many adult women in the crown villages were short of husbands.

And yet that was not so. Direct measurement of the impact of conscription on marriage is difficult because the populations from which men were conscripted, and among whom crown peasant women married, were very different. All conscripts were taken locally, but two-thirds of the crown peasants' wives came from outside the parish, and two-thirds of their daughters who married, married away from the parish. The population within which Kuplia crown women circulated in marriage was many times larger than the population from which Kuplia crown conscripts were taken. I can, however, offer a hypothetical measure: if all young crown peasant men and women had been determined to marry, and to marry only within their parish, would conscription have left a shortfall of adult men, and if so, how many adult women would have been left without husbands?

The hypothetical crown peasant population of Kuplia parish consists of all the real men and women born in the parish and listed in the tax censuses from 1763 to 1795. In the hypothetical parish, all men and women born in the parish marry within the parish, and they marry universally—no man or woman remains single willingly. In the hypothetical parish, 156 real crown peasant women lived to twenty (the threshold marriage age) or beyond between 1763 and 1795, as did 164 real crown peasant men. As in the real parish, conscription took 7 men who were twenty-five or older; by our hypothesis, they were all married. Their conscription produced no spinsters; the soldiers' wives suffered, but conscription of married men did not reduce any other woman's prospects for marriage. As in the real parish, conscription took 9 crown peasant men who were ages twenty to twenty-four from the hypothetical parish. If we say that the proportion of men in that cohort who were married was the same in the hypothetical as in the real parish—44 percent—then the parish lost 5 unmarried men to the army. That left 159 men for the 156 women to marry, a slight male surplus.

The thirteen conscripted teenagers are not taken into account here, and that may have turned out to be a problem for the women of the next generation; we actually cannot calculate whether more women than men crossed over the marriage threshold at age twenty after 1795 because the next tax census, in 1812, enumerated only men. But if we are trying to identify possible reasons why, among the real crown peasants of Kuplia parish in 1795, so many women twenty-five and over remained single, conscription cannot have been a major part of the explanation. Along with other factors that in the real world reduced the number of marriageable young men, conscription (of men in the entire population living within ten kilometers of Kuplia parish) may have made it difficult for some young crown peasant women to marry but not many. We might have drawn the same conclusion simply by acknowledging that, across broad swaths of Russia, men were conscripted at the same rate as in Kuplia parish and yet peasant women there actually did marry universally, as seen on the estates in Riazan province discussed in chapter 1. To minimize conscription's impact on marriage scarcely mitigates the enormous economic and social carnage that it (or the real culprit, the Russian state's international and imperial ambitions) inflicted on the crown peasant villages of Kuplia parish and on peasants across Russia.

The distribution of unmarried adult women among the three crown peasant villages by itself demonstrates that, at the level of the village, there was no relationship between conscription and the number of adult women who never married. Peshkovo, in which only two (6.0 percent) of thirty-three women twenty-five and over in 1795 never married, lost eleven of the fifty-four men (20.3 percent) who turned fifteen between 1763 and 1795. Sluchkovo, twenty-seven of whose sixty-one women twenty-five and over

(44.3 percent) in 1795 had never married, lost only six of the thirty-nine men (15.4 percent) who had turned fifteen since 1763. Most women in Peshkovo managed to marry despite the fact that their village hemorrhaged men. In Sluchkovo and Aleshkovo (Aleshkovo lost 20.5 percent of its men who survived to fifteen, while 37.7 percent of its adult women in 1795 had never married), fewer men were conscripted away from the village than spinsters who remained. Obviously, many women in those villages thought about marriage differently than their Peshkovo sisters.

THE OLD BELIEVER HOUSEHOLDS OF SLUCHKOVO AND ALESHKOVO

The tax census returns for 1763 show that women in Sluchkovo had begun to resist marriage by at least 1715–25, women in Aleshkovo by 1725–35. As of 1763, nine of thirty-three Sluchkovo women twenty-five and older (27.3 percent) had never married, while in Aleshkovo six of thirty-six women in that age group (16.7 percent) had never married. In Aleshkovo, the two oldest were in their early fifties; in Sluchkovo, the three oldest were said to be in their eighties. The ages of those three were certainly exaggerated; the ages of two other Sluchkovo single women, listed as in their sixties, may also have been exaggerated, but in later censuses with more reliable female ages, there were usually a few women sixty and older. If some of the Sluchkovo spinsters were in fact in their sixties, they had come of marriageable age sometime between 1715 and 1725; Sluchkovo women may have avoided marriage even before that, but if so, the pioneers had probably died by 1763. The oldest spinsters in Aleshkovo had reached marriage age between 1725 and 1735, and they were likely among the first in the village to shun marriage.

We know that almost all the women who resisted marriage in Aleshkovo were Old Believers and that they were members of a religious community that emerged in the 1760s. In 1777, the Kuplia parish priest grouped ten (of the twenty-one) Aleshkovo households as "registered schismatics" at the end of the annual confession register.[28] Those ten households accounted for seven of the eight Aleshkovo women twenty-five and older who had never married as of 1782 and for eleven of the twelve women who had never married as of 1795. Back in 1763, the six unmarried women lived in six different households, only one of which was schismatic in 1777. One of the Orthodox spinsters lived to 1794; the others all died before 1782. Up to 1795, all the other women born into those Orthodox households married before turning twenty-five. In 1763, on the other hand, the households that later made up the "registered schismatic" group had many daughters not yet twenty-five who would become the single adult women of 1782 and 1795. This pattern suggests that women who avoided marriage prior to 1763 made individual choices at variance with the conception of marriage held by others in their households, whereas after 1763, female aversion to marriage was a defining feature of the households and community that the priest identified as registered schismatics.

Marriage resistance among the Aleshkovo Old Believers gained force over time. In 1782, only five of the ten Old Believer households in Aleshkovo held unmarried women twenty-five and over. By 1795, seven households were contributing unmarried daughters to the total.[29] In 1782, two of the three brothers Ivanov (their patronymic; no peasants in Kuplia parish had family names) living in two separate households each had an unmarried daughter over twenty-five; they also had an unmarried sister. All three spinsters survived to 1795, when they were joined by the third Ivanov's daughter, age thirty-two, who also never married. In 1782, the widow Fevronia Afanaseva had three unmarried daughters, ages twenty-seven, thirty, and thirty-one, as well as a thirty-five-year-old bachelor son. She and her son both died in 1794, but the daughters were still alive in 1795. Before she died, Fevronia adopted a son, Prokhor, age twenty in 1795, from the family of Grigorii Ignatiev, presumably in order to provide male labor for her aging daughters. Grigorii was himself an Aleshkovo Old Believer who in 1795 had a twenty-eight-year-old spinster daughter, Agafia; another daughter, also Agafia, age fourteen; and another bachelor son, Matvei, age twenty-five. Giving up an adult son to help sustain a co-religionist's household was, for a peasant family in which male labor determined household well-being, an act of extraordinary generosity. It must also have been an example of solidarity among Aleshkovo Old Believers. Taken together, the two Ivanov and the Afanaseva households accounted for six of the eight unmarried Aleshkovo Old Believer women over twenty-five in 1782 and seven of the eleven in 1795. The other never-married adult women lived, like Grigorii Ignatiev's daughter Agafia, one to a household.

Identifying Old Believer households in Sluchkovo is more complicated, but by the 1790s, they had clearly become the majority. The Kuplia parish priest listed no registered schismatics in Sluchkovo in 1777, but in 1779, he identified four men and nine women individually as schismatics. They made up a majority in three of the twenty-two households in the 1777 register,[30] but there were more Old Believer households than that. All the members of three other households, for example, failed to appear at Lenten confession in 1777. When a different priest compiled the 1800 register, he listed twelve of the original twenty-two households, as well as another fifteen Sluchkovo men and thirty-three women, as registered schismatics and five more men and fourteen more women as "Old Believers."[31] That was the official designation of members of the Edinoverie chapter of the Orthodox Church, established in 1798; Old Believers who joined that chapter could use the pre-Nikonian books and practice the old rituals, so long as they recognized the canonicity and authority of the official church. The priest in 1800 did not group the dissenters by household, but most of those sixty-seven men and women can be connected to one or another of the twenty-two households of 1777. The 1763–95 census returns list three additional households—one missing from all three confession register, two missing from the 1777 and 1779 registers, but with some of their members listed in 1800.[32] Of the twenty-five households in the 1795 tax census, the members of fourteen were predominantly Old Believers, with some nominally Orthodox scattered among them. The other eleven were, according to the confession registers, overwhelmingly Orthodox, but with at least a few acknowledged schismatics.

In 1763, the first two generations of Sluchkovo women who had refused to marry were on the verge of extinction. Two disappeared quickly, leaving the twenty-five households of 1782. One consisted only of an eighty-year-old spinster; the other, a married couple and a spinster, died out in 1767. There was also an agglomeration of mostly elderly spinsters (forty-five, sixty-two, and eighty-seven) and widows (seventy-eight and eighty-five), the last of whom died in 1775. The census taker described them as "widows and maiden daughters [left] after deceased peasants"; they were survivors of households that had collapsed earlier.[33] Some may have been living on their own; others may have been sheltering with neighbors. Probably the enumerator thought it better to list them separately than to dangle them at the ends of lineages not their own. We cannot say for sure whether any of these unmarried women were Old Believers, but some probably were. We can be more confident, for example, that the unmarried female members of Fedor Nikitin's household were Old Believers. Fedor himself was only eighteen in 1763, living with his forty-six-year-old widowed mother and three unmarried aunts: his mother's sisters, thirty-five and twenty-six, and his father's sister, age sixty. Only twenty-six-year-old Elena survived to the 1782 census;

she also survived to be listed as a registered schismatic in 1800. The only other woman in Sluchkovo who had never married as of 1763 and survived until 1782 was forty-seven and living in what from 1777 was nominally an Orthodox household.

In Sluchkovo, as in Aleshkovo, marriage resistance increased rapidly after 1763. Only two of the nine single Sluchkovo women twenty-five or older in 1763 survived to 1782, but by then, they had been joined by a new and much larger generation of twenty women who were twenty-five and over and never married. By 1795, there were twenty-seven of them. In 1782, sixteen of the never-married women lived in eleven identifiably Old Believer households; six lived in three nominally Orthodox households. Nine lived in households in which they were the only single adult women; the other sixteen lived between two and four to a household. Some young men had also chosen not to marry. There had been no single men twenty-five or older in 1763; in 1782 there were eight, ages thirty to forty-two. Six were living in households with unmarried adult women. In Sluchkovo, refusal to marry had begun earlier than in Aleshkovo, had spread to more households, and had been taken up by men as well as women. In 1795, seventeen never-married women lived in ten Old Believer households, ten in five supposedly Orthodox households. Two of those households, their Orthodoxy very much in doubt, held three unmarried adult women each. The number of unmarried adult men, by contrast, had declined. One of the eight from 1782 had at last married; four had died. The three other survivors from that generation were the only unmarried adult men in the village. Male aversion to marriage had lasted a single generation.

Differences in family structure point to at least three different marital and reproductive strategies in Sluchkovo and Aleshkovo. Of course, uncontrollable demographic variability—how many children of which sex were born and how many survived into adulthood—affected household outcomes, and except for extinction, all outcomes were temporary, changing from census to census. Nevertheless, the contrasts in 1795 were so stark that they reveal human choice.

The extremes are easy to identify: households in which, after a certain point, no adults married and reproduction ceased and those in which every child married and reproduced. As of 1795, seven Sluchkovo households (two of them Old Believer) and fifteen Aleshkovo households (four Old Believer) practiced universal marriage and, in principle, reproduced themselves. They were not all thriving. The household of Grigorii Ivanov in Aleshkovo, for example, consisted of only sixty-one-year-old Grigorii himself after he gave a daughter in marriage sometime after 1782 (when she had been twenty) and his wife died in 1786. The couple had another daughter, who had married before the 1782 census, but no sons. The household would soon expire, for reasons beyond Grigorii's control.

Other households—at least six in Sluchkovo (all Old Believer) and at least six more in Aleshkovo (one of them nominally Orthodox)—had ceased to give or take women in marriage and stopped reproducing. In the census returns, they appear to be celibate. To take the only case in which commitment to celibacy is not completely obvious, in 1782 the Sluchkovo brothers Kozma and Semen Zinoviev and their two sisters, ages thirty-one and forty-two, had never married. A third brother, Gerasim, thirty-four, had a wife, Lukeria, thirty-eight. However, that couple had probably opted for celibacy; they were childless as of 1782. By 1795, the bachelor brothers had died, and the only child in the house was a three-year-old abandoned baby boy whom the family had taken in. (The women of the household were too old to have been the mother.) Except for that foundling, by 1795 the celibate households had no young children and only one teenager, a fourteen-year-old girl whose twenty-eight-year-old sister and two older brothers had not married. The youngest members of celibate households were usually in their late thirties or early forties. These households chose extinction for themselves. Some of the households that disappeared between 1763 and 1782 may also have succumbed to celibacy, but there isn't quite enough information in the 1763 census return to be sure.

Most of the other households—one in Aleshkovo, twelve in Sluchkovo—procreated but contained one or more unmarried women twenty-five or over. The priests labeled some of them schismatic, others Orthodox. The only demographic distinction among them was that some had only one younger reproducing couple while the others had two, and that difference was in most cases (other than recent household division) probably not something over which they had control. But the decision that one or more of their daughters and sisters never marry was deliberate. A few remnant households—without surviving married couples—cannot confidently be assigned to any group.

The distinction between Orthodox and Old Believers was demographically relevant only among the celibate and the reproducing, but even the celibate included one household whose Orthodoxy was obviously spurious. Both Orthodox and Old Believer households were among those in which everyone married and those in which men married but their sisters did not. Some of the nominally Orthodox households harbored covert Old Believers, though others may have been genuinely Orthodox. The celibate and universally marrying Old Believers certainly had different beliefs about marriage, and they probably belonged to different Old Believer covenants.[34] The households in which men married and women didn't may have belonged to yet another Old Believer covenant; however, it is just as likely that they and the celibate confessed the same anti-marriage creed but that those with marrying men were more pragmatic: in order for a household to survive and provide sustenance for the elderly, sons had to marry.

The eighteenth-century documents at our disposal allow us to chart the growth of marriage aversion in Sluchkovo, Aleshkovo, and Kuplia parish more broadly but do not explain it. Why did they shun marriage? Since most Old Believers in most of Russia did in fact marry (even if state and church refused to recognize their often heterodox unions), the fact that so many Sluchkovo and Aleshkovo crown peasants were Old Believers is not the explanation. What sort of Old Believers were they? Probably many of them were Spasovites. We know from the 1830 confession register that the overwhelming majority of Kuplia parish Old Believers were Spasovites as of that year. But that, too, was a (temporary) outcome; not all of the Spasovites of 1830 necessarily had eighteenth-century Spasovite forebears.

REPERCUSSIONS

Russian peasant society was organized around marriage and married couples—the household was a collectivity of married couples, the village a collectivity of households. Men and women entered adulthood and assumed adult responsibilities after marriage; if they did not marry, they were marginal to the adult social world. Marriage structured hierarchy and relationships within the household. A household generally received its share of village resources (land, for instance) based on the number of its married couples.[35] Preparation for marriage, and marriage itself, was the focal point of much of peasant folklore.

Widespread refusal to marry, therefore, had major repercussions within the family, the village, and beyond. Celibate households, which rejected everything central to peasant life, removed themselves from the peasant world. Households in which sisters and daughters rejected marriage but whose young men married were in a socially and culturally more complex— not to mention schizophrenic—situation. Could the women of the house who avoided marriage for religious reasons be treated with the same disdain as in conventional households? When, as regularly happened, one or two married adult males and their wives lived with two or three single adult women, what would the dynamics and the hierarchy in the household have been? They could not much resemble social dynamics in a household in which all adults were married couples and a very occasional old maid a misfortune. Every peasant household like that would have had to work out for itself how authority and responsibility were distributed, because there was—at least in the eighteenth century—no precedent to follow. When the young men of the house married, what role did the single women play in the preparations and celebration (if they played any role, if there was any sort of celebration)? How exactly did the conflict between the embeddedness of marriage in peasant culture and their faith's evident hostility to marriage work itself out? Alas, the tax and parish censuses offer no answers to these questions. I pose them simply to suggest how refusal to marry at the rate that obtained in Sluchkovo and Aleshkovo at the end of the eighteenth century necessarily and profoundly destabilized peasant society. The tax census returns do, however, illuminate other repercussions of widespread refusal to marry—one that had fully emerged by the 1790s, another that would shortly crash through Sluchkovo and Aleshkovo.

Sluchkovo peasants' refusal to marry created tensions with their neighbors. So far, I have presented figures on non-marriage in the conventional way, the proportion of adult women living in the village who never married: in Sluchkovo, 44 percent as of 1795. A better measure, or at least the measure peasants in the neighborhood must have used when they evaluated what was going on in Sluchkovo, is the percentage of women *born* in Sluchkovo who never married—that is, not counting the many women who married into the village but counting women who married away. Of the forty Sluchkovo women who turned twenty-five between 1763 and 1795, twenty-eight (70 percent) never married.[36] There was, correspondingly, a sizeable imbalance in the flow of brides into and out of Sluchkovo. In crown villages with low levels of marriage aversion, peasants imported the majority of their wives and exported the majority of their brides; over time, the numbers balanced. Peshkovo, for instance, imported twenty-eight brides and exported twenty-eight between 1763 and 1795, with an import surplus before 1782 and an equal export surplus after. In those same years, Sluchkovo imported twenty-six women and exported only eight, on average just one every four years.[37] The village was a sink hole for women: many entered, few emerged.

Peasants in surrounding villages seem to have retaliated. There is overlapping, albeit indirect, evidence that by the 1780s, Sluchkovo had a reputation as a village in which women didn't marry and that fathers in other villages turned away Sluchkovo suitors. Why do a favor for a household in a village that contributed scarcely any of its own women to the marriage market? Peshkovo, in which almost all women married, sent four brides to Sluchkovo between 1763 and 1782 but none between 1782 and 1795. Peshkovo also provided four brides for Aleshkovo between 1763 and 1782, none between 1782 and 1795, despite the fact that Aleshkovo in those years was a net exporter of women. Evidently, Peshkovo peasants' hostility to families that would not surrender their daughters extended to all households in the village. Between 1763 and 1782, Sluchkovo men had to travel more than ten (crow-flies) kilometers only twice to find the fifteen women they married. Between 1782 and 1796, they traveled more than ten kilometers to find four of sixteen. Between 1763 and 1782, only one of the fifteen Sluchkovo men who married took a serf for a wife. Between 1782 and 1795, five of sixteen Sluchkovo men married serfs. By the 1780s, Sluchkovo men had to search farther, and some had to resort, in effect, to purchasing brides. I have no data on the bridal departure fees that serf-owners in the district charged in the 1780s and 1790s, but these were the decades in which departure fees elsewhere rose to the level of the purchase price of a marriageable serf woman.

We might suppose that the difficulties Sluchkovo men apparently encountered when they sought wives were due less to resistance than to their own choosiness. Did Sluchkovo Old Believers look for spouses, whether wives or husbands, primarily among their coreligionists? In the extreme case, did men from families whose daughters refused to marry prefer to take wives from other families whose daughters shunned marriage? That preference could have been met rarely, at best. Did they settle for a wife from any Old Believer household? Any woman from an Orthodox household who agreed to join their particular Old Believer covenant? Any available woman, irrespective of creed?

The evidence from the census returns is slight but probably indicative. Between 1763 and 1782, one Sluchkovo bride moved from an Old Believer to an (at least nominally) Orthodox household in the village, while another moved between two Orthodox households. One Old Believer and two Orthodox Sluchkovo households took wives from Orthodox Peshkovo households. (At least that's what the Kuplia priest considered them, and those households did practice universal marriage.) Another Orthodox household took a bride from a Peshkovo household where all the women married, but two men over twenty-five had not; that may have been an Old Believer household. Between 1782 and 1796, one Sluchkovo Orthodox woman married into a local Old Believer household, while another moved from Old Believer to at least nominally Orthodox. Sluchkovo Old Believers seem to have been willing to marry any woman available and to have allowed their daughters to marry into nominally Orthodox households or unable to prevent them from doing so. The problem Sluchkovo men faced was that two-thirds of Sluchkovo women weren't willing to marry anyone, and Sluchkovo men, therefore, encountered resistance when they searched for wives in villages nearby.

All Sluchkovo men who became marriageable between 1782 and 1795 did marry; however, they had to work harder at it than their fathers had, and it cost their fathers more than their fathers' marriages had cost their grandfathers. Probably they managed to establish connections in, and fetch wives from, distant villages because so many men in that part of the Gorokhovets district traveled to make a living. Probably they used their off-farm earnings to purchase serf brides.

The other, and very obvious, social consequence of widespread nonmarriage was household collapse and the burden of providing for individual survivors. Within Sluchkovo and Aleshkovo, this problem had not fully emerged as of the 1790s, but it was signaled by a cluster of nine women among the Old Believers whom the Kuplia priest listed as living in Sluchkovo at the very end of his 1800 census register. They ranged in age from ten to eighty-eight (so they claimed or the priest guessed). The priest called six of them, including the ten-year-old, "maidens"; the others were "widow," "old lady" (*zhenka*, here meaning widow), and "aunt" (of the ten year old). Five of the nine were forty-four or older. Unlike the many other Old Believers and registered schismatics in the 1800 register, they cannot be found in any of the preceding tax censuses or in confession registers dating back to the late 1770s. They were, apparently, outsiders.

I infer that they were refugees from marriage-averse households that had collapsed in other villages and that they had found shelter in Sluchkovo households that shared their faith. The priest listed them in the confession register because they lived in Sluchkovo and were, therefore, nominally his parishioners (they were not just visiting). But they had not been born in or married into long-standing Sluchkovo households, so they were not counted in the 1795 census. The census taker did list some households and individuals who moved to the village, but only when a move was officially sanctioned (as when a crown peasant family moved from one crown village to another) or officially commanded. For instance, the 1782 census return includes three runaway serfs, two men and one woman, who had turned themselves over to the authorities and been sent to Sluchkovo by decision of the Viazniki Lower Court. The census return includes notations to that effect. The census taker would not have written into the census elderly women who had simply taken up residence in Sluchkovo households. If they were counted in the 1795 census at all, they would have been listed on returns from the villages from which they had come and where they had previously been entered on the census rolls. One did not have to be physically present in a village to be listed in the census: men and women working or otherwise away from their home villages at census time were listed with their natal or marital households.[38] I read the evidence this way in part because we will encounter an identical phenomenon—a substantial number of women listed in the parish records but not the census returns—between 1830 and 1850.

Some Sluchkovo households that curtailed or entirely renounced marriage collapsed, but as of 1795, most of the older single women were still living in households with men of working age—some of advanced working age, for peasants. One household, however, had experienced calamity. When Grigorii Alekseev died at age seventy-one in 1787, he left three single daughters who were ages forty-five to fifty-five by 1795. How long could they hold on? Over in Aleshkovo, Fevronia Afanaseva had made a premortem arrangement for the support of her three unmarried daughters by adopting twenty-year-old Prokhor Grigoriev. Prokopii Vasilev of Sluchkovo, thirty-four in 1795, had a twenty-five-year-old wife (probably his second) and a nine-year-old daughter and was supporting as well his widowed mother, seventy-one; two never-married sisters, thirty-six and thirty-three; his sister-in-law (her husband had been conscripted), forty; and her two sons, three and five. What would that mob do if something happened to Prokopii?

Table 3.3 Age Table for Sluchkovo, 1795.

	Men		Women	
	Married	Not married	Married	Not married
Under 20	0	28	1	31
20–24	3	1	1	3
25–29	3	0	9	3
30–34	6	0	3	4
35–39	4	0	5	3
40–44	4	0	5	6
45–49	6	2	1	4
50–54	3	1	4	5
55–59	3	0	2	2
60 and over	5	0	5	0
Totals	37	32	36	61

Sources: GAVO, f. 301, op. 5, d. 202, ll. 58a–63ob.

What must it have been like for Prokopii to support all of those women even while he was of prime working age? The five Zinoviev brothers and sisters had at one point tied the future of their household to the one brother who married, but when he and his wife produced no children, the Zinovievs, too, were doomed to a wretched old age. Their three-year-old foundling could not grow up fast enough to save them.

The reason many households in Sluchkovo were only approaching rather than already in the abyss had to do with the rhythm with which marriage aversion had developed in the village: two smaller generations of single women had mostly died out by the 1770s, while the next and much larger generation of marriage-averse women reached adulthood mostly in the 1770s and 1780s. Table 3.3 provides the distribution of male and female ages for Sluchkovo (the nine apparent refugees from other villages listed in the 1800 confession register *not* included).

A disproportionate number of women in their forties and fifties never married: seventeen unmarried compared to twelve married women, for a total of twenty-nine. Married or single, the survivors would need support within a decade from younger family members, if they had any, or relatives or neighbors. There were also nineteen men in their forties and fifties, and most of them would shortly require support, too. There were only seventeen men in their twenties and thirties, and they would bear most of the burden of supporting the forty-eight men and women in the older generation (fifty-three, if we count the five apparent survivors, age forty-four and older, of household collapse elsewhere who had found refuge in Sluchkovo).

The bleak future starkly visible in a few households as of 1795 was, in fact, the future of the entire village. The burden resulted from the many women who had never moved away through marriage and was aggravated by the only partly fortuitous circumstance that there were not many men in the younger generation. The declining number of children because of celibacy was one problem; another was that roughly 20 percent of the men who might have been available to support the elderly had already been or soon would be conscripted. If the six normally functioning households (everyone marrying and reproducing) refused to help any but their own elders, the prospects of the other nineteen were grim. In Aleshkovo, the immediate future was not quite so bleak. Fifteen of its twenty-four households were, as of 1795, reproducing normally, and the oldest unmarried woman in the village was only forty-nine. But Aleshkovo would suffer a similar demographic and social crisis in a generation, when its six celibate households—just like the six celibate Sluchkovo households—would collapse.

Younger widows and single women could, with some difficulty, eke out a living for themselves, but the elderly could not. They could not perform the farm labor that was backbreaking for men, and probably very few of them had the strength or skills to support themselves through craft production or migrant labor. An Old Believer woman who taught Old Believer children to read might manage to feed herself through her own labor, but very few other women, or men, in their sixties could. Elderly Old Believer women also supported themselves by providing ritual services, but our evidence on that point comes largely from urban communities. And Spasovites shunned most rituals (see chapter 5). Whether they continued to occupy their own cabin or slept on a bench in a household that agreed to provide shelter as well as food, the elderly women of Kuplia parish, when they reached penurious old age, must as a group have depended on the charity of their community.

THE REST OF KUPLIA PARISH AND BEYOND

The extremely elevated levels of marriage aversion in Suchkovo and Aleshkovo in the late eighteenth century were not representative of Kuplia parish as a whole. In Peshkovo, the other crown village, both men and women married close to universally (as can be seen in tables 3.1 and 3.2). Although there

Table 3.4 Marriage Aversion in Kuplia Parish among Serf Men Twenty-Five and Older, 1777–1800.

		Kuplia	Kharlakovo	Khoroshevo
1777	Married	18	11	32
1777	Never married	0	0	0
1800	Married	27	20	30
1800	Never married	0	2 (9.1%)	1 (3.2%)

Table 3.5 Marriage Aversion in Kuplia Parish among Serf Women Twenty-Five and Older, 1777–1800.

		Kuplia	Kharlakovo	Khoroshevo
1777	Married	17	11	33
1777	Never married	0	0	3 (8.3%)
1800	Married	27	23	34
1800	Never married	0	1 (4.2%)	8 (19.0%)

Sources: Tables 3.4 and 3.5: GAVO, f. 556, op. 111, d. 108, ll. 187–98; op 107, d. 73, ll. 169–710b.

was a bit of a perturbation at the time of the 1782 census, both in 1763 and in 1795, only one man and two women in Peshkovo ages twenty-five and above never married. Kuplia priests identified none of the villagers in Peshkovo as schismatics in 1777 and only one married couple as "Old Believer" in 1800.[39]

Tables 3.4 and 3.5 provide the levels of marriage aversion in the parish's serf villages. The statistics are based on the 1777 and 1800 confession registers, which state ages unreliably. Nonetheless, while the numbers of men and women under and over twenty-five may be inaccurate, the differences among the villages and the change over time are substantial enough to override random error in the underlying data.

The only serf village in which aversion to marriage took hold was Khoroshevo. In Kuplia village during the last quarter and probably during the entire second half of the century, all men and women who reached the age of twenty-five married.[40] Two unmarried Kharlakovo men and one unmarried woman show up in the 1800 confession register, but they were more likely the result of random variation than a sign of budding marriage resistance. As of 1830, only one of the seventeen women over twenty-five in the village had never married.[41] In Khoroshevo, if the age given for the two oldest spinsters in 1777 (forty) were close to actual age, women had begun to shun marriage shortly before or after 1760, and aversion increased steadily. Only one of the three spinsters of 1777 survived to 1800; however, by then, five of nineteen nominally Orthodox households held seven unmarried women twenty-five and older, and one "Old Believer" was also a spinster at age thirty-four. The priest identified three other Khoroshevo "Old Believer" women—one married at thirty-nine, the others unmarried at nineteen and twenty-one—as well as five men and three women as registered schismatics, all over thirty-eight and married. In Khoroshevo, marriage resistance arose chiefly among the nominally Orthodox, not the declared dissenters. Yet Khoroshevo was the only one of the three serf villages with more than two declared Old Believers of any sort, so there was probably a connection between the presence of Old Believers and aversion to marriage.[42]

It was probably not a coincidence that Khoroshevo was the only one of the serf villages without a resident owner. In 1777, Aleksandr Babkin owned four households, Petr Babkin owned five, and Maria Shekhovskaia owned fourteen; all of the unmarried adult women resided on her portion. By 1800, three of the nine nominally Orthodox households then owned by Shekhovskaia contained five spinsters (one held three never-married sisters, ages twenty-nine to forty-nine), while among the Babkin brothers' now ten households, two had unmarried women twenty-five and above and three others had unmarried twenty-four-year-old women who were strong candidates to become lifelong spinsters.

The one resident serf-owner in Kuplia parish as of 1800 was Vasilii Bychkov. He and his wife were listed as parishioners and had no fewer than twenty-five house serfs in the parish.[43] He owned shares in Kuplia village (two households) and Kharlakovo (six households). The fact that Kharlakovo's population doubled between 1777 and 1800 suggests that he moved serfs there. Bychkov, it would seem, was an active manager interested in expanding his new holdings. If his serf women had exhibited marriage aversion, he would likely have done everything he could to compel them to marry, as other hands-on serf-owners were doing at the time. It is at least possible that his absentee co-owners had asked him to keep an eye on their properties, too.

As of the late eighteenth century, marriage resistance in seven randomly selected crown peasant villages within ten kilometers of Kuplia parish was

Table 3.6 Proportion of Never-Married Adult Women Twenty-Five and Older in Crown Peasant Villages in the Gorokhovets District, 1763–95 Tax Censuses.

	1763	1782	1795
Shubino	19.6%	31.1%	26.8%
Vetelnitsy	12.2%	22.5%	21.9%
Kupreianovo	2.2%	17.4%	17.9%
Svetilnovo	7.1%	14.3%	15.2%
Arefino	3.4%	13.9%	7.4%
Kniazhichi	15.2%	5.4%	6.5%
Luchinskovo	5.4%	2.6%	6.1%
In the aggregate	9.6%	18.0%	16.7%

Sources: GAVO, f. 301, op. 5, d.120, ll. 108–380b, 1490b–64, 175–82, 1910b–200; d. 202, ll. 109–520b, 161–640b, 173–780b.

lower overall than in Sluchkovo but, by comparison with what we think of as the traditional pattern of Russian peasant marriage, startlingly high.

Female aversion to marriage in villages in Kuplia's neighborhood varied considerably, just as it did within Kuplia parish. Marriage resistance in Shubino tracked marriage resistance in Aleshkovo closely, while Vetelnitsy trailed only a bit behind. Luchinskovo (also known as Gorodishche), Kniazhichi (after 1763), and Arefino (except in 1782) more or less matched Peshkovo, with what, for this district, were very low numbers of women who spurned marriage. Kupreianovo and Svetilnovo fell in between. Overall, however, the level of marriage resistance was strikingly high, especially if we remember that table 3.6 measures resistance in populations that included both native-born women who wouldn't marry and imported brides. Just as marriage aversion among women born in Sluchkovo was not 44 percent but 70 percent, marriage resistance among women born in the villages in table 3.6 may have been half again as high: up to 40 percent in Shubino, 30 percent in Vetelnitsy, well over 20 percent in Kupreianovo and Svetilnovo, and perhaps around 25 percent in the seven villages taken together. Marriage resistance among crown peasants here was both high and sustained. The one way in which the villages in table 3.6 differed from crown peasant villages in Kuplia parish was that marriage aversion seems to have hit a ceiling and leveled off after 1782, whereas in Sluchkovo and Aleshkovo, it continued to rise.

As in Kuplia parish, serf women elsewhere in the district were less prone to reject marriage or perhaps less able to resist successfully. For instance, in Miachkova Sloboda parish, fourteen (crow-flies) kilometers northeast of Kuplia, the rate of female resistance to marriage among the "economic" peasants of Miachkovo itself was 11.8 percent in 1800 and 14.2 percent in 1815, according to the parish confession registers. (In two other economic villages not in the parish, Rostovo and Rytovo, 18.9 and 7.0 percent of women twenty-five and over were unmarried in 1795.[44]) In the two serf villages in Miachkovo parish, Vyezd and Shchalipino—both owned by the Lazarev family—the registers for both 1800 and 1815 report that all women twenty-five and older had married.[45]

In Florovo parish, there were many small serf villages, almost all with a number of very small ownership shares (down to individual households); ownership changed, as did parish boundaries, excluding some and including other villages. There was continuity in six serf villages and one portion of a seventh between 1800 and 1815. Some had a few adult unmarried women in one year but none in the other; overall, the proportion of women who never married was stable: in 1800, 8.6 percent and 8.9 percent in 1816. In Malinovo, the most marriage-averse serf village, the figures for 1800 and 1815 were 19 and 21 percent (and had been 18.4 percent in 1779). The parish's "economic" village, Manilovo, had an almost identical rate of marriage aversion: in 1800, 22.0 percent and, in 1815, 21.2 percent.[46]

Probably, the variation among villages should be attributed primarily to differing attitudes toward marriage among the serfs themselves (as among economic and crown peasants) rather than to the attitudes of estate owners (none resident) or managers. The entire twenty-five-kilometer-long, eight- to twelve-kilometer-wide zone of settlement in which Kuplia parish was located seems to have been a center of female resistance to marriage. Intensity varied from village to village, but no one lived very far from a village in which large numbers of women refused to marry.

DAUGHTERS DECIDE

Was it fathers and mothers who decided that their daughters would not marry, or did the daughters, one by one, make that decision for themselves? The initial assumption might be that eighteenth-century peasant parents must have exercised their traditionally firm control over their children's marriages. But those same parents, in adopting a religious doctrine that (we may assume) encouraged women to shun marriage, had themselves overturned social and cultural norms; they had shattered the cake of custom.

Girls growing up in such households may not have submissively accepted their parents' views. In fact, their parents embodied contradiction: they had married but now (we may again assume) urged their daughters not to. In Sluchkovo and Aleshkovo—indeed, in all villages nearby—some girls married while others did not. Perhaps our initial assumption should be that young women in that situation were actually forced to choose—at least to reject—one option or the other.

Evidence that might tell us who chose, parents or daughters, is sparse and indirect. For instance, the age at which both serf and crown peasant women in Kuplia parish married—most of them in their early twenties—made it more likely that they would have preferences about whether to marry or not and to whom and would be able to exert their will in a way that fifteen- or sixteen-year-old girls could not. By their early twenties, they had been of marriageable age for five or more years; ordinarily they would have taken part in the spring round dances since age fifteen. That was when and how Russian peasant parents presented their daughters as potential brides. Parents in marriage-averse households likely held their daughters back. But would they have locked them in a cupboard so that they neither saw nor heard what was going on?

Although they note peculiarities rooted in the local economy, reports on courtship from the Gorokhovets district in the mid-nineteenth century (apparently the earliest available) describe the more or less standard practices of the Orthodox and say nothing about the way in which local Old Believers conducted courtship and marriage, let alone about courtship of daughters from marriage-averse families.[47] Descriptions of courtship among Old Believer peasants in the nineteenth century are from other districts and do not necessarily tell us anything about how peasant boys and girls of Sluchkovo and Aleshkovo may have courted in the eighteenth. The earliest such report on Old Believer courtship I have found, from January 1800, was sent by the manager of the Baki estate in the Varnavin district of Kostroma province, just acquired by Countess Charlotte Lieven. It is relevant because, on that estate, as in Kuplia parish, many women were marriage averse and single adult women piled up. On that estate, too, there were many Old Believers, both priested and priestless. The newly appointed manager observed, disapprovingly, that during winter evenings maidens gathered to spin, young men visited them, and the parties lasted until the early morning hours. He ordered that they end no later than 10:00 p.m. and that boys be excluded.[48] Even in villages with many non-marrying Old Believer women, young Orthodox and Old Believer men still courted, and it is likely that girls from marriage-averse households socialized with other girls and possibly with boys as well.

Pavel Melnikov, after investigating Old Believers in Nizhnii Novgorod province for many years, claimed in his voluminous 1854 report for the Ministry of Internal Affairs that Old Believers were very un-Russian in their aversion to singing and dancing. That precluded round dances and most courtship games. But he also reported that in the trans-Volga districts, Old Believers (there, mostly priested) married exclusively through elopement. That eliminated all of the customary public rituals involved in contracting, preparing for, and celebrating a wedding.[49] However, elopement necessarily meant that there was courtship of some sort and that girls were making marital decisions for themselves. According to Melnikov and others who described the custom in the elopement districts, the bride's parents were not told in advance but often knew what was about to happen. Girls were often stolen away from the winter evening gatherings. Sometimes their parents protested, but there was a ritual for begging forgiveness that always eventually elicited a parental blessing.[50]

Marriage by elopement (*ukhodom*), also called bride theft (*uvodom*) if the groom were deemed the more culpable, was widely reported in provinces north of Moscow, among the Orthodox as well as Old Believers, while evidence of bride theft south of Moscow is scant. Bride theft was associated with locale rather than confession. The Gorokhovets district was not far from elopement country, which overlapped the Nizhnii Novgorod forests from which the Spasovite covenant had emerged. However, there are only vague suggestions of bride theft or elopement from a few locations in Vladimir province, none of them in the Gorokhovets district.[51] That does not necessarily mean that Sluchkovo girls did not elope, but since there is no positive evidence, I must assume they did not.

Census returns provide some clues about how young people came to be married in Sluchkovo and so, inferentially, about why others never married. Most young women did not marry, but some had sisters who did. For example, the 1782 return tells us that Ivan Alekseev's oldest daughter, thirty-six-year-old Mavra, never married, while the younger daughters, another Mavra and Avdotia, married sometime after 1763. All five daughters of Grigorii Alekseev (no relationship to Ivan) were over twenty-five; four of them never married, but the second daughter, Matrena, did. In Ivan Stepanov's household, the older daughter married; the younger did not. While there were no similar split decisions in Sluchkovo households between 1782 and 1795 and and no split decisions at all in Aleshkovo from 1763 to 1795, in other nearby villages where large proportions of women shunned marriage, some sisters married and others didn't.[52] That was not common, but neither was it rare.

How did those daughters come to be married? Fathers may have made arbitrary decisions about which of their daughters would marry and which wouldn't, but more likely some daughters were making their own decisions. The fact that these marriages were exceptions to the norm in the household and local religious community in itself suggests that the daughters who married took the initiative. And if the marrying daughters chose to marry, then their non-marrying sisters also chose, in not following a sister's or a neighbor's example. No doubt strong parental views on the impropriety of female marriage influenced the choices many daughters made, and some fathers and mothers probably resorted to more than moral suasion to keep their daughters at home. Nevertheless, in an Old Believer community with, we can assume, a strong religious conviction that women should not marry, it is not surprising that most daughters chose spinsterhood.

The irrelevance of sibling order is additional evidence of choice: in the three Sluchkovo households, younger daughters married, the oldest married, and a daughter in the middle married. The same absence of a rule held among split-decision households in other villages. Yet in peasant households not averse to marriage, it was an almost invariable rule that daughters married in their order of birth, to avoid the impression that an older sister had been passed over. In households in Sluchkovo and neighboring villages, where most daughters never married but some did, a younger sister's fate did not depend on her older sister's fate or choice. At the very least, where seniority played no part in decisions about marriage, young women had more leeway to follow their own wishes than did their counterparts in more conventional peasant households.

If women like Mavra and Matrena chose to marry, then they almost certainly chose whom to marry. If the default understanding in a household was that women should not marry, Mavra had to take some initiative or her father would turn away every Ivan and Andrei who turned up (which perhaps indicates that some girls in the village did elope). Probably Ivan's representative would approach Mavra's father only after she and Ivan had already reached an agreement. Moreover, if Mavra's father, for whatever reason, took the initiative and tried to force an unwanted suitor on her, she could always reject marriage on religious grounds that her parents, and her larger community, would probably find compelling.

I have pulled this thread of inference to its breaking point, so I will stop with what may seem to be (but is really not) a paradoxical conclusion: I am convinced (and convincing, I hope) that it was precisely in marriage-averse households, as early as the second half of the eighteenth century, that enough Russian peasant girls to matter acquired, probably by default, the right to make their own nuptial decisions.[53] In villages where everyone married, girls had no choice but to marry. In Sluchkovo, both marriage and spinsterhood were options. Once women had the opportunity to choose whether to marry or not, they automatically also acquired some capacity to choose their own partners. The less interest fathers took in seeing their daughters married, the more decisions devolved to daughters.

NOTES

1. *Slovar' geograficheskii Rossiiskogo gosudarstva*, part 2, vol. p. 675.

2. GAVO, f. 301, op. 5, d. 120, ll. 68–730b, 1640b-1720b, 1820b-191; f. 556, op. 111, d. 108, ll. 187–98. The priest seems not to have enumerated most young children.

3. Dubenskii, *Vladimirskaia guberniia*, p. 33. On the extent of marshland and swamps in general, see pp. 8–10, 14, 21–22, 31.

4. I am indebted to Andrei Petrovich, a former Soviet land reclamation engineer and native of Gorokhovets who worked on marsh drainage during the Soviet era and drove me around the accessible portions of the parish in July 2012.

5. Dubenskii, *Vladimirskaia guberniia*, pp. 13–14, 88–90; *Topograficheskie izvestiia*, vol. 1, part 2, pp. 127–29; *Slovar' geograficheskii*, part 2, col. 80; *Geografichesko-statisticheskii slovar'*, p. 676.

6. "Nakaz kupecheskogo obshchestva," pp. 177–78.

7. Andreev, *Gorokhovetskaia*, pp. 32–37; Andreev, *Kotel'shchiki*, pp. 13–56.

8. Zenkovsky, *Russkoe staroobriadchestvo*, pp. 144–56, 271–77, and Rumiantseva, *Narodnoe antitserkovnoe dvizhenie*, pp. 66–81, are the major sources. Some others are useful: Smirnov, *Vnutrennie voprosy v raskole*, pp. xxxii–xxxiv; Crummey, *Old Believers in a Changing World*, pp. 52–67; Shul'gin, "'Kapitonovshchina,'" pp. 130–39; Borodkin, "Istoriia staroobriadchestva Verkhnevolzh'ia," pp. 31–37.

9. Borodkin, "Istoriia" p. 38.

10. Rumiantseva, *Narodnoe antitserkovnoe dvizhenie*, pp. 143–71, 204; Andreev, *Gorokhovetskaia*, pp. 28–32. Documents on the 1665–66 operation on the Kliazma are

in Rumiantseva, *Narodnoe antitserkovnoe dvizhenie v Rossii XVII veka. Dokumenty*, pp. 50–102. On Old Believers around Viazniki in the seventeenth and early eighteenth centuries, see Morokhin, *Arkhiepiskop Nizhegorodskii*, pp. 102–4.

11. Andreev, *Gorokhovetskaia*, p. 28.

12. GAVO, f. 556, op. 11, d. 119, l. 122, household 90; op. 107, d. 73, l. 152, household 116; op. 14, d. 254, l. 776, household 45.

13. Except for children who were born after one tax census but died before the next. These child ghosts can be recovered from the parish confession registers, if extant.

14. The classic study of the tax censuses is Kabuzan, *Narodonaselenie*. Kabuzan devotes considerable attention to the number of persons omitted and the almost ceaseless efforts to discover men missed in the first round. In the end, most were counted. The crown peasant returns from Kuplia parish show no evidence of subsequent insertions of individuals or households. (Returns from other districts and villages do have such insertions.) Despite what might seem to be the likelihood that young girls would be carelessly omitted because they were not taxed, the Kuplia parish returns seem complete. No woman was omitted in one census and then added in the next because, for example, in the interim she had married or become the mother of a male taxpayer.

15. The November 28, 1761, decree on the tax census did not explain the requirement that women be enumerated but referred to a May 13, 1754, decree that in the next tax census women be listed, along with married women's villages of origin and where daughters had been given in marriage (after 1763), in order to make it easier to sort out disputes over ownership of runaway serfs and their offspring (*PSZ*, vol. 14, p. 85; t. 15, p. 837).

16. The 1763 census is found in RGADA, f. 350, op. 2, d. 824, ll. 128–137, 176–97ob. The 1782 and 1795 censuses: GAVO, f. 301, op. 5, d. 120, l. 68–730b, 1640b–720b, 1820b–91; d. 202, ll. 58–630b, 153–600b, 165–700b.

17. For the Serpukhov district, see Bushnell, "Did Serf Owners Control Serf Marriage?," pp. 441–42.

18. Mironov, "Ispovednyi i metricheskii uchet," pp. 11–16, provides an overview of the origins and evolution of the confession register, as does Mel'nikov, "Schislenie raskol'nikov," pp. 384–88. The major legislatation is found in *Russkaia istoricheskaia bibliotek*, vol. 5, cols. 904–5 (Metropolitan Kornilii, 1690); *PSZ*, vol. 3, p. 415 (Patriarch Adrian, 1697); *PSZ*, vol. 5, pp. 166 (February 8, 1716), 200 (February 18, 1716; this edict summarizes and reiterates the 1714 edict, the text of which has not survived), 545 (February 17, 1718); *PSZ*, vol. 10, pp. 111–125 (April 16, 1737; legislation on the confession register and the model reporting form). On late seventeenth-century efforts to compel annual confession, see Michels, *At War*, pp. 116–17, 188–89 and passim.

19. GAVO, f. 556, op. 111, d. 73, ll. 187–98.

20. See the original presentation of this method in Hajnal, "Age at Marriage," pp. 111–36.

21. For 1763, see RGADA, f. 350, op. 2, d. 824, ll. 128–37, 176–97ob. For 1782 and 1795, see GAVO, f. 301, op. 5, d. 120, ll. 68–730b, 1640b–720b, 1820b–91; d. 202, ll. 58a–630b, 153–600b, 165–700b.

22. For 1777, see GAVO, f. 556, op. 111, d. 108, ll. 187–98. For 1800, ibid., op. 107, d. 73, ll. 160–710b.

23. In a random sample of six villages from which Kuplia parish's crown peasants took wives, three of seventeen women ages twenty-five to twenty-nine unmarried in 1763 were married by 1782, while eight of the twenty-six single women in the twenty-five to twenty-nine cohort in 1782 were married by 1795. After age twenty-nine, women in those villages also ceased to marry. The villages were Svetilnovo, Shubino, Vetelnitsy, Kupreianovo, Arefino, and Kniazhichi (GAVO, f. 301, op. 5, d. 120, ll. 108–38, 1490b-164, 175–82, 1910b–200; ibid., d. 202, ll. 102–320b, 143–520b, 161–640b, 173–780b).

24. Mironov, *Sotsial'naia istoriia*, vol. 1, p. 172.

25. The wives of conscripts were free (if serfs, emancipated) to leave their husbands' villages in search of work, to return to their parental home, or to follow their husbands.

26. Beskrovnyi, *Russkaia armiia i flot v XVIII veke*, pp. 33–39, 293–302.

27. In a sample of seven villages (Luchinskovo, Svetilnovo, Morozovki, Shubino, Vetelnitsy, Kupreianovo, Kniazhichi, and Arefino) from 1763 to 1782, conscription took 6.0 percent of the men listed in the 1763 census (GAVO, f. 301, op. 5, d. 120, ll. 102–64, 175–82, 1910b–200). In a sample of five villages (Svetilnovo, Shubino, Vetelnitsy, Kupreianovo, and Kniazhichi), from 1782 to 1795 conscription took 5.8 percent of the 1782 male population (ibid., d. 202, ll. 104–320b, 143–520b, 173–780b).

28. GAVO, f. 556, op. 111, d. 108, ll. 1950b–970b. The priest listed eleven registered schismatic households, but the tenth household was officially resident in Arefino at the time. According to the 1795 census, it moved from Arefino to Aleshkovo sometime between the 1782 and 1795 censuses. I count it among the Aleshkovo Old Believers in 1795 but not in 1782.

29. By 1795, one of the original ten Old Believer households had died out, but another had moved from Arefino to Aleshkovo.

30. GAVO, f. 556, op. 11, d. 108, ll. 191-1920b (1777); ibid., d. 119, ll. 126–27, 133 (1779).

31. GAVO, f. 556, op. 107, d. 73, ll. 164–65, 170–71.

32. The priest listed fourteen Sluchkovo households in 1800, but two of those do not appear in the census returns. Because the censuses tracked the movement of crown peasant households from village to village, these two households may have moved into the village after 1795 or been a different category of peasant, listed on a different census return. There is no obvious explanation for the priests' omission of one to three households listed in the census records. While priests generally treated even registered Old Believers as members of their parishes for record-keeping purposes, they did sometimes ignore households that had been schismatic for a very long time.

33. RGADA, f. 350, op. 2, d. 824, l. 136. The last men of those women's households must have died before the previous census in 1744; if they had been alive in 1744, their names and ages in 1744 would have appeared in the 1763 return.

34. The two groups that the priest indentified in the 1800 confession register—registered schismatics and "Old Believers"—do not correlate with the different Old Believer marriage regimes.

35. Moon, *Russian Peasantry*, pp. 165, 167–79, presents a nearly identical formulation in his adumbration of the reasons for universal marriage among Russian peasants. For a particularly grim view of the economic and social pressures that forced peasants into early and nearly universal marriage, see Mironov, "Traditsionnoe demograficheskoe povedenie," pp. 83–104. In his *Sotsial'naia istoriia Rossii*, vol. 1, pp. 160–164, Mironov adds the overwhelming moral and religious pressure to marry young and universally.

36. This and the following statistics on Sluchkovo marriages do not include four Sluchkovo wives whose villages of origin the censuses do not identify. By contrast, only 32.5 percent of the women who turned twenty-five in Aleshkovo between 1763 and 1795 never married because of the lower level of aversion as of 1763 and a very large number of daughters who came of age between 1782 and 1795.

37. The 1795 census gives Sluchkovo as the village of origin of one woman who married, but neither she nor a father whose name matches her patronymic can be located in the 1782 census. I have included her among the women imported.

38. Women such as these might have been listed as members of a lineage, their actual isolation not being evident from the census return; in the nineteenth century, they might have appeared as the sole survivors in "virtual households" that existed only in the census returns, artifacts of the technique the census used to track individuals from one census to the next. See the discussion of virtual households in chapter 6.

39. GAVO, f. 556, op. 111, d. 108, ll. 194–950b; ibid., op. 107, d. 73, ll. 162–64, 170.

40. Ibid., op. 111, d. 108, ll. 1920b–930b; op. 107, d. 73, ll. 165–660b.

41. Ibid., op. 111, d. 108, ll. 188–1880b; op. 107, d. 73, ll. 1660b–670b. For 1830, see ibid., op. 107, d. 212, ll. 882–85.

42. Ibid., op. 111, d. 108, ll. 1890b–91; op. 107, d. 73, ll. 1670b–690b, 1700b–71.

43. Ibid., op. 107, d. 73, ll. 160–1600b. I have not included the house serfs in the statistics on marriage. They and the peasants had little in common when it came to either family structure or marital practices.

44. GAVO, f. 301, op. 5, 202, l. 2300b–42, 3060b–17.

45. GAVO, f. 556, op. 107, d. 73, ll. 154–590b; op. 14, d. 254, ll. 117–240b.

46. Ibid., op. 107, d. 73, ll. 134–520b; op. 14, d. 254, ll. 772–830b. The Manilovo data for 1779 is found in ibid., op. 111, d. 119, ll. 120–1200b, 141–420b.

47. Borisoglebskii, "Svadebnye obriady," pp. 92–94; Veselovskii, "Svadebnye obriady," pp. 17–40; Dobrotvorskii, "Krest'ianskie iuridicheskie obychai," 322–49; Posokha, "Svadevnyi obriad," pp. 133–54.

48. LP 47422, f. 44v.

49. Mel'nikov, "Otchet," pp. 273–74.

50. For example, "Pokhishchenie nevest"; Kordatov, "Samokrutka"; *Russkie vedomosti*, no. 25, January 31, 1875.

51. The Tenishchev Ethnographic Bureau, circa 1900, asked respondents explicitly whether bride theft or elopement were local practices. Four Vladimir province respondents denied that was so, and a respondent from the Shuia district said, "They are extremely rare." The overwhelming majority of respondents ignored the question,

almost certainly because they had no knowledge of such practices in the districts from which they were reporting (*Byt velikorusskikh krest'ian-zemlepashtsev*, pp. 244–45).

52. GAVO, f. 301, op. 5, d. 120, ll. 114ob (Svetilnovo, 1763–82), 119–119ob, 120, 120ob, 122, 125 (Shubino, 1763–82), 125ob, 128, 130, 133, 134ob (Vetelnitsy, 1763–82), 150, 150ob, 151, 157, 162ob (Kupreianovo 1763–82); ibid., d. 202, ll. 113ob, 116ob (Shubino, 1782–95); ibid., l. 163 (Arefino, 1782–95).

53. "Marriage-averse" households can be expanded to include those of priested Old Believers who favored marriage but not by Orthodox priests; girls from such households often married in Orthodox churches by elopement. I expand on this point in chapter 6. Elopement by priested girls probably became significant in the second half of the eighteenth century, too.

CHAPTER 4

Kuplia Parish, 1830–50: Demographic Crisis and the Resumption of Marriage

From at least the first quarter of the eighteenth century, women in the crown village of Sluchkovo became increasingly marriage-averse. By the end of the century, 70 percent of the adult women born in the village—priestless Old Believers all of them, surely—had refused to marry. It was practically impossible for the rate of marriage aversion in Sluchkovo to climb any higher, and the nineteenth century data show it did not. In the crown village of Aleshkovo, marriage avoidance among women began a decade later and continued to rise until it peaked at the Sluchkovo rate sometime around 1830. In Peshkovo, marriage avoidance was so infrequent in the eighteenth century that physical or mental incapacity might have explained why a few women remained single, but between 1800 and 1830, the women of the village stampeded into spinsterhood. By 1830, the proportion of adult women in Peshkovo who shunned marriage had reached 37 percent, close to the level it had taken more than half a century to achieve in Sluchkovo and Aleshkovo. And then, around 1830, in all three villages, in many households in which women had been marriage-averse for generations, young women suddenly returned to the Russian peasant tradition of universal marriage.

That reversal occurred in households that the priests identified as Spasovite in 1830 and 1850 or that were home to individual Spasovites. In other households that priests identified as belonging to the Pomorsk covenant, female marriage avoidance began sometime after 1800 and continued unabated down to 1850. At the very least, that is a curiosity—young women in identifiably Pomorsk households shunned marriage in the nineteenth century, though their eighteenth-century grandmothers had married universally. We cannot be certain, however, that the eighteenth-century grandmothers of the nineteenth-century Pomorsk women had themselves been Pomorsk: they practiced universal marriage, lived in households the eighteenth-century priests considered Orthodox, and may have been Orthodox. Or they may have dissembled, as many covert Old Believers in the parish did. It was only in the early nineteenth century, when they stopped marrying and the priest identified them as Pomorsk, that they became visible.

Both Spasovite and Pomorsk marital behavior in Kuplia parish was paradoxical. I deal with Spasovite marital practices at some length in chapter 5 because it requires close interpretation of very sparse evidence to explain why large numbers of Spasovite women for a long time shunned, and then resumed, marriage. Here, for context, I provide a précis. When the Spasovites emerged as a priestless covenant in the trans-Volga forests of Nizhnii Novgorod in the late seventeenth century, they held, like all other priestless covenants at the time, that since there were no longer priests to administer the marriage sacrament, there could be no marriage. Living together without benefit of marriage was fornication—better than marriage in a heretical church, perhaps, but still a grievous sin. That was Spasovite doctrine until at least 1730, but by the end of the eighteenth century, it was firmly established that the covenant condoned marriage by Orthodox priests in Orthodox churches. Other Old Believers thought that practice outrageous, and it does seem to have been theologically contradictory. In chapter 5, I offer a possible explanation, but for present purposes, what is significant is that at about the same time that the covenant sanctioned marriage, increasing numbers of Spasovite women in Kuplia parish rejected marriage. I explore in chapter 5, as well, a possible explanation for the collapse of Spasovite marriage aversion in the parish—a schism among the Spasovites that came to a head in the 1840s.

Pomorsk households in Kuplia parish adopted the local Spasovite rule on nuptiality—men marry, women don't—at exactly the same time that the national Pomorsk covenant officially accepted marriage. During the eighteenth century, Pomorsk leaders in their Vyg Lake monastery in North Russia (the Pomorsk Vatican) consistently opposed marriage. They argued not just that there were no longer priests to administer the sacrament and that without sacramental blessing marriage was mere fornication but also that as the Second Coming and the Last Judgment approached, only a celibate life was appropriate. They were, however, tolerant of the corporeal frailties of their married followers and made no attempt to expel married couples or force them to remain celibate (as the Fedoseev covenant did, for instance); they merely required married couples to stand outside the chapel during worship and to use separate tables and tableware at mealtime. Indeed, the Old Believer peasants who settled in the Vyg Lake region during the eighteenth century to be close to their religious center married freely, as the tax census returns from the second half of the century show. By 1763, most of the single adult men and women in the small settlements in the vicinity were elderly survivors of the first flush of religious zeal who had arrived in those precincts in the early eighteenth century. The norm by 1763 was the multigenerational family in which all young men and women married.[1]

By the middle of the eighteenth century, some Old Believer preachers (or ideologues) associated with but not necessarily members of the Pomorsk covenant had become champions of marriage. They argued that marriage was a gift from God, that God had commanded humanity to "be fruitful and multiply," and that priests were not needed because it was God who performed the sacrament when couples exchanged vows of fidelity unto death. In the 1770s, the Pomorsk community in Moscow favored marriage, and its lay leader, Vasilii Emelianov, welcomed married couples into the community as full members. In the 1780s, he composed a priestless marriage service and began to wed Pomorsk couples by parental blessing, mutual consent, and the exchange of vows. After a series of confrontations between Emelianov and the Vyg elders, Vyg (which depended on donations from Moscow's Pomorsk merchants) surrendered in 1798 and pronounced marriage permissible.[2] Almost all local communities that had held out against marriage soon adopted the practice. The Moscow Pomorsk aggressively promoted marriage as a way to recruit Old Believers from covenants still hostile to marriage, and at least by the 1830s, peasants in the Gorokhovets district were themselves celebrating priestless weddings with the Pomorsk marriage service.[3] Pomorsk women in Kuplia parish stopped marrying just when their covenant overwhelmingly adopted a pro-marriage position, just as Spasovite women in the parish had ceased to marry as their covenant condoned marriage. I attempt to resolve this dual conundrum in chapter 5.

The fact that Spasovite women in Kuplia parish began to marry, universally, around 1830 is easy to miss. The instrument I have been using to measure marriage resistance up to this point—the percentage of single women over twenty-five—is too blunt. While that measure may seem to capture propensity to marry (or not) at any given point in time, that is not so. In 1795, 44.3 percent of adult women in Sluchkovo were single because of decisions they had made over the previous forty years; the tables measuring proportion married in 1795 summarize the local history of marriage aversion, not nuptiality as of 1795. Spasovite women resumed marriage abruptly around 1830, but the historical measure of female marriage resistance changed very slowly. When the women born in Sluchkovo, Aleshkovo, and Peshkovo began to marry, most of them married away from their native villages. And anyway, there could be no more adult married women in the village than there were adult married men, and as of 1830, all the men were already marrying. The proportion of never-married women declined slowly as, one by one, elderly spinsters died and young women married away from their villages.

Analysis of marriage by cohorts has to be supplemented by tracing what happened to girls and teenagers carried forward—or disappeared—from one census to the next. Here we face two problems. One is that the 1812 census enumerated only men, while the 1816 census returns from Kuplia parish villages have been lost. We are left only with the 1834 and 1850 census returns. The other problem is that the nineteenth-century tax censuses listed only the women who were currently legal residents in the village. Men were still listed in two columns: one enumerating men alive at the previous census, with explanations of their disappearance (death, conscription) before the current census; the other, the current population. The 1834 census lists only current female populations; it tells us nothing about the women of 1816. We can identify women who disappeared between the 1834 and 1850 censuses, but we cannot say, in the case of the children and adolescents of 1834, whether they had died or married away sometime before 1850. We can only estimate which explanation is the more likely at any given age. A girl recorded as several weeks old in 1834 but missing in 1850 had almost certainly died; a girl of sixteen in 1834 had almost certainly married away. Most estimates are not so easy as those.

Spasovites in Sluchkovo, 1800–50: Separation, Collapse, and Resumption of Marriage

Between 1816 and 1830, there was a revolution in household arrangements in Sluchkovo, but we cannot reconstruct why or exactly when it happened. In 1830, the Kuplia priest listed ten Spasovite households in Sluchkovo (they

Table 4.1 Spasovite Household Number Eleven, Sluchkovo, 1830.

Simion Vasiliev, 52
  Wife Avdotia Kozmina, 53

Maiden Agafia Nikitina, 64
  Her niece Akulina Gerasminova, 44
  Her niece Maria Gerasimova, 34

Widow Matrena Grigorieva, 60
  Her daughter maiden Vasia Ilina, 32

Vasilii Kozmin, 54
  Wife Matrena Dementiev, 52
    Their daughter Evdokia, 21

Conscript's wife Agrafena Mikhailova, 62
  Her son Ivan Mikhailov, 15

Widow Anna Andreeva, 64
Widow Varvara Iakovleva, 33
  Her son Abram, 11
  Her daughter Praskovia, 8

Source: GAVO, f. 556, op. 107, d. 212, l. 895ob.

are numbered two through eleven; Spasovite household number one was in Peshkovo). Those ten households held almost twice as many people as the fourteen listed on the Orthodox pages of the confession register: forty-seven male and seventy-one female Spasovites (of all ages), as against forty men and twenty-seven women among the Orthodox.[4] The priest listed another man and four women in a separate Pomorsk group; they may not have formed a separate household. As the gender imbalance among Spasovites suggests, many of their households were oddly constructed. Seven of the ten bear some resemblance to households in the 1834 tax census, but three of those seven had substantial additional portions that were listed with other households in 1834.[5] And three of the Spasovite households of 1830 were entirely composite, stitched together from portions distributed among up to six different census households in 1834. The households in the 1834 census look normal; the Spasovite households of the 1830 confession register appear quite abnormal. Spasovite household eleven is the oddest of them all.

Spasovite household eleven was a conglomeration of unrelated family fragments distributed in six separate households in the 1834 census. The Kozmins, Vasilii and Avdotia, were not brother and sister; Vasilii was listed in the Sluchkovo census returns in 1782 and 1795, but Avdotia was not. There are, in fact, no discernable kinship links among the household's six component parts. Twelve of the sixteen members of the household were female, five of them were single adults, and three more were widows. Vasilii Kozmin and Simion Vasiliev were nearing the end of their working lives with no sons to take their places. Ivan Mikhailov was just beginning his working life. The number of eaters was so much greater than the number of workers that the household was not viable, unless it had substantial resources beyond the three men, who themselves barely qualified as able-bodied adult laborers. It might have become sustainable within a few years if the two men were skilled craftsmen and could keep working until Ivan, fifteen, and Abram, eleven, grew into adulthood and if the elderly women died quickly. If the men died first, the survivors would be forced to seek refuge in other households. From the peasant point of view, everything about this household was wrong.

Yet there is no reason to doubt that in 1830, Spasovite household eleven was just as the priest enumerated it or that many of the households in the 1834 tax census—including the six in which the census taker placed the members of Spasovite eleven—were fictional. While the nineteenth-century tax censuses enumerated peasants by what look like (and probably were in most villages, most of the time) real households, the census taker's primary concern was enumeration of men, and the surest way to avoid omitting any was to record them in family groups, which could be checked against the preceding census returns. Just as in the eighteenth century, the 1834 census listed in the left-hand column all the men (but not the women) from the preceding census; that dictated the organization of the right-hand column enumerating current population. The census enumerator placed Spasovite eleven's members into the households where they had been at the time of the 1816 census. As a matter of fact, the law required him to do so in cases, including this one, when households had divided or re-formed without permission.[6]

By contrast, priests had no reason at all to construct artificial households for the Old Believers: in Kuplia parish, they more often listed their Old Believer parishioners individually rather than in households because (as can be verified from other lists from other years) openly declared Old

Believers were usually distributed among many households, not concentrated in a few. When the priests listed Old Believers by household, as they did for Aleshkovo in 1777 and for Sluchkovo in 1830, we can be certain they did so because those were the actual living arrangements. Indeed, in the 1830 confession register, the same priest who listed Sluchkovo's Spasovites by household listed Sluchkovo's Pomorsk and Aleshkovo's Spasovites not in household formation but as numbered individuals. In any case, if the 1830 priest had constructed fictitious households, he would never have come up with one as absurd as Spasovite household eleven.

Thus, sometime between 1800 and 1830, most of Sluchkovo's Old Believers declared themselves to be Spasovites, and at some point between 1816 and 1830, Spasovites in mixed households moved to other Spasovite households or came together to create entirely new households. We know that the separation occurred after 1816 because in that year, census enumerators were instructed to list people in the households in which they actually lived as of that date rather than listing them in the households of 1812.[7] Using the household data from 1816 in the 1834 census as the reference point, we see that between 1816 and 1830, Spasovites from one household had divided themselves between two existing Spasovite households and from another they divided themselves among three Spasovite households. Only one household (husband, seventy; wife, sixty; daughters, forty-two and thirty-one) had definitively ceased procreating, but in another, the youngest child was ten. Four large households had four or more young children, and all but the celibate household and Spasovite household eleven included a married couple who had produced a child within the preceding decade; Spasovite eleven did have a widow with two young children. This Spasovite community, in other words, continued the practice that had emerged among the Sluchkovo Old Believers by the end of the eighteenth century: the men of the household married, the women didn't, and there was usually at least one reproducing couple in a household.

Spasovite men all married—all twenty-five of those twenty and over were married in 1830—while their women remained as averse to marriage as they had been between 1795 and 1800 (table 4.2).[8]

The only plausible way to interpret these numbers is to assume—as we more or less know to be true, since in general peasant women who did not marry remained in their natal households—that the twenty-five Spasovite women who had never married were all born (or had taken refuge)

Table 4.2 Marriage Aversion among Sluchkovo Women Twenty-Five and Older, by Denomination, 1830 Confession Register.

Denomination	Married	Never married
Orthodox	11	0
Spasovite	26	25
Pomorsk	1	4
Sluchkovo total	38	29 (43.3%)

Source: GAVO, f. 556, op. 107, d. 212, ll. 889–900b, 894–950b.

in Sluchkovo, while all or almost all of the twenty-six Spasovite wives had been imported from other villages or perhaps from a neighboring Orthodox household or two. Because the nineteenth-century censuses did not track women's movement through marriage, we cannot be sure that literally every girl born into a Spasovite household had refused to marry, but that "every or almost every" girl refused is certain. But that meant, too, that Spasovite households were almost entirely dependent on the willingness of peasants beyond Sluchkovo to send their daughters to households that did not reciprocate. We can only assume that Spasovite men experienced the same difficulty finding wives between 1795 and 1830 as they had between 1782 and 1795.

Another conclusion to draw from table 4.2 is that aversion to marriage among Sluchkovo women had proven to be quite enduring: the proportion of single women had scarcely changed at all between 1795 (44.3 percent) and 1830 (43.3 percent). Since the 44.0 percent never-married rate had been reached by 1795 only because 70 percent of the women born in the village who had turned twenty-five since 1763 had avoided marriage, we can say that by 1830 almost all declared Old Believer Sluchkovo women had shunned marriage over at least three or four generations. Of the twenty-one Sluchkovo women who were registered schismatics in 1800, only six had ever married; the youngest was thirty-nine (and married sometime after 1782), the next youngest was forty-eight (and likely married around 1770), and neither of those women had been born in Sluchkovo.[9]

The priest did not arrange Sluchkovo's registered schismatics into households in 1800, and the fact that there were only eight, mostly elderly, schismatic men probably explains why: no household was then composed exclusively of declared schismatics. That, of course, makes it more difficult to trace possible connections between the households of 1795–1800 and 1830–34. So does the fact that some households had gone extinct (including all of the celibate households of 1795) while others had grown and divided. And the composite character of a majority of the Spasovite households of 1830 adds another layer of complexity.

Nonetheless, linking the lists of Sluchkovo inhabitants from 1795, 1800, 1830, and 1834 as best as possible shows that the Spasovites of 1830 were indeed both the biological and religious descendants of late eighteenth-century households—some nominally Orthodox, some openly schismatic—most of which, as of 1795–1800, sheltered adult women who had never married. It is not a surprise that some nominally Orthodox households subsequently turned Spasovite, as we have already deduced that in the late eighteenth century, some villagers concealed their true beliefs from their priest. Furthermore, many late eighteenth-century households had mixtures of identifiably Orthodox, registered schismatic, and "Old Believer" (Edinoverie) individuals. Indeed, before they rearranged themselves into religiously homogeneous households sometime after 1816, many of the Spasovites lived as minorities in what by 1830 had become equally homogeneous Orthodox households.

What is perhaps counterintuitive is that for most of the period over which we can trace the history of the Old Belief and Spasovites in Sluchkovo, so many Old Believers and Orthodox shared households. Spasovites, like all other Old Believers, proscribed praying with and eating from the same table and tableware as the Orthodox (and others not of their covenant), as well as some kinds of food and clothing common among the Orthodox.[10] Life in mixed households must have been difficult. But there is a likely explanation for this intermingling: in all of the lists of households and individuals, the Old Believers were preponderantly female and preponderantly elderly. This is a familiar pattern in other societies (the Soviet Union, for instance) in which officially disapproved beliefs are either prosecuted or persecuted: working-age men are at greater risk than any other group. Probably Sluchkovo Spasovites could tolerate living with their officially (if only nominally) Orthodox kin because their kin were sympathizers and because (being mostly female and elderly) they couldn't live without them. It would be nice to know what precipitated the physical separation of Spasovites and (as we will see, nominally) Orthodox sometime after 1816, but the documents available offer no clues.

As of 1830–34, the division between Orthodox and Spasovite households in Sluchkovo aligned perfectly with marriage practices: all men and women in households the priest considered Orthodox now married, which had not been true in the eighteenth century; in Spasovite households, daughters didn't marry, but all sons did. Spasovite households, therefore, accumulated women, often two generations of them. Sometimes these were the sisters and daughters of the head of the household, but as can be seen in Spasovite household eleven, they could also be the sisters and daughters of other households or from other villages. The 1830 confession register lists eight Spasovite women, ages sixteen to seventy-nine, who were not in the 1834 census return. The five Pomorsk women, too—one a widow and four spinsters—are missing from the 1834 census roll. Some of the elderly may have died between 1830 and 1834, and the sixteen-year-old may either have married or died; however, probably the majority of these women were (like the women missing from the 1795 census return) refugees from collapsed Spasovite and Pomorsk households in other villages. That certain expectation of, and absolute aversion to, marriage of women born into Orthodox and Spasovite families, respectively, is starkly visible in the tax and parish censuses.

That does not necessarily mean that Orthodox and Spasovite villagers themselves understood the opposing marriage practices to be the principal difference between them. Nor should we take the diametrically opposed positions on female marriage to represent an impenetrable barrier between the Orthodox and Spasovites. Even after they had sorted themselves into homogeneously Spasovite and Orthodox households, almost everyone in Sluchkovo had kin in the other camp. Indeed, Spasovites continually acquired new Orthodox kin precisely because their own women avoided marriage.

By 1850, the separate Spasovite community had disappeared. The parish priest listed twenty-six Sluchkovo households in the Orthodox section of the 1850 confession register, with eighty-two male and eighty-nine female residents. He listed separately one male and twelve female Spasovites as individuals rather than by household.[11] His list of households largely coincided with those in the 1850 tax census.[12] A few of the Orthodox census households consisted almost entirely of former Spasovites, while other former Spasovites and those who still acknowledged being Spasovites were distributed among other Orthodox census households. The fact that the entire older generation of Spasovite had died by 1850 may be the reason why most of the survivors retreated back into mixed households—there were either no or too few men left to provide support. The small celibate household had expired. If the Spasovite households of 1830 had still existed, one married man would have been supporting his own family and six elderly widows and spinsters. If Spasovite household eleven had survived, the fifteen- and eleven-year-old boys of 1830, now both married, would have been supporting their own families and three elderly spinsters; in that and a few other cases, the demographic situations of the Spasovite households might actually have improved, but that would have depended entirely on the sequence of death among the middle-age and elderly women, which nineteenth-century tax census returns do not reveal. In any event, the demographic crisis that had already been at hand in 1830 must have destroyed many Spasovite households by 1850.

Nevertheless, the unbearable burden that working-age Spasovite men had assumed in the quest for Spasovite self-segregation and self-sufficiency is probably only a part of the explanation for the Spasovites' retreat to mixed households. It may be that the younger Spasovite men who perforce took over the households when their elders died or became incapacitated had affiliated with the Spasovites partly in deference to their parents or grandparents; the economic strain may have made it easier for them to effect a generational shift in their households' public religious identities. This was, in any case, much more likely a retreat into covert religious dissent than an actual conversion to Orthodoxy. None of these newly minted Orthodox went to confession in 1850. In fact, only twelve men and women from seven of the twenty-six Sluchkovo households then identified as Orthodox made the obligatory Lenten confession. Even the peasants who had been listed as Orthodox in 1830 in their overwhelming majority abstained from confession in that year and probably every year thereafter. By that measure, Sluchkovo remained at heart, if not in public declaration, an almost entirely Old Believer village in 1850, as in 1830 and 1800.

The retreat of the Sluchkovo Spasovites into mixed households coincided with another change: a sharp decline in aversion to marriage among Spasovite (or formerly Spasovite) women. There are two different measures of the change. Table 4.3 shows a sharp drop in marriage aversion in the village as a whole.

Table 4.3 Married and Unmarried Sluchkovo Women Twenty-Five and Older, by Age
Cohort, 1850 Tax Census.

	Ever married	Never married
25–29	5	1
30–34	4	4
35–39	5	0
40–44	7	0
45–49	9	4
50–54	6	4
55–59	2	6
60 and over	3	3
25 and over	41	22 (34.9%)
25–44	21	5 (19.2%)
45 and over	20	17 (45.9%)

Source: GAVO, f. 556, op. 5, d. 460, ll. 824ob–35.

In 1850, the proportion of adult women in the village who had never married remained high at 34.9 percent, but if we look just at those who were
ages twenty-five to forty-four—that is, those who had turned twenty-five
in the twenty years that had passed since 1830—the proportion of women
never marrying (19.2 percent) was less than half of what it had been in 1830.
The change was sharp and decisive: during the 1830s, all twelve women
who turned twenty-five married. It is true that in 1830, there was only one
Spasovite girl who was of the right age to belong to the cohort of forty- to
forty-four-year-olds in 1850, and we cannot know whether she had actually
married because she was a refugee taken in by Sluchkovo Spasovites and
was listed neither in the 1834 nor the 1850 census returns nor in the 1850 confession register; if she had married, she married out of the parish. There may
seem to have been a return to marriage aversion in the early 1840s since four
of the five women in the age thirty to thirty-four cohort never married, but
two of those four were sisters in a household that must still have stubbornly
retained the old Spasovite practices. The next cohort, ages twenty-five to
twenty-nine in 1850, exhibited what, for Sluchkovo, was a very low rate of
aversion to marriage.

That the numbers in table 4.3 are not misleading becomes clear when
we look for the girls listed in the 1830 confession register (with their ages
taken from the likely more accurate 1834 census) in the 1850 census return.

Six Spasovite girls in 1834 had been ages ten to seventeen; all but two were missing from the 1850 census—they had either died or married away from their households. Five girls in 1834 were ages five to nine, and all were missing in 1850; three were under five, and only one was missing from the 1850 census. (The oldest of the others was twenty in 1850, just crossing the traditional marriage threshold age.) The majority of the missing girls, certainly, had married, probably bringing a more or less definitive end to Spasovite female marriage avoidance in Sluchkovo.

The decade when Spasovite women began to marry was probably when they began to make the transition back to at least nominal Orthodoxy and to retreat into mixed Spasovite-Orthodox households. The resumption of marriage and willingness to embrace the Orthodox Church publically— and thus to live with the nominally Orthodox—are at least logically, though not necessarily, connected. That this was just a coincidence will become clearer when we consider the simultaneous resumption of marriage by Spasovite women in Aleshkovo and Peshkovo. In any case, female marriage aversion declined as the number of declared Spasovites declined, and as Sluchkovo headed into the second half of the nineteenth century, there was a good chance that something approaching universal marriage would return more than a century after the onset of marriage aversion in the village.

ALESHKOVO: SPASOVITES VERSUS POMORSK

In Aleshkovo, the proportion of women over twenty-five who never married rose from 30.8 percent in 1795 to 40.1 percent in 1834, just a bit below Sluchkovo's 43.3 percent in 1830, and then apparently held steady. At the time of the 1850 census, marriage aversion in Aleshkovo had risen a bit to 42.3 percent. However, disaggregating the gross totals shows that in Aleshkovo, too, Spasovite women had begun to marry by the early 1830s. It was Pormorsk women who continued to shun marriage.

As in Sluchkovo, refusal to marry was concentrated in Aleshkovo's Old Believer households, but unlike in Sluchkovo, some women in nominally Orthodox households also avoided marriage. Unfortunately, it is more difficult to distinguish Old Believers from Orthodox in Aleshkovo than in Sluchkovo. The 1830 confession register is defective; it is missing at least one sheet (two pages) from both the beginning and end. It breaks off after listing four Spasovite women (all in their seventies) in Aleshkovo; the list obviously continued onto at least one more page, which probably also listed the Pomorsk living in the village.[13] The 1850 parish register lists six Aleshkovo Spasovites (one seventy-eight-year-old man and five women ages twenty-seven to seventy-nine) and four Pomorsk households with four men and sixteen women. But according to the 1850 census, the Pomorsk households held fourteen men (eight of them twenty-five and older) and twenty-two women (twelve of them twenty-five and older).

However, the 1850 census, which labeled the men of the Pomorsk households "schismatic of the priestless sect," treated their wives as mere cohabitants because they had not been married by an Orthodox priest in an Orthodox church. Those wives were listed not with their husbands but in their natal households; their children—all characterized as illegitimate— were left in the husbands' households. Only in the tax censuses of 1850 and 1858 were wives not married in an Orthodox or Edinoverie church banished from the census household. This was a byproduct of an 1839 decision by the St. Petersburg Secret Committee on Old Believers, ratified by Nicholas I, to consider the children of marriages not consecrated in either an Orthodox or Edinoverie church as illegitimate and to consider the mothers, as a matter of law, not to be living with the fathers.[14] Four such women were missing from three households in Aleshkovo's 1850 return. However, the 1850 confession register identifies all four; they were not listed in any census household in Aleshkovo, so they must have arrived from other villages. I have added the four to the census total of married females in Pomorsk households; there were actually twenty-six women in the Pomorsk households, sixteen of them twenty-five and over.[15] I have grouped all of them, as well as all of the men and women in the three census households that held the six Spasovites, into an Old Believer population. And I have treated the same households as the village's likely Old Believer population in 1830. Table 4.4 compares marriage resistance in the two populations.

Both the "Orthodox" and the "Old Believer" groups are approximations; they would be better described as "households in which identifiable Old Believers lived" and "households in which no identifiable Old Believers lived." The Old Believers group may have included a few Orthodox, and certainly at least some Old Believers resided in some of the Orthodox households in which adult women never married. Without a doubt, table 4.4 understates the actual differences between the two groups. Nevertheless, table 4.4 shows that Orthodox and Old Believers approached marriage

Table 4.4 Marriage Aversion Among Old Believer and Orthodox Women Ages
Twenty-Five And Older, Aleshkovo, 1834–50, According to the Tax Censuses

	Orthodox		Old Believer	
	Married	Never Married	Married	Never Married
1834	24	15 (38.5%)	8	10 (55.6%)
1850	24	6 (20.0%)	11	16 (59.3%)

Source: GAVO, f. 301, op. 5, d. 560, ll. 7960b–805; d. 602, ll. 52–59.

differently. In 1834, marriage resistance was at a minimum almost 20 percent lower among the Orthodox than among Old Believers, and the proportion of Orthodox women who never married had fallen by at least half by
1850. Old Believers seem to have become just a bit more marriage averse by
1850, but the records are misleading. A single Pomorsk household accounted
for almost the entire apparent increase in Old Believer marriage resistance
in the village. In 1850, it held five men twenty-five and over, two of them
bachelors, and seven women twenty-five and over, six of them unmarried—
three more than in 1834. Younger marriage-averse daughters had grown up
to become never-married adults.

Far more significant demographically, comparison of the three 1834
and 1850 census households that we know held Spasovites and the four
households we know held Pomorsk shows that while Pomorsk women up
to 1850 continued resolutely to refuse to marry, young Spasovite women
had entered the marriage market by 1850. The three identifiably Spasovite
households of 1834 held only four unmarried women under age twenty-five
(ages five, ten, thirteen, and thirteen), and none of them were listed in the
1850 census. Certainly at least two or three of them had departed through
marriage rather than death. By contrast, all but one of the ten women under
twenty-five (ages six to twenty-three) in identifiably Pomorsk households
in 1834 remained in those households in 1850. The exception was a twenty-
three-year-old, and since she was approaching the local ceiling age for marriage in 1834, she is more likely to have died than to have married.

As of 1834, Spasovite households in Aleshkovo were under almost as
much stress as in Sluchkovo. Unlike Sluchkovo's Spasovites, however,
nineteenth-century Aleshkovo Spasovites had never withdrawn from
mixed households because, apparently, their households were homogeneously Spasovite, whatever the priest may have thought, and had been so

for a long time. Two of the three households can be traced surprisingly easily back through the censuses of 1795 and 1782 to the cluster of registered Old Believer households in Aleshkovo in the 1777 confession register. The Kuplia parish genealogy of the third Spasovite household begins only in 1791, when it moved from Vetelnitsy to Aleshkovo; there is no indication that it held any Old Believers in 1795 or 1800, but it probably did. Stressed demographically as they may have been, these Spasovite households survived to 1850. At that point, two of the households, while still burdened by elderly unmarried women, were on a path toward demographic recovery; the other, reduced to a sixty-two-year-old man and his unmarried twenty-five-year-old daughter, was approaching extinction. The signal change among the Aleshkovo Spasovites around 1830 was the resumption of female marriage. While that was demographically pragmatic, the decision does not seem to have been based on demographic circumstances.

Aleshkovo's Pomorsk women continued to avoid marriage more or less universally up to 1850. It is probably not relevant that Pomorsk households in Aleshkovo were under less demographic (and therefore economic) stress. In part, that was fortuitous. In both 1834 and 1850, they held proportionately more married men of working age than their Spasovite neighbors. Just as important was that Pomorsk and Spasovite households had very different histories. Two of the three Spasovite households were the sole survivors of Aleshkova's ten registered Old Believer households of 1777; the others had died out either because they had become celibate in the eighteenth century or because the growing imbalance of men and women had made them unsustainable. The ancestors of the Pomorsk of 1834 had lived in households that, in the 1795 tax census and the 1800 confession registers, held no identifiable Old Believers of any sort. Because of the shorter time over which their daughters had not married, the Pomorsk households of 1830–34 had been accumulating adult women for no more than thirty years, and even in 1850, most were still demographically sustainable, because of their many married adult sons.

PESHKOVO: A COMPRESSED HISTORY OF AVERSION, AND RETURN, TO MARRIAGE

While marriage resistance in Sluchkovo and Aleshkovo had been increasing steadily since before the 1763 tax census, in Peshkovo it was only in the nineteenth century that women began to shun marriage in numbers too large to represent random variation. In 1795, two of the thirty-three women twenty-five and over (6 percent) had never married; by 1830, the figures were twenty of fifty-four (37 percent) and in 1850, twenty of sixty-two (32.3 percent).[16] If the priest identified any Peshkovo villagers as Old Believers in the annual confession register in 1830, he did so on the missing last page. In 1850, the priest listed individually one seventy-four-year-old Spasovite widower; three never-married women, ages forty-four to fifty-four; and twenty-eight members of the Pomorsk covenant, including nine never-married women ages twenty-six to fifty-nine. According to the 1850 priest, with the exception of one seventy-two-year-old woman, everyone else in the village who was seven (the age at which confession became obligatory) or older had gone to confession.[17]

If we sort the Spasovites and Pomorsk into the census households in which they were listed in 1834 and 1850 and take into account the unmarried adult women in Orthodox households (some of them obviously filled with covert Old Believers), as shown in table 4.5, we can see that the total number of adult Old Believer women who never married rose slightly between 1834 and 1850, that the number of marriage-avoiding Orthodox women declined slightly (more than slightly if we consider the growth of the Orthodox contingent by 1850), and that the level of marriage resistance in Peshkovo appears to have stabilized at 32 to 37 percent. With so small a number of adult women in the village, there was bound to be some random fluctuation over time.

But the appearance of stabile marriage aversion is illusory. The total number of unmarried adult women had indeed leveled off, but it would soon begin to decline steadily, just as in Sluchkovo and Aleshkovo, because after 1830, in Spasovite households with marriage-averse adult women, young women became willing brides. Again, we cannot tell from the census rolls exactly why young unmarried women listed in the 1834 census return were not in the 1850 return, but the odds are that the majority of them had married away from their households and village. In the three Spasovite households in 1834, there had been only two unmarried girls under twenty-five, ages twelve and twenty. Both had disappeared by 1850, and at least one must have married away. In the six nominally Orthodox households with unmarried adult women in 1834, there had been two girls unmarried at ages twelve and sixteen, and they had both left by 1850, almost certainly through marriage. There had also been four girls ages from one week to five years, and all

Table 4.5 Marriage Aversion by Confession among Women Twenty-Five and Over, Peshkovo, 1834–50, According to the Tax Censuses.

	Orthodox		Spasovite		Pomorsk	
	Married	Never	Married	Never	Married	Never
1834	22	9 (29.0%)	2	4 (66.7%)	10	7 (41.2%)
1850	28	6 (17.6%)	4	4 (50.0%)	10	9 (47.4%)

Source: GAVO, f. 301, op. 5, d. 460, ll. 789–96; d. 602, ll. 197–207.

of them, too, had disappeared. While the one-week-old had certainly died (she would have been just sixteen, the minimum legal marriage age after 1830, if she had survived), as had, possibly, one or two of the three others, probably at least one had survived to marry away from Peshkovo.

The resumption of marriage by girls both in the three Spasovite and in the six nominally Orthodox households suggests that at least those six households were covertly Spasovite. By contrast, five young Pomorsk women ages fourteen, fourteen, sixteen, twenty-one, and twenty-four in 1834 were still unmarried in 1850. Two Pomorsk girls, nine and twenty in 1834, had disappeared by 1850; even if they had both married, female abstention from marriage remained the dominant practice among the Peshkovo Pomorsk women, as among Pomorsk women in Kuplia parish at large. This is, of course, further evidence of the Pomorsk and Spasovite divergence in marital ideology and practice after 1830 and of the likelihood that Spasovites within Kuplia parish had more or less unanimously and simultaneously returned to the conventional peasant practice of universal marriage around 1830–34.

THE SERF VILLAGES

In 1800, in the three serf villages in Kuplia parish, only the women of Khoroshevo had demonstrated more than an insignificant level of marriage aversion: eight of the thirty-four women twenty-five and over (19.0 percent) had never married. Not much changed thereafter. In 1830, Khoroshevo was still divided among three owners, one of them new since 1800. There were spinsters on all three portions, but the total had fallen to six of thirty-nine (15.4 percent), one of them in a household the priest identified as Spasovite. Between 1830 and 1850, ownership of all three shares changed, but the rate of female marriage aversion held almost steady at eight of fifty (14.0 percent), none of them in the Spasovite household.[18] These were minor fluctuations, apparently unaffected by ownership turnover.

For Kuplia village, enumerated at the front of the confession register, the first four households are missing along with the first leaf of the 1830 confession register; in the remaining eighteen households, only two of thirty-two women twenty-five and over in 1830 (6.3 percent) had never married. The owner's name disappeared with the missing leaf, but the same anonymous noble in 1830 owned Kharlakovo, where only one of seventeen women twenty-five and over (5.9 percent) had never married.[19] In 1850, Kuplia had a resident owner, Pavel Kodin, and a nonresident owner, Dmitrii Izvolskii; there was an old maid in each portion, and together they made up 5.5 percent of the village's total female population ages twenty-five and over.[20] Of course, the numbers for Kuplia village are small, but the fact that in both 1830 and 1850 there were two households each holding an unmarried woman over twenty-five was a departure from the utterly universal marriage of Kuplia village women during the eighteenth century. In 1850, Kharlakovo was no longer part of the parish.

A TELESCOPIC VIEW OF MARRIAGE RESISTANCE IN KUPLIA PARISH

From the middle of the eighteenth century to around 1830, the number of appanage peasant women in Kuplia parish who avoided marriage increased steadily. In 1834, about when marriage aversion peaked, 73 of the 177 appanage women twenty-five and over (41.2 percent) had not married and never would (that does not include the refugee women missing from the 1834 census return); by 1850, the number of never-married adult women had declined to 64 of 180, but that was still a very high 35.6 percent. Keeping in mind that many of the women in the appanage villages had been imported into the parish as brides, the proportion of adult appanage women born in the parish who never married was probably around 60 percent in 1834 and still around 50 percent in 1850. Marriage aversion had first surfaced in Sluchkovo in the first quarter of the eighteenth century, spread to Aleshkovo in the second quarter of the century, and, after a delay, grew very quickly in Peshkovo in the early nineteenth century. Marriage aversion had also spread to the serf village of Khoroshevo in the second half of the eighteenth century, but only minimally to the other two serf villages.

Women in households that the parish priests labeled either registered schismatic or, in 1800, adherents of the "Old Believer" (Edinoverie) chapter of the Orthodox Church were those most likely to reject marriage, but in both the eighteenth and nineteenth centuries, nominally Orthodox women did so, too. They and many members of their households were certainly covert Old Believers. The priests did not identify the covenant or covenants to which the Old Believers belonged until the nineteenth century, but by tracing household genealogies, we can be confident that most of the eighteenth-century Old Believers in Sluchkovo and Aleshkovo were Spasovites. In Kuplia parish, the history of the Pomorsk began early in the nineteenth century. There may have been some secret Pomorsk pretending to be Orthodox in the eighteenth century, but none of the identifiably Pomorsk households in the nineteenth century had origins in eighteenth-century households with single adult women. Since the Pomorsk seem to have emerged at the same time in all three appanage villages, it may be that those who married universally had secretly been Pomorsk earlier and that for some reason their women stopped marrying at the same time that they acknowledged their creed publically.

The eighteenth-century census returns show clearly, if indirectly, that when the daughters of Old Believer households withdrew from the marriage market in large numbers, peasants in neighboring villages where almost all daughters married retaliated. The households withholding daughters, after all, reduced the number of women (in Kuplia parish, dramatically) available for multilateral bride exchange. That complicated the search for brides. Households whose daughters all married were reluctant to let them marry into households that did not reciprocate. This retaliation, in turn, made it especially difficult for daughter-withholding households to secure brides for their own sons. Because the nineteenth-century census returns include no information about where wives came from, we have no nineteenth-century evidence (from Kuplia parish, at least) of tension between communities in which daughters did and did not marry. Nevertheless, we should assume that tension at the very least continued and perhaps mounted.

Evidence of the demographic difficulties that arose when households held on to their own women and acquired additional women through marriage is striking. Where women had first and in greatest numbers withdrawn from marriage—such as in Sluchkovo—the burden on adult male laborers had approached the breaking point by the late eighteenth century; the households that had adopted celibacy all died off in the early nineteenth century, and then many of the households in which men married but women did not collapsed or merged with others. Household collapse set off small cascades of female refugees, through their own communities and outward to neighboring villages, as evidenced by the many women listed in the parish confession registers of 1800 and 1830 but not accounted for in the tax censuses of 1795 and 1834. Household collapse in fact struck Aleshkovo first and hardest, because six of the ten to fourteen original Old Believer households there (the larger number includes nominally Orthodox households in which women had stopped marrying) had chosen celibacy. The Pomorsk, who began to accumulate unmarried women in their households only in the early nineteenth century, did not, even by 1850, experience anything like the demographic implosion that destroyed much of the Spasovite community in the 1830s and earlier.

It is tempting, in fact, to link the resumption of female marriage in Spasovite households to the demographic and (since demography accounted for almost everything else) economic catastrophe that befell them. Sending daughters away in marriage, which in the immediate future could only prevent the further accumulation of single women, did not end the crisis but certainly was a pragmatic response. However, the way in which Spasovite women in all three appanage villages resumed marriage simultaneously points to a decision at the level of the religious community and almost certainly not in Kuplia parish alone. That decision reversed what must have been the religious principle that women should not marry. As we will see in the next chapter, a schism in the Spasovite covenant that erupted in the 1840s was likely already brewing in the 1830s. One of the many points of doctrine over which the Spasovites divided was marriage: the breakaway Spasovites said marriage was a very good thing, not something to be avoided or merely tolerated. That doctrinal innovation is visible in the demographic records from Kuplia parish when we know what to look for.

Beyond Kuplia Parish

While I have held the demography of marriage in Kuplia parish up to a microscope, this was much more than a local story involving just a few villages. The Spasovite and Pomorsk women of Kuplia parish resisted marriage to such an extent that for a time, they achieved close to universal nonmarriage, but many other peasant women in the Gorokhovets district also avoided marriage. In the late eighteenth century, women in some crown peasant villages avoided marriage at about the same rate as in Aleshkovo, and women in other crown villages resisted marriage at rates that would seem extraordinary if it weren't for the examples of Sluchkovo and Alesh-kovo. In yet other crown villages, there was only minimal female resistance to marriage. In the comparison group of seven crown villages within ten kilometers of Kuplia parish, 16.7 percent of adult women went unmarried in 1795, which suggests that roughly a quarter of all the women born in those villages never married (see table 4.6). There were "economic" villages in which female marriage aversion was in the middle of the crown peasant range, and in some serf villages, too, roughly 20 percent of women (or perhaps 30 percent of those born in the villages) never married.

If the demographic data from the eighteenth century seem to show crown peasant villages beyond Kuplia trailing in the wake of Sluchkovo and Aleshkovo, their histories diverged in the nineteenth century. By 1850, women in the now-appanage villages of Kuplia parish had resumed marriage, but that was decidedly not the case in other appanage villages in the vicinity, as table 4.6 illustrates. Although I use for comparison the same set of villages as in chapter 3 (table 3.6), two of those villages—Kupreianova, which had only twelve women twenty-five and older in 1850, and Vetelnitsy, whose entire population in 1850 consisted of three never-married middle-age women—had emptied out. The other five villages, however, were fully comparable to their 1795 iterations, and the population of the set as a whole was quite substantial in 1850. It is remarkable that marriage aversion had escalated dramatically in Arefino, Kniazhichi, and Luchinskoe, which had been at the low end of the marriage-aversion spectrum in 1795, and that, setting Vetelnitsy and Kupreianovo aside, the other villages were close to the cluster average of 26.1 percent. Moreover, that average was not a lagging indicator, elevated by large numbers of single women in the older cohorts, as was the case in the Kuplia parish villages in 1850. In the junior cohorts, ages twenty-five to thirty-four (women who came of marriage age in the 1840s), single women accounted for twenty-four of the ninety-seven women of those ages—that is, 24.7 percent of the total. They shunned marriage at the same rate as their elders. Indeed, to judge by the figures for survivors in the older cohorts, that was roughly the rate at which women who turned twenty-five in those villages had avoided marriage since at least the second decade of the nineteenth century.

Table 4.6 Marriage Aversion among Women in Appanage Villages, 1795 and 1850.

	1795	1850
Shubino	26.8%	25.2%
Vetelnitsy	21.9%	100.0%
Kupreianovo	17.9%	33.3%
Svetilnovo	15.2%	26.1%
Arefino	7.4%	18.8%
Kniazhichi	6.5%	29.6%
Luchinskoe	6.1%	26.3%
In the aggregate	16.7%	26.1%

Source: GAVO, f. 301, op. 5, d. 602, ll. 48ob–51730b-82, 1000b–113, 1590b–62, 1680b–74, 2580b–59, 2610b–76.

There are a number of possible explanations for the divergence in the nuptial behavior of the majority of appanage peasant women within ten kilometers of Kuplia parish and in Kuplia parish itself. In the first place, in none of these villages did the rate of marriage aversion come close to the roughly 44 percent rate (or universal in Old Believer households) that obtained in Sluchkovo and Aleshkovo circa 1830–34 or even the 37 percent in Peshkovo in the same years. The demographic and therefore economic difficulties that so many appanage households encountered in Kuplia parish were likely less acute in villages beyond the parish. Alternatively, if the Old Believers in those villages were Spasovites, they may have belonged to the branch that continued to resist female marriage after 1830. Finally, the Old Believers outside Kuplia parish may have been predominantly members of the Pomorsk rather than the Spasovite covenant, and like the Pomorsk in Kuplia parish, their women may have continued to avoid marriage after 1830 even when Spasovite women trooped to the altar. This might seem to be an especially likely explanation for the post-1800 surge in marriage aversion among the women of Arefino, Kniazhichi and Luchinskoe: like the Pomorsk in Kuplia parish, they began to avoid marriage only around 1800. On the other hand, the 1850 census returns from those villages list no households from which wives were removed because they had married in a priestless wedding service, as was the case in the Pomorsk households in Aleshkovo. Most likely, different combinations of these factors were at work in the different villages. There appear to be no sources that might explain why when most Old Believer women in Kuplia parish resumed marriage, their sisters in neighboring parishes did not.

I can offer only a much cruder measure of female resistance to marriage in the first half of the nineteenth century—the ratio of female to male population—beyond that comparison set. In no village was there a stable relationship between the proportion of women twenty-five and above who never married and the balance between the sexes in the village population at any time from 1763 to 1850. Women's refusal to marry was only one of many reasons why there might be more women than men. In small populations, there will always be sharp fluctuations in the sex ratio—conscription had a varying impact on the male population from one small village to another, men's different occupations produced more widows in some villages than in others, and the crown, and then appanage, administration from time to time transferred households from village to village. On the other hand, the random sample of seven villages in tables 3.7 and 4.5, with the addition of Sluchkovo, Aleshkovo, and Peshkovo (the villages in Kuplia parish were my first random choice), yield roughly similar relationships (with variations from plus 4 to minus 6 percent) between the percentages by which women exceeded men and women eschewed marriage. In 1763, women outnumbered men in the ten villages by 15.3 percent, while 11.6 percent of their adult women never married; in 1782, the figures were 18.5 percent and 20.0 percent; in 1795, 23.9 percent and 20.1 percent; in 1850, 23.7 percent and 29.5 percent.

Using the female-to-male ratio as an approximation of the proportion of adult women who never married—likely within 5 percent of the actual ratio—allows us to broaden the focus. The twenty-four villages subordinate to the Krasnoe Selo appanage administration (which included the three in Kuplia parish and the comparison set of seven) stretched across most of the habitable portion of the Gorokhovets district south of the Kliazma River. Women outnumbered men 2,291 to 1,852 (23.7 percent) in 1834; in 1850, women outnumbered men 3,742 to 2,889 (29.5 percent).[21] The latter figure was probably greater than the rate of female marriage aversion but does suggest that the 26.1 percent rate in the seven sample villages in 1850 was probably close to the rate for the entirety of the district's appanage peasant population. In 1834, in the forty-two state peasant villages (which now included the former "economic" villages) scattered all over the Gorokhovets district—much larger in the nineteenth century than today; in the north, it covered what is now eastern Ivanovo province as well as part of what is now Nizhnii Novgorod province—women outnumbered men 3,559 to 3091 (15.1 percent).[22]

Of course, the farther we move from Kuplia parish, the less confident we can be that the sex ratio approximates the proportion of adult women who never married. And within the rather miscellaneous set of state peasant villages situated in diverse ecological zones and no doubt with diverse economies and—more critically—different local religious histories, there was considerable variation both in sex ratio and most likley in female marriage resistance. Nevertheless, 15.1 percent is large enough to indicate that state peasants both in the Kuplia neighborhood and well beyond experienced some degree of female marriage aversion in the first half of the nineteenth century. That is the larger story in which the peasants of Kuplia parish played a small but illuminating part.

NOTES

1. RGADA f. 350, op. 2, d. 2379, lists only the male population in 1748, but the majority were old and apparently single. There were also male children and adolescents. The 1763 tax census (ibid., d. 2422), which lists both men and women, shows that by 1763 multigenerational, procreating families were the norm. See also Sokolovskaia, "Krest'ianskii mir," pp. 270–74; Staritsyn, "Starovercheskie poseleniia Kargopol'ia," pp. 160–67.

2. There is a very large, and polemical, manuscript literature on Pomorsk marriage. For the eighteenth-century intra-Pomorsk debate and the 1780s wedding service, see RGB OR, f. 17, no. 393, especially ll. 29–710b, 740b–82, 1380b–246, 295–3020b; f. 98, no. 1597, ll. 1–5, 450b–62. There is also a large body of nineteenth-century scholarship, mostly Orthodox, on this history. A short summary of the history that gets details wrong but the major developments right is in Popov, ed., *Materialy dlia istorii*, vol. 1, part 2, [pages numbered separately], pp. 1–8, 17–45, 114–27. A much fuller discussion is in Nil'skii, *Semeinaia zhizn' v russkom raskole*, vol. 1. An excellent recent account is in Mal'tsev, *Staroobriadcheskie bespopovskie soglasiia*, pp. 126–29, 267–396. A good summary in English can be found in Paert, *Old Believers*, pp. 47–49. Paert, "Regulating Old Believer Marriage," pp. 558–61, provides a short survey of the marriage practices of both priested and priestless Old Believers. On the confrontations between the Vyg Lake and Moscow Pomorsk leaders, see Khval'kovskii and Iukhimenko, "Pomorskoe staroverie v Moskve," pp. 314–43; Iukhimenko, *Pomorskoe staroverie v Moskve*, pp. 1–27.

3. GAVO, f. 93, op. 2, d. 171, ll. 42, 223–230b, 2240b, 225–2250b, 229, 231–320b, 2330b, 3330b, 397, 4090b–10, 433–435, 469–710b, 481–489.

4. GAVO, f. 556, op. 107, d. 212, ll. 889–900b, 894–950b.

5. GAVO, f. 301, op. 5, d. 460, ll. 8240b–35.

6. *PSZ* 2, vol. 8, pp. 348–49; t. 25, p. 20. Gorlanov, *Udel'nye krest'iane*, pp. 11–18, and Gorlanov, "Udel'nye krest'iane," pp. 91–109 and passim, discuss the appanage administrative structure; at the local level—as in the area south of the Kliazma in the Gorokhovets district—officials were chosen from the appanage peasantry, but to ensure their loyalty, they were given privileges (their families were no longer subject to conscription) and reasonably good pay. It is possible that priestless Old Believers were among the officials.

7. *PSZ*, vol. 33, p. 209. The decision not to recapitulate the 1812 household structure in the 1816 census was due to the considerable displacement of population in European Russia during Napoleon's invasion in 1812 (Kabuzan, *Narodonaselenie Rossii*, p. 72).

8. The figures from the 1834 census were approximately the same: among women twenty-five and over, thirty-eight had married and twenty-eight (42.4 percent) had not (GAVO, f. 301, op. 5, d. 460, ll. 8240b–35).

9. GAVO, f. 556, op. 107, d. 73, l. 1700b; f. 301, op. 5, d. 120, l. 720b; d. 202, l. 620b.

10. Pavel, *Nikol'skogo edinovercheskogo monastyria inoka Pavla*, p. 55; Pavel, "Kratkie izvestiia," p. 567.

11. GAVO, f. 556, op. 1, d. 1503, ll. 849–82 (numbering skips from 8490b to 880), 887–88.

12. GAVO, f. 301, op. 5, d. 602, ll. 126–40.

13. GAVO, f. 556, op. 107, d. 212, l. 8950b.

14. Varadinov, *Istoriia Ministerstva vnutrennikh del*, vol. 8, pp. 613–14; *Sobranie postanovlenii po chasti raskola*, 2nd ed., pp. 274–75, 428, 528; Paert, "Regulating Old Believer Marriage," pp. 564–71.

15. In practice, this rule seems to have been applied only to couples married since 1834; the oldest of the four men identified in the census as a "priestless schismatic" and listed without a wife but with illegitimate children was thirty-six. It was no doubt impractical both to try to establish the legality of the marriages of the grandparental generation and to list grandmothers in what was left of their fathers' households.

16. GAVO, f. 301, op. 5, d. 460, ll. 7890b–96; d. 602, ll. 197–207.

17. GAVO, f. 556, op. 1, d. 1503, ll. 884–880b.

18. Ibid., op. 107, d. 212, ll. 8860b–89, 894 (1830); op. 1, d. 1503, ll. 8460b–849, 887 (1850).

19. GAVO, f. 556, op. 107, d. 212, ll. 882–85.

20. Ibid., op. 1, d. 1503, ll. 841–440b. I have not included house serfs in the totals.

21. GAVO, f. 301, op. 5, d. 460, ll. 695–950b (1834 table of contents); and from the unnumbered table of contents in ibid., d. 602 (1850).

22. Ibid., d. 460, l. 133–1330b.

CHAPTER 5

SPASOVITES: THE COVENANT OF DESPAIR

Spasovites, so far as we know, did not produce any works on their own history prior to the nineteenth century, and the earliest known Spasovite
historical chronicle, composed sometime after 1848, is spurious. All other
Spasovite histories of the covenant derive from that fictitious original. The
original is preserved only as it was incorporated, apparently verbatim, into a
longer polemical tract around 1874. A third version, considerably reworked
and with many differences in detail, dates from around 1894.[1] And a final
version, which in large part reproduces the 1874 polemic and chronicle,
was incorporated into *Vechnaia Pravda* by Avvakum Komissarov (better
known at the time by his patronymic, Onisimov), published by an underground press in 1895.[2] In all four versions, the chronicle does little more than
trace an alleged genealogy of Spasovite monks. According to these chroni-
cles, the monks who founded the covenant arrived in the Olonets forests in
the Russian North in the late seventeenth century and established a skete
(a monastic community consisting of scattered dwellings). Those origi-
nary monks tonsured successors, who in turn begat others. They founded
sketes in Kostroma and then Nizhnii Novgorod provinces, the succession of
sketes culminating in the Osinovsk skete in the Semenov district of Nizhnii
Novgorod province.

In 1848, the Russian government seized that skete, scattered the few
Spasovite women living there, and, in 1849, turned it into a Edinoverie nunnery. The Osinovsk skete actually existed, and a few other details may (but
also may not) be based on oral tradition and may bear some resemblance to
reality.[3] But the central thrust of the chronicle is false: the Spasovites, prior
to the 1840s, did not have tonsured monks. Their sketes held lay elders and

eldresses, who led monastic lives but did not claim to be monks and wore plain dark dress, not monastic habit.

The chronicle was a byproduct of a schism among the Spasovites in the 1840s. It was produced by a breakaway group that included Avvakum Onisimov (Komissarov) in order to fabricate a lineage for itself and to demonstrate that Spasovites had a continuous history of monasticism that stretched back to the pre-Nikonian Orthodox Church. They came to be called the Spasovites of the Great Rite, and I will return to them later. As it happens, one of the innovations the Great Rite Spasovites wanted to introduce was monasticism, but they could not do that unless they could demonstrate that a Spasovite monastic lineage stretched back to the ancients in an unbroken chain.[4] By the beginning of the twentieth century, there were probably Great Rite leaders who believed that the practices of their covenant were the same as those of the original Spasovites, but on occasion, when pressed, they admitted that there were no historical records on Spasovite monasticism earlier than the chronicle itself and that the chronicle was based on an oral tradition. Other Great Rite leaders insisted on the chronicle's authenticity and veracity.[5] Of course, the chronicle is authentic, in its own way. Though it tells us nothing about the early history of the Spasovites, it does reveal a great deal about the origins of the Great Rite covenant.

There may be fewer than a handful of Spasovite sources from which to reconstruct the history of the covenant in the eighteenth and early nineteenth centuries. Other sources provide very sparse information; most of them simply repeat what others had written earlier.[6] Prior to the recovery of the spurious accounts of early Spasovite history in the twenty-first century, there was a consensus among the few historians of the Old Belief who paid serious attention to the Spasovites that the founder of the covenant was a "virtually illiterate" peasant, Kozma, who appeared in the Kerzhensk forests of Nizhnii Novgorod province in the late seventeenth century and by the early eighteenth century had become important enough to lead a covenant bearing his name, the *Kozminshchina* (Kozma-ites). Historians have plausibly identified this Kozma as the Kozma Andreev who, according to Grigorii Levshutin, had two thousand followers in the forest and directed two large sketes, one for men the other for women. Levshutin was a Cossack deserter who denounced Kozma to the governor of Nizhnii Novgorod province for *lèse-majesté* (Kozma called Peter I the Antichrist) in 1714. Kozma and some of his associates were arrested, and he died in Moscow in 1716 after being tortured. According to information Levshutin gathered from Kozma Andreev's followers and Kozma's own testimony when interrogated, he had been born a peasant but came to Moscow as a boy, worked as a small tradesman and craftsman there, and had been an Old Believer before fleeing to the forest in the 1680s. He was, in fact, literate and was probably well read in the religious literature that circulated among Old Believers. When seized, he had eight published and nine manuscript books in his cabin, as well as primers for instruction in reading. He not only read but also taught others to read. His followers arrested in the same case also had large numbers of books and manuscripts.[7]

Sources quite independent of each other reveal that Kozma was known beyond the Kerzhensk forest by the early eighteenth century, before Cossack Levshutin met and denounced him. Metropolitan Dmitrii of Rostov was told of the presence of Kozma-ites around Kerzhensk in 1708.[8] According to Dmitrii, they taught that marriage was fornication (as it would be, according to priestless Old Believers, because there was no authentic priest to administer the sacrament); the church of the saints, priests, and the holy sacrament existed nowhere on Earth; and they did not pray for the tsar.[9] Ivan Pososhkov also mentioned Kozma's covenant, which he called *Koz'movshchina*, in his anti–Old Believer tract *Zerkalo ochevidnoe* (*The Manifest Mirror*), completed by 1708 (but first published in the nineteenth century). To that point in his life, Pososhkov had lived only in Moscow and its environs and in what is now Tula province—in any case far from where Kozma preached. He himself grew up Orthodox, but his sister spent much of her life as a priestless Old Believer. Pososhkov may have learned about Kozma from her, but it was more likely from the Old Believers he questioned and debated (many mentioned by name but not identified by covenant in *The Manifest Mirror*).[10] Pososhkov has nothing to say about Kozma's teachings, but like Metropolitan Dmitrii, he does tell us that by 1708 Kozma and his covenant were already known in Russia's historic center.

Neither Cossack Levshutin nor Kozma under interrogation had much to say about the doctrine Kozma preached, either. What they did say amounted to standard priestless fare, on the presence of the Antichrist, the need to cleave to the pre-Nikonian rituals and texts, and the expiration of the priesthood. The earliest, if very terse, statement of what was distinctive about Kozma's teachings comes at the very end of a rejoinder by Feofilakt (Lopatinskii) to what is known as the *The Pomorsk Responses* (*Pomorskie otvety*), a defense of priestless doctrine compiled by the Old Believers at Vyg Lake in reply to questions put to them by an emissary from the official Orthodox Church. The Vyg elders delivered their tract to a government official in 1723. Feofilakt, in his capacity as the synod's specialist on schismatics, answered with a manuscript written in 1725 but published only in 1745 as *Oblichenie nepravdy raskolnicheskoi* [*sic*] ("Denunciation" or "Exposé of Schismatic Error"). Appended at the end of the exposé are brief characterizations of a number of Old Believer covenants, among them the *Netovshchina* (Nothing-ites), a name that we know from other sources was synonymous both with Spasovites and Kozma-ites. They believed that "God's grace is not in the churches, not in reading, not in chanting [that is, not in the church service], not in icons, not in anything, it has all been taken up to heaven, and we can only hope and trust to be saved."[11]

So condensed a summary obscures the radicalism of Kozma's views: God had withdrawn his grace from the world. Neither worship service, nor icons, nor holy writ, nor anything else offered access to God's grace or provided the means by which believers might work toward their salvation. No other priestless covenant taught its adherents not only that they lived in a world over which the Antichrist reigned but also that God had pulled up the sacramental ladder that had once given access to heaven. They might hope that they would nevertheless be saved, but there was nothing they themselves could do to achieve salvation. It was the assertion that God's grace was entirely absent, and that there was no sacramental source of salvation, that led other Old Believers, apparently, to dub Kozma's followers *netovtsy*—that is, nothing-ites—a name that later Spasovite peasants commonly called themselves.

A somewhat fuller, if still spare, account of Kozma Andreev's teaching is found in *Oblichenie na raskolknikov* [*sic*] ("Denunciation" or "Exposé of the Schismatics"), written by a one-time priested Old Believer turned Orthodox deacon, Vasilii Florov, in 1737 but published only in 1894. Florov had lived in the Kerzhensk and adjacent forests for many years, until he fled in 1718 or 1719, and he outlined the doctrines of many of the covenants active there.[12] He called Kozma Andreev's followers the *Kuzminshchina* (Kozma-ites) or *Netovshchina* (Nothing-ites). According to Florov, what distinguished Kozma-ites from other priestless Old Believers was that they believed the Eucharist sacrament had been taken up to heaven and no longer existed on Earth and that monasticism had expired for the same reason. They did not pray for the conversion of heretics and schismatics (that is, for the conversion of the officially Orthodox, who in the Old Believer view were the true schismatics), and they had renounced chanting and worship service ("how can we sing to the Lord in this alien land!") and did not rebaptize converts, as almost all other Old Believers did.[13] Florov probably misunderstood Kozma's teaching on the sacraments: not just the Eucharist but all sacraments had vanished, as Feofilakt's summary and all other sources state.

Serge Zenkovsky posited that Kozma Andreev took his doctrine from the disciples of the radically ascetic monk Kapiton, who had dispensed with clergy and ignored Orthodox liturgical practices in the first half of the seventeenth century.[14] Kozma could not have met Kapiton, who died in the Viazniki forest in the early 1660s. What is known about Kozma's biography does leave room for an encounter with Kapiton's followers in the forest north of Viazniki and Gorokhovets, although that is not attested. Nevertheless, Kozma spent many years in the forest, and like others, he probably moved about the Old Believer settlements taking part in the ongoing arguments over doctrine; therefore, it is entirely possible that he did meet up with Kapiton's disciples or disciples of disciples. One we know about is Kozma Medvedevskii, who taught in the vicinity of Kostroma.[15] According to Evfrosin, an Old Believer who wrote a polemic against self-immolation in 1691 and angrily denounced those Old Believers who encouraged it, Kozma Medvedevskii preached that both the priesthood and the sacraments were no more. He and his followers had also ceased to pray.

Another was Vasilii Volosatyi (Hairy Vasilii, so called because he never cut or combed his hair), mentioned both by Evfrosin and Vasilii Florov; according to Florov, Vasilii (like Kozma Andreev) did not rebaptize converts, taught his followers that they need not confess or repent, and urged those who intended to commit suicide to consume or destroy all their property in order to leave nothing to the Nikonians. And there were others in the forests who shared at least some of Kozma Andreev's beliefs.[16] Quite possibly Kozma Andreev drew on the teachings of the Kapitonites and others, but by the early eighteenth century, the belief that the sacraments had departed this world was firmly associated with the covenant that bore his name.

None of the earliest accounts of Kozma's covenant—including those by Cossack Levshutin, Vasilii Florov, and Feofilakt—give it the name Spasovite. Subsequently, Spasovites and Nothing-ites were names employed interchangeably, while *Kozminshchina*, based on the founder's name, eventually fell out of use.[17] Kozma was arrested in 1714, and Florov fled the Kerzhensk forest in early 1719 at the latest. It is quite possible that the covenant had not yet adopted the name Spasovite while Florov was present. The crusading anti–Old Believer bishop Pitirim of Novgorod referred to the covenant exclusively by the name *netovshchina* in his 1721 anti-schismatic tract, "The Spiritual Sling" (*Prashchitsa dukhovnaia*).[18] Writing in 1725, Feofilakt apparently did not know that was the decade in which the covenant adopted the name Spasovite. The paucity of sources on the early history of the covenant means, of course, that this can be no more than a hypothesis, but given Florov's interest in naming and describing the beliefs of the forest covenants, if the Kozma-ite Nothing-ites had also been known as Spasovites before he left the forest, he would almost certainly have said so. Indeed, toward the middle of the 1720s, Florov lived for a time among a group he identified as Spasovites in the steppe north of the Azov Sea but did not realize that they belonged to the same covenant as the Kozma-ites he had known in the Kerzhensk forest.[19]

A partially preserved Spasovite polemical letter written sometime between 1723 and 1742 suggests why the covenant eventually adopted the new name. The letter asserts that, although the sacraments were no more, their "trust in the Savior" gave them hope in a time of sacramental want.[20] There is no such suggestion in Florov's account of their creed. Feofilakt's 1725 summary of the Nothing-ite creed does state that they could hope for salvation even in the absence of sacraments but does not identify the Savior as the source of hope. He may simply have neglected to mention that article of faith. Again, the paucity of early sources permits only a hypothesis, but it seems likely that placing hope in the Savior became a central tenet of Spasovite doctrine sometime after Florov left the forest in 1718–19 and that this innovation prompted the covenant to adopt Spasovite (Savior-ite) as its formal name. Florov met Spasovites in the 1720s, and by the second half of the 1720s, the name was well established—that was when a priest near Domodedovo, south of Moscow, reported to the Holy Synod that there were secret Old Believers of the Spasovite covenant among the crown peasants in his parish and that they did not accept the validity of the sacraments.[21] One of those Spasovites, Iakov Rodionov, was sent to the Schismatic Office in Moscow for questioning, and he revealed that he had learned Spasovite teachings from laborers who came from the Kerzhensk forest to work for a friend of his. He also said that he neither worshipped nor associated with the

Orthodox because he didn't consider them Christians. Spasovites obviously shunned the Orthodox, just as other Old Believers did.[22]

The Spasovite practices of infant baptism and marriage were later frequently commented on, but neither Cossack Levshutin nor Feofilakt nor Vasilii Florov had anything to say about them. Kozma Andreev made a distinction between his followers, who lived apparently celibate lives in the forest, and laymen living in the world, for whose conversion it was useless even to pray.[23] In such a community, neither marriage nor infant baptism were pressing issues. However, as the covenant emerged from forest thickets and spread to worldly villages, marriage and infant baptism became problematic, and Spasovite teaching evolved. By the end of the eighteenth century, Spasovites were marrying, and their children were being baptized in Orthodox churches by Orthodox priests, despite the fact that Spasovites denied the validity of those sacraments and the sanctity of those priests. The Spasovite document from 1723 to 1742 says of baptism that it could not be performed by immersion in water (that was Orthodox practice, employed by most Old Believer covenants as well) but could be administered by making the sign of the cross and reciting an appropriate prayer.[24] The author seems to have been referring to infant baptism.

In 1727, Iakov Rodionov, the Spasovite from the Domodedovo crown property, told the Schismatic Office that Spasovites forbade marriage, so he and his wife lived in separate cabins. He had sent his two daughters to live celibate lives in a Kerzhensk skete. Rodionov also said that Spasovites banned use of bathhouses so that they would not see each other naked.[25] If Rodionov stated accurately the Spasovite teaching on marriage, then it was only sometime after 1730 that Spasovites began to resort to Orthodox priests for marriage, as reported in all sources from the late eighteenth and early nineteenth centuries. By then most Spasovites had also decided that infants could be baptized in the official Orthodox Church (or that midwives, but not parents, could baptize them). There are nineteenth-century reports that Spasovites prayed for the Savior to make good the sacramental deficiencies and that they performed minor acts of penitence (seven ritual bows) to cleanse themselves of the impurity that adhered to them when they had contact with the official Orthodox Church. Those practices, too, probably originated in the eighteenth century, but it is not clear whether all subgroups of what was a fissiparous covenant accepted them.

The use of Orthodox priests to perform sacraments that the Spasovites did not recognize to be sacraments was quite pragmatic—it not only made married life possible but also allowed members of the covenant to conform outwardly to official Orthodoxy—but was theologically perplexing, as the adherents of rival covenants pointed out. Yet however pragmatic or deceptive marriage and baptism in the Orthodox Church may seem, there was a theological justification. Although no known source actually sets it out, the justification follows directly from the Spasovites' core beliefs. The other priestless covenants held that any contact with the official church, which was at best heretical and at worst the domain of the Antichrist, endangered their immortal souls. But they believed that baptism and confession could be administered by laymen in a time of need—for example, when priests were lacking. Spasovites, who insisted that God's grace and all of the sacraments had expired, could not use that sacramental loophole.

On the other hand, since there was nothing at all that they could do to save themselves from eternal damnation, the use of an official Orthodox priest as a matter of convenience put them in no more danger of perdition than they already faced. We know from the Fedoseev leader Feodosii Vasiliev that other priestless Old Believers reasoned in that way. In 1701, he wrote a letter reprimanding Fedoseevites who justified taking the Eucharist alongside the officially Orthodox because "in the present communion there is neither holiness nor profanation."[26] Spasovite elders probably constructed an analogous syllogism about resorting to Orthodox priests for marriage and baptism. The thinking of Spasovite peasants was probably summed up in Spasovite sayings on the matter of baptism by a heretical priest: "He may be a heretic, but he's a priest"; "He may be Satan himself, but he's in chasuble and it's not a simple peasant who's baptizing."[27] They could have said the same thing about the Orthodox priest who married them: a priest added dignity and ceremony to the occasion.

Two other witnesses who spent time with the Old Believers in the Nizhnii Novgorod forests in the second half of the eighteenth century tell us something of the Spasovites after their initial phase. Gavriil Andreev, a student who ran away from the Slaviano-Latin School in Nizhnii Novgorod, spent most of 1760 listening to talk by the many different Old Believers in the forests. Gavriil, age twenty-one when interrogated in the diocesan consistory in December 1760, reported that Old Believer elders frequently gathered for disputations, during which "they cursed each other and fought." He found it difficult to follow their arguments, he said, but he did understand the difference between the Nothing-ites and those he called Rebaptizers, which in this context most likely refers to the Pomorsk covenant. Unlike other priestless, the Nothing-ites did not rebaptize converts, said Gavriil, because, in their view, "there are no sacraments on Earth, they have been taken up to heaven."[28] His description of relations between Spasovite (and other) lay elders and their followers out in the world is more interesting. Parties of followers came to the forests for instruction in the faith for several weeks at a time, and sometimes husbands and wives alternated: when the husbands returned home, their wives and children trooped to the woods.[29] By the 1760s, the Spasovites, as well as other Old Believer covenants, had sturdy networks linking their religious centers to the surrounding lay population.

According to an account published in 1794 by Andrei Ioannov (also known as A. I. Zhuravlev), an Old Believer who became an Orthodox priest, "entire regiments of monks and nuns" traveled through those same forests, while "mobs of single women and wives who have destroyed their marriages through permanent celibacy" wandered about.[30] Surely that is hyperbole, but given Gavriil's earlier testimony, there is no reason to doubt that in the late eighteenth century, the Nizhnii Novgorod forests were both dense with sketes and heavily trafficked by pilgrims. A 1788 report from the Semenov district court to the governor of Nizhnii Novgorod province put the number of Old Believer sketes in the district at fifty-four and the number of their permanent inhabitants at eight thousand.[31] Probably there were more residents than that, since the forests in the Semenov district were notoriously impenetrable and the forest-dwellers went into hiding when government or church officials approached. Ioannov-Zhuravlev claimed that most of those traveling the woods were priested Old Believers, and all sources agree that the priested far outnumbered the priestless in Nizhnii Novgorod's trans-Volga districts. He had little more to say about the Spasovites than what was already known: they had originally been called Kozma-ites, and they believed the Antichrist reigned, the end times had begun, God's grace and sacraments had vanished, and they could do no more than put their trust in the Savior. About marriage he said only that the Spasovites, like the Filippovtsy, treated their married followers indulgently.[32] Spasovites married in Orthodox churches, probably followed by a penance.[33]

Ioannov-Zhuravlev's testimony is a useful reminder that Spasovite women were not the only ones who chose never to marry or, if married, sometimes took up a celibate life. In Kuplia parish, as we know, nineteenth-century Pomorsk women were also marriage-averse. The unmarried women whom Ioannov-Zhuravlev describes as tramping about the forest seem to have included not only those committed to a full-time religious life but also others who were short- or long-term visitors to the forest, not permanent dwellers in sketes. For all we know, single and married-but-celibate crown peasant women from Kuplia parish who lived not many days away from some of the skete-filled forests of Nizhnii Novgorod province may have joined in the pilgrimages that Gavriil Andreev described and Ioannov-Zhuravlev implied.

Nineteenth-century sources tell us that Spasovite marriages were celebrated by Orthodox priests and that even though Spasovites did not consider the marriage ceremony to be a sacrament, they held marriage to be both binding for life and sacred. Because confession and communion were requirements for an Orthodox marriage, Spasovites acted out those sacraments in an Orthodox church but did penance afterward. Most used either Orthodox priests or midwives to baptize infants, although there were some who baptized their own children, practiced self-baptism, or avoided baptism altogether. Those who turned to Orthodox priests for infant baptism distributed "sacramental alms" to members of their covenant during the baptism and asked the recipients to pray that God make good the sacramental imperfection. They read rather than chanted (the Orthodox manner) worship service. In fact, they did not hold community worship; they believed it a usurpation of priestly office for a layman to lead a service or to chant like a priest. Instead, they read services individually (and presumably also as families). Rather than gathering for worship, Spasovites gathered for discussion. They confessed their sins individually, sometimes to pre-Nikonian icons, sometimes to each other, sometimes in the open air. One subcovenant, known as the Hole-in-the-Wallers (*dyrniki*) confessed outdoors facing east or, during inclement weather, through a hole in the eastern wall of their cabins. At least some of them confessed by reciting a confessional text used by hermit monks: an extended prayer for the absolution of multiple but unspecified sins.

Spasovites accepted converts based on a few repetitions of seven ritual bows and the promise to pray with no one other than fellow Spasovites. In principle, they were to avoid association (eating, drinking, worshiping) with the officially Orthodox and members of other priestless covenants, but we know that in practice, in households of mixed faith, shunning was not always practical. They were forbidden to consume food made with yeast or hops, potatoes, and some other fare. They wore plain dark clothes; particolored garments were banned, as were particolored sacks. The crown of Spasovite men's heads was shaven when they came of age. Most of these practices surely dated from the eighteenth century. As was the case in every other Old Believer covenant, some Spasovites adopted different rules, based on their own understanding of pre-Nikonian Orthodox texts, or because (as with the many variations on baptism) there was no obviously correct way to live a Christian life in a world devoid of sacraments.[34]

One reason for the local variations in confessional and baptismal practice was that Spasovites lacked—at least insofar as available sources tell us—institutionalized leadership. Some sources deny they had any leaders at all, but government officials who investigated Old Believers in the mid-nineteenth century could name a few, and we can identify at least some of the leaders of the conflicting Spasovite parties at the time of the schism in the covenant in the 1840s. What does seem to be true is that there was no acknowledged central leadership (such as the priestless Fedoseevites and Pomorsk had, for instance) that ruled on matters of doctrine and that Spasovite communities in the villages generally had no chosen or appointed pastoral leaders (*nastavniki*). That was a clear departure from practice in other Old Believer covenants. Identifiable local leaders were, for the most part, urban merchants, and their positions were probably based as much on their socioeconomic standing as on their religious authority.[35]

In the 1840s, the main body of Spasovites split into the Spasovites of the Great Rite (*Bol'shogo nachala*), sometimes called Neo-Spasovites (*Novospasovtsy*), and the Spasovites of the Lesser Rite (*Malogo nachala*), also known as the Underground netovtsy (*Glukhaia netovshchina*).[36] *Glukhaia* here refers to the way in which Spasovites were difficult to detect because of their occasional resort to Orthodox priests and other practices that concealed them from view, such as not gathering for worship and not registering themselves as schismatics (which makes the openly declared Spasovites of Kuplia parish truly exceptional).[37] The split was triggered, at least in part, by a dispute over the ritual through which Spasovites admitted converts—not by rebaptizing them, as was the practice in most other priestless covenants, but by requiring the convert to perform one or more repetitions of the rite of seven deep bows. Shaken by the constant attacks by polemicists from the rebaptizing covenants, who pointed out that "except a man be born of water and of Spirit, he cannot enter the kingdom of God" (John, chapter 3, verse 5), some sought an alternative. Those who broke with Spasovite tradition continued to reject the rebaptism of converts, on the grounds that some ecumenical councils had ruled that heretics who had received Trinitarian baptism ("in the name of the Father, and of the Son, and of the Holy Spirit") need not be rebaptized, but at a council in the city of Gorokhovets (within hailing distance of Kuplia parish) sometime in the 1840s, they replaced the seven-bow rite with a ritual established in the early seventeenth century in which a rightly baptized but otherwise heretical convert formally abjured his heresy. They became the Spasovites of the Great Rite, with Avvakum Onisimov (Komissarov) at some point becoming their spiritual leader. Because of their conversion ritual, they were popularly known as Abjurers (*otritsanty*). Lesser Rite Spasovites pointed out that the abjuration ritual also required that a priest anoint the convert with myrrh and that since neither priest nor holy myrrh were available, the innovation was uncanonical.[38]

The Great Rite Spasovites also made many other changes to long-established Spasovite beliefs and practices. They introduced monasticism (while claiming monks had founded and had always been at the center of the Spasovite covenant), an innovation that trailed only the differences in the conversion ritual in polemics between the rival Spasovite covenants. They introduced elders who functioned much like and were popularly called priests, creating something like a hierarchy; chapels and community worship; confession in the presence of elders in place of solitary confession[39]; baptism of infants by the elders rather than by Orthodox priests or midwives; and a priestless marriage ceremony based on parental blessing. Indeed, the Great Rite Spasovites banned any contact with Orthodox priests. And while from some time in the eighteenth century the Spasovites had tolerated marriage, Onisimov-Komissarov taught that marriage was a positive necessity.[40]

A lengthy 1874 Great Rite manuscript, *The Book of Rules* (*Kniga naritsaemaia pravila*), sets out theological justifications for most of those innovations and more; it treated spiritual communion (rather than physical consumption of the Eucharist) and anointment with myrrh, as well as baptism, marriage, and confession, as genuine sacraments.[41] The Great Rite Spasovites had created an entirely new covenant that bore no resemblance to the original. They clung to the name as the warrant of their historical legitimacy. They could support that claim only with their spurious chronicle of monks descended from the founders of the covenant at the very origin of the schism in the Russian church, and the chronicle itself was the final component of *The Book of Rules.*

The arguments between Great Rite and Lesser Rite Spasovites, at least as they have been preserved in early twentieth-century texts, centered on the conversion ritual and monasticism.[42] Those texts are completely silent about marriage. The one hint that marriage was a point of contention comes in the account of an outsider, allegedly an Old Believer peasant who spoke at length with representatives of both rites but, in the end (so he claimed), reasoned his way to accepting the legitimacy of the official Orthodox Church. He quoted Onisimov (Komissarov) as saying (in denunciation of the Fedoseev and Filippov covenents, which formally rejected marriage) that "inasmuch as death exists among us, marriage is indispensable; with its end, the human race would also end in one century. Against God's commandment, *be fruitful and multiply, and fill the earth, and possess it* (Gen. 1), they are destroyers of the human race."[43] Komissarov was not criticizing the Lesser Rite Spasovites because they did accept marriage, but his was not a position that would welcome widespread abstention from marriage by the women of his covenant. In reporting this and other discussions with Spasovite leaders, the alleged peasant must, of course, have fabricated the dialogue, but much of what he says, and the leaders of both rites he names, are reported in other sources as well.

What little we know about the origins of the Spasovite schism indicates it was preceded by years of debate at a number of conclaves in cities along the Volga. It seems likely that the council in Gorokhovets that codified the practices of the Great Rite covenant created the new creed not from scratch but by stitching together heterodox practices (heterodox in the Spasovite context) that had already been adopted by one Spasovite group or another. The person credited with introducing the renunciation rite, Aleksandr Svetov of Simbirsk, on the middle course of the Volga, learned of it while spending time with his brother, who was conducting business in the Ottoman Empire. Svetov also tonsured himself a monk while there. He then wrote to two acquaintances in the city of Gorbatov, urging them to adopt the renunciation ritual, and they invited him to come to Gorbatov because they knew nothing about it.[44]

Gorbatov, on the Oka River just over the border between Vladimir and Nizhnii Novgorod provinces, is only twenty-four straight-line kilometers due east of Gorokhovets (but more than seventy kilometers by river, southward down the Kliazma, northward up the Oka). Gorbatov both abutted the Gorokhovets district and was home to presumably authoritative Spasovites whom Svetov assumed to be sympathetic to the changes he wanted to introduce in the covenant. Other leaders of the Great Rite Spasovites were located in Kovrov, roughly one hundred kilometers west of Gorokhovets on the Kliazma River. Onbisimov-Komissarov, some years later, regularly spent time in a cell near Kovrov.[45] And although we do not know the names of any Spasovites in Gorokhovets itself, there must have been some because they hosted the council that formally adopted the Great Rite rules.

This evidence warrants the hypothesis that the abrupt reversal of the avoidance of marriage by Spasovite women in Kuplia parish around 1830–34 had something to do with a gathering reform movement among the Spasovites in that part of Vladimir province and neighboring Nizhnii Novgorod province. Such a connection would explain the apparent simultaneity with which Spasovite women in the three appanage villages of the parish began to marry around 1830; unlike the gradual spread of aversion to marriage in Sluchkovo and Alshkovo in the eighteenth century, the resumption of marriage seems to have been an immediate response to a change in doctrine. And it appears, too, that most Kuplia parish Spasovites welcomed the change, with only a few young women continuing stubbornly to avoid marriage.[46]

In the early nineteenth century, the Spasovites there had emerged from the underground and declared their true beliefs. (They may have done the same in the eighteenth century, even as the priests then labeled them generic schismatics.) Spasovites so open about their beliefs were just the sort likely to welcome the remaking of the covenant and may indeed have been among those who championed the reforms. We know further that in the second half of the nineteenth century, at least one of the Spasovite leaders in the Gorokhovets district was associated with a Great Rite leader in Kovrov. We know, too, from our sources for the second half of the nineteenth century— reports by anti–Old Believer missionaries—that Spasovites were then the most numerous of all Old Believers in the district; unfortunately, the missionaries did not distinguished between Great and Lesser Rite Spasovites and may not have known the difference.[47] On the other hand, we know that at least through 1850, Kuplia Spasovite men continued to marry in the Orthodox Church because the 1850 census enumerator left young Spasovite wives in their census households rather than omitting them, as he did Pomorsk wives.

The resumption of marriage may not have been particularly controversial because women in many traditional Spasovite communities soon began to marry, too. A Ministry of Internal Affairs official who investigated Old Believers in Iaroslavl province in the 1850s reported, for example, that Spasovites considered sexual relations between spouses to be sinful after a certain age.[48] He did not mention which branch of the Spasovites held this attitude; probably he was referring to Lesser Rite Spasovites and did not understand that this attitude was actually a marriage practice already adopted by some other priestless Old Believers—that is, marriage and procreation while young, with spousal separation sometime in middle age followed by celibacy and the status of fully fledged members of the faith.[49]

As a particularly well-informed source, Archimandrite Pavel "Prusskii" of the Edinoverie St. Nicholas Monastery in Moscow—a member of the Fedoseev covenant by birth, a monk and head of a Fedoseev monastery in the Mazurian Lakes district in East Prussia in the 1850s, and a pro-marriage Pomorsk Old Believer in the 1860s before affiliating with the Edinoverie chapter of the official Orthodox Church in 1867—reported in the mid-1880s, that was precisely the practice among Lesser Rite Spasovites.[50] Other reliable sources from the second half of the century report that Lesser Rite Spasovites, like their Great Rite opponents, had introduced a priestless marriage service.[51] On the other hand, a brief Fedoseev denunciation of Spasovite errors, published in 1915, singles out baptism and marriage by Orthodox priests as especially grievous Spasovite malpractices.[52] Probably the Fedoseevite was recycling a traditional but now largely outdated indictment, but there were, in fact, some Spasovites (referred to as "Underground" or *Glukhaia* Nothing-ites) who continued to wed and baptize their children in Orthodox churches.[53]

The schism among the Spasovites provides the likely context in which to understand the resumption of marriage by women from Spasovite households but does not explain why they stopped marrying in the eighteenth century. In fact, nothing we know about Spasovite doctrine, from the moment sometime after 1730 when they decided marriage in an Orthodox church was legitimate, required or even encouraged Spasovite village women to practice celibacy. Very few sources even demonstrate an awareness that large numbers of Spasovite women refused to marry. Pavel Prusskii wrote that when Lesser Rite Spasovites baptized their newborns in an Orthodox church, their *keleinitsy*—single women, characteristic of many Old Believer covenants, who lived in small cabins called cells outside the village or sometimes near their family's cabins and often taught the faith as well as reading and writing—handed out alms to poor old men and women and asked them to pray that God make complete the baptism in the church.[54] He did not go on to suggest that single adult women were unusually numerous among the Spasovites. So far as I know, only the eighth volume of the official history of the Ministry of Interior, published in 1863 and devoted entirely to the ministry's efforts to combat schismatics, noted of the Spasovites (in Simbirsk and Saratov provinces) that "unmarried maidens, enjoying great influence, are especially numerous" among them.[55] That information came from an unusually observant government official in the 1850s.[56] Of course, it may be that by the 1850s, most younger women in both Spasovite covenants were marrying and that most of the Spasovite spinsters the official noticed were women who had avoided marriage in the 1830s, 1840s, and earlier.

Vladimir Mainov, a specialist in Mordva ethnography who also wrote about Russian religious dissidents, apparently stumbled upon a Spasovite community whose views, although divergent from the Spasovite mainstream, may help us understand the earlier Spasovite attitude toward marriage.[57] Around 1870, Mainov sought out these Spasovites in northern Olonets province because he had heard that they practiced self-immolation; their settlement was five days' travel (he claimed) from the nearest village, through forest and bog and unknown to government officials.[58] Their elder, Abrosim, told Mainov that while his group respected the early Old Believer self-immolators, he did not approve of suicide because it accomplished nothing. Like other traditional Spasovites, he believed there were no sacraments, thus no way to win God's favor; in Abrosim's view, God was as indifferent to martyrdom as to prayer. He did say, however, that if the government tracked the community down, they would have no choice but to commit collective suicide by fire. Members called themselves *Zhivye pokoiniki*—the Living Dead—which Mainov's guide, one of the community, explained actually meant "those living in peace" (*pokoi*).[59] That was an obvious deception (although apparently not obvious to Mainov), probably what members of the group had been instructed to say when anyone asked them about their beliefs. Their songs revealed a singularly morose view of life on earth:

> *There is no salvation on earth, none!*
> *Deceit alone rules, deceit!*
> *Death alone can save us, death!*
> *Not even God is in the world, not!*
> *The madness can't be numbered, can't!*
> *Death alone can save us, death!*
> *There is no life in the world, none!*
> *Only vengeance have the brothers, vengeance!*
> *Death alone can save us, death!*[60]

Although their religious roots were in the Spasovite covenant, the Living Dead, like other small Spasovite subgroups, held some singular beliefs. Elder Abrosim, for instance, preached a Manichean view of good and evil: God was responsible for everything good, the equally powerful Satan for everything evil. The Living Dead were also indifferent to the various proscriptions that other Spasovites and almost all Old Believers imposed to stave off the pollution and impurity so easily transmitted in a world over which the Antichrist presided, because, like prayer, they were pointless. As Abrosim explained, "It's not a sin because there's no one to sin against."[61] This uncharacteristically liberal attitude toward the practices of daily life was founded on the hopelessness of the Spasovites' situation. For that matter, the Living Dead had removed themselves from most sources of pollution by living in profound isolation.

The belief that they lived in a world of pervasive, unremitting evil that could be escaped only by death, and with no sacramental tools that offered a connection to God, naturally shaped the Living Dead's attitudes toward birth and death and certainly toward marriage, too, but Mainov failed to follow up on any of the relevant clues. One member of the community died while Mainov was visiting, and he noticed that the funeral was not accompanied by the customary lamentation; in fact, those in attendance seemed happy. Death as welcome release was obviously no mere consoling phrase but a conviction so strongly held that it made mourning utterly inappropriate. Mainov counted only four children in the community (he does not tell us how many adults there were or in how many households they lived; however, the impression he leaves is that this was a rather substantial village for those parts, so there may have been twenty or more households), and he asked why that was so. His guide told him that women swallowed a powder that prevented pregnancy. Abrosim said that was nonsense and attributed the infertility of the women to climate, heavy labor, and food shortages (though Mainov observed that the village looked remarkably prosperous). Abrosim added that when a child was born, the entire village lamented because "for us life is a bitter misery."[62] When Mainov pointed out that such an attitude would eventually lead to the demise of humanity, Abrosim replied, in effect, "So what?" Obviously, the Living Dead were deliberately limiting births, either by avoiding marriage altogether or by avoiding pro-creation within marriage. Abrosim himself claimed to have been married for thirty-eight years and to have had no children.

We can extrapolate, cautiously, from the self-isolated Living Dead to Spasovites alive in the world. Pavel Prusskii, for instance, asserted that the Lesser Rite, traditionalist Spasovites, were the most religiously strin-gent of all Old Believers, with the greatest number of pollution-deflecting proscriptions. He singled out their dark dress bereft of all ornament as the symbol of their zealous rigor.[63] Spasovite traditionalists themselves most likely understood their plain dark dress to be an emblem of despair at living in a joyless world abandoned by God. It was but a short step from existen-tial hopelessness to skepticism about the propriety of marriage and not just because marriage involved an inappropriate gratification of the flesh in a sorrowful world, as some other priestless Old Believers held (or had earlier, in the eighteenth century). Was it right, Spasovites may have asked, to bear children condemned to live in a world without God, sacraments, and a fight-ing chance for salvation?

A different conjecture might locate Spasovite women's rejection of marriage in the long-standing Orthodox tradition that privileged monas-ticism over marriage. Old Believers, who considered themselves the only true Orthodox, considered that tradition theirs. Yet a monastic life, even as a member of a lay female community (in Old Believer sketes, for instance), required withdrawal from the world and from dangerous contact with the opposite sex. A lesser tradition placed celibacy within marriage above pro-creation, but in the village, that could be no more than a hypothetical ideal, not a reality, as witnessed in the termination of celibate marriage among Kuplia Spasovites after a single generation. There was also a lay tradition, among both Orthodox and Old Believer village women, of celibacy as a religious calling, but no precedent for the staggeringly large number of Kuplia parish spinsters.[64] Orthodox teaching on celibacy may have provided the general backdrop, but there was nothing in Orthodox doctrine or practice that anticipated the celibate Spasovite women in Kuplia parish. That suggests a specifically Spasovite impetus.

Because so little is known about Spasovites in the eighteenth century, it is in principle possible that some leaders of the covenant, after they had decided that marriage could be celebrated by Orthodox priests, nevertheless encouraged women to avoid marriage. It is more difficult to explain away the complete lack of evidence of an anti-marriage doctrine among nineteenth-century Spasovites because from the middle of the eighteenth century onward, polemics over marriage within and between covenants roiled priestless communities. Moreover, if an Old Believer covenant opposed marriage (and refused to pray for the health of the ruler), government and official church classified it as "especially harmful," meriting special scrutiny.[65] It is true that Spasovites have not attracted much scholarly attention; it is conceivable that Spasovite documents recommending that women not marry may eventually be found.

However, from what we do know about Spasovite teachings on marriage, it is more reasonable to presume that Spasovite laywomen pioneered resistance to marriage in the villages and that whoever made such decisions among the Spasovites approved but—pragmatists that they were—did not make a ban on female marriage an article of their creed. Refusal to marry was certainly compatible with Spasovite doctrine. While marriage by an Orthodox priest (or, in the second half of the nineteenth century, a priestless wedding ceremony) was acceptable, Spasovites (of the Lesser Rite) never conceded that marriage was a sacrament. Many also believed the Antichrist was present and that the end times had begun, central pillars of anti-marriage theology in other covenants.[66]

It is not difficult to imagine how anti-marriage sentiment took hold among Kuplia parish women. The Old Belief took root around Gorokhovets before the end of the seventeenth century. A huge schismatic-ridden forest lay just to the north, and the even vaster Nizhnii Novgorod forests began not far to the east. Those forests were the site of intense debates among Old Believers of all sorts. We know that many women took up residence in forest skites, where they (or most of them, probably) led celibate lives whether they had married earlier or not. Certainly some women eventually returned from the forest to their native villages; certainly female pilgrims such as those reported by Gavriil Andreev in 1760 sought religious counsel in the forests. In an atmosphere of deep religious anxiety, amid rumors of the Antichrist and anticipation of the Second Coming, it is not at all surprising that marriage-denouncing elders persuaded a few women in Kuplia parish in the early eighteenth century that marriage was a great sin, one to be avoided so they could prepare themselves for the end of days. Or the women may have made the decision by themselves without prompting. There is no way to know whether that first generation of marriage-averse village women belonged to any particular covenant. Perhaps they were generic Old Believers who had difficulty distinguishing one covenant from another.

Something changed early in the second half of the eighteenth century, when the number of women avoiding marriage in Sluchkovo and Aleshkovo surged and the tax censuses and confession registers suggest that the Old Believer households had a separate community life. In those two villages, female marriage aversion then grew steadily and had become wellnigh universal in Sluchkovo by 1795 and among Spasovites in Aleshkovo by 1830, by which date it had swamped Peshkovo as well. Almost certainly what changed was that in the second half of the eighteenth century the Old Believers became an organized community (or communities), within which female marriage-avoidance became the norm. We don't know what precipitated the formation of these communities. Perhaps charismatic missionaries used free-floating suspicion of the official church and anxiety about marriage to gather Kuplia parish Old Believers into an organized group or groups. Perhaps the change was brought about by the cumulative impact of years of organized peasant contact with forest elders. The fact that it took half a century for female abstention from marriage to become universal among the Spasovite households of Sluchkovo, and longer still in Aleshkovo, is further, indirect evidence that non-marriage was adopted by local initiative of the Spasovite women themselves rather than in obedience to their covenant's teachings.

The Pomorsk women who resisted marriage in Kuplia parish in the nineteenth century probably did so because of the Spasovite example. They knew that their covenant accepted marriage: their brothers married and, at least by the 1830s, did so using the Pomorsk priestless wedding service. Pomorsk women must have eschewed marriage because, around Kuplia, the local Spasovite rule—men marry, women don't—had become the gold standard of female righteousness and religious zeal. That was no doubt the reason, in the story I extracted from confession registers back in chapter 3, the nominally Orthodox Matrena Gerasimova, her son Aleksei and her granddaughter Vassa had over time carefully falsified their biological relationships so that in the parish records they appeared to be celibate siblings. If Pomorsk women followed the lead of Spasovite women, among Spasovites the pressure on young women not to marry must have been even more compelling. Indeed, while in the late eighteenth century we can identify women from presumptively Spasovite households in and around Kuplia parish who chose to marry, I can find no such examples in the early nineteenth century—until the 1830s, when almost all Spasovite young women married. If, as I have argued, Spasovite parents did not control their daughters' marital choices in the late eighteenth century, it seems that their local religious community increasingly, and ultimately completely, did. Yet most of the young women who avoided marriage probably thought they had good reason to remain single, believing as they did that they lived in a God-forsaken world devoid of God's grace and sacraments where they could only hope that their indifferent maker might, for reasons only he could know, take an interest in them. That sort of thinking would have been fully in accord with the existential despair that underlay Kozma Andreev's teachings and that continued into the second half of the nineteenth century among the Living Dead in the Olonets woods.

NOTES

1. The document from 1874 is in IaGIAM, in two identical texts: Sobranie rukopisei, no. 9056, ll. 724–39, and no. 17149, ll. 25–40. It is discussed and quoted from in Mal'tsev, "Maloizvestnyi istochnik," and Mal'tsev, *Staroobriadcheskie bespopovskie*, pp. 410–13. The chronicle from circa 1894 is in Rudakov, "'Drugopriemnoe postrizhenie.'"

2. Kamisarov [*sic*], *Vechnaia Pravda*, ll. 230–2410b. Pages are numbered manuscript-style, on the recto side only. Komissarov claimed that the text was a written version of answers that he had given to eight questions posed by Orthodox clergy at an 1892 disputation in the Poshekhonie district; it lays out—on both sides of 392 pages—the basic issues that produced the schism in the Russian Orthodox Church and a theological defense of practices peculiar to Komissarov's branch of the Spasovites. Komissarov was from the Poshekhonie district, and such a disputation may have taken place. The spelling of his name is subject to considerable variation: his patronymic is sometimes given as Anisimovich, e.g., on the title page of *Vechnaia Pravda*; in the nineteenth century, his surname was usually spelled Komisarov.

3. For analysis of the various texts, and of the sources that the defenders claim support their version of Spasovite history, see Bushnell, "Proiskhozhdenie Spasova soglasiia." On the Osinovsk skete, see Mel'nikov, "Otchet," pp. 137–38. Mel'nikov was the official who destroyed it.

4. Komissarov argues that point in *Vechnaia Pravda*, pp. 243–254ob. Part of his argument is that "simple" monks—monks who were not priests—had the right to tonsure. He cites numerous texts to support that contention. This was critical to his argument, because all Spasovites believed that the Nikonian reforms had eliminated the possibility of a consecrated priesthood.

5. *Besedy staroobriadtsev Spasova soglasiia, byvshie v Nizhegorodskoi*, pp. 115–18. Andrei Antipin, the Lesser Rite leader, challenged Andrei Konovalov, speaking for the Great Rite, on the claim that there had been Spasovite monks from the beginning; Konovalov admitted that he could not offer proof because there were no documents, only a tradition (*Besedy staroobriadtsa Spasova soglasiia V. A. Voikina s A. A. Antipinym*). Voikin, speaking for the Great Rite, steadfastly defended the claim early in the third session, which was devoted entirely to the issue of monasticism.

6. I did not myself make an exhaustive search for manuscript sources, but both Nikolai Ivanovskii, *Rukovodstvo po istorii*, part 1, p. 127, a scholar specializing in the Old Belief, and especially A. I. Mal'tsev, *Staroobriadcheskie bespopovskie*, p. 410, a prodigious researcher in Old Believer manuscripts, noted the paucity of Spasovite sources. So did Sergey Zenkovsky, *Russkoe staroobriadchestvo*, p. 474, but he had no access to archives.

7. "Barely literate" is the characterization of an early hostile witness (Florov, *Oblichenie na raskolnikov*, p. 25); Florov was in the Kerzhensk district at the same time as Kozma, but he may never have met him and may simply have repeated what he heard from others. Zenkovsky, *Russkoe staroobriadchestvo*, p. 473, repeats Florov's assertion. Smirnov, *Vnutrennie voprosy*, pp. 085–090, seems to have been the first to demonstrate that the Kozma of Levshutin's denunciation was indeed the founder of the covenant later known as the Spasovites. There is a lengthy account of the interrogation of Kozma in Esipov, *Raskol'nich'i dela*, vol. 1, pp. 557–608. Both Levshutin and Florov (*Oblichenie na raskolnikov*, p. 25) reported that Kozma Andreev had a close associate, also named Kozma. That is the basis for concluding that Kozma Andreev was the founder of the covenant.

8. Dmitrii, Metropolitan of Rostov and Iaroslavl', *Rozysk o raskol'nicheskoi*, pp. 64–65.

9. Ibid., p. 606.

10. Pososhkov, *Zerkalo ochevidnoe (Redaktsiia polnaia)*, vol. 1, pp. vii, 265; vol. 2, p. 51; Kafengauz, *I. T. Pososhkov*, pp. 18–19.

11. Feofilakt (Lopatinskii), *Oblichenie nepravdy raskolnicheskoi, Obiavleniia*, separately paginated at the end, l. 40b. The date of writing is given in ibid., l. 60b— the last page in the book—where Feofilakt wrote: "The above described fruits of malice . . . having grown from 1666 to 1725." It is unclear why the book wasn't published immediately. For most of the decade from 1730 to 1740, Feofilakt was either

under investigation or incarcerated in connection with an unrelated conflict with Feofan Prokopovich. He was released in 1740 and died in 1741. On Feofilakt's life, see *Russkii biograficheskii slovar'*, t. 25, pp. 457–66. For a brief discussion of *The Pomorsk Responses*, see Crummey, *Old Believers and the World of the Antichrist*, pp. 85–89.

12. Florov does not say how long he spent in the forest. However, he was chosen by his covenant, the *D'iakonovtsy*, to respond to questions presented to them by Pitirim—then an anti–Old Believer missionary, subsequently bishop of Nizhnii Novgorod—in 1716. According to Gurii, *Skazanie o missionerskikh trudakh*, pp. 42–43, Florov was chosen because of his ability to write; presumably he had been associated with the Diakonovites long enough to be entrusted with so important, and also dangerous, a task. The Old Believer bibliographer Pavel Liubopitnyi claimed that the Pomorsk leader Andrei Denisov composed the answers for the Diakonovites (Liubopytnyi, "Istoricheskii slovar'," p. 123).

13. Florov, *Oblichenie na raskolnikov*, pp. 2–4, 24–25. Florov claimed that the netovtsy believed that the Eucharist and monasticism had disappeared after the Seventh Ecumenical Council (Second Council of Nicea), the last of the ecumenical councils recognized by the Orthodox Church. Florov also asserted that the netovtsy tonsured themselves and placed monastic robes in front of an icon of the Savior and then put them on. Since they believed that monasticism had expired, the habit was probably meant to signify asceticism and withdrawal from the world. Shaving the crown of the head and plain dark clothing was required of all Spasovite adult men in the nineteenth century. Levshutin testified that Kozma said there was no reason to pray for those who died out in the world; this is perhaps how Levshutin understood Kozma's teaching that there was no reason to pray for reunification with the Orthodox (Esipov, *Raskol'nich'i dela*, t. 1, p. 561).

14. Zenkovsky, *Russkoe staroobriadchestvo*, pp. 155–56, 473–74.

15. Ibid. Zenkovsky suggests that Kozma Medvedevskii and Kozma Andreev may have been one and the same person, but even the evidence he cites does not support that hypothesis. Smirnov, *Vnutrennie voprosy*, p. 090, and in a somewhat different way "Proiskhozhdenie samoistreblenia," pp. 628–29, also suggests that Medvedevskii and Andreev may have been one and the same Kozma. For that argument to hold, however, the story of Kozma Andreev's life as he and as his followers told it would have to have been entirely fictitious.

16. Evfrosin, *Otrazitel'noe pisanie*, pp. 10–11 (Evfrosin also accused Kozma's followers of gluttony, fornication, and the use of women as preachers); Florov, *Oblichenie na raskolnikov*, p. 26; Smirnov, *Vnutrennie voprosy*, pp. xxiv–xxv, pp. 88–90.

17. One brief account of Spasovite beliefs published in 1786 calls the covenant both Spasovites and netovtsy while asserting that the founder was unknown (Bogdanovich, *Istoricheskoe izvestie*, p. 39).

18. Pitirim, *Prashchitsa dukhovnaia*, ll. 110b, 30, 380, 408.

19. Florov, *Oblichenie na raskolnikov*, p. 84. The only thing he said about these Spasovites was that they were priestless. He characterized them that way as if to explain who they were, since he had not mentioned Spasovites earlier in his narrative.

If he had known Spasovites and netovtsy were one and the same covenant, he would have said so.

20. Mal'tsev, *Staroobriadcheskie bespopovskie soglasiia*, pp. 413–15. The writer does not name the covenant whose beliefs he defends, but Mal'tsev deduces, I believe correctly, that those beliefs were distinctly Spasovite.

21. *Opisanie dokumentov*, vol. 10 (1730), col. 648–49.

22. *Polnoe sobranie postanovlenii*, vol. 6, pp. 166–69; *Opisanie dokumentov*, vol. 8, col. 308–9.

23. Esipov, *Raskol'nich'i dela*, vol. 1, p. 561.

24. Mal'tsev, *Staroobriadcheskie bespopovskie soglasiia*, pp. 415–16.

25. *Polnoe sobranie postanovlenii*, vol. 6, pp. 166–69; *Opisanie dokumentov*, vol. 8, col. 309.

26. Smirnov, *Spory i razdeleniia*, p. 142.

27. Pavel, *Nikol'skogo edinovercheskogo monastyria inoka Pavla*, l. 170b. The author was most commonly referred to as Pavel Prusskii, but his lay name, Petr Lednev, is sometimes used for bibliographical purposes. While this is a printed book, pages are numbered manuscript-style, on the recto side of the page only.

28. "Rebaptizers" (*perekreshchevantsy*) could also refer to Fedoseevites or any other of the priestless sects that insisted on rebaptizing those converting from official Orthodoxy. This was a term commonly employed in government, official Orthodox, and Old Believer documents of the eighteenth and first half of the nineteenth centuries.

29. TsANO, f. 570, op. 554, 1760, d. 11, ll. 2–5. According to Gavriil, when Pomorsk and Spasovite women came to the forest, they committed adultery—"which they call an act of love and do not consider a sin"—with the schismatic novices. That seems to have been an unprompted statement, but it was possibly an answer to a question put to him by consistorial officials fishing for information that would confirm the widespread Orthodox conviction that priestless Old Believers were fornicators.

30. Zhuravlëv, *Polnoe istoricheskoe izvestie*, p. 212. This is the sixth edition; authorship in the first two editions (1794, 1795) was under his given name and patronymic, A[ndrei] Ioannov. Priested Old Believers did have monks and nuns, and Ioannov-Zhuravlev may have included in their numbers the elders and eldresses living in sketes.

31. Mel'nikov, "Otchet," pp. 111–12. The Semenov district certainly had more sketes than many other districts in the province but not all of them.

32. Zhuravlëv, *Polnoe istoricheskoe izvestie*, pp. 120, 123. Ioannov-Zhuravlev also observed that Spasovites were divided into three groups, but he did not describe them.

33. Ibid., pp. 122–23. He implies but does not state directly that Spasovites married in Orthodox churches. Another late eighteenth-century source confirms that by then Spasovites did so (*Nastavlenie pravil'no sostiazat'sia*, p. 24). This source was a manual on the basic doctrines of the various Old Believer covenants, with the biblical and other texts refuting those doctrines, so that seminary graduates would be prepared to confront Old Believers in their parishes. Bishop Simon of Riazan, who commissioned it,

died in 1804. Probably the work was first composed at the Riazan seminary in the eighteenth century.

34. GAIaO, f. 230, op. 1, ed. khr. 12878, ll. 12, 16, 27, 36, 44; Sipitysn [Introduction], *Sbornik pravitel'stvennykh*, pp. 10–12; Sipitsyn, "O raskole v Iaroslavskoi gubernii," pp. 90–93 (Sipystin was a Ministry of Interior official sent to investigate the state of the schism in Iaroslavl province in 1852); Mel'nikov, "Otchet," pp. 9, 104, 110, 232, 262, 269, 275; Pavel, *Nikol'skogo edinovercheskogo monastyria inoka*, ll. 150b–180b; *Krest'ianina Ivana Aleksandrova razgovory*, p. 28; Pavel, "Kratkie izvestiia," pp. 566–68; Pavel, "O imenuemoi glukhoi netovshchine," pp. 29–32; Smirnov, *Istoriia russkogo raskola*, pp. 122–24; Ivanovskii, *Rukovodstvo*, pp. 128–30; Ivanovskii, "Iz staroobriadcheskogo mira," pp. 323–24; "Prisoedinenie iz raskola"; Strel'bitskii, *Istoriia russkogo raskola*, pp. 125–26. A published edition of the confessional text Spasovites used was *Skitskoe pokaianie* [1909], a republication of a 1650 edition.

35. Zenkovskii, *Russkoe staroobriadchestvo*, p. 476; Sipitsyn, "O raskole v Iaroslavskoi gubernii," pp. 90–93; Mel'nikov, "Otchet," p. 104; *Krest'ianina Ivana Aleksandrova*, pp. 23, 29; A-v, "Nechto o bezpopovskikh sektakh, pp. 31–37; Ageeva, Robson, and Smiljanskaja, "Staroobriadtsy spasovtsy," p. 103.

36. "Lesser Rite" was probably a term coined by the Great Rite Spasovites. Traditional Spasovites, for good reason, considered Great Riters not to be Spasovites at all and so had no reason to adopt new terminology to distinguish themselves from those who had broken away. Nevertheless, these names were employed in some accounts of the Spasovites from the second half of the nineteenth century onward. I use them so that it will be clear which Spasovite covenant I am discussing.

37. That is one interpretation of the meaning of *glukhaia* in this phrase; see Smirnov, *Istoriia russkogo raskola staroobriadstva*, p. 121 (Smirnov gives a somewhat different interpretation of the term in *Vnutrennie voprosy*, p. 086); Ivanovskii, *Rukovodstvo*, p. 128. It is also supported by an early twentieth-century leader of the Great Rite Spasovites who argued, mendaciously, that the Lesser Rite Spasovites had descended not from real Spasovites but from a separate *glukhaia netovshchina* that had tried to remain concealed. See *Besedy staroobriadtsa Spasova soglasiia V. A. Voikina*, third discussion. Most commentators in both the nineteenth and twentieth centuries took *glukhaia* to be a reference to the Spasovites reading (silently or inaudibly) rather than chanting the service; see, for example, *Krest'ianina Ivana Aleksandrova*, p. 28, and *Staroobriadchestvo. Litsa, sobytiia*, p. 189. That seems more likely to be a folk etymology, although it is quite possible that some of the Spasovite folk explained the term that way.

38. *Krest'ianina Ivana Aleksandrova*, pp. 23–27, 29; Pavel, *Nikol'skogo edinovercheskogo monastyria inoka Pavla*, ll. 140b, 20; A-v, "Nechto o bezpopovskikh sektakh," pp. 32–35; Smirnov, *Istoriia russkogo raskola staroobriadst*, pp. 121, 123. *Besedy staroobriadtsa Spasova soglasiia V. A. Voikina* treats this issue at great length, as does *Besedy staroobriadetsev Spasova soglasiia*. There is a lengthy refutation of the Great Rite conversion ritual, which takes the form of responses to questions allegedly put by Spasovites with lengthy answers by a member of the Pomorsk covenant. Archivists at

the Manuscript Division of the Russian State Library have dated it to circa 1800, which cannot be correct; it probably dates from the 1840s (RGB OR, f. 98, no. 1552/1556).

39. The matter of confession comes up in the Great Rite genealogical chronicle. According to the author of the version written around 1874, reports that Spasovites did not confess to their elders were false. Rather, he said, when questioned by the authorities Spasovites never revealed who their confessors ("spiritual fathers" is the Russian phrase) were and, in fact, claimed they had none and that they confessed in isolation (IaGIAM, Sobranie rukopisei, no. 17149, l. 39). Mal'tsev, *Staroobriadcheskie bespopovskie*, p. 416, was taken in by this deceit.

40. It may be that the text of the priestless wedding service that the writer Nikolai Leskov published, which he identified as the service the Pomortsy used up and down the Volga and, he said, was first employed in the 1840s, was Spasovite rather than Pomorsk (Leskov, "Blagoslovennyi brak, pp. 499–515"). It bears no resemblance at all to any of the identifiably Pomorsk wedding services. If it did, in fact, begin to circulate during the 1840s, that would put its composition in the decade in which the Great Rite Spasovites established their new covenant and composed their genealogical chronicle. It seems unlikely that the service was Pomorsk in origin. It may, of course, have been used by some Pomorsk communities. Leskov himself said that it was used both by Pomorsk and mixed Old Believer communities. Leskov, very knowledgeable about Old Believers, was unaware of the earlier Pomorsk marriage services. On the marriage service and other practices of the Great Rite Spasovites, see A-v, "Nechto o bezpopovskikh sektakh," pp. 35–36; Pavel, *Nikol'skogo edinovercheskogo monastyria inoka*, l. 150b; Pavel, "Kratkie izvestiia," p. 568; Pavel, "Razgovor o vere," pp. 34–36; *Krest'ianina Ivana Aleksandrova*, pp. 21–22, 30, 49–50, and passim; Ivanovskii, *Rukovodstvo*, p. 131; Ivanovskii, "Iz staroobriadcheskogo mira," pp. 324–27; Strel'bitskii, *Istoriia russkogo raskola*, pp. 126–27; Murtaeva, "Staroobriadtsy," pp. 113–17; Ageeva, Robson, and Smiljanskaja, "Staroobriadtsy spasovtsy," pp. 104–7.

41. "Kniga naritsaemaia pravila" (IaGIAM, no. 9056, 747 ll.). This is the same manuscript that includes a copy of the spurious Neo-Spasovite chronicle of Spasovite monks.

42. Nizhnii Novgorod archaeographers have also collected late nineteenth-century disputational texts from the province. They are reviewed in Klochkova, "Put' samoopredeleniia." There were Spasovites who practiced (or defended as valid, in some circumstances) self-baptism.

43. *Krest'ianina Ivana Aleksandrova*, pp. 21–22; emphasis in the original.

44. Ibid., pp. 28–29; Smirnov, *Istoriia russkogo raskola*, p. 123; A-v, "Nechto o bezpopovskikh sektakh," p. 33.

45. *Krest'ianina Ivana Aleksandrova*, p. 13.

46. Perhaps they remained members of the Lesser Rite covenant. Some of the Lesser Rite leaders of the opposition to the Great Rite were from the same general area in Vladimir province, and an account from later in the nineteenth century puts members of both rites in the province (*Krest'ianina Ivana Aleksandrova*, pp. 23–26; Smirnov, *Istoriia russkogo raskola*, p. 124).

47. Ankudinov, "Gorokhovetskii uezd," pp. 266–68.

48. Sipitsyn, "O raskole v Iaroslavskoi gubernii," pp. 90–93.

49. That practice was known among the Filippovtsy, as reported (as long-standing practice) early in the second half of the nineteenth century. Efimenko, *Obychai i verovaniia*, pp. 527, 534 (originally published as *Materialy po etnografii russkogo naseleniia Arkhangel'skoi gubernii*, part 1, Moscow, 1877). That information came from the Pinega district of Arkhangelsk province. The same practice had taken root among Pomorsk in Viatka province, perhaps influenced by Filippovites in the same general area who called themselves Old Believers of the Pomorsk Heritage of the Filippovite Covenant (Ageeva et al., *Rukopisi Verkhokam'ia*, pp. 7–8). See also Rogers, *Old Faith*, pp. 47–48, 60–69, who describes the same Viatka Pomorsok practice. He argues that it was an adaptation to the particularly harsh persecution of marriage (or cohabitation) outside the Orthodox Church by the Stroganov overlords of much of that area. The fact that the same practice is reported among other covenants in other areas would seem to rule out that explanation.

50. Pavel, "Kratkie izvestiia," p. 568; Pavel, "O imenuemoi glukhoi netovshchine," p. 32.

51. *Krest'ianina Ivana Aleksandrova*, p. 30; Klochkova, "Put' samoopredeleniia," p. 219; see ibid., p. 226, for marriage services among the self-baptizing Spasovites. TsANO, f. 5, op. 50, d. 20055, ll. 1–19, is a 1911 investigation of a Spasovite community in the Ardatov district; the elected pastor (*nastavnik*) both performed the Spasovite marriage ceremony and baptized infants; this seems to have been a Lesser Rite congregation, but the documents do not identify it as such. Another case from the same year, in the Lukoianov district, is in TsANO, f. 5, op. 50, d. 20058.

52. Tulupov, *Istoriko-dogmaticheskii ocherk*. That Tulupov was a Fedoseevite at the time (he joined the Pomorsk covenant later) I take from Tulupov, *Put' zhizn*, pp. 6–7.

53. Klochkova, "Put' samoopredeleniia," p. 219. TsANO, f. 570, op. 559, 1886, d. 37, ll. 1–2, is a report on just such a Spasovite community that continued to use the local church for baptisms and weddings.

54. Pavel, "Kratkie izvestiia," p. 567. On Archimandrite Pavel up to his adherence to the official church, see Berenskii, *Arkhmandrit o. Pavel*, pp. 1–95.

55. Varadinov, *Istoriia Ministerstva*, vol. 8, p. 543. The volume's only other comment on Old Believer resistance to marriage was that among the Wanderers (*Stranniki*) in Iaroslavl province, women were disinclined to marry and, if they were serfs, their fathers sought to purchase their manumission so they could lead single lives undisturbed (ibid., p. 535). The Wanderers were numerically a much smaller covenant than the Spasovites. In the village of Sopelki, across the Volga from Iaroslavl and the center of the Wanderers' covenant between the late eighteenth century and at least the 1850s, 18 percent of the women twenty-five and above had never married in 1838, by Russian standards a very high level of resistance to marriage but far short of the level of resistance among the appanage peasants of Kuplia parish at the same time (GAIaO, f. 230, op. 1, d. 13639, ll. 489–93). I have not counted women living in the two Sopelki merchant households registered in Iaroslavl. This covenant was discovered,

by accident, only in 1849; as of 1838, there was no external pressure on or persecution of the Sopelki Wanderers.

56. *Sobranie postanovlenii po chasti raskola*, vol. 2, pp. 710–11.The report on the Old Believers in Simbirsk province was passed along to the synod, which then sent instructions to the Simbirsk bishop to take special measures against the schismatics, mentioning in particular the "spinster *keleinitsy*" and the Spasovites in general, who concealed themselves by accepting Orthodox baptism and marriage.

57. Mainov, "Zhivye pokoiniki."

58. Ibid., p. 747. To not reveal where this community lived, Mainov did not specify the province. However, two of the Spasovite songs he quotes in the article first appeared in his *Poezdka v Obonezh'e i Korelu*, p. 158. He inserts them at a point in the text when he is conversing with a peasant in whose cabin he was spending the night, near the ruins of the Pomorsk Vyg Lake monastery. The peasant tells the story of the persecution of a former nun of the former Pomorsk Leksa nunnery nearby and remarks that such persecution could only drive peaceful Pomorsk believers into the arms of sects with extreme views illustrated by the songs. Mainov implies but does not actually say that his interlocutor recited them, nor does he there identify the group whose views they were supposed to illuminate. Probably he encountered the Spasovite community on that same journey of exploration and perhaps sought them out because of what he had learned from the peasant that night. In the article, he says he heard rumors of the group while living in St. Petersburg.

59. Abrosim's group is not to be confused with the Skoptsy, who practiced castration and sometimes called themselves *zhivye mertvetsy* and were sometimes called *zhivye smertniki*—phrases that also translate as "the living dead" (Engelstein, *Castration*, pp. 14, 81, 253n104). Mainov had written earlier about the Skoptsy and had a good grasp of their history, beliefs, and practices (Mainov, "Skopcheskii eresiarkh"). If Abrosim's group were Skoptsy, he would have said so.

60. Mainov, "Zhivye pokoiniki," p. 765.

61. Ibid., p. 761.

62. Ibid., p. 757.

63. Pavel, *Nikol'skogo edinovercheskogo monastyria inoka*, ll. 8, 200b; Pavel, "O imenuemoi," p. 29.

64. Levin, *Sex*, pp. 36–88; Tul'tseva, "Chernichki," pp. 80–82; Gromyko, *Traditsionnye normy*, pp. 103–4.

65. See Mel'nikov, "Pis'ma o raskole," pp. 26–30 (originally published in *Severnaia pchela* in 1862). The question of whether the Spasovites should be classified as especially harmful was ruled on at least twice. In 1835 and 1857, Nicholas I and Alexander II, respectively, following the advice of Ministry of Interior officials, ruled that would do more harm than good (*Sobranie postanovlenii po chasti raskola*, 2nd ed., pp. 234–36, 525.

66. Pavel, "Kratkie Izvestiia," p. 566. Some Spasovites believed the Antichrist would appear physically only at the end of the world; others, that he was already present in the world in spirit.

CHAPTER 6

Baki: Resistance to Marriage on a Forest Frontier

In May 1799, Emperor Paul gave an estate at Baki, Kostroma province, as a gift to Countess Charlotte Lieven, former governess to his children. In January 1800, Lieven's manager Karl Hennemann issued a set of orders to the estate's serfs. Among them: fathers must give their daughters in marriage. He prefaced the order with an explanation. Charlotte's son Christoph had looked at the returns from the 1795 tax census, observed that there were many unmarried men and women, and ordered Hennemann to find out why that was so. The serfs had given a variety of explanations: their previous owner, Princess Elena Alekseevna Dolgorukova, had allowed parents to make the decisions about their children's marriages; parents, especially mothers, kept daughters at home for their labor; local priests charged more for marriage services than they could afford to pay. The count thereupon told Hennemann to ensure that all single men ages twenty to thirty-five and all single women from eighteen to twenty-five marry during the approaching Shrovetide.

Thus the order. Hennemann continued: Parents must put no obstacles in the way of marriage or try to bribe estate officials, and daughters must not abuse their right to consent. Girls who refused to marry worthy grooms by the appointed time would be sent to the countess in St. Petersburg and taught a trade, unless there were compelling reasons why they could not marry. Single women between twenty-five and thirty-five, depending on circumstances, would be put to work for the owner. If they were of bad conduct, however, they would be exiled, as would disorderly men. If a father was too poor to arrange his son's marriage, he would receive an interest-free loan from the communal charitable fund; if he was of good repute, the loan would be forgiven.[1] Hennemann also said he had a copy of the March 17,

1765, imperial decree establishing what priests could charge for each of the sacraments and would send copies to all the villages.[2]

Hennemann had already learned that Baki serfs and their three priests did not get along. On December 9, 1799, the priests complained that parishioners from Baki and other villages seldom attended church and that they died unconfessed and without receiving the sacraments. On December 11, a delegation of peasants from Baki and other estate villages countered that the priests were ruining them by illegally charging a great deal of money for burials, marriages, prayers, christenings, and other rites. In the notebook in which he recorded requests and decisions, Hennemann observed that he did not know what to make of these complaints because he had just received a letter from the district's supervisory priest praising the estate's serfs for attending church assiduously and for confessing and taking communion annually. He decided (he wrote) to do nothing. And then on December 25, Gavrilo Matveev, one of the Baki priests, complained that Andrei Demenov, a Baki serf, had insulted him. Hennemann reprimanded Andrei.[3] The Baki peasants of course exaggerated the impact of their priests' charges. Nevertheless, when in February 1801 priests from the neighboring Ilinskoe estate, which Charlotte Lieven had purchased in 1800, asked that some of Baki's parishioners be reassigned to them, they pointed out that Baki priests charged fifty kopeks for the cleansing prayer for the mother after birth and again for baptism (the fee the government established in 1765 was three kopeks), though they themselves charged only ten kopeks.[4]

Hennemann, a Baltic German like the Lievens, may not have understood the extent to which Russian priests were corruptible, especially when their parishioners were Old Believers. Many serfs on the Baki estate, including the most prosperous, were in fact Old Believers—Hennemann may not yet have known that, either—and they had certainly paid the supervisory priest to extoll them to their new manager, either in order to create a good impression or in anticipation of what their own priests would say. Their nonattendance was due to religious dissent. However, under Dolgorukova, Baki serfs had paid the clergy 40 kopeks annually for every male on the estate; at one thousand or so male souls as of 1795, that amounted to 400 rubles, a very good income for the priests and lesser clergy (priests ordinarily earned 20 to 40 rubles annually), and Baki serfs accounted for fewer than half of the priests' nominal congregants. The villagers wanted to continue that arrangement under the Lievens.[5] They were willing to pay the priests; what they did not want to do was to accept sacraments from them.

Table 6.1 Married and Unmarried Men and Women Twenty-Five and Older on the Baki Estate, 1795.

Village	Men		Women	
	Married	Never Married	Married	Never Married
Baki	98	6 (5.8%)	112	30 (21.2%)
Afonasikha	19	1 (5.0%)	17	0 (0.0%)
Chashchikha	25	3 (10.7%)	21	2 (8.7%)
Iaksharikha	8	0 (0.0%)	6	1 (14.3%)
Liady	10	2(16.7%)	10	0 (0.0%)
Zubilikha	14	1 (6.7%)	16	7 (30.4%)
Korovikha	13	7 (35.0%)	21	10 (32.3%)
Villages west of the Vetluga River above, east of the river below.				
Iadrovo	17	2 (10.0%)	17	0 (0.0%)
Kirilovo	39	1(2.5%)	35	2 (5.4%)
Dranishnoe	56	6 (9.7%)	47	12 (20.3%)
Staroustie	62	17 (21.5%)	54	38 (41.3%)
Izhma	49	5 (9.3%)	36	18 (30.1%)
Estate totals	410	51 (11.1%)	392	118 (23.1%)

Source: LP 47421, ff. 45–103.

Probably Hennemann soon learned the priests were telling the truth, that many of the estate's peasants did shun the church. Probably he reported this to the Lievens, and probably Charlotte Lieven told him to command her peasants to attend services. Admittedly, there is no record of such an exchange. The earliest surviving document ordering attendance at church is a terse report on an assembly of Baki peasants in January 1806, at which Ivan Oberuchev, who had replaced Hennemann in 1803, conveyed an order from Charlotte: "Peasants should attend God's church on Sundays and other holy days for devotions."[6] In that particular context, the command seems to have been a pro forma repetition of a standing order, perhaps issued at the beginning of every year as Lenten confession season approached. Earlier that same month, Oberuchev had sent a letter reminding the Baki serfs of the standing order that children who had come of age were to marry before Lent.[7] Baki peasants' reluctance to attend church, and to marry, were interconnected.

Table 6.1 presents the problem that Christoph Lieven spotted when he looked at the 1795 census returns. Of course, he constructed nothing like this table, but it was impossible to miss the fact that an alarmingly large number of Baki women were single. He would, in fact, have thought the problem far more serious than table 6.1 suggests, because he would have lumped the women twenty-five and over together with the much larger number of younger single women.[8]

I have listed the villages in the order of their distance from Baki, beginning with Afonasikha, which was just to the south on the west bank of the Vetluga, and Iadrovo, on the east bank and somewhat downstream, because both distance from Baki and the side of the river on which the villages were located correlated loosely with nuptial behavior. Lieven probably did not know where any of the villages were located. But he could not miss the large numbers of single men and women on the estate. He assumed that many men couldn't marry because women wouldn't or because the women's parents kept them at home.

Neither the Lievens nor Hennemann ever raised the possibility that conscription was in any way responsible for the large number of spinsters, and it wasn't. Between 1763 and 1795, 419 men and 398 women either turned fifteen in the eight (of twelve) villages from which the census returns are complete or were fifteen to twenty—ages when Baki serfs began to marry—as of 1763. It is likely that most of the 28 conscripts taken between ages twenty and thirty-four were married when conscripted; possibly some of the 17 teenagers were, too.[9] That is, even after conscription, the numbers of marriage-age men and women on the Baki estate were in balance. At Baki, as among the crown peasants in Kuplia parish in the same years, conscription of single men cannot have been responsible for the large numbers of never-married adult women.

Conscription nevertheless had consequences: the conscript cohort that turned fifteen between 1763 and 1772 had lost 26 men (22.6 percent) by 1795. The class of 1773–82 lost 13 men (13.8 percent), though the class of 1783–92 had lost only 6 (4.5 percent) by 1795. That last class, at least, would lose many more subsequently. Still, this was a lower rate of conscription than among the crown peasants of Kuplia parish: 45 of 347 men, or 13.8 percent of those who turned fifteen between 1763 and 1795, compared to 18.9 percent among Kuplia's crown peasants over the same years. I suspect that wealth generated by the local economy financed the purchase of substitutes, and that concentration of wealth in Baki village explains why it lost proportionately fewer men than the other villages that became part of the Lieven estate (11.7 percent versus 14.1).

The Vetluga Basin Frontier

The Vetluga River flows south into the Volga about 150 straight-line kilometers due east of Nizhnii Novgorod. In the fifteenth century, the Vetluga lay beyond the Russian frontier. In the trans-Volga region (north of the Volga), the border then ran more or less along the Unzha River, roughly 100 kilometers to the west. In the fifteen century, the central Vetluga basin was controlled by the Cheremis (Mari, their own name for themselves), who were, in turn, subject to the Kazan Tatar Khanate. Into the sixteenth century, Tatars and Cheremis raided westward to the Unzha and northward toward Velikii Ustiug. Russians raided into Cheremis territory in return. What Russians there were in the Vetluga basin as of the fifteenth century had descended along rivers from the Russian North and lived on the upper stretch of the Vetluga.[10] Local historians insist that Varnava, a priest from Velikii Ustiug, traveled down the central Vetluga sometime in the second half of the fifteenth century and built a cell on a hill on which the Varnavin Trinity Monastery was later built.[11] The settlement that grew up around the monastery became the small city of Varnavin, capital of the eponymous district in which Baki was located, in 1778. Baki was 38 post-road kilometers south of Varnavin, about 125 straight-line kilometers north of the Volga but about 225 kilometers as the Vetluga twists and turns.[12]

The monastery may (or may not) have been built on Varnava's hill sometime in the first half of the sixteenth century. Perhaps in 1530, Grand Prince Vasilii III granted the monastery an extensive tract of forest, perhaps at that time there were seven homesteads in the vicinity of the monastery, and perhaps in 1551, Tsar Ivan IV (the Terrible) confirmed the grant. All the information in the preceding sentence comes from documents known only as quoted in authentic seventeenth century documents generated by property disputes involving the Varnavin monks. However, the language and terminology employed in the quotations are from the seventeenth century, not the sixteenth. The supposed 1530 document asserts, for instance, that the deed was issued by the Pomestnyi prikaz, which may have existed at the time but not by that name; down to the early seventeenth century, it was called the Pomestnaia izba. One reputable historian has suggested that the author of a 1664 petition rewrote the quotations in more familiar contemporary language. Since Russians of the time were literalists not just in religious matters but in copying, that hypothesis seems weak.[13]

It is also rather suspicious that the supposed document of 1530 refers to the settlement of Minin and the other six as *pochinki*—that is, homesteads in newly cleared forest—just as genuine documents from 1635 and 1645 did.[14] The designation *pochinok* could persist beyond the first generation of settlers, but after a century, Minin ought to have been called a village, even if it were tiny. And it is next to impossible that the cluster of homesteads endured without addition or subtraction for over a century. Indeed, the archimandrite of another monastery accused the Varnavin fathers of purchasing forged documents from yet a third monastery.[15] But it really doesn't matter (except to a handful of local historians) whether or not there were a few tiny Russian settlements around a monastery on Varnava's hill in the early sixteenth century. The key word is *tiny*.

The center and south of the Vetluga basin became safe for Russian settlers only after Ivan IV conquered Kazan and destroyed the Kazan Khanate in 1552. The land along the river itself was now frontier in the sense of being open for settlement. In the late sixteenth century, Tsar Fedor Ivanovich (or Boris Godunov, acting in his name), invited peasants and beekeepers to settle "in the empty places" along the Vetluga and granted tax immunities to encourage them.

Tax surveys conducted by government officials early in the seventeenth century suggest that both before and after Fedor's invitation, Russians settled along the central stretch of the Vetluga.[16] The upheaval in central Russia at the opening of the seventeenth century—the Time of Troubles, involving famine, civil war, and invasion by Swedes and Poles—caused many to flee eastward. Others went east to escape serfdom. The schism in the Russian church in the second half of the seventeenth century set off another major wave of settlement, as Old Believers moved in large numbers into what later became the trans-Volga districts of Nizhnii Novgorod province. Some of them pushed farther north into what became Kostroma province in the late eighteenth century; this included the Varnavin district. In 1719, the Vetluga district, among others, was made a part of the Nizhnii Novgorod diocese; the newly appointed bishop, Pitirim, was a relentless crusader against schismatics, and the Vetluga region was a schismatic stronghold. Indeed, Old Believers fleeing Pitirim's persecution moved up the Usta River—which flows into the Vetluga below Baki—and surrounded their forest sketes with pitfalls.[17] In the nineteenth century, it was conventional wisdom in Varnavin that the district had been settled in the seventeenth and eighteenth centuries century primarily by runaway serfs and Old Believers moving deep into the forest to hide from Russian church and state.[18]

Like many others, the Vetluga frontier was turbulent. The vast forest along the central portion of the Vetluga stretched continuously east and west for scores of kilometers and was sometimes referred to as the "wild forest" (*dikii les*), just as the steppe south of Moscow into which Russians were moving at the same time was called the "wild prairie."[19] In the aftermath of the Time of Troubles, the newly elected tsar, Mikhail Fedorovich, granted the land along almost the entire central and northern course of the Vetluga to Prince Fedor Mstislavskii, head of the Boyar Duma (or Boyar Council). That land was soon re-deeded, divided, and deeded again. Since none of the properties were surveyed and outer boundaries faded into forest, noble proprietors (or their representatives—none of the early owners resided along the Vetluga) engaged in a continual frontier land grab, snatching up unsettled and lightly settled territory and taking their quarrels to government officials.

The Varnavin monastery was engaged in such disputes from the early seventeenth century and also had to fend off charges from peasants that the monastery was intruding on land that was theirs. The peasants living on land distributed by the tsars became serfs, and many of them escaped by pushing farther into the wild forest. In 1610–11, local peasants refused to pay the Varnavin monastery their dues, broke into and burned the monastery, destroyed the documents enserfing them, and drove the brethren away.[20] Settlement in the Vetluga region remained sufficiently sparse that the dissident monk Kapiton, seeking isolation in the wilderness, established a monastic community there in the 1620s.[21]

Russians call this process of settlement *osvoenie*, the literal meaning of which is "making ours" and which they understand as peaceful Russian movement into and development of land not meaningfully inhabited. Seizure is what really happened and was anything but peaceful. Some Russian historians write of the Cheremis withdrawing eastward after the Russian conquest of Kazan as though they did so of their own volition. In fact, the Russian government constructed fortresses with permanent garrisons on the south bank of the Volga, opposite Meadow Cheremis territory (the Hill Cheremis lived south of the Volga). A history of the Kazan Khanate, composed in the 1560s by a Russian who had lived in Kazan as a captive for twenty years, described the Meadow Cheremis as living "deep in the forests, they neither sow nor reap, they feed themselves by catching beast and fish, and by war, and they live like savages."[22] They demonstrated their ferocity in rebellions in 1573, 1574, and 1582–84.[23] The Cheremis rebelled again in 1606–10 during the Time of Troubles and, together with other non-Russian peoples and Russians along the central Volga, temporarily occupied or besieged small towns from Cheboksary (south bank of the Volga, east of the Vetluga) to Sviazhsk (upriver from Kazan), and to Kotelnich on the Viatka River and Vychegda in what is now in southeastern Arkhangelsk province. They stopped paying in-kind taxes (the *iasak*) and rebelled once more when tax collectors attempted to collect arrears and additional emergency taxes in 1615–16.[24]

Russian settlers, meanwhile, pushed ever deeper into Cheremis country. In 1667, Cheremis appealed to the tsar against the Makariev Trinity Monastery on the Unzha and the Varnavin monastery on the Vetluga, both of which had established serf settlements east of the Vetluga, and against Russian nobles whose serfs had intruded into Cheremis land. According to the Cheremis, the Russians

> beat and cripple [the Cheremis] in their fields and abuse them in every way and shoot at them with guns and have killed many Cheremis. And because of those [monastic] elders many dwellings have been abandoned and their inhabitants have scattered. And now the elders Varlam [Makariev Monastery] and Gurii [Varnavin Monastery] with their brethren and with peasants . . . have seized fishing spots and beaver runs for [a hundred kilometers] and more. . . . And many [Vetluga nobles'] peasants from various places have settled in villages and clearings in Cheremis lands and fields and inflict no end of violence and abuse on the Cheremis.[25]

Since the Vetluga region was the frontier, and since peasants were being enserfed—or enserfed again—all along the river, it is not surprising that Stenka Razin's great Cossack–peasant–Old Believer frontier rebellion of 1670–71 surged briefly up the Vetluga. In October 1670, Iliushka Ivanov (aka Ponomarev, aka Dolgopolov), a minor Razin lieutenant, led a party of 150 or so Cossacks, newly recruited rebels, and Cheremis up the Vetluga. Serfs in and around Baki welcomed him enthusiastically. Under interrogation when captured, Iliushka claimed that 370 serfs had joined his force, which grew to a total of 400 men; the numbers in the various accounts naturally do not match, but Iliushka's estimate of the serfs who joined his band is the lowest. Iliushka encamped at Baki and sent letters to estates in the district instructing serfs to hold their stewards in chains until he arrived to deal with them. His men killed 10 stewards, beat others, and drove the rest away. They also killed the resident owners of some small estates.

Iliushka claimed his men had killed only stewards the peasants asked them to. Stewards from estates some distance upriver, forewarned by Iliushka's letters, organized their own armed force and in early November (this is the stewards' account) captured some of Iliushka's emissaries and then drove his band south to Baki, where, with the support of many peasants, Iliushka regrouped. The stewards withdrew to their own estates and dispatched a letter begging for help. Also in November, Iliushka captured the city of Unzha on the Unzha River but immediately withdrew because government troops were approaching. He sent his band back to the Vetluga while he himself tried, unsuccessfully, to disappear. The commander of the government force reported he had destroyed Iliushka's bands, killing five hundred in various places and capturing seventy-five.[26]

Government retribution was ferocious: about 150 participants in the Vetluga uprising, including Iliushka, were hanged, whipped, or lost right thumb and ear to the executioner's axe. On December 17, 5 were hanged at Baki and another whipped, and on December 18, another 56 were executed, whipped, and lost thumbs and ears, again at Baki. Only one of those hanged was from Baki, while another Baki serf lost thumb and ear, and a serf from nearby Zubilikha, later part of the Lievens' Baki estate, was whipped. Many of the others were from nearby settlements.[27]

These public executions and whippings were meant to inspire fear, and probably did, but scarcely eliminated social tensions. In 1708–10, peasant bands inspired by the Bulavin Rebellion (1707–9) in the Don region terrorized the districts along the Volga from Nizhnii Novgorod up to Tver. The leader of one was a runaway serf from Pritykhino, on the northern stretch of the Vetluga. His men—many of whom must have been serfs from the Vetluga basin—destroyed gentry manors in the Vetluga and Unzha districts, as well as many other places; camped outside of Nizhnii Novgorod; and roamed farther up the Volga as well.[28] One consequence of all this marauding was an accumulation of men who could not return to their villages; they provided fuel for a long history of brigandage along the Vetluga. That included robbery at Baki and the murder of the steward in broad daylight in 1744.[29] When in 1761 Mikhail Lomonosov wrote about the heightened danger of brigandage in areas far from cities, he singled out the basin of the

Vetluga, "which stretches for [656—actually 889—kilometers] from head-waters to mouth without cities," without troops or police apparatus, and over the winter sheltered marauding boat haulers.[30]

The one sort of social tension only weakly present on this frontier, at least according to the peasants' testimony, was among the peasants themselves. Through the seventeenth century, the potential for intra-peasant conflict was attenuated by the natural resources available to what was a very small population. In 1664, when the Varnavin monastery elders complained that the serfs of Prince Stepan Tataev, whose holdings abutted monastery property on all sides, were intruding on monastery land and doing harm to the monastery's serfs, the government official sent to investigate summoned the "best peasants"—old inhabitants, peasant elders, and representatives of serfs belonging to neighboring nobles. They swore that they and the monastery serfs "possessed the property in such a way that everyone clears meadows for themselves, because land and forest and hay fields and all the resources are not marked off, and they have never been marked off, and there have never been disputes because of this."[31]

It is true that this is the testimony of serfs from neighboring properties and that the monastery's serfs may not have had a chance to speak, but the words nevertheless ring true. You might move farther into the forest and seize clearings and fields and beaver runs from the Cheremis—the point was to chase the Cheremis away—but the forest was, for the time being, practically boundless. Russian peasants knew that whenever they needed a new field, they could slash and burn a clearing. Serious intra-peasant tension would come only with a new social and political order, when small communities had to select some of their number for the Petrine army and when the economy changed and some peasants began to hire others as labor.

The Baki estate that Charlotte Lieven received in 1799 bore the imprint of the frontier throughout the eighteenth century. The property out of which the Lieven estate was carved was over twice as large as hers. It had belonged to Mikhail Golovkin (the disgraced vice-chancellor whom Empress Elizabeth exiled to Siberia), was given to Prince Iurii Dolgorukov in 1746, and then in 1747 to his widow, Elena, "for her provisioning"—that is, as a life grant, not hereditary property.[32] Because the Baki tax census returns from the 1720s and 1744 have been lost, the earliest document describing the property (quoted in an 1804 ruling in a property dispute) is a list of the villages, with their populations, that Dolgorukova received in 1747: 267 men and 306 women living in twenty-six very small villages. Six of them were designated *pochinki*—that is, they were of recent origin. Baki, with only 20 men and 22 women, was the second-largest village. Staroustie, a *pochinok*, had 33 men and 32 women. By 1799, according to the count of an appanage official just before Lieven received her portion, there were thirty-seven villages with a total male population of 2,352. The male population had increased almost nine-fold (as no doubt had the female population) in just over fifty years.[33]

Natural increase cannot account for that growth. The oldest surviving census is from 1782.[34] It identifies everyone living in the villages as of 1763 but only identifies newcomers who had arrived between 1763 and 1782. In the villages that went to Charlotte Lieven, almost all were said to have arrived from other villages on the Dolgorukova estate or to have married in; the same was true of newcomers in what became the Lieven villages between 1782 and 1795. There is no evidence that Dolgorukova moved anyone from distant estates onto her Baki property, nor is there any reason to suppose that, with the property hers only on lifetime loan, she would have wanted to do so. I presume that, throughout the eighteenth century, runaway serfs, soldiers deserting the army, peasants designated for conscription, and Old Believers continued to move into the forests around Baki and were eventually entered on estate rolls. The way tax censuses were conducted was meant to preclude such deceptions, but both wandering peasants and estate officials had good reason to conceal that sort of population movement.

That was what happened on the estates of the Kazhirov monastery along the Vetluga, several hundred kilometers to the north but in a natural environment identical to Baki's. Runaways could not be stopped from settling in the woods—soldiers sent to round them up were often beaten back. Peasants fled to hideouts prepared in advance and could not be found. Sometimes the monks themselves led the resistance to the troops. Some peasants were forcibly removed from the Kazhirov properties, but the estate population nevertheless increased steadily due to the constant inflow of migrants. Once they had been there for years, their status—illegal migrant or permanent resident—became ambiguous.[35] The government was, in the end, more interested in entering newly found taxpayers on the census rolls than in trying to discover where they or their parents had come from many years earlier.[36]

The appanage official who compiled the list of former Dolgorukova villages with their male populations in 1799 noted that the population of every village had changed since the 1795 census because after those returns had been handed in, "many moved by the household and one by one from village to village on their own."[37] With so much movement among villages, it would have been easy to claim that newly arrived peasants were actually transferees from another village on the property—with so many serfs, and so many villages, it would have been difficult to cross-check all the returns. More importantly, it is evident that down to the end of the eighteenth century Baki peasants were pushing ever deeper into the forest, just as their parents, grandparents, and more distant ancestors had for the last two centuries.

Old Believers on Charlotte Lieven's Baki Estate

After Elena Dolgorukova died early in 1799, the property reverted to the appanage administration. In May 1799, Emperor Paul granted Charlotte Lieven somewhat less than half of the estate: Baki and eleven other villages (Lieven received all four of largest), with—officially—a population of exactly 1,000 male souls, based on the 1795 tax census. The summary total from the 1795 census was actually 1,010.[38] The official who counted the population of the villages that had made up the Dolgorukova estate in 1799 put the total male population in Lieven's twelve villages at 1,087.

Baki and six small villages were strung out on the higher right (western) bank of the Vetluga, on or close to the road connecting Varnavin to the north with Semenov in Nizhnii Novgorod province. Korovikha, the most distant from Baki, was only seven kilometers away. (Distances are those peasants walked; I have taken them from a nineteenth-century directory of Kostroma province settlements, which gives distances along postal roads and footpaths for villages away from the roads.[39]) Until the eighteenth century, all known settlement in the Baki area, and almost all settlement along the central Vetluga, was on the west bank, because spring floods inundated the low and boggy east bank, at Baki, for instance, to a distance of two kilometers or more.[40] The village of Iadrovo (not on the 1747 list of villages and referred to as a *pochinok* in the 1782 tax census), eight kilometers downriver from Baki, was on the left (east) bank, at the edge of the floodplain that extended two kilometers from the river channel. Also on the eastern side, in a line running south along the Usta River (here, roughly parallel to and six to ten kilometers distant from the Vetluga) were Kirilovo (eighteen kilometers from Baki), Dranishnoe (twenty kilometers), and Staroustie (twenty-five kilometers); and then farther down the Usta and northeastward up the

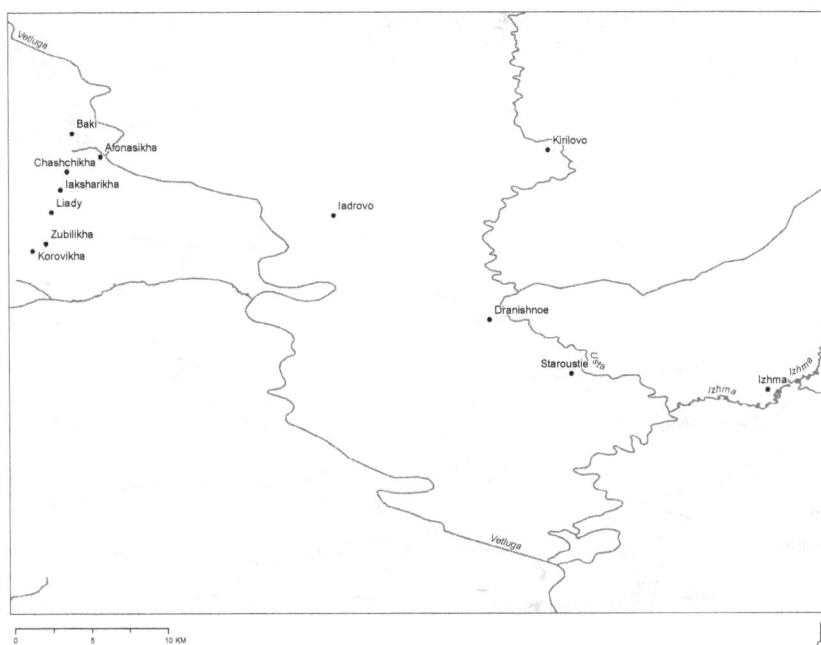

Map 6.1 Charlotte Lieven's Baki Estate. Contains information from OpenStreetMap, which is made available at https://www.openstreetmap.org under the Open Database License (ODbL). Modified by Kelsey Rydland, licensed under CC BY-SA 2.0.

Izhma River was Izhma (forty kilometers from Baki). Those two rivers were navigable, for small boats and rafts of logs, only during the spring flood. Peasants from Dranishnoe, Staroustie, and Izhma cut across forest and bog above Dranishnoe to get to the Vetluga around Iadrovo and then Baki. Charlotte Lieven's newly acquired serfs clung to riverbanks along a very long, very thin line of settlement, deep in the forest. All of those settlements originated in the eighteenth century, but there were small concealed communities of runaways and Old Believers (with their pitfalls) there already.

Information in the 1782 and 1795 tax censuses on the movement of women shows that most brides in Baki and the six small villages in the Baki cluster married within Baki and the cluster or were exchanged with other nearby villages on what was then the giant Dolgorukova estate. Peasants east of the Vetluga searched for brides within a range of twenty (Iadrovo and Kirilovo) to forty (Izhma) kilometers.[41] Peasants east of the Vetluga had chosen to live in relative (in the case of Izhma, almost total) isolation, but that preference had costs. Only peasants from Baki married serfs from nearby estates, probably because they were more prosperous than peasants in the other villages that later made up the Lieven estate.

Immediately after she received the estate, Lieven sent an agent to inspect the property. In July 1799, he wrote back that there was a surfeit of crop- and meadowland but that many of the peasants did not themselves farm, instead hiring others to work the fields. The foundation of the Baki economy was the forest: peasants barged logs and lumber downriver, along with barrels of tar and pitch, bast mats and "various trifles." Traveling down the Volga, they bought fish at Kazan and Astrakhan for sale in towns farther north. Many of the peasants, he noted, had capital in the thousands of rubles.[42] Edgar Melton has filled in many of the details in an excellent account of the Baki estate economy, based on Lieven estate papers from the early nineteenth century. As of 1812, sixteen timber dealers from Baki village controlled the trade, paying teams of loggers in advance for their winter work in the forest and hiring many men to work the barges. Well over half of the other Baki village households had incomes (in addition to whatever they harvested) of 100 to 150 paper rubles and more, in wages and the sale of craft products, as well as baked goods at the weekly market; Baki was the second most important commercial center on the Vetluga. The wealthy controlled Baki village and probably much of what went on in the entire estate, including conscription, because they hired everyone else. They ensured that their own sons, and the men who worked their barges, were spared while the sons of the poor went to the army. The two wealthiest lumber dealers, Andreian Osokin (worth 50,000 rubles, with an annual income of 15,000 rubles) and Vasilii Voronin (also 15,000 rubles per year, with a capital of 25,000 rubles), were both priestless Old Believers but rivals in Baki politics.[43]

The forest industries that provided many Baki peasants a reasonably good income were also ruinous to their health. An observer who knew the estate well reported in 1856 that scurvy and scrofula were endemic. Possibly the morbidity was the result of an extremely limited diet, almost entirely lacking in vegetables during the winter months they worked in the forest, and pestilential living conditions in their winter forest dugouts (their shirts literally rotted on their backs), often so far from their villages that they went for months without an opportunity to clean up in a steam bath.[44]

No Baki confession registers have survived, but the compiler of the 1782 tax return identified many of the peasants on the Dolgorukova estate as registered schismatics. He was not required to do so—neither the instructions nor the model forms for the 1782 census contain a word about schismatics, and in 1782, Catherine II revoked the double tax on Old Believers.[45] Nevertheless, in some places enumerators assumed the double tax still held. The Baki enumerator no doubt carried registration information forward from the 1763 tax census; the 1763 notations were themselves likely carried forward from the 1744 tax census.[46] As of 1782, the information was woefully outdated and, in any case, applied only to peasants who at some point in the past had decided to register as Old Believers and pay the double tax. Probably few Baki Old Believers reported themselves. In 1812, the Varnavin court accepted (at Charlotte Lieven's request) two lists of the estate's Old Believers who wanted to register, including five priested and four priestless households in Baki village. Most of them descended from extended families not identified as Old Believers in the 1782 census. Together, these two different sources—the 1782 census and the 1812 lists of the newly registered—identify fourteen of Baki village's extended families in the 1782 tax census as Old Believers. Family and household were not the same. The 1782 census returns were organized by lineage. Five priested and two priestless households of 1812 descended from one in which no Old Believers had been registered in 1782.[47] The two other priestless households of 1812 descended from two different lineages.

Not surprisingly, priested and priestless Old Believers had different nuptial regimes: among the priested in Baki village in 1812, all six men and all four women twenty-five and over had married; among the priestless, all five men in that age group had married, but five of the eight women had not. Among the Old Believers from four other villages who registered in 1812, all of them priestless, eight of nine men twenty-five and over had married, while eight of seventeen women twenty-five and above had not.

Table 6.2 encapsulates the eighteenth-century history of priestless Old Believer marriage in Baki village but requires interpretation. Women in self-declared Old Believer families were avoiding marriage by the 1720s. In the 1763 census, the three oldest never-married women were listed at sixty to seventy, though their ages were probably overstated. If women had turned twenty-five without marrying prior to 1720, they had likely died by 1763. In the 1730s, three priestless men avoided marriage; they were listed in 1763 at fifty-two to fifty-four. Those ages were reasonably accurate, as the men would have been listed at thirty-three to thirty-five in 1744 and in their early

Table 6.2 Marriage Aversion among Women Twenty-Five and Older in Old Believer and Other Families, as Identified in the 1782 Census and 1812 Lists, Baki Village, 1763–95.

	Old Believers*		Others		Baki as a whole	
	Married	Single	Married	Single	Married	Single
1763	8	12 (60.0%)	75	18 (19.4%)	83	30 (26.5%)
1782	11	13 (54.2%)	93	15 (13.9%)	104	28 (21.2%)
1795	17	10 (37%)	95	20 (19.0%)	112	30 (21.1%)

*Both priestless and priested.
Source: GAKO, f. 200, op. b/sh, d. 546, ll. 76–352; LP 47421, ff. 45–103.

teens in the census conducted in the early 1720s. After 1750, however, every declared Old Believer male who turned twenty-five married. By then the declared priestless families had adopted the Spasovite rule: all sons married, but (most) daughters did not. Marriage aversion among priestless women concealed within nominally Orthodox lineages tracked resistance among the registered priestless closely. On the other hand, aversion to marriage among (some) nominally Orthodox Old Believer men began only around mid-century; by the 1790s, all of them were again marrying, too.[48]

The fact that some men would not marry affected the ratio of married to unmarried women. For instance, if the eight never-married Old Believer males in the 1763 returns had all married, their eight wives would have produced married majorities among Old Believer women in both 1763 and 1782. If we correct for that distortion, the proportion of never-married women in the Old Believer households held relatively steady from 1763 to 1795. If we add the missing wives of five unmarried, nominally Orthodox men between 1782 and 1795, the never-married proportion of women in the village as a whole would have changed little from 1763 to 1795.[49]

Priestless Old Believer households in Baki village had made definitive choices between marriage and non-marriage (female and male both) by the middle of the eighteenth century, earlier than in any other village community I have examined. As in Kuplia parish, a small minority of men trailed women in choosing not to marry, but within a generation or so, all men married once again. In Baki, we see that happening among registered Old Believers in the first half of the century and among the unregistered—or perhaps the newly converted—in the second half of the century. Because the eighteenth-century censuses enumerated the population by lineage, the actual households within which men and women made those decisions are only partially visible. Nevertheless, even in family aggregations, the results of men and women both choosing celibacy are starkly visible: of the fourteen extended families I have classified as Old Believer as of 1763, two had died out and five consisted of a single elderly man or woman by 1795.

The six villages in the cluster south of Baki were individually too small for their numbers to have much meaning. Korovikha is missing from the 1782 return, so we do not know whether or not it held registered Old Believers. Setting Korovikha aside and considering the others collectively, 12 percent of men twenty-five and over were unmarried in 1763 and 10 percent in 1795. Among women, 20 percent were unmarried in 1763 and 14 percent in 1795. On balance, those proportions were close to Baki's, although the percentage of unmarried men was higher and that of unmarried women lower. There were few registered Old Believers: one family with a spinster in Liady and three elderly spinsters in three separate families in Iaksharikha as of 1795. The association between aversion to marriage and priestless Old Belief is clear, as is the fact that most Old Believers in these villages never registered.

Loss of some of the 1782 returns from Dolgorukova's Baki estate hampers reconstruction of the history of marriage resistance in the villages east of the Vetluga. They end with an incomplete, almost entirely bleached register of the population of Dranishnoe. The returns from Iadrovo and Kirilovo are missing; they must have followed Dranishnoe's. The 1795 census returns from the Baki estate do list all of the inhabitants in those three villages as of 1782, but provide no information about who among them were self-declared Old Believers. There may have been no registered Old Believers in Iadrovo and Kirilovo, where almost all adults were married in both 1782 and 1795. The loss of the 1782 return from Dranishnoe is particularly unfortunate, because 20 percent of its women 25 and older were unmarried in both 1782 and 1795, while in 1782, fully 22 percent of men in that age group were unmarried, a proportion that had fallen to just under 10 percent by 1795. I suspect that Dranishnoe had a history of Old Belief and marriage resistance much like Staroustie's downriver. Similar to Staroustie, Dranishnoe was called a *pochinok*, a recently established settlement, with a population of only fifteen men and ten women in 1747. Most likely settlers had cleared, or emerged from, the forest early in the eighteenth century.[50]

Table 6.3 Marriage Aversion among Women Twenty-Five and Older in Old Believer and Other Families, as Identified in the 1782 Census, Staroustie, 1763–95.

	Old Believers		Others		Staroustie as a whole	
	Married	Single	Married	Single	Married	Single
1763	19	11 (36.7%)	34	5 (12.8%)	53	16 (23.3%)
1782	18	20 (52.6%)	45	7 (13.5%)	63	27 (30.0%)
1795	14	24 (63.2%)	40	14 (25.9%)	54	38 (41.3%)

Source: GAKO, f. 200, op. b/sh, d. 546, ll. 306–3280b; LP 47421, ff. 83–900b.

Deep in the woods to the east of the Vetluga, Staroustie and Izhma, the villages farthest from Baki at twenty-five and forty kilometers, had by far the largest proportion of families identified as Old Believers and by far the largest proportion of women who refused to marry. Deep woods, Old Belief, and extreme aversion to marriage were interconnected. Staroustie was of relatively recent origin but grew rapidly. The 1747 document describing the Dolgorukova estate gave Staroustie's population as 33 men and 32 women.[51] By 1763, the population had risen to 289. Quite likely, its founders were Old Believers deliberately putting rugged distance between themselves and Russian church and state.

In 1763, as table 6.3 shows, women in Staroustie's twelve avowedly Old Believer families were roughly three times more likely to avoid marriage than women in families not identified as Old Believers, and between 1763 and 1795, the rate of refusal to marry among schismatic women rose from 36 to 63 percent.[52] The rate at which nominally Orthodox women avoided marriage rose from 12 percent in 1763 to just short of 26 percent in 1795, putting them at the same marriage-avoiding level as some of the Spasovite-laden villages around Kuplia parish in the same year. If we set aside all those who arrived via marriage, and also those whose families arrived between censuses, we find that of the ninety-one women raised in the village between 1763 and 1795, forty (44 percent) never married and that the rate of resistance rose over time: 38 percent of native Staroustie women avoided marriage between 1763 and 1782, 51 percent between 1782 and 1795.[53]

Quite unusually, the proportion of unmarried adult men in Staroustie held steady at just over 20 percent between 1763 (twelve of fifty-three) and 1795 (seventeen of seventy-nine), and it is remarkable that in both 1763 and 1795, the proportion of single men among the schismatics and the supposedly

Orthodox was almost identical. Perhaps we should not assume that all never-married Staroustie men were so by choice. Perhaps in Staroustie—ten kilometers down the Usta from Dranishnoe, fifteen kilometers from Izhma up the Izhma River, both villages with very high rates of female marriage aversion—some men failed to secure wives because so many of the locally accessible women would not marry. Nevertheless, it is likely that most men avoided marriage out of religious conviction. In 1795 for example, there was an Old Believer family in which three males ages thirty-four to sixty had never married, and there was a dubiously Orthodox family with two bachelors and a spinster sister.

The census returns chart a very clear history of marriage resistance in Staroustie. Aversion among men and women both had set in by the 1720s or earlier, probably around the same time Staroustie was founded. Almost all of the increase in female marriage aversion down to 1782 occurred among declared Old Believers, while between 1782 and 1795 nominally Orthodox female aversion rose from 14 to 26 percent. Because women ages twenty-five and above as of 1782 had already made irrevocable choices to marry or not, so sharp an increase in the level of Orthodox aversion required an extraordinary increase in marriage aversion among women who turned twenty-five between the 1782 and 1795 censuses. Such a surge there was: of the nominally Orthodox women who turned twenty-five to thirty-four by 1795, over half (ten of nineteen) never married; in the same cohort, four of five Old Believer women remained single. In the decade preceding 1795, the Orthodox made the greater contribution to the increase in female marriage resistance simply because there were more of them in the village.

In Izhma, hostility to marriage was even more pronounced than in Staroustie as of 1763, because the tiny population—forty-six in all—was probably homogeneously schismatic. The 1782 census classified members of five of the seven families who had lived there in 1763 as schismatic; the other two, while officially Orthodox, included unmarried adult men and women, almost certain evidence of their religious heterodoxy. Izhma was not on the list of villages compiled in 1747 when the property went to Elena Dolgorukova. Either the pioneers had not yet arrived, or they had not yet come to the attention of census enumerators.

Izhma certainly was, as the 1782 census return called it, a *pochinok*. It was at the eastern extremity of what would become Charlotte Lieven's Baki estate, deep in a trackless forest that even in the early twenty-first century extended another forty kilometers to the east without human habitation. That isolation was surely what the original Old Believer settlers sought. The isolation, and the resulting interdependence of the few founding households, is probably further evidence that, whatever their public posture, the two nominally Orthodox households were actually Old Believers. They could not attend the Orthodox Church in Baki, two river crossings and a forty kilometer hike away over difficult terrain, and had they been truly Orthodox, the other families would not have welcomed them. Izhma's immediate neighbors were the bear, wolf, elk, and otter in the forest and waterways. Our mid-nineteenth-century source on Baki-area forest life reports that by then the lynx had disappeared.[54] He did not even recall the vanished beaver, important to the Cheremis in the seventeenth century but probably exterminated in the first half of the eighteen, victim of the same relentless Western European demand for beaver pelts that devastated beaver populations farther north and west in Russia earlier and in colonial New England. And it was probably during the eighteenth century that the demand for lumber and forest products in the prairie provinces south along the Volga spawned the logging economy along the Vetluga, Usta, and Izhma Rivers. This was very thinly settled frontier, yet the Izhma peasants who had tried to lose themselves in the forest nevertheless lived in a world buffeted by national and international markets.

Izhma grew rapidly. Between 1763 and 1782, the population more than tripled, from 46 to 159; by 1795, it had grown by another 53 percent, to 243. The 1782 and 1795 census returns characterize the families who had arrived since the preceding census as "transferred" (*perevedeny*), which implies that, after the Old Believers had settled Izhma, estate management began to send other serf families there. However, as the official who compiled the list of villages on the former Dolgorukova estate in 1799 pointed out, Baki-area peasants were in the habit of moving from one place to another (and also of carving out new settlements) as they saw fit. "Transferred" as the term for explaining why a serf household had moved from one village to another lent a dignified veneer of management control to what the serfs did without asking permission. At least up to 1782, it is much more likely that most families moved to Izhma on their own initiative: they were, for the most part, multigenerational, with many elderly members. These may, in fact, have been families who had emerged from forest hideaways. A few of the families who moved to Izhma between 1782 and 1795 were of the same large variety,

Table 6.4 Marriage Aversion among Men and Women Twenty-Five and Older in Izhma, 1782–95.

	Old Believers		Orthodox	
		Men		
	Married	Never Married	Married	Never Married
1782	9	5 (35.7%)	18	1 (5.3%)
1795	12	4 (25.0%)	37	1 (2.6%)
		Women		
1782	5	13 (72.2%)	20	8 (28.6%)
1795	8	7 (46.7%)	28	9 (24.3%)

Sources: GAKO, f. 200, op. b/sh, d. 546, ll. 3280b–3370b; LP 47421, ff. 91–96.

but more were nuclear families, with a working couple (or widow/widower) with a young child or two. These small families may have been ordered to move by estate managers intent on expanding the Izhma labor force.

Comparing the demographic behavior of Izhma's Old Believer and nominally Orthodox populations is relatively simple, at least in 1782 and 1795, when a few more avowedly schismatic families had joined the five declared Old Believer families of 1763 and there were enough nominally Orthodox to constitute a meaningful population. In brief, marriage resistance among Old Believers declined but remained very high, marriage resistance among Orthodox men was minimal, and marriage resistance among Orthodox women receded slightly from a high of 29 percent to a still high 24 percent (table 6.4). However, such a comparison is not necessarily meaningful because of the uninterrupted flow of new families into the village. In terms of the families composing it, Izhma in the census years was three different villages.

Comparison of the nuptial behavior of the three successive Izhmas is more revealing. In 1782, for instance, of the eighteen women aged twenty-five and above who descended from the original seven households, eleven (61 percent) never married. Of the twenty-seven women in that age group whose families arrived in Izhma after the 1763 census, ten (37 percent) never married. Of course, among those newcomer women were many who were already married when they arrived. Among newcomer women aged twenty-five to thirty-nine in 1782, seven of eleven (64 percent) never married. It would be nice to know exactly when those families arrived, but we don't. Of the eight newcomer women from twenty-five to thirty-four, the cohort most likely to have chosen to marry or not after their arrival, seven of eight (88 percent) never married. Nuptial behavior in established and newcomer families as of 1782 was more or less identical. Whether avowedly Old Believer or nominally Orthodox, their families had surely moved to Izhma in order to live in a community whose women shunned marriage out of religious conviction. The families who arrived between 1782 and 1795 were very different: only one of the eighteen women over twenty-five was single. It may be that estate management deliberately sent to Izhma families known for their adherence to Orthodoxy, marriage, or both.

While in Kuplia parish and in most of the villages on the Baki estate, resistance to marriage seems to have spread from household to household by example and serial conversion, Izhma seems to have gathered in families already antipathetic to female marriage up to 1782. In Izhma—and to a somewhat lesser extent in Staroustie—the number of marriage-averse women grew because the village attracted marriage-averse women (with their families) from other villages or from the forest. Families who arrived after 1782 overwhelmingly favored female marriage. But that still left Izhma with almost one-third of its women (sixteen of the fifty-two who were twenty-five and over) stubbornly averse to marriage in 1795.

While the eighteenth-century histories of the Old Belief and marriage aversion in each of the twelve villages that became Charlotte Lieven's Baki estate—to the extent that we can reconstruct them—were different, there were some clear patterns. By the 1720s at the latest, priestless Old Believers opposing marriage had appeared in Baki village and deep in the forest, in homesteads both known and unknown to census enumerators. In most of the villages there was a period, early in community formation, in which an appreciable number of men as well as women shunned marriage, but among the registered Old Believers of Baki village, that tendency both peaked and ended earliest, by 1750. It is not a surprise that in the six small villages clustered near Baki, marriage resistance reached roughly the same proportions as in Baki. More interesting is that all of the statistical outliers were also geographical outliers. Both Kirilovo and Iadrovo, where marriage aversion was practically nonexistent, were on the eastern side of the Vetluga, as were Staroustie and Izhma, where aversion was most pronounced. Probably Dranishnoe should be included in the latter group. The geographical distribution suggests that self-segregation was involved: genuinely Orthodox or pro-marriage priested Old Believers may have crossed to the eastern side of the Vetluga to separate themselves from Baki's many marriage-averse priestless Old Believers, while by mid-century priestless Old Believers had pushed the frontier of settlement ever deeper into the forests along the Usta and Izhma Rivers.[55] While in Baki village marriage avoidance had peaked by 1763, it was still rising in Staroustie in the late eighteenth century.

Unlike the villages in Kuplia parish, Charlotte Lieven's twelve Baki villages were not a separate administrative unit in the eighteenth century; they were part of the much larger Dolgorukova estate. Nevertheless, in both the Baki cluster and most of the future Lieven villages to the east of the Vetluga, a majority of the peasants married into or away from villages Charlotte Lieven received in 1799. Of the 153 women in the twelve villages who married between 1782 and 1795, 105 (69 percent) married into the Lieven twelve. Of the 193 men who married in those years, 88 (54 percent) took wives from the Lieven twelve. Only a bare majority of men took wives from the twelve villages because so many women in those villages would not marry. Those men made good the local bride deficit by draining women from other Dolgorukova villages and other properties reasonably nearby or, in other words, by exporting their bride deficit.

The returns from the 1782 and 1795 censuses do not reveal the sort of tension between bride-withholding and bride-donating villages that we saw in Kuplia parish, and perhaps there was none. The large bride-withholding villages on the east bank were so remote from almost all the others on the Dolgorukova estate that many villagers may not even have been aware of the extraordinarily high level of female marriage aversion in Staroustie and Izhma. Or perhaps they were (as many who moved to Izhma and Staroustie between 1763 and 1795 certainly were), but they were unconcerned because those villages lay beyond the range within which they sought brides. The future Lieven villages strung out south of Baki were too small to be of much concern to anyone. Only Baki itself, by far the largest village on the Dolgorukova estate and with a high level of female aversion to marriage, was both visible to all and sufficiently large that its women's nuptial choices had an impact on its neighbors. But Baki seems to have exchanged brides with almost all of the villages in its immediate vicinity, most of which did not become Lieven property in 1799. Whether or not the neighbors were concerned, however, the choices made by the women in the twelve Baki villages must have made it more difficult for men elsewhere on the Dolgorukova estate to find wives. But then, there is no reason to think that women in the other Dolgorukova villages married universally; they, too, probably contributed to a bridal deficit that could be made good only by drawing on women over a very extensive territory.

Once Again: Did the Girls Decide?

Baki census returns reveal the same nuptial pattern as in Kuplia parish: some daughters decided against, others for marriage. In Baki village, Ivan Fedorov's daughter Anisia, fourteen in 1782, never married, while Elena, twelve in 1782, had married by 1795. In Afonasikha, Galaktion Kozmin's daughter Varvara, seventeen in 1782, never married, but Paraskovia, sixteen in 1782, married; Mikhail Sergeev had an older daughter who married, a younger who did not. In Dranishnoe, both Makar Vasiliev and Maksim Eremeev had older daughters who married, younger who did not. So did Vasilii Andreev in Staroustie. In Staroustie, Kozma Andreev's two oldest daughters never married, but his youngest did. Also in Staroustie, the widow Tatiana Fedorova's oldest daughter married, but her two younger daughters did not. In Izhma, Petr Leontiev's oldest daughter never married; her two younger sisters did.[56] There are other cases in which some daughters married and others didn't, as well as cases that are ambiguous because a daughter age twenty-four in 1795 may subsequently have married or died single.

I have argued that the same pattern of nuptial choice—some girls from a family marrying, others not; sometimes younger and sometimes older daughters marrying while their sisters remained single—suggests that the young women in Kuplia parish made their own decisions about marriage. That argument is inferential but seems stronger than the opposite assumption—that parents were deciding which of their daughters would marry and which would remain single and at home. For Kuplia, the weak link is the absence of evidence about how young women in marriage-averse households might have escaped the parental domain.

At Baki, the escape mechanism was elopement. In 1836, gendarme Second Lieutenant Pavel Averkiev, supervising the Baki estate in the aftermath of a rebellion against estate management, reported that according to the local marriage custom, grooms were expected "without fail" to take girls to church for marriage "secretly"—that is, without the girls' parents being told. A girl signaled her assent beforehand by giving her beau a pledge: towel, kerchief, ribbon, or, most often, the cross she wore around her neck. They then agreed on the date the lad would steal his betrothed away.[57] The groom must also have made arrangements with the priest. Elopement with prior pledge (in fact, courtship, pledge, elopement) was a widespread custom in some provinces north of the Volga River. While it was common among Old Believers, it was not specific to them. However, in the trans-Volga districts of northern Nizhnii Novgorod province, just south of the Varnavin district and heavily populated by priested Old Believers, elopement was reported to have been almost universal in the first half of the nineteenth century.[58] That was probably an exaggeration, but elopement may have been the modal route to the altar. On Second Lieutenant Averkiev's evidence, the Baki area was a northern extension of Nizhnii Novgorod's trans-Volga elopement country.

In fact, government officials investigating Kostroma province Old Believers reported in 1852 that elopement was common practice in much of the Varnavin district and identified the Uren area, northeast of Baki and notorious for the density of its priestless Old Believer population, as the site of elopement followed by unwedded cohabitation rather than a church wedding.[59] Eloping couples at Baki and around Uren—the former heading to the altar, the latter not—almost certainly belonged to different Old Believer covenants. Around Uren, Filippovites were numerous.[60] In Baki, the frequency of elopement with marriage in a church suggests a Spasovite presence, since the Spasovite covenant permitted church weddings. However, eloping priested couples at Baki probably also married in the church.

Priested Old Believers' children did not elope because their parents objected to marriage. Defense of the continuing legitimacy of marriage and family life divided priested from priestless even before the two Old Believer currents had separated.[61] However, through the first half of the nineteenth century, the only priests available to Old Believers were "fugitive priests," who abandoned the official church and were cleansed of the Nikonian heresy by reanointment. They were hunted by the government, always in short supply, and, for most peasants, inconveniently distant when available at all. In the absence of an Old Believer priest, a trans-Volga priested couple anxious to marry could do so in a nearby Orthodox church, where the priest was first supposed to make them promise to convert to Orthodoxy and raise their children in the official church. Priested couples had no difficulty finding Orthodox priests who would marry them, whether or not they extracted the empty promise.[62] Elopement was a device by which the bride's parents—who must almost always have known their daughter was being courted, who may well have married by elopement themselves—could feign ignorance of what she was doing and so avoid responsibility for her marriage by a priest whom they considered heretical.[63] The groom's parents, on the other hand, must always have given their consent beforehand, because he returned to the family household with the bride.

However, if marriage on the sly was, south of the Varnavin district, associated chiefly with the priested, there was no reason why a priestless couple could not marry in the same way, whether or not the bride's parents gave tacit consent. At least occasionally, priestless peasants in the trans-Volga districts eloped and married in an Orthodox church.[64] In Moscow in the second half of the eighteenth century, priestless couples married by elopement in Orthodox churches with the foreknowledge of their parents, who nevertheless acted out surprise and dismay, precisely in order to disclaim responsibility for their children's actions.[65] At and around Baki, as in other trans-Volga districts to the south, marriage by elopement among priested Old Believers could only have provided a tempting example to priestless girls who wanted to marry. There were certainly Orthodox priests in the province willing to marry Old Believers without any promise to convert.[66] Priestless parents may have genuinely objected to their daughters' marriages, but short of imprisoning them in the household, there was little they could do to prevent their daughters from forming attachments to local boys and slipping away to marry. At Baki, the pattern of nuptiality in presumably priestless Old Believer households, and the local custom of marriage by elopement, fit together seamlessly.

Spasovites in the Varnavin District and at Baki

All we can say with certainty about the Old Believers in and around Baki in the eighteenth century is that they included numerous priested and priestless and that most of the many women who never married were certainly priestless Old Believers, registered or not. We also know that there were some Old Believer skete in the district in the eighteenth and early nineteenth centuries. They were destroyed in 1840, but all the skete-dwellers moved to forest hideouts or villages—including a group of women who settled in the village of Pesoshnoe, to the east of the Vetluga and twenty kilometers from Baki—and continued to provide religious services for the local population. Our source does not tell us whether any of the sketes had been populated by Spasovites.[67]

It is also clear, although the evidence is only impressionistic, that in the eighteenth century, Old Believers made up a very substantial proportion, perhaps a majority, of the population of Kostroma province and certainly a majority and probably an overwhelming one in the Varnavin district. Because statistics on Old Believers provided by church and state were risible—evidence only that they were in deep denial—I cannot prove those assertions. Nevertheless, the available evidence (as, for instance, from Baki, where the priests complained to Karl Hennemann in 1800 that hardly any of their parishioners attended church) does lend support.

The bishop of Kostroma asserted in 1792 that at various times, government officials had sent him for admonition over 1,500 schismatics of long standing and more than 400 recent converts. The bishop also claimed that during the 1782 tax census, schismatic enumerators had persuaded so many parishioners to declare themselves Old Believers that in the Iurevetsk district almost all of the peasants in nine parishes had left the church. Village heads, he said—referring to the province as a whole rather than to Iurevetsk district alone—were themselves schismatic, recruited peasants for the schism, and were complicit in the establishment of Old Believer cells in fields and forests, as well as the construction of Old Believer chapels.[68] In the 1860s, according to the priest in the village of Chernaia, all of the peasant officials in the area were Old Believers. At mid-century, the governor's staff in Kostroma knew the major centers of the Old Belief and the names of some of the leaders, but local officials procrastinated when ordered to investigate. Most cases were closed either without reaching any conclusion or without punishment for the Old Believers under investigation.[69] Local officials were reluctant to prosecute Old Believers, probably because they were sympathizers or bribed.

Around Uren in the Varnavin district northeast of Baki, there was a major insurrection in 1829–30 involving (so the rebels claimed in one petition) villages with a total population of five thousand. The insurrection had nothing to do with religion; it began as a protest against the appanage administration's effort to control and tax slash-burn agriculture in appanage forests. However, the religious solidarity of these priestless peasants ("being schismatics of various sects rejecting the sacraments," as they said in another petition) is certainly what sustained it for almost a year after they drove appanage officials from their offices in Uren in July 1829 and briefly took control of the entire settlement in early 1830. From January through May 1830, armed mostly with clubs, they forced officials leading small detachments of soldiers out to the villages to retreat. In June, the arrival of an armed force of about one thousand men finally allowed the authorities to prevail. But while over two hundred participants were punished—running the gauntlet, whipping, conscription, exile to Siberia—many escaped, including one of the leaders, and the investigation dragged on inconclusively in the usual Kostroma way, until it wound down and pronounced sentences in 1831. The governor, quite properly, suspected that one of the investigating officials had been bribed to ignore orders to capture the rebel leader. The Uren appanage peasants continued to protest and petition down to 1836.[70]

According to Petr Brianchaninov and Lev Arnoldi, two Ministry of Internal Affairs staffers posted to Kostroma province in 1852 to collect information on Old Believers, at the local level church and state officials neither attempted to count nor were they concerned about Old Believers. Priests profited by levying a small charge to list them as present at confession and the Eucharist during Lent, thereby giving them an Orthodox cover. Arnoldi, in a diary offering some particulars that did not appear in the formal report, noted that one priest charged 150 rubles to record an Old Believer couple's marriage in the parish register though they had never set foot in the church. Priests also connived with Old Believers' pastors (*nastavniki*) and "heresiarchs," presumably for payoffs. Old Believers were, according to Brianchaninov and Arnoldi, the priests' principal source of income. They also observed, without noting it as a Spasovite practice, that many Old Believers were baptized and married in a church and thus obtained Orthodox status.

Brianchaninov and Arnoldi provide the most realistic estimates in their 1852 report: 20,587 self-declared schismatics of both sexes, 27,485 secret schismatics, and 57,571 "infected" with the Old Belief, probably secret Old Believers. Of the 105,643 likely Old Believers in the province, they put 20,555 in the Varnavin district (out of the district's total population of 69,089, both sexes, in 1858), second only to the neighboring Makariev district's 25,209.[71] But they declared that their count was woefully incomplete and that only when the governor's staff conducted a thorough review would it be possible to determine "how insignificant the number of true sons of the Orthodox Church is" in Kostroma province.[72]

Their figures were indeed far too low, as the 1866 diocesan report on those who had and had not confessed revealed. The report categorized non-confessants in a way that minimized the number of schismatics, which was put at 13,973. There was no separate count of those who avoided confession because of "inclination to the schism" (a standard formula used in parish confession registers of the time); they were lumped in with all those who skipped confession: 195,017. The Ministry of Internal Affairs would have counted them all as schismatics, and that figure does not include anyone who gave an acceptable reason for not confessing, such as being away from the parish on business or being sick. Together, the declared Old Believers and those of age to confess (seven and above) who did not, amounted to 22.6 percent of the supposedly Orthodox population in the diocese.[73] And that does not take into account those who bribed priests to list them as confessing, or who confessed but were secret Old Believers. At a minimum, one quarter of those whom the church classified as Orthodox in Kostroma province were Old Believers.

Brianchaninov and Arnoldi's estimates on membership by covenant are the best available but rest on an estimate for all Old Believers that was at a minimum low by a factor of two and probably by much more than that. They put the number of priested Old Believers in the province at 41,336. Among the priestless, Spasovites were most numerous at 33,305, while "rebaptizers" (Pomorsk and Fedoseevites together) numbered 30,479.[74] Brianchaninov and Arnoldi left out the Filippovites, who were particularly strong in the Uren area of the Varnavin district in both the eighteenth and nineteenth centuries, possibly because the Filippovites called themselves Christians–Old Believers of the Pomorsk Heritage of the Filippovite Covenant (or some variation thereon).[75] The number of officially registered Old Believers in 1861 was only 12,209 (of the priestless: 4,531 Pomorsk, 2,016 Spasovites, 319 Fedoseevites). Of those, two-thirds—8,095—lived in the Varnavin district.[76] Arnoldi identified in his diary a number of parishes in the Varnavin district in which almost everyone was a schismatic, including the village of Semenovo, where no more than 200 of 3,680 were genuinely Orthodox. He asserted that "a similar proportion applies to most of the district."[77]

There is later evidence, too, that the Varnavin district teemed with Old Believers and that Spasovites were particularly well represented at Baki. The Holy Synod's annual report for 1883, for instance, referred optimistically to reports from Kostroma that even in the Varnavin district, "the very focal

point" of the schism in the diocese, schismatics no longer shunned Orthodox priests.[78] And in an account of the progress of an Orthodox missionary
who engaged in discussions with Old Believers in fourteen parishes in the
Makariev and Varnavin districts in May–June 1894, we learn that he held
two discussions in Baki

> *at which Spasovites appeared. In the Varnavin district the schism spreads
> because, among other reasons, in this district there are few Orthodox churches,
> and there are villages 30 kilometers distant from their parish churches. In those
> distant villages live Austrian priests [that is, priests of the Old Believer hierar-
> chy established by a renegade Greek Orthodox Metropolitan in Habsburg ter-
> ritory in 1846] and priestless pastors and, taking advantage of the remoteness of
> these villages from churches, they do whatever they will with utter impunity.[79]*

This chronicle of discussions with schismatics generally identified just one
covenant as participating in the encounter in a given parish. Baki was the
only parish in which Spasovites and only Spasovites took part, so we can
assume that they were a major presence there, but we can be sure there were
still priested Old Believers about. Brianchaninov and Arnoldi noted in their
1852 report that among the appanage peasants of the Varnavin district and in
the neighboring property of Prince Lieven, meaning the Baki and Ilinskoe
estates that Christoph and then his brother Karl had inherited, the rebaptizers were particularly strong and that in the district's appanage properties,
almost all marriages were by elopement and without the administration of
the sacrament by a priest.[80] According to a report from 1879, hardly anyone
in the Varnavin district attended an Orthodox church, Old Believer priests
performed most of the marriages, the schism spread openly, and women in
particular were easily recruited into one covenant or another.[81]

That there was a sizeable number of Spasovites at Baki in both the eighteenth and nineteenth centuries seems certain, as does the presence of a
sizeable number of priested Old Believers and probably members of other
priestless covenants. However, the various reports are inconsistent. For
instance, the assertion that in the first half of the nineteenth century, marriage in Varnavin district appanage properties was almost universally by
elopement and that in the same district in the second half of the century,
marriage was almost always performed by Old Believer priests were probably both exaggerations. Up to the 1830s or 1840s, the Spasovites around
Baki and in neighboring appanage properties would likely have employed
Orthodox priests for marriage (as the eloping couples reported by Second

Lieutenant Averkiev did), but it is possible that Spasovites, both then and in the second half of the century, considered Old Believer priests to be just as suitable as Orthodox priests. It is also possible that in the second half of the century, many of the Spasovites were actually Neo-Spasovites, or Spasovites of the Great Rite, whose pastors, while not formally considered priests, did celebrate weddings. Both Spasovite covenants were said to have been present in Kostroma province in the second half of the nineteenth century.[82] Unfortunately, none of those reporting on the Varnavin district seem to have been aware that from the 1840s on, two quite different covenants called themselves Spasovites.[83]

Baki Estate Managers, Marriage Aversion, and Serf Unruliness

We already know that manager Karl Hennemann, urged on by Christoph Lieven, adopted aggressively pro-marriage policies when he assumed responsibility for Baki estate. He had ordered unmarried girls eighteen and over and young men twenty and over to marry by Lent of 1800, and he reported the results to the Lievens: ninety-one marriages and, not counting those too ill or disabled to marry, nineteen men and forty-three women remaining unmarried (he probably meant men and women in the targeted age group, roughly those between twenty and thirty). All had pledged to marry soon, he said.[84] Hennemann must already have known that not all of those promises would be kept. On February 8, 1800, he noted in the punishment log that he had fined Grigorii Markov five rubles for not presenting his daughter Marfa to the estate office, so it had been impossible to arrange her marriage.[85] We can infer from that entry that Hennemann had summoned fathers with their unmarried daughters and had overseen the matches himself. The estate papers include a list of all ninety-two of the marriages celebrated in early 1800, with the names and (in ninety cases) ages of brides and grooms: the mean age of both brides and grooms was twenty-one (grooms were fractionally older); median age of brides was twenty to twenty-one and of grooms, twenty-one; modal age of brides was nineteen and of grooms, twenty. Only seven brides and eight grooms were twenty-five or over.[86] There is not much doubt about the normal age at marriage on the Baki estate. For the most part, these were not the single men and women who most concerned Christoph Lieven.

Probably shortly after Charlotte Lieven bought the neighboring Ilins-koe estate in March 1800, she sent the bailiff and elders there instructions for managing the estate; Lieven ordered that in October, they should tell the peasants that every man over twenty-five should marry and that those who weren't married by February would pay a ten-ruble fine. If a bachelor remained single because he could not find a willing bride, and if he were of good conduct, the bailiff and elders would choose one for him. If the appointed bride stubbornly refused to marry, and if she were over twenty-five, she would be fined five rubles annually. Only those girls kept at home by their parents because there was no other adult labor in the household were exempted from marriage and fine.[87]

Although no similar instructions for the Baki estate have survived, surely Lieven had decided that Hennemann's threat to send unmarried women to St. Petersburg was impractical and had adopted the policy employed by other serf-owners of her day: bailiff and elders should first try to compel marriage; if that didn't work, collect an annual fine. Lieven also adopted another standard practice, having reports on unmarried men and women sent to her annually. Three such lists, dated 1800, 1802, and 1804, have survived from the Baki estate.[88] Only the 1804 enumeration seems more or less complete: 129 men ages fifteen to thirty-five, 225 women ages fifteen to seventy-two.[89] In the 1802 list, he identified 18 of the 92 women ages seventeen to thirty-three as crippled or ill: fits, bent, feeble minded, lame, crippled, weak heart, weak in limb, deaf, and short. Fourteen of 51 unmarried men ages nineteen to thirty-five suffered from similar defects, as well as blindness and axe wounds. As we know from many other sources, peasants did not think all of these ailments actually precluded marriage, but we can understand why Hennemann might think so.

A household inventory for Baki village, based on the 1812 tax census return, but with women as well as men listed, perhaps provides some insight on how effectively the Lievens imposed their marriage regime.[90] Table 6.5 shows that Baki management had increased nuptiality in the village only marginally: among women ages twenty-five to thirty-nine in 1812 (those who had been subjected to management pressure to marry since 1800) eight of sixty-four (12.5 percent) had avoided marriage, whereas among women forty and over, fourteen of ninety-five (14.7 percent) never married. With only two exceptions all Baki men twenty-five and over were married in 1812, but that had nothing to do with management pressure—Baki men had married universally since the 1780s.[91]

Table 6.5 Marriage Aversion among Men and Women Twenty-Five and Older in Baki Village, 1812.

Age	Men		Women	
	Married	Never Married	Married	Never Married
25–29	21	0	17	2
30–34	22	1	20	3
35–39	15	0	19	3
40–44	13	0	18	2
45–49	9	0	15	2
50–54	10	1	17	3
55–59	10	0	11	0
60 and over	15	0	20	7
25 and over	115	2 (1.7%)	137	22 (13.8%)

Source: LP 47424, ff. 135–143v.

The 1812 household inventory is the first extant document that groups Baki residents by household rather than lineage. That offers us a better measure of the extent of marriage resistance than the number of extended families that held single adult women distributed over an unknown number of households. In 1812, of the unmarried women twenty-five and older, two households had three each, four had two each, and eight had one each. Fourteen of 126 households (11 percent) accounted for all the never married women twenty-five and over.[92] That is close to the 13.8 percent of adult women who had never married.

That same inventory, which divided households into five income groups, from wealthy (the 2 households in that group had annual incomes of 15,000 rubles) to poor (which included begging for a living), allows us to evaluate the income of both Old Believers and households with unmarried women twenty-five and over. The two wealthiest household heads, Andreian Osokin and Vasilii Voronin, were both priestless Old Believers. The 5 registered priested households all fell into the second group, the merely prosperous, with incomes of 1,000 to 1,200 rubles per year.[93] Those 7 registered Old Believer households accounted for 7 of the 12 households in the wealthy and prosperous categories. But registered and priestless Old Believers were disproportionately poor. The widow Varvara Vasilieva, forty-two and registered, lived alone and survived on the property her husband had left; since she and her husband apparently had no adult children to contribute to household well-being, her husband was not likely to have left her much beyond the cabin and its furnishings. The other registered priestless Old Believers—three spinsters ages forty-two to sixty-three and a widow, thirty-seven, with a nine-year-old son—shared a household. They survived by selling baked goods and nankeen. The two older women hired themselves out as sowers and the widow did a bit of farming; it is difficult to imagine that they lived much above the subsistence level.[94] But registered priestless households accounted for only two of the thirteen Baki village households with women who had passed through marriage age and remained single. Of those thirteen, one (Osokin's) was wealthy, one was prosperous, three were moderately well-off, one was not well-off, and seven were poor.[95] Just more than half of the presumably priestless households were poor, while among the 122 universally marrying households, 27 (22 percent) were poor.[96]

The priestless and other poor households had characteristics in common, most importantly a lack or shortage of adult male labor. Women in those households, single or not, lived by hiring themselves out as sowers (something even elderly women could do, though they could not have earned much), baking, stitching, and begging. What priestless aversion to marriage did was to double the odds that a household would end up in that unfortunate situation and would, sooner or later, collapse. Since the preceding tax census (1795) was not organized by household, we have no idea how many households collapsed in the interim. But many of the poor priestless households of 1812 could not have survived much longer.

The Lievens monitored Baki nuptial behavior just as vigilantly after 1812 as before. There are no lists of the unmarried in the Lieven papers between 1804 and 1836, but managers may have continued to compile them, as well as related reports. In May 1817, the "most humble slaves and peasants" of Baki reported that there had been thirty-seven marriages so far that year; in September, they reported that there had been no marriages that month.[97] More conclusively, in 1814 Charlotte Lieven sent a reminder to Ivan Kremenetskii, appointed manager at Baki in 1813:

> *In the instruction I issued I ordered that you not compel maidens to choose grooms, they can marry whom they wish. But this refers only to their choice of grooms, and bachelor men's choice of brides, which I now confirm, but does not*

*in the least change my earlier order that you should see to it that lads and maid-
ens not remain single for too long, and thus give themselves over to a shameful,
sinful, dissolute life. For that reason I instruct you to declare to all peasants
my order that men remain single no later than age 21 or 22—unless they stand
to be conscripted soon—and peasant maidens no later than age 20, by which
time men should have found themselves brides and girls grooms. If not, summon
them to the office with their parents, give them another year to find brides and
grooms, and then order them to marry appointed brides and grooms even if
those be contrary to their wishes.*[98]

On the other hand, the Lievens at least occasionally manumitted Baki
women for marriage. In the surviving documents the subject comes up
first in the rough draft of a July 1820 letter Charlotte Lieven sent to Aleksandr Alalykin, who was overseeing Baki. Vasilii Voronin, the wealthy
priestless Old Believer, had requested that his daughter Anna be freed so
that she could marry away from the estate. Lieven wrote that while she
had previously forbidden the practice, if the girl were "truly disposed to
marry" (a note of skepticism), then she would manumit Anna upon receipt
of the departure fee, the amount of which she did not then specify. However, she added, if the matchmaking was not in conformity with rules she
had laid down earlier (unspecified here), then she would not manumit the
girl. And, she concluded, "in the future I have no intention of manumitting
any of my peasants."[99] Alalykin's reply apparently reassured Lieven, for a
July rough draft of the manumission paper freed Anna to "live where she
pleases and marry according to her own wishes." In September, Alalykin
reported that Voronin had delivered a 300-ruble departure fee and received
the paper.[100]

From this exchange, we may infer that at some point the Lievens had
established a 300-ruble departure fee (Alalykin apparently did not have to
be told what it was) but had subsequently banned departure through marriage, probably because they suspected fathers were paying for their daughters' manumission precisely in order to protect them from marriage—hence
Lieven's skepticism about Anna's true intentions. (She did, in fact, marry.)
Before Charlotte Lieven took over the estate, priestless fathers had not needed
to purchase their daughters' immunity. Under the new marriage regime,
some priestless Old Believers must have purchased manumission papers
to put their daughters beyond reach of estate management. The 300 rubles
Lieven charged was at least twice the market price of a marriageable serf girl.
Charlotte Lieven, in her own formulation, made a compassionate exception

to her ban on manumission for marriage, but her true motive was, probably, to bestow a favor on one of the most influential men on the estate.

Christoph Lieven, who inherited the estate in 1828, also occasionally manumitted women for marriage: he charged 350 rubles in 1836, for instance, when he manumitted twenty-one-year-old Arina Ivanova from Baki village so that she could marry a Don Cossack who had settled in Varnavin as a merchant.[101] But we know that Lieven gave his Baki managers power of attorney to manumit serfs: the manager from 1833 to 1835, Lieutenant Colonel (retired) Ivan Grekov, manumitted at least two women without Lieven's knowledge but necessarily with a document permitting him to do so.[102] While there is a gap in the Lieven papers from 1820 to 1835, it is likely that managers then, too, had the same power of attorney and that, at least from time to time, they manumitted women, sometimes with the Lievens' express consent, sometimes perhaps without.

The Lievens also regularly exchanged brides with neighboring appanage villages. In January 1836, Second Lieutenant Averkiev, the gendarme officer temporarily managing the estate, wrote to General Leontii Dubelt, chief of staff of the Corps of Gendarmes, that the Baki estate had for a very long time exchanged brides with neighboring appanage properties and that the balance of trade favored the Lievens: they had acquired more brides from appanage villages than they had yielded in return.[103] A local appanage manager had asked that a Baki girl be allowed to marry an appanage lad; he claimed that the groom fully expected Lieven to give permission. Later in the month, another gendarme officer wrote Averkiev that Lieven had done so.[104] There is no mention of a departure fee in this exchange, which does not necessarily mean that no fee was collected. But it may well have been that around Baki, as elsewhere, when properties routinely exchanged brides in roughly equal numbers, no money other than the peasants' own bride price changed hands. However, manumission papers (and the appanage administration equivalent) would have been issued. Probably the Lievens considered such manumissions to be qualitatively different from transactions involving marriage onto other serf estates, or properties more distant, from which Baki might not receive brides.

The rebellion in 1835 churned up considerable information about marriage at Baki. Lieutenant Colonel Grekov took over management in the second half of 1833. Two years later, on July 10, 1835, estate peasants "almost to a man" (Grekov's words) converged on Baki, beat the serf estate clerk Ivan

Kalinin, locked him in chains, and deposed all of the other serf officials (bailiff, treasurer, village elders, police) because they had not been chosen by the community.[105] They berated Grekov but did not touch him; they told him they intended to send emissaries to lay their complaints before Christoph Lieven. Grekov wrote to Lieven that he had not called in the authorities because he did not know whether Lieven would approve and had allowed the emissaries to set out for St. Petersburg.[106] Grekov could not have blocked them had he tried. The serfs had taken over the estate.

In St. Petersburg, the Baki serfs accused both Grekov and clerk Kalinin of a considerable number of misdeeds. Grekov had ordered every dues-paying unit to prepare a log for the construction of a sawmill, and the logs were now rotting (Grekov: the peasants didn't want to build a sawmill on the Usta River near Staroustie; he had explained they would not be paid for the work but would later earn money hauling logs to the mill. Baki peasants: we once tried to build a mill there, but it couldn't be properly anchored and there are no longer suitable trees in the vicinity). In 1834, Grekov had contracted out one hundred men for sluice-work two hundred kilometers from the estate (later specified to be in the Viazniki district). The men had labored day and night, surviving on bread and water, before slipping away—some immediately, others within a few weeks. The previous winter, Grekov had sold 1,500 rubles' worth of firewood to a merchant. He had probably kept the money for himself, though serfs had provided the firewood in lieu of quitrent and had then been ordered to transport it. Clerk Kalinin had told Izhma villagers that an appanage inspector was going to charge them with producing pitch and tar from trees on appanage property and had persuaded them to give the inspector a 420 gold ruble bribe. They had given the money to the clerk, but the inspector said he never received it. In reality—the peasants claimed—they had worked trees on Lieven property.[107] Since both the extortion of 420 gold rubles and the preparation of logs to construct the mill must have fallen most heavily on the Usta River villages of Dranishnoe and Staroustie, as well as on Izhma, it is not surprising that peasants from those villages were said to have organized the insurrection.[108] The Baki serfs complained subsequently that Kalinin ran the local market and profiteered at their expense.[109]

As became clear shortly, Grekov had also monumentally defrauded Lieven. According to a letter from Dubelt, Grekov had suggested the income-generating innovations complained about and others, but Lieven had considered only one useful: an increase in the annual quitrent, from 10 to 20 rubles. When the Baki serfs complained, Lieven (in Dubelt's account) had agreed to a transitional rate of 15 rubles at Grekov's suggestion, but Grekov had, in fact, collected the 1834 quitrent at the 20-ruble rate—which Lieven had not known—and had pocketed the 11,500 extra rubles as recompense for fictitious expenses. Grekov had also, without authorization, hastened to St. Petersburg in the aftermath of the rebellion, at a time when his presence on the estate was critical. He told Lieven that he was in St. Petersburg to take care of personal affairs.[110] Lieven fired Grekov in late 1835. He wrote to his Baki serfs that every one of their complaints against Grekov was justified but their rebellion was unforgivable.[111]

The insurrection was over by the end of July. On July 21, Ivan Kalinin was freed from chains and sent to Varnavin for questioning by the district court. On July 24, district police chief Pavel Zbruev, in Baki, demanded other peasants turn themselves over for questioning, but they refused. After three days of persuasion and threats, the bailiff and other Baki serfs surrendered, and ten or so suspected instigators were taken to Varnavin for investigation. Chief Zbruev, in a letter to Lieven, promised not to report the rebellion to higher authorities unless Lieven wanted him to. Lieven did not.[112] In effect, the Baki serfs had achieved their purpose. Some of them must have been punished, but Zbruev did keep the affair out of the courts, and the serfs had effected a complete change of estate management: Grekov was fired, Kalinin was permanently removed from the clerkship, and Lieven eventually appointed a new bailiff.[113]

It was from the Baki emissaries that Lieven learned that one of Grekov's many misdeeds involved marriage: he had collected 500 rubles in manumission fees from two estate serfs (a total of 1,000 rubles). The Baki peasants suspected, correctly, that Grekov had not informed Lieven and had pocketed the money.[114] Grekov had also added 150 to 200 rubles to Lieven's departure fee. Lieven commented, "This is a circumstance of the sort that happens frequently with [estate] managers. An abuse of that kind holds no danger for the perpetrator, because the grateful beneficiary will not disclose it."[115] One of the beneficiaries was the (now deceased) priestless Old Believer Vasilii Voronin's son Tikhon; just like his father, he paid for the manumission of his daughter.

In the aftermath of the rebellion, Lieven asked his brother-in-law Alexander Benckendorff, head of the Third Section (Russia's security service), to send an officer to investigate the insurrection and to take over management for a time, and Gendarme Chief of Staff Dubelt selected Second Lieutenant Pavel Averkiev, then serving in Kostroma. Averkiev arrived in Baki in early January 1836.[116] We have already met him—he is our source on the exchange of brides between Baki and appanage villages and on the local predominance of marriage by elopement. We would not have known about the elopement custom had Averkiev not arrived just prior to the peak wedding season and had he not been an inquisitive young man eager to prove himself by restoring tranquility to the estate.

According to Averkiev, Baki peasants made decisions on marriage without any intervention by estate management, and their customs were both bizarre and perverse. It was not just that they married by elopement. In fact, young men complained and older residents confirmed that as of early 1836, young women often gave young men tokens of their agreement to marry—in the past, sacrosanct—and then reneged, after which they and their girlfriends made fun of the would-be grooms. Men thus dishonored became unmarriageable, said Averkiev. Jilted grooms asked Averkiev for help, and he tried to reconcile couples but seldom could. At that point, the girls' parents forbade marriage, and the girls obeyed.[117]

Women's aversion to marriage, at least in Averkiev's mind, was associated with immorality. He claimed that single women were depraved, especially in Baki village, and that "they consider debauchery something permissible." Few of them became pregnant, however, because—so he said he had learned by secret but reliable inquiry—they aborted fetuses at the first sign of pregnancy, and many had "rendered themselves infertile beforehand" or practiced infanticide.[118] Averkiev proposed that unmarried adult women ages twenty to thirty be fined. The earlier fines on unmarried women had been abandoned—long before Grekov's brief tenure, surely—as had every other measure to compel marriage. Another gendarme officer approved Averkiev's suggestion and proposed that Lieven impose an annual fine of twenty-five rubles.[119]

Averkiev associated sexual disorder with both religious and social disorder. He linked sexual promiscuity to religious heterodoxy, especially in Dranishnoe, Staroustie, and Izhma, the three villages east of the Vetluga that in the eighteenth century had been particularly associated with female marriage aversion and in which, Averkiev claimed, most serfs had fallen away from the church and professed a false and immoral faith. It was in those villages, he said, that the rebels of 1835 had first plotted insurrection.[120] There may well have been a connection between what Averkiev considered religious and sexual immorality. While irregular marriage was certainly not a proximate cause of the 1835 insurrection, the serfs on the estate had a history of ungovernability stretching back to their arrival on the forest frontier in the seventeenth century. The association between marital and social disorder was more than metaphorical.

The 1835 insurrection may have been the most serious upheaval on the estate, but not by much. Grekov, in his first report on the outbreak, sought to deflect responsibility from himself by claiming there had been a similar rebellion in 1833, prior to his appointment as manager, when the Baki peasants had deposed the bailiff, the clerk (Ivan Kalinin in that year, too), and other serf officials and had written to Kostroma governor Lanskoi protesting Lieven's intention to increase their quitrent. There is no other information on that disturbance, but the documents from 1835 to 1836 state that Lieven decided to raise the quitrent only in 1834, at Grekov's suggestion, and none of the documents referring to Grekov's appointment suggest that it occurred in the aftermath of a rebellion. If any disturbance such as Grekov described actually did occur in 1833, it was most likely one of a long series of tumults that grew out of conflict among the serfs themselves. Averkiev implied that the same may have been true in 1835. He blamed both Old Believers and the wealthy, who hoped that their wealth would protect them, for fomenting the rebellion. The likely instigators Police Chief Zbruev identified were in fact among the estate's wealthiest serfs.[121] It may be indicative that Grekov claimed that in 1833 the serfs chose Vasilii Ivanov Voronin—a priested relative of the priestless Voronin family who had been at the center of intra-estate conflict since the beginning of the century—as their new clerk.[122]

In 1813, serf opposition to Ivan Oberuchev (and his many real misdeeds) led to his dismissal as manager; the serf clerk, son-in-law to the wealthy priestless Vasilii Voronin, was apparently removed at the initiative of the serfs themselves, and Voronin lost influence over communal affairs. In 1817, intrigues by both Vasilii Voronin and his rival Andreian Osokin, and likely other of the wealthy serfs angered by Ivan Kremenetskii's insistence that their sons be subject to conscription or that they contribute disproportionately to the purchase of substitutes, led to Kremenetskii's resignation.[123] In 1818, the serfs, apparently prompted by one of Osokin's sons, replaced the Baki bailiff again. Manorial documents refer to this as an insurrection, involving both Baki and Lieven's neighboring Ilinskoe estate. In the after-math, some of Voronin's male relatives were designated for conscription, while Osokin and his entire family were expelled from the estate and forced to purchase their manumission for 10,000 paper rubles.[124] Baki serf families had long histories of ignoring the decrees of church, state, and owner. Only a few documents from 1820 to 1834 have survived, but it is unlikely that the serfs were any less unruly between those dates than before and after. Con-flicts among the serfs themselves almost always fueled the upheavals but also always turned into rejection of management authority.

The evidence generated by the 1835 rebellion demonstrates conclusively that at some point—probably after Ivan Krementskii's resignation in 1817—managers abandoned the effort to achieve universal marriage on the estate. In October 1836, Christoph Lieven ordered Averkiev to compel women to marry and to fine those who refused twenty-five rubles annually. In Feb-ruary 1837, the estate clerk reported to Lieven that seventy-two women had married in the just-concluded wedding season. Most would have been teenagers and women in their early twenties and probably married of their own volition.[125] Unfortunately, the estate papers break off in 1837, and the promised lists of those who had married and those who had paid the fine on singleness have not been preserved. Nor do we know what other efforts, if any, Christoph and his brother Karl, who inherited in 1839, made to force universal marriage on the estate. All we can say for certain is that the 1836 order and any others that may have followed had no perceptible effect.

NUPTIALITY, 1795–1858

By 1834, the ceiling age for women (and men) in Baki village had risen to thirty, as table 6.6 shows, so the cohort of those thirty to forty-four best reveals current nuptial practice at the date of the census. Marriage resis-tance had risen somewhat from its 1812 nadir, 13.8 percent, to 15 percent. By 1858, it had declined again (as measured by the cohort of thirty- to fory-four-year-olds) to 12.7 percent. In 1795, 21.2 percent of women in Baki village had been marriage averse. Over the course of three generations, women's resis-tance to marriage had declined significantly.

As table 6.7 shows, that was true across the estate. The key cohort is, again, women ages thirty to forty-four, whose rate of marriage aversion declined by about 60 percent between 1795 and 1858. However, the decline was far from uniform. In 1834, marriage aversion in the six west bank

Table 6.6 Marriage Aversion among Women by Age in Baki Village, 1834–58.

Age	1834		1858	
	Married	Never Married	Married	Never Married
25–29	42	18 (30.0%)	34	14 (29.2%)
30–44	68	12 (15.0%)	89	13 (12.7%)
45 and over	68	12 (15.0%)	110	19 (14.7%)

Source: GAKO, f. 200, op. 3, d. 462, ll. 6520b–683; op. 13, d. 30, ll. 4710b–522.

Table 6.7 Marriage Aversion among Women by Age in the Other Eleven Baki Estate Villages, 1795–1858.

Age	1795		1834		1858	
	Married	Never Married	Married	Never Married	Married	Never Married
25–29	62	21 (25.3%)	122	34 (21.7%)	93	38 (29.0%)
30–44	113	40 (26.1%)	204	41 (16.7%)	310	40 (11.5%)
45 and over	127	46 (26.5%)	187	19 (9.2%)	277	63 (18.5%)

Sources: LP 47421, ff. 45–103; GAKO, f. 200, op. 3, d. 462, ll. 6880b–788; op. 13, d. 22, ll. 1140–123; d. 30, ll. 5220b–552, 5600b–592, 6020b–651.

villages was 15.6 percent, just a bit lower than the 18 percent of 1795. In the east bank villages of Dranishnoe, Staroustie, and Izhma, aversion had fallen from its 1795 level of 38.4 percent to 17.5 percent (in Dranishnoe, to a meager 5 percent). In Kirilovo and Iadrovo, also on the east bank but with minimal marriage aversion in 1795, aversion rose to the same 17.5 percent. Nuptiality rates in the different clusters on the estate, previously sharply divergent, had converged.

Between 1834 and 1858, nuptiality rates diverged again, because female marriage aversion continued to fall in Staroustie, Izhma, and Dranishnoe to 11.2 percent (thirty- to forty-four-year-olds), while remaining steady at 16.3 percent in the six west bank villages. The rate in Kirilovo and Iadrovo had fallen back to 7 percent. The lower level of aversion among women forty-five and over in 1834, and the higher level in 1858, were echoes of an earlier history.

Neither the considerable decline of marriage aversion deep in the woods east of the Vetluga nor the rise and decline in Kirilovo and Iadrovo had anything to do with management policy on marriage. Changing rates of nuptiality in the eleven villages were due to choices peasants made themselves. Since Averkiev singled out Dranishnoe, Staroustie, and Izhma as schismatic strongholds in 1836, the fall in marriage aversion there did not signal a return to Orthodoxy. Most likely, women remained priestless but, as among the Spasovites of Kuplia parish, began to marry—perhaps around the same time and just as precipitously as at Kuplia, if the universal marriage among thirty- to thirty-four-year-old women in Izhma and Dranishnoe in 1834 is indicative. The spike in marriage aversion in Kirilovo and Iadrovo might have been due to the emergence of marriage aversion, as among the Pomorsk of Kuplia parish, but it did not last long. Lacking actual evidence that might explain these trends, we can only speculate. It does seem to have been the case that at any given moment from 1795 to 1858, somewhere on the Baki estate women were reconsidering their attitude toward marriage.

MARRIAGE-AVERSE WOMEN, HOUSEHOLD PERIL, AND SPECTRAL HOUSEHOLDS IN BAKI VILLAGE

Documents from Baki offer particularly useful insight into the conditions that could turn even a single unmarried adult woman into a household catastrophe. In July 1836, Averkiev produced a list of households divided into four categories on the basis of wealth and moral qualities. He described the first two classes (24 and 43 households in Baki village) as doing well; the third (51 households) included households "that are not in great need, but are significantly poorer than the peasants in class two." The fourth class, only 17 households, consisted of peasants with "nothing at all, which includes the elderly, orphans and peasants of depraved conduct, of whom many don't even have their own homes and from childhood wander from village to village."[126] Depravity was represented by two households total-ing, in 1834, three women with an illegitimate child each. Averkiev identi-fied only the oldest male in each of the 135 households.

Linking those households to the 1834 census return, we find that twenty-five (18.5 percent) held at least one unmarried woman twenty-five and over in 1834. Households with unmarried women accounted for (in descending order) 17, 16, and 14 percent in the top three classes. In the fourth class, seven (41 percent) included unmarried adult women. They accounted for 28 percent of all marriage-averse households on Averkiev's list, while the other ten fourth-class households account for only 9.9 percent of the universally marrying households.[127] We might conclude that in the 1830s, households with unmarried adult women were three times more likely to be utterly destitute and in imminent danger of disintegration than households in which all adults married. In 1812, the risk of destitution had been only a bit more than double for households with unmarried women, but given the relatively small number of utterly destitute households in 1812 and 1836, the difference was probably due to random fluctuation.

Yet there was a category below destitution. Missing from Averkiev's 1836 list were sixteen of the households in the 1834 census. Only one contained an adult male; the others were composed of widows, single women, and minor children.[128] Those households almost certainly did not actually exist, either in 1834 or in 1836; how would they have supported themselves, and why would Averkiev not have included them among the destitute? They were artifacts of the 1834 census return: wherever those women and children were actually sheltering, the census enumerator inserted them into former, now virtual, households, which survived in the census returns for tracking purposes, until every last person who had ever lived in them had died or otherwise disappeared. Unlike the wandering destitute, these remnants had been absorbed into existing households. In Kuplia parish from 1830 to 1834, the Sluchkovo census return concealed the households in which Sluchkovites actually lived. The priest's confession register revealed them. Averkiev's 1836 list of Baki households reveals neither agglomerations nor remnants tacked to viable households but points to their presence—where else might those sixteen households have gone?

For a better measure of the impact of both random demographic misfortune and female marriage aversion at Baki, I add the virtual households to those listed by Averkiev, for a nominal total of 151; they had all been functioning households sometime in the past, otherwise they would not have had their own boxes in the 1834 census return.[129] The 15 households and virtual remnants with unmarried adult women at the level of destitution, or no longer actually existing, accounted for fully 45.5 percent of the 33 households and ghosts with unmarried women in the 1834 census. The 18 currently destitute and virtual households in which all women twenty-five and over had married represented 13.6 percent of those that practiced universal marriage. In addition, according to the 1834 census, 5 of the households listed in the 1816 census had disappeared.[130] Counting them together with the universally marrying households of 1834 (the 1812 household inventory seems to justify that assumption), 17.2 percent of universally marrying households collapsed, or reached the point of no return, between 1816 and 1834. It is perhaps surprising that random demographic misfortune destroyed close to 20 percent of Baki village households that (at least between 1816 and 1834) held no unmarried adult women. It is stunning that at Baki even a single unmarried adult woman pushed a household's likelihood of collapse toward 50 percent.

By 1858, most of the ghost households—12 of the 16 from 1834 to 1836—had disappeared from the census return because all of the survivors had died. Another 6 households also disappeared from the census. Seven of the households in which everyone had died had held spinsters—19.4 percent of the 36 households with unmarried adult women. The other 11 accounted for 9.8 percent of the 112 households listed in the 1834 census in which all women twenty-five and over had married. Without any source with which to compare the 1858 Baki village census return, we have no way to identify its virtual households. We can, however, identify many that may have been mere census specters or in danger of imminent disappearance: 39 held solitary men and women (elderly widows, spinsters), childless elderly couples well beyond the age of reproduction, or middle-age widows with young children, or faced demographic peril for some other reason. Ten of those households held unmarried adult women, 27.7 percent of the 36 marriage-averse households in the 1858 census return. The 29 universally marrying but demographically imperiled households represented only 19.8 percent of the 146 universally marrying households of 1858.[131] Those are just estimates of households in peril; some middle-age couples may later have adopted an heir to support them in their old age or found some other way to prolong household life. Some of the 39 endangered households probably existed, but many of them certainly did not. Whatever measure we use, unmarried adult women significantly increased the odds of penury and household collapse.

Those odds were conditioned by other choices Baki peasants made—most importantly, to live in small family units. In 1834, the mean size of the census households at Baki was 5.48 individuals (148 households, 372 men, 439 women). I provide that standard measure for comparative purposes only, ignoring the fact that 16 of those households were ghosts, their supposed members distributed among the rest; the actual mean size was 6.1. Published calculations of mean household size in other villages must also often have been based on household counts that included ghosts. In any case, 5.48 was appreciably lower than the mean household size of 6.80 (an average of villages studied) in the mid-nineteenth century in Russia's central industrial zone, of which Kostroma province was a part, but by no means was it the lowest reported.[132]

We get a better sense of household preferences at Baki if we set aside the 34 census households of 1834 that no longer contained married couples. The average size of the remaining 114 was 6.3 individuals. The modal household was the single married couple (not always with children): 56 of the 114. Another 27 couples lived with a widowed parent. Those should be grouped with the 19 households with father-and-son married couples because they followed the same life courses: couple with children, father-son married couples, couple with a widowed parent. Most of the one-couple households, too, would turn later into two-couple and then couple-with-widowed-parent households. The other arrangements—four pairs of married brothers, three households with three married couples, and some minor variants (grandparents living with a grandson and wife, for instance)—were exceptions. Single adult women lived as sisters, daughters, aunts, and nieces in both the two- and three-generation households. All of the couples in nuclear families had probably spent some short time after marriage in the parental household before breaking away. The overwhelming majority of all Baki peasants—including those in remnant households as of 1834–36—had chosen either to marry and stay in the groom's parental household or marry and move out. Household preferences in 1858 were almost exactly the same. The not quite invariable rule was that only one younger couple remained with the parental couple. In the demographic literature, this household pattern is known as the stem family.[133]

Small families were especially vulnerable to demographic mischance. For Baki men, the odds of early death were heightened by work in the forest and along rivers and travel for commerce and work. In 1834, there were only seven widowers at Baki, but forty-six widows, four of them in their twenties and thirties. In 1858, there were nineteen widowers and seventy widows. The youngest widows were nineteen and twenty-eight, eight more were in their thirties, and thirteen were in their forties. In 1812, there had been nine widowers and forty-two widows. Male mortality was so great that it could denude even three-generation households of adult men (a few households had no adult men but two generations of widows), but nuclear households, whether or not containing never-married adult sisters, nieces, or aunts, were most at risk.

Analysis of household structures does not immediately suggest why unmarried adult women would have been so strongly associated with household destitution and collapse. In 1834, there were both small and large households (up to twelve members in universally marrying households, up to nine in households containing marriage-averse women) in Averkiev's top three wealth classes. Moreover, mean household size in the top three classes was larger among the marriage-averse than among the universally marrying—7.1 versus 5.8—which suggests that households with marriage-averse women achieved on average the same labor capacity as households not burdened with unmarried adult women. Mean household size in Averkiev's fourth class, however, was clearly associated with destitution: among the destitute, universally marrying households' average size was 4.6, among marriage-averse households' only 4.Among the sixteen household remnants not on Averkiev's list, there was only one adult male.

Household remnants were one likely source of the danger faced by households with unmarried adult women: most could not possibly have sustained themselves and must have been an added burden to households that sheltered or fed them. Existing marriage-averse households were those most likely to provide shelter for refugees from collapsed marriage-averse households; that was the pattern among Spasovites in Kuplia parish. Since there were far fewer marriage-averse than universally marrying households to provide shelter, refugees from collapsed marriage-averse households at the bottom likely cascaded upward, in turn pulling third-class households that offered the refugees shelter toward destitution and eventual destruction. And then a new set of survivors must have sought shelter upward. The only evidence that directly supports this conclusion is Averkiev's observation that homeless destitute households wandered from village to village—wandered, of course, in search of at least temporary shelter in functioning households. The spectral household remnants, most of which consisted of only one or two members, must have found permanent refuge.

However, a slow cascade of wretched survivors through marriage-averse households need not be the only explanation for their extraordinarily elevated rate of destitution and extinction. Mean household size among the seven marriage-averse households in Averkiev's third, struggling, category was an above-average 6.28, but if we set aside the unmarried adult women (two households had two each), mean household size falls to 4.86 (assuming they sheltered no refugees from extinct households). Three marriage-averse households had only two members at least twenty-five years old other than unmarried adult women: husband and wife (ages sixty-one and fifty-eight in 1834), an unmarried daughter (age twenty-seven), and a bachelor son (age twenty-two); husband and wife (ages fifty-four and fifty), with unmarried daughters (twenty-five and twenty-nine); and a couple (ages forty-six and forty-eight), the husband's spinster sister (thirty-one), daughter (twenty-five), and bachelor son (twenty-one). The other four marriage-averse households in class three—by Averkiev's definition, "not in great need"—could quite accidentally fall over the edge, but those three would almost inevitably descend into destitution or worse. Either or both of the parents in all three would soon die, leaving spinsters to fend for themselves in one case and leaving an unmarried young adult male in each of the others; the fact that they had not yet married, despite the obvious urgency, suggests that one or both of them either would not or could not.

There were, likewise, households in class two that were candidates for relegation to class three or lower, at least based on demographic indicators, but they obviously had resources beyond labor power. Households whose only resource was labor, including almost all of those in the third class, could not forestall descent into destitution if they contracted to unmarried women and an unmarried young adult male, whether or not he married later. Healthy widows and spinsters might contribute to household earnings but could not fell trees or render them into tar and pitch over the winter. Nor could they successfully till the miserable local soil. The one adult male must often have had little choice but to wrest sustenance from resistant earth rather than earn money by rafting or in other off-farm pursuits.[134] And that was the most favorable, not the most likely, outcome. If such a household took in a refugee widow or spinster, if winter forest work ravaged the health of the adult male, prospects were grim.

Conscription, too, contributed to household mortality. Between 1816 and 1834, seventeen substitutes were purchased and sent to the army to satisfy part of the conscript levy on the estate as a whole.[135] On the evidence of Baki village, the principal beneficiaries were the wealthy households, which individually or collectively provided the money: no conscripts were taken from the twenty-four households Averkiev put in the first class in Baki village in 1836. Baki village conscripts were taken from seven of the forty-three second-class households (17.3 percent), seven of the fifty-one third-class households (13.7 percent), and one of the seventeen destitute fourth-class households (5.9 percent). The wealthy households aside, there seems to have been an effort to distribute the damage caused by conscription more or less equitably. Nevertheless, conscription was probably responsible for the destitution of the one class-four household that lost a son to the army.

Conscription had also destroyed two other households by 1834. One conscript perhaps left a wife (freed when her husband was conscripted and so not listed on the Baki census return) and certainly left a daughter who was thirteen in 1834, as well as a forty-four-year-old never-married sister. The other household perhaps consisted of only the conscript's nineteen-year-old daughter (but perhaps also his wife).[136] The available evidence on conscription at Baki between 1816 and 1834 suggests that the most unfortunate Baki households were not singled out but that those were the households conscription was most likely to destroy. Conscription, like elevated male mortality, was an inescapable reality at Baki and, like death, sometimes stripped households of the male labor needed to survive.

All Baki households with an unfavorable balance of production capacity to consumption requirements struggled, but small households with one or two marriage-averse women were more likely to experience a labor deficit than those without. In the bottom 50 percent of the households—Averkiev's categories three and four—the risks were magnified for households with only a single married couple or with a young couple and aged or widowed parents. The potentially rewarding but demographically threatening forest economy added to the risk. Conscription had the same effect. Many Baki households sank to the bottom, but those with an unmarried woman or two did so at two to three times the rate of universally marrying households.

NOTES

1. LP 47422, f. 42v. Work for the owner (*gospodskaia rabota*) probably meant work at the estate rather than being sent to the countess as house serfs.

2. The law is available in a Holy Synod decree of February 28, 1765 (*Polnoe sobranie postanovlenii i rasporiazhenii*, vol. 1, pp. 265–66). Also see Freeze, *Russian Levites*, pp. 165–67, who suggests that the lawful fees for rites would have produced, on average, an annual income of two to three rubles. Naturally, priests continued to charge far more than was lawful.

3. LP 47422, ff. 47–48v.

4. LP 47428, f. 68–68v.

5. On payment to the priests, see LP 47428, ff. 7–8. On various statistics on the number of parishioners, see ibid., f. 68–68v; 47424, f. 133. On the average money income of priests, see Freeze, *Russian Levites*, pp. 166–67. On how a priest earned forty

rubles per year in the second half of the eighteenth century, based on the notebook of a priest in a village near Iaroslavl, see Semevskii, "Sel'skii sviashchennik," pp. 507–14. That priest also received approximately forty rubles' worth of in-kind payments and contributions.

6. LP 47424, f. 5.

7. Ibid., f. 3.

8. I use twenty-five as the ceiling age at Baki, as in Kuplia parish, because that facilitates comparison. But at Baki, a few women did marry between ages twenty-five and twenty-nine. The table therefore slightly overstates marriage aversion. A handful of Baki girls married at thirteen or fourteen, and many older teenagers also married. Marriage began earlier than in Kuplia, and the ceiling age was higher.

9. Data for 1763 to 1782 are from the 1782 tax census (GAKO, op. b/sh, d. 546, ll. 76–1090b, 1510b–59, 175–870b, 234–45, 2770b–840b, 306–3370b). For the eight villages from 1782 to 1795, see LP 47421, ff. 45–103.

10. Platonov, *Ocherki po istorii*, pp. 32–34; Liubavskii, *Obrazovanie*, p. 94; Ivina, *Vnutrennee osvoenie*, p. 152; Baldin, *Varnavinskaia starina*, pp. 15–17.

11. For Varnava arriving in the fifteenth century, see Baldin, *Varnavinskaia starina*, p. 16–17. Antonov, "Iz istorii," p. 150, observes that among all the documents (real and forged) that the monks offered in their disputes over land, the first to associate the monastery with Varnava dates from 1607; he concludes that Varnava could not have arrived before the sixteenth century and may have been entirely legendary.

12. Morokhin, *Po reke Vetluge*, p. 10.

13. See the extensive quotations from and remarks about the text in Shumakov, *Obzor "Gramot,"* vol. 4, pp. 135–37. On possible modernization rather than fabrication, see Ivina, *Vnutrennee osvoenie*, p. 152.

14. Shumakov, *Obzor "Gramot,"* vol. 4, pp. 137–38.

15. Antonov, "Iz istorii," p. 150.

16. Ivina, *Vnutrenee osvoenie*, pp. 152–53; Got'e, *Zamoskovnyi krai*, p. 335.

17. Makarii, *Istorii nizhegorodskoi ierarkhii*, pp. 64, 79, 90, 97; Begunov and Panchenko, "Arkheograficheskaia ekspeditsiia," pp. 387–88.

18. Kititsyn, "Staroobriadcheskie skity," pp. 174–75; Kititsyn, "Iz proshlogo," pp. 351–52. Present-day Kostroma historians concur. See, for example, Nagradov, *Raskolot' "raskol,"* p. 92.

19. Shumakov, *Obzor "Gramot,"* vol. 4, p. 151; Antonov, "Iz istorii," p. 152.

20. Ivina, *Vnutrenee osvoenie*, pp. 153–54; Antonov, "Iz istorii," pp. 148–49, 154; Baldin, *Varnavinskaia starina*, pp. 22–26.

21. Rumiantseva, *Narodnoe antitserkovnoe dvizhenie*, p. 71. Her source is the Life of Kornilii of Vyg, published by Breshchinskii, "Zhitie Korniliia," pp. 68–70. Kornilii did not say exactly where along the Vetluga Kapiton settled.

22. *Istoriia o kazanskom*, col. 304. The original has not survived. This volume provides two of the well over one hundred known manuscript versions. There are very helpful introductions by the editor of the original 1903 publication and the editor of the 2000 republication.

23. *Riazradnaia kniga 1559–1636 gg.*, pp. 217–20, 347–48; *Razriadnaia kniga 1475–1598 gg.*, p. 252; Morokhin, *Po reke Vetluge*, p. 105. Evidence on these rebellions is fragmentary, but Ermolaev, *Srednee Povolzh'e*, pp. 32–36, provides a persuasive account based on the few surviving Muscovite records.

24. *Istoriia o kazanskom*, cols. 169, 185–86, 320–21, 354, 392, 407; Ermolaev, *Srednee Povolzh'e*, pp. 76–102; *Akty, sobrannye*, vol. 2, pp. 163–64, 167–70, 216–22, 278–79, 322–23, 352–53; *Polnoe sobranie russkikh letopisei*, vol. 14, p. 86; *Dvortsovye razriady*, vol. 1, col. 205. See also Dimitriev, "Vosstanie iasachnykh," pp. 109–19. For some reason, Dimitriev, after quoting the source identifying the Cheremis involved in 1616 as those from the Meadow side, misidentifies them as the Hill Cheremis (Dimitriev, "Vosstanie iasachnykh," p. 114).

25. Shumakov, *Obzor "Gramot,"* vol. 4, p. 151.

26. *Krest'ianskaia voina*, vol. 2, ch. 1, pp. 201–2, 226–28, 248–51, 277–82, 285–86, 315–17, 346–47, 362–63, 404–5, 407–10. Partly summarized in Baldin, *Varnavinskaia starina*, pp. 33–35.

27. *Krest'ianskaia voina*, pp. 431–34, 476–78.

28. Lebedev, "Krest'ianskoe dvizhenie," pp. 62–63, 65–66; Chaev, *Bulavinskoe vosstanie*, pp. 113–14; Pod"iapol'skaia, *Vosstanie Bulavina*, pp. 96, 121, 195; Lebedev, *Bulavinskoe vosstanie*, pp. 116–17.

29. Baldin, *Varnavinskaia starina*, p. 37. On brigandage, whether by outlaws or by individuals and groups of peasants moving into the area, see Kupletskii, "Beglye krest'iane," no. 6, pp. 178 and passim; Kupletskii, "Beglye krest'iane," no. 7, pp. 348–50 and passim.

30. Lomonosov, *Sochineniia*, p. 457.

31. Shumakov, *Obzor "Gramot,"* vol. 4, p. 137.

32. LP 47428, f. 124.

33. Ibid., f. 20.

34. GAKO, f. 200, op. b/sh, d. 546, ll. 76–352.

35. Kupletskii, "Beglye krest'iane," no. 6, pp. 171–91; no. 7, pp. 339–56.

36. Pyzhikov, *Grani russkogo raskola*, pp. 112–15, 132–38.

37. LP 47428, f. 20.

38. Ibid., ff. 20, 52–55; ibid., 47421, f. 103.

39. *Kostromskaia guberniia. Spisok.* I have also used the very detailed *Nizhegorodskaia oblast': topograficheskaia karta.*

40. *Kostromskaia guberniia. Spisok*, pp. vi, viii, xvi; Zarubin, "Zametki," pp. 392–94.

41. GAKO, f. 200, op. b/sh, d. 546, ll. 76–352 (1782); LP 47421, ff. 45–103 (1795).

42. LP 47428, ff. 1–2. There are useful descriptions of the harvesting and shipping of forest products along the Vetluga in *Kostromskaia guberniia. Spisok*, p. xvi, and Tsvetkov, "Geografiia vnutrennikh lesnykh rynkov," pp. 98–100. Smith, "Sustenance and the Household," pp. 165–79, provides a complementary description of two Iusopov villages in the Varnavin district.

43. Melton, "Household Economies," pp. 564–78. On the religious affiliations of Osokin and Voronin, see LP 47428, f. 254v. Melton gives Osokin's annual income as

1,500 rubles and Vorinin's as 1,000 to 1,500 rubles annually, but I read both figures as 15,000 (LP 47424, f. 140-140v, households 65, 88). On Osokin's net worth, see LP 47419, f. 170v. On Voronin's, see LP 47429, f. 237. On the regional importance of the Baki market, see *Kostromskaia guberniia. Spisok*, p. xvii. A report from 1836 describes the very impressive array of goods available at the market (LP 47432, ff. 303v-5).

44. Zarubin, "Zametki," p. 420. On the impact of winter forest work on health in the Vetluga district just north of the Varnavin district, see Malygin, "Materialy po osmotru." The forest economies were identical, but Malygin was writing about conditions in the early twentieth century. Although the squalid conditions in the dugouts appalled Malygin, he did not mention scurvy and scrofula as health problems. In his 1870s novel *V lesakh*, pp. 214–19, set in the mid-nineteenth century, Melnikov describes the same living and working conditions, but with a slight romantic gloss, in a winter logging camp not far from Varnavin; Ogloblin described the same conditions, without the romanticism, in 1903 in *Vetluzhskie burlaki* (Nizhnii Novgorod, 1903), as quoted in Morokhin, *Po reke Vetluge*, p. 126.

45. *PSZ*, vol. 21, pp. 304–6, 344–52, 745.

46. Neither the instructions nor the model reporting forms for the 1763 census, issued in November 1761, mention Old Believers, but the model form for summary reports of totals by category of the population does provide a space for the total number of Old Believers subject to the double tax (*PSZ*, vol. 15, pp. 834–40). Only in March 1764 were instructions issued to submit lists of Old Believers (*PSZ*, vol. 16, pp. 596–97), by which date most of the census returns had already been filed. The reasoning behind this late instruction was that the information on Old Believers in the preceding tax census (1744) must have been out of date. In any case, if the Baki returns were submitted in 1763 (likely), the information on Old Believers would have been copied from the 1744 return. At the then crown estate of Sidorovo in western Kostroma province, the 1763 census return file includes a separate list of Old Believers at the beginning, compiled in 1764; the 1763 census return does not itself identify the Old Believers (RGADA, f. 1454, op. 1, d. 46, ll. 7–140b).

47. The lists are found in LP 47428, ff. 253–55. I have identified their households in an 1812–13 household list (LP 47424, ff. 135-143 ob). The household list is not dated, but it was based on the 1812 tax census return, with change of status down to 1813, and contains much additional information.

48. Of the five unmarried nominally Orthodox men listed in the 1795 census, the three youngest, ages twenty-five to twenty-seven, probably married subsequently. They are not on the list of unmarried men and women in Baki as of 1804 (LP 7422, f. 55). Of course, they may also have been conscripted.

49. Of the eight unmarried male Old Believers in 1763, only one was still alive in 1795. There were two perhaps never-married elderly Orthodox males in 1763, two generations older than the next "Orthodox" adult single males. In 1795, three of the five unmarried Old Believer men age twenty-five and more were about to marry. See the preceding footnote.

50. The 1782 populations for Iadrovo, Kirilovo, and Dranishnoe are in LP 47421, ff. 45–103. The figures for Dranishnoe in 1747 are in LP 47428, f. 124.

51. Ibid., f. 124v.

52. Sixteen families in the 1782 tax census had at least one identified Old Believer, but four families had only a single avowed Old Believer each during the thirty-two years between 1763 and 1795, two of them fleetingly. One Old Believer woman, for instance, married sometime between the 1763 and 1782 censuses and was quickly sent into exile, at age sixteen; the census return notes her brief passage but does not include her in the population count. Some of the families I have counted among the Old Believers included adults who were not labeled schismatics, but those families held two or more schismatics and exhibited marriage avoidance across the generations. I have divided one family into two. Vasilii Vasiliev was labeled a schismatic and had schismatic descendants, but his brother Andrei, or any of his many descendants, was not labeled a schismatic. Only one of them never married. I have placed Andrei and his descendants in the "Orthodox" population.

53. I have included among the never-married a few women who turned twenty-five between the census years but died prior to the following censuses; the 1782 and 1795 censuses give their dates of death. I have not counted women in families that moved away from the village.

54. Zarubin, "Zametki," p. 397.

55. A gendarme source from 1836 characterizes Kirilovo as a schismatic stronghold. If true, nuptial behavior points to the priested Old Belief (LP 47432, ff. 306–7).

56. LP 47421, ff. 49, 63v, 66, 76v, 81v, 84v, 86v, 87v, 90v, 94.

57. LP 47432, f. 297–97v.

58. See the discussion in chapter 3.

59. Brianchaninov and Arnol'di, "O raskole," pp. 300–301. Brianchaninov and Arnoldi asserted that the girls' parents consented to this. However, they also said that the girls were called *samokrutki*, meaning that they put on the married woman's headdress by themselves; that term was always associated with elopement. Formal parental consent was no doubt given after the fact, not beforehand. As late as the early twentieth century, Old Believer chapels outnumbered Orthodox chapels in the Uren area twenty-three to five (Begunov and Panchenko, "Arkheograficheskaia ekspeditsiia," p. 388).

60. See note 75 for sources.

61. Smirnov, *Vnutrennie voprosy*, pp. 170–81, 077–081.

62. There is considerable documentation of this traffic in the papers of the Nizhnii Novgorod Diocese. For example, there are two cases from 1830 (TsANO, f. 570, op. 557, 1830, dd. 38, 39). Cases of this sort were also investigated by the Nizhnii Novgorod governor's office (e.g., TsANO, f. 5, op. 46, 1839, d. 55, ll. 16–180b; 1841, d. 55). On the requirement that Old Believers swear to join the Orthodox prior to marriage by an Orthodox priest, see *PSZ*, vol. 6, p. 741 (a senate and synod decree of July 16, 1722); *PSZ*, vol. 9, p. 791 (a senate decree of March 22, 1736); *Polnoe sobranie postanovlenii i rasporiazhenii, [Seriia 5]*, vol. 1, pp. 444–45 (a synod ruling of 1830).

63. Old Believer and Orthodox parents deflected responsibility for giving their daughters in marriage in many ways. See, for instance, Bushnell, "Bor'ba za nevestu." The North Russian bridal lament was a ritualized denial by the bride that she was in any way responsible for marrying away from her family and usually absolved her parents of responsibility as well.

64. TsANO, f. 5, op. 46, d. 46.

65. RGB OR, f. 17, no. 595, ll. 1–36; Vishniakov, "Novozheny," pp. 93–97. A similar custom is reported from the city of Torzhok in the early nineteenth century (A. N., "O Bezhetskom uezde," pp. 195–96).

66. Prokof'eva and Nagradov, "Istoriia staroobriadchestva," p. 114.

67. Kititsyn, "Staroobriadcheskie skity," pp. 174–75.

68. *Polnoe Sobranie postanovlenii i rasporiazhenii, [Seriia 4]*, pp. 563, 565.

69. Prokof'eva and Nagradov, "Istoriia staroobriadchestva," pp. 51, 67; Nagradov, *Raskolot' "raskol,"* pp. 62–63, 98.

70. *Krest'ianskoe dvizhenie v Rossii v 1826–1849 gg.*, pp. 161–73, 653–54; Nagradov, *Raskolot' "raskol,"* pp. 91–95; Nagradov, "Urenskii miatezhnyi," pp. 207–11; Gorlanov, "Udel'nye krest'iane," pp. 283–85.

71. Brianchaninov and Arnol'di, "O raskole," pp. 295–97, 324. Population: Krzhivoblotskii, *Materialy po geografii*, p. 176. Corrupt priest (just one of many examples): "Iz dnevnika Kollezhskogo Assesora Arnol'di," p. 21. See also Brianchaninov, "Iz dnevnika Nadvornogo Sovetnika," pp. 23–27.

72. Brianchaninov and Arnol'di, "O raskole," p. 297.

73. *Pamiatnaia kniga dlia Kostromskoi eparkhii*, Otd. 2, pp. 103–4. I have corrected arithmetical errors in the published figures. The percentage for the peasant estate counted separately is identical.

74. Brianchaninov and Arnol'di, "O raskole," pp. 298–301; Nagradov, *Raskolot' "raskol,"* pp. 83–84, provides a few details on the work of the investigative committee.

75. Nagradov, *Raskolot' "raskol,"* pp. 242–43. Most information on the Uren Filippovites comes from sources on Filippovites in Viatka province, who traced their lineage back to Uren; ten manuscript copies of what is called *Urenskii sbornik*, which tells that story, have been found, and into the second half of the nineteenth century, the Viatka Filippovites appealed to Uren Filippovites to help sort out their internal conflicts. A review of the history, a version of *Urenskii sbornik*, and other documents, as well as references to earlier scholarship, can be found in *Materialy k istorii staroobriadchestva Iuzhnoi Viatki*, pp. 19–24, 71–103, 106, 116,130, 133, 144. Pochinskaia, "O bytovanii rodoslovnii," pp. 424–30, is particularly clear on the dating of Filippovites around Uren in the eighteenth century.

76. Krzhivoblotskii, *Materialy*, p. 176. The count by the Orthodox Church, based on the annual reports from Kostroma clergy, was not much better: 16,433 Old Believers in the province in 1859. Nagradov, *Raskolot' "raskol,"* p. 144.

77. Arnol'di, "Iz dnevnika," p. 19.

78. *Izvlechenie iz Vsepodanneishego otcheta Ober-Prokurora . . . 1883 g.*, p. 235.

79. "Vtoraia poezdka missionera-sleptsa," p. 558.

80. Brianchininov and Arnol'di, "O raskole," pp. 300–301.

81. Kititsyn, "Staroobriadcheskie skity," pp. 174–75.

82. Smirnov, *Istoriia russkogo raskola*, p. 124; Pavel, "Kratkie izvestiia," p. 568.

83. There is almost an exception: in the early twentieth century, the police chief of the neighboring Makariev district reported on a Spasovite community that he characterized as "singing Spasovites," as the Great Rite Spasovites were sometimes called because they chanted worship services (Nagradov, *Raskolot' "raskol,"* pp. 245–46).

84. LP 47422, f. 45. This report is undated, but it follows immediately after the document recording Hennemann's January 1800 order that the unmarried marry immediately.

85. Ibid., f. 46v.

86. Ibid., ff. 53–54v.

87. LP 47428, f. 22.

88. LP 47422, ff. 55–55v (1800); 47428, ff. 75–78 (undated, but from 1802—ages are two years higher than in the list from 1800), 131–134 (1804).

89. LP 47428, ff. 131–134.

90. LP 47424, ff. 135–46v.

91. The strikingly larger number of ever-married women than men was due to widowhood: forty-two widows but only nine widowers. I have counted men enrolled in the militia as figuratively present, the men taken through regular conscription as no longer on the estate.

92. The document lists only 125 households, but the economic note for household 49 states that the household was actually divided and that the unmarried sisters, ages seventeen, twenty-eight, and thirty-one, lived separately and supported themselves; I have counted the sisters as a separate household (LP 47424, f. 139). The notes describe another woman, in household 91, as actually homeless; I have not counted her as a separate household.

93. LP 47424, f. 140–140v, households 66–70.

94. Ibid., ff. 139, 140v, households 52 and 65.

95. Ibid., ff. 135–143v, households 23, 25, 29, 35, 49, 52, 55, 78, 88, 94, 96, and 117. Only one of the seven poor households was so labeled. The others, by implication, were beneath the poverty level; the household inventory describes how they eked out a living.

96. I have adjusted the statistics calculated by Melton, "Household Economies," p. 566.

97. LP 47427, ff. 150v, 160v.

98. LP 47429, f. 143v. The preceding directive to which Lieven alludes is not in the surviving Baki papers.

99. LP 47431, f. 84v.

100. Ibid., ff. 93, 97–97v.

101. LP 47432, ff. 105–9v.

102. Ibid., f. 16v.

103. Dubelt's superior was Alexander Benckendorff, chief of the Third Section and brother of Christoph Lieven's wife, Dorothea. Benckendorff was willing to deploy members of his small security force to sort out problems on the Baki estate. On the Lieven and Benckendorff families, see *J. Siebmachers grosses und allgemeines Wappenbuch*, Bd. 3, abt. 11, pp. 14–15, 32–33; Hyde, *Princess Lieven*, pp. 13–22.

104. LP 47432, ff. 101–2, 105–106v.

105. The police (*sotskie*) were appointed by and answerable to the district court for up to a year; they were not estate officials.

106. Grekov's letter to Lieven, July 15, 1835, LP 47432, ff. 18–12v; Zbruev's letter to Lieven, September 29, 1835, LP 47432, f. 45–45v.

107. LP 47432, ff. 3–6, 11–12v, 16–17, 18v–19, 34–35, 61–64v, 200v–201. The amplification of the peasants' complaint about the sawmill is in a letter to Lieven in June 1835, after Grekov had announced that Lieven had ordered it built (ibid., f. 11–11v).

108. Ibid., f. 330v.

109. Ibid., ff. 30v, 34v, 90. The Baki serfs subsequently complained, too, that Kalinin had sold foreigners a permit to log in Lieven's forest and had taken (or extorted) bribes during the previous conscription (ibid., f. 88).

110. Ibid., ff. 30v–31, 52–54, 57–60v. On the accounts and the evidence of Grekov's fraud, see ibid., ff. 72, 77v–78, 84–85, 92v, 112–13.

111. Ibid., ff. 93–94.

112. Ibid., ff. 30–30v, 41–45, 49–49v, 50–51.

113. Averkiev attempted to retain Kalinin as clerk despite his misconduct, because of his writing skills, but the hostility to him was so great that Lieven (on Averkiev's recommendation) replaced him in May 1836 (ibid., ff. 157, 215).

114. Ibid., f. 36, provides a copy of a receipt (dated January 5, 1845) for 300 paper rubles received from Tikhon Voronin for the manumission of his daughter, but this is part of a very disorderly list of receipts that Grekov may have composed after his misdeeds had been discovered; a subsequent "complete accounting" of the money Grekov had collected while managing the estate included 650 rubles in departure fees for the two women who married off the estate (ibid., f. 74v).

115. Ibid., f. 16v.

116. Ibid., ff. 57–60, 81v.

117. Ibid., ff. 297v–98.

118. Ibid., f. 298–298v.

119. Ibid., ff. 299, 330v.

120. Ibid., f. 329.

121. Ibid., f. 307 (Averkiev's assertion). Zbruev identified the instigators in a letter to Christoph Lieven (ibid., ll. 44–44v). I have used an 1836 list of households on the Baki and Ilinskoe estates organized in four wealth classes (ibid., ff. 249–60v) and the 1834 tax census for the Baki estate (GAKO, f. 200, op. 3, d. 462, ll. 650–788) to identify their wealth status. For a discussion of the 1836 household list, see the subsequent section on Baki demography. Of the three identifiable instigators from the Baki estate,

two were in the top category, one in the second; the two identifiable instigators from the Ilinskoe estate were both in the top category.

122. LP 47432, ff. 3–4v, 11–14v, 16–19v. According to the serfs, Kalinin's father had been bailiff while Charlotte Lieven was still alive and had been whipped as punishment for abusing them, and he and his entire family forbidden even to attend estate assemblies (ibid., ff. 34v–35). In 1836, Lieven, on Averkiev's recommendation, appointed as bailiff another priested Voronin, Egor Pavlov (ibid., ff. 156v, 170v). The genealogy of the Voronin families can be traced through the 1795 tax census, the 1812–13 Baki village household list, and the 1834 tax census. Their religious affiliations are in the 1812 petitions to register as Old Believers.

123. Melton, "Household Economies," pp. 573–76, covers the changes of management in 1813 and 1817. (For some time after 1817, serf bailiffs were in charge.) For Kremenetskii's summary account, see LP 47430, ll. 117–20v. He blames Voronin and the "wealthy peasants" in general, the village scribe who was Voronin's nephew, and the bailiff—that is, the Baki elite.

124. LP 47430, ff. 201–6v, 215–17, 228–43, 257–60, 274v–75; LP 47431, ff. 2–12, 18–19.

125. LP 47432, f. 365.

126. Ibid., l. 247ob (the descriptions of the classes); ibid., ll. 250–52ob (the list for Baki village).

127. GAKO, f. 200, op. 3, d. 462, ll. 652ob–682ob. Averkiev did not himself indicate which households held unmarried adult women.

128. Averkiev did include in his list a few with teenage boys and widowed mothers that he presumably deemed at least potentially viable. One unlisted household consisted of an unmarried nineteen-year-old woman; I have not counted that household among those with unmarried adult women, since any single woman under twenty-five or thirty might marry.

129. According to Averkiev's list, 3 of the 148 households in the 1834 census had divided, which accounts for the difference in households counted and uncounted in 1834 (148) and 1836 (151). They may have divided after the census, or the census taker may have refused to recognize them as divided in 1834.

130. That does not include two Osokin households that had been expelled from the estate in 1819.

131. GAKO, f. 200, op. 13, d. 30, ll. 471ob–522.

132. See the summary figures from a number of different studies in Moon, *Russian Peasantry*, p. 159, and Mironov, *Sotsial'naia istoriia Rossii*, p. 221. Dennison, *Institutional Framework*, p. 63, calculated mean household size at Voshchazhnikovo in the Rostov district, with a predominantly non-agriculture economy, as 4.93 in 1834.

133. Thus, at Baki, the usual household partition options were not premortem and postmortem household division, but premortem partition and household inheritance. For discussion of premortem and postmortem partition, see Moon, *Russian Peasantry*, pp. 177–83.

134. I base this assessment of household prospects on the 1812–13 descriptions of how poor households with limited male labor power eked out a living (LP 47429, ff. 135–143v).

135. GAKO, f. 200, op. 3, d. 462, ll. 6820b–6870b. The 1834 census lists fifteen of them at the end of the return from Baki village (no substitutes are listed at the end of returns for other villages), but they clearly substituted for men from other villages as well. I have not counted them as part of the population of Baki village, although for census purposes they were. Two other substitutes died before they could be handed over to the army. The 1834 census also lists another two men, ages twenty-eight and twenty-nine in 1816, conscripted in 1818. They are not in the 1812–13 Baki household list. They must have been bought for conscription prior to 1816, their purchase described in the 1816 census but not in that of 1834 (ibid. l. 6820b).

136. In the 1834 return, these are households 43 and 64 (GAKO, f. 200, op. 3, d. 462, ll. 6610b–62, ll. 6660b–67). In the 1812–13 household list, these are households 36 and 49, which subsequently divided (LP 47424, ff. 138, 139).

CHAPTER 7

Steksovo and Sergei Mikhailovich Golitsyn:
Marriage Aversion in a Context of Prosperity

Any account of female resistance to marriage that follows the stories of Kuplia parish and the Lievens' Baki estate will seem anticlimactic. Marriage resistance on Sergei Golitsyn's Steksovo estate in Nizhnii Novgorod province never came close to the levels that obtained in Sluchkovo or Aleshkovo—or Staroustie and Izhma—in the late eighteenth century. In 1795, the rate for the Steksovo estate as a whole was 14.5 percent (of all women twenty-five and over, including those who had married onto the estate). That statistic is misleading, however, because marriage aversion arrived at Steksovo only around 1760. The rate of refusal to marry among women between ages twenty-five and fifty-four—women who had passed through marriage age between 1760 and 1795—was 18.5 percent.[1] Nevertheless, on the estate as a whole, female marriage aversion never quite rose to 20 percent, although it peaked above that rate in three of five villages. We need to remind ourselves how extraordinary a 20 percent rate of female abstention from marriage was against both the background assumption that Russian peasants married universally and the reality that in much of Russia that was actually so.

Steksovo differed from Kuplia and Baki in some instructive ways. For instance, the pronounced demographic perils of marriage aversion observed in Kuplia parish and around Baki were largely skirted at Steksovo. The census returns and manorial household inventories from the nineteenth century do show that many households contracted to remnants without married couples and then expired. However, they seem seldom to have collapsed and cast elderly survivors on the mercy of the community; indeed, some remnant households were prosperous. Steksovo's economy, and in particular the substantial amount of privately owned land that Steksovo serfs accumulated, offered insurance against collapse. Sergei Golitsyn, too, may have helped to fend off demographic disaster. After he inherited the estate in 1804, he sought to stamp out marriage aversion. While he never came close to that goal, a gradual decline in the rate of marriage resistance on the estate may have owed something to his efforts.

While marriage resistance in the five villages on the estate rose in parallel and to roughly the same levels in the eighteenth century, marriage aversion in the villages diverged as sharply as on the Baki estate in the nineteenth.[2] Unlike the Kuplia confession registers, none of the few surviving registers from Steksovo identify the Old Believer covenants to which schismatic households belonged. Nor do any of the surviving eighteenth-century Steksovo census returns identify registered schismatics. Sharp variations in nuptiality from one village to another nevertheless provide some clues and certainly demonstrate that Steksovo serfs belonged to more than one Old Believer covenant. As in Kuplia parish, Spasovite women were the most likely to shun marriage. And as in Kuplia parish and at Baki, parents in Spasovite and perhaps other marriage resistant households seem to have allowed their daughters to decide whether to marry or not.

Sergei Golitsyn's Steksovo

Steksovo, located in what became the Ardatov district of southern Nizhnii Novgorod province in 1779, belonged to the Golitsyns from at least the early seventeenth century. By the 1780s, most of the original estate was in the hands of two Golitsyn widows, Daria and Praskovia.[3] Sergei Mikhailovich Golitsyn (1774–1859) received—through his father, Mikhail Mikhailovich—the portion that had once belonged to Daria, while most of Praskovia's portion had passed to the Obolenskii and Bibikov families by the 1820s. Sergei Golitsyn thus shared ownership of the estate's three parish seats—Steksovo, Pisarevo, and Piatnitskoe—and two satellite villages with unrelated proprietors. In 1845, his Steksovo estate consisted of 213 households with a total of 1,293 male and female serfs.[4]

During Sergei Golitsyn's tenure, his serfs performed corvée labor (growing grain), paid quitrent, and were relatively prosperous. In the Ardatov district as a whole, agricultural conditions were middling. In the mid-nineteenth century, three-quarters of the district was under forest, much of the land was marsh, and there was little good soil. Grain yields were reported to range from 3:1 to 5:1, about average for the central industrial region of which the province was a part. Because of the infertility of most of the soil, Ardatov district peasants engaged in craft production at home or left their villages to earn money. While Steksovo itself sat on a patch of fertile black earth and was reputed to have the best gardens in the district, it was off-farm earnings that made some Steksovo peasants prosperous and many others comfortable. The estate lay near the intersection of two commercially important roads: one from Nizhnii Novgorod to Tambov, the other from Moscow to Simbirsk. According to the 1845 household inventory, most of the 69 households belonging to Golitsyn in Steksovo village engaged in both agriculture and some trade: driving cattle from Orenburg province to Nizhnii Novgorod and Moscow, cartage, milling, butchering, blacksmithing, production and sale of hemp oil, grain trading, and so forth. Ten of those 69 households had estimated annual earnings of between 1,000 and 8,500 paper rubles; the median income for all households was 450 rubles. The few households engaged only in farming earned well below the median. In the other 144 households on the estate, only 6 earned 1,000 or more rubles per annum, but median income was a respectable 400 rubles.[5] As of 1843, Steksovo estate serfs were expected to pay 16,000 paper rubles in annual quitrent, or just over 75 rubles per household on average. For most, that would not have been a particularly onerous burden.[6]

Relative prosperity at Steksovo was nothing new. Since 1778, the date of the first surviving household inventory, around 90 percent of the households in Steksovo and the other villages on the estate had been engaged in commerce and crafts. They had also been steadily purchasing land.[7] In 1845, forty-one of the sixty-nine households in Steksovo village owned farmland. Twelve households owned 5 *desiatiny* (13.5 acres; 5.5 hectares) or fewer, another fifteen owned up to 20 *desiatiny* (54 acres; 23 hectares), and three owned 100 or more *desiatiny* (270 acres; 109 hectares). Fedor Groshev owned just short of 1,118 *desiatiny* (3,018 acres; 1,229 hectares), or better than 4.7 square miles (12.2 square kilometers) of land. Like the Groshevs, many Steksovo families had accumulated property over the generations.[8]

Land-ownership strongly correlated with household well-being. In Steksovo village (1845), only ten of the thirty-two families (31 percent) with incomes under 450 rubles owned any land, while thirty-one of thirty-seven (84 percent) with incomes of 450 rubles or more were landowning. Of the sixty-nine households, forty-one contained just one married couple (some with a widowed parent as well) or none at all. Twenty-six of those forty-one households earned under 450 rubles; fifteen had incomes of 450 rubles and above, which conforms to the rule of thumb that small households were on average poorer than large households. But in Steksovo, property ownership could compensate for small household size: twelve of the fifteen small households (80 percent) in the upper bracket owned land, while only eight of the twenty-six (31 percent) in the lower bracket did. Or, to put that another way, twelve of the twenty small households (60 percent) that owned even a small amount of land had annual incomes at or above the median.

Although Sergei Golitsyn probably never set foot on his Steksovo estate—Steksovo had no manor house—he personally corresponded with his Steksovo stewards on matters both managerial and religious, and his religious convictions had a direct effect on the lives of his serfs. He was a very prominent public figure, the "last of the Moscow lords" who spent unstintingly on banquets, balls, and other entertainments. He was an intimate of the ruling family, helped to manage and was himself a benefactor of the imperial charities in Moscow from 1807 on, and served as chair of the Moscow Board of Guardians (*Opekunskii sovet*) from 1830 until his death in 1859. His wife, Evdokiia (aka Avdotia)—who separated from him in 1800, just a few months after their marriage—was the famous *Princesse Nocturne*, who hosted a nighttime salon in St. Petersburg. For his Steksovo serfs, what was most important about Golitsyn was his devotion to Orthodoxy and his intimacy with the leaders of the church. He corresponded with Metropolitan Filaret of Moscow from 1823 to 1858, and the subjects they covered included the danger posed by, and prospects for converting, Old Believers. While some considered his demonstrative piety hypocritical, the Steksovo manorial correspondence testifies at the very least to his abiding hostility to the Old Belief.[9]

The Old Belief and Marriage Aversion at Steksovo

When Sergei Golitsyn inherited the Steksovo estate in 1804, he also inherited the practice of imposing fines on the fathers of single, marriageable women. Probably Aleksandr Mikahilovich Golitsyn or his widow, Daria, began the practice in the 1770s or 1780s in response to the outbreak of marriage aversion after 1762.[10] In 1809, the Steksovo bailiff, Andrei Iakovlev, reported that peasant Ivan Vilkov had asked that the twenty ruble annual fine he had just paid for keeping two unmarried daughters at home (ten rubles per daughter) be refunded on the grounds that they were beyond marriage age. Iakovlev advised the Moscow office to reject the request. Other fathers had unmarried daughters just as old as Vilkov's, and if an exception were made for him, they would all demand refunds. The estate needed to collect these fines, Iakovlev explained, because the money was used to purchase free women (*vol'nye devki*) for men too poor to secure brides on their own. An assembly of "the best peasants" (most prosperous) had agreed that Vilkov's petition should be rejected.[11]

There were in fact many unmarried adult women on the estate, but they had appeared two to three generations later than the marriage-averse women of Kuplia parish and Baki estate. There had been almost none in 1762. In that year, on the portions owned by Aleksandr Mikhailovich Golitsyn (husband of Daria) that Sergei Mikhailovich would inherit forty-two years later, of 302 women ages twenty-five and over, only 10 (3.3 percent) had never married. Seven of those were in the village of Pisarevo (9.2 percent of the 76 ages twenty-five or older in the village). The 3 in the other four villages represented just 1.3 percent of women of that age.[12] They may have been disabled. Only in Pisarevo had a degree of marriage aversion set in prior to 1762.[13] By 1778, 27 of 304 women twenty-five or older (8.9 percent) had never married.[14] By 1795, 55 of the 298 women on the estate ages twenty-five to fifty-four (those who had turned twenty-five since 1765), or 18.5 percent, had never married, while of the 89 women fifty-five and over, only 2 had never married. Among the men ages twenty-five to fifty-four, 7 of 254 (2.8 percent) had never married.[15] Fining the fathers of never-married women had failed to check the spread of marriage aversion but may have raised considerable funds for purchasing brides elsewhere. To judge by the best peasants' reaction to Vilkov's petition, there was probably a consensus among universally marrying households that daughter-withholding households should be punished, at least by paying for harboring young women who wouldn't marry.

Notes in the 1795 tax census on the origins and destinations of daughters who married between 1782 and 1795 seem to show that almost all Steksovo estate girls, if they married at all, married young men from the estate. Although notations on where wives came from as of 1795 are missing for 27 percent of the married men, men mostly found wives on the estate. It was a large estate, after all, and local wives were likely less expensive than outsiders. Nevertheless, some wives were outsiders. Fifteen of the married or widowed women were identified as "my master's serf" or "my master's as of old" rather than from a particular village; they may have been brought to Steksovo from distant Golitsyn properties in order to marry Steksovo men. Ten others had arrived from other nobles' estates, and another was the daughter of a peasant living (or perhaps only registered) in the city of Arzamas. She was the only woman who might have been a "free maiden" marrying onto the estate, and it is possible that she had been acquired from her father for a bride price equal to the purchase price of a marriageable serf woman. Otherwise, the purchase of non-serf maidens to which bailiff Iakovlev apparently alluded in 1809 makes little sense. There were also merchants and townsmen registered in Arzamas and Ardatov but living in Steksovo, and in the years Sergei Golitsyn owned the estate, his serfs occasionally married local townsmen's daughters.[16] However, as of 1795, the only candidate for such a marriage was the daughter of the Arzamas peasant, who may actually have been living in Steksovo.

More likely, the money from fines was used to purchase, perhaps in the form of high departure fees, serfs from other estates, among them the ten imported serf women listed in 1795. We do know that at least occasionally Steksovo serfs purchased other serfs. In 1809, when bailiff Iakovlev forwarded a request from Petr Nikiforovich Koloskov (three sons, three daughters, net worth 1,200 rubles that year) that a daughter be issued a certificate of manumission so she could marry off the estate, he pointed out that this same Koloskov, together with his brother, had asked to be allowed to purchase a girl (*devushka*: of marriageable age) for 80 rubles.[17] Perhaps the Koloskovs intended to employ the girl as a servant, but it is also possible that they wanted to buy a wife for a son. The Koloskovs asked for no financial assistance, but some Steksovo households would have needed a subvention.

At some point, Sergei Golitsyn abolished the fine; by the 1820s, the manorial correspondence no longer mentions it. Probably Golitsyn understood that the fine was just a minor tax on singleness, the payment of which actually authorized women to avoid marriage. He required, in order after order to a succession of stewards, all his serfs to marry. He did, however, leave a loophole: a father could protect his daughter from marriage by purchasing her freedom, always in the guise of paying Golitsyn "departure money," ostensibly so that the daughter could wed off the estate. Koloskov probably paid 500 paper rubles for his daughter's manumission in 1809. That was the standard price Golitsyn extracted from other well-to-do serfs (not just at Steksovo) who sought their daughters' freedom; he charged the same of Ivan Groshev (income 2,500 rubles as of 1845) for a daughter in 1823.[18]

Koloskov and Groshev may have purchased their daughters' freedom not so they could marry off the estate but so that they could avoid marriage altogether.[19] Like the serfs on the Orlovs' Romanovo estate, Steksovo serfs bought their daughters' freedom on false pretenses. And Sergei Golitsyn knew that, at least by the time he abolished fines but offered the far more expensive alternative of manumission. As he informed steward Daniil Nikolaev in 1840, "Peasants of this estate redeem their daughters not so they can be given in marriage off the estate, but so they can forever remain in their heresies, have their cells, and celebrate schismatic rituals, and also so that they not be given in marriage to grooms on the estate."[20] While he told Nikolaev to compel peasants to marry, he also reaffirmed the price that peasants had to pay to secure their daughters' freedom from marriage: 500 rubles from the wealthiest peasants, 350 rubles or 250 rubles from less well-to-do households.[21] That was extortion—Golitsyn was charging far more for manumission than the market price for a marriageable serf woman, at the time probably around 150 to 200 rubles. His manumission charges were, however, no higher than those levied by other serf-owners.

While Golitsyn seems never to have missed an opportunity to profit from a prosperous Old Believer's desire to save a daughter from marriage, he and his Steksovo managers worked hard to force others to yield their daughters. In early 1823, Prokofii Krotov traveled all the way to Moscow to complain that steward Feripont Popov was trying to force him to give his fifteen-year-old daughter, Avdotia, to Ivan Golubkin's son. Claiming that his wife was sickly and that he had three young sons who needed to be cared for, Krotov asked to be allowed to keep Avdotia at home for another year. Steward Popov responded that Krotov was a crude and stubborn man, that he would never voluntarily hand over his daughters in marriage, that he had earlier yielded another daughter only under duress, that Golubkin could find no other bride for his sixteen-year-old son, and that Krotov should be forced to surrender Avdotia. In this instance, the home office ordered that Avdotia's marriage be put off for the year requested. And in the end, Golubkin found another young woman for his son.[22] Krotov may have wanted to keep Avdotia at home for religious reasons; while Avdotia was no longer in his household by the time of the 1834 tax census and had presumably either married or died, in that same year Krotov's fifty-three-year-old spinster sister was living with him.[23] However, he may have genuinely needed Avdotia's contribution to the household, he may have objected to the proposed match, or he may have thought she was too young to marry. On the other hand, steward Popov—in dealing with both of Krotov's daughters—certainly acted in the interest of other serfs who had asked him to secure wives for their sons.

The manorial correspondence about marriage and Old Believers overlaps. The overwhelming majority of Steksovo serfs were officially Orthodox, but in their actual religious practice, they were heterodox. As steward Popov wrote to Golitsyn's Moscow office in 1823, there was an Old Believer (by which he meant a Edinoverie) church in the village of Pashutina, and its parisioners attended church faithfully. Many other peasants, however, "out of laziness and their schismatic delusions" worshiped neither at the Edinoverie church nor at the Orthodox churches in Steksovo, Pisarevo, or Piatnitskoe, nor did they take part in the required annual confession and communion. So few peasants worshiped at the Orthodox church in Steksovo that parish income did not cover even the cost of candles, wine, and incense, let alone the construction of a stone church to which all of the masters who shared in the ownership of the village expected their serfs to contribute. The Moscow office instructed Popov to fine those who didn't attend church.[24] In 1824, a Nizhnii Novgorod diocesan investigation confirmed that Steksovo serfs were unwilling to contribute to construction of a new church.[25]

The estate's serf officials were often (probably mostly) Old Believers and at least some of them led the resistance to Orthodoxy. In 1822, for instance, Golitsyn's Steksovo village bailiff denounced the Orthodox priest in Pisarevo, Stefan Petrov, for routinely canceling church services and thereby depriving parishioners of sacraments. Petrov responded that he could prove he had conducted all the required services and included with his letter to the diocese a statement supporting him from the 115 Bibikov serfs in Pisarevo. Petrov claimed that the Steksovo bailiff, whose authority extended to Pisarevo's Golitsyn serfs, was a schismatic intent on recruiting them to the Old Belief.[26]

Pavel Melnikov, who spent the years 1847 to 1855 investigating Old Believers in Nizhnii Novgorod province and wrote a lengthy analysis for the Ministry of Interior in 1854, reported that 60 percent of the population of Steksovo village were Old Believers and that Steksovo parish was one of a cluster of sixteen parishes straddling the border between the Ardatov and Arzamas districts that were thoroughly infected by the Old Belief. According to Melnikov, half of the population in those parishes was schismatic. Pisarevo and Piatnitskoe parishes, parts of which were on Golitsyn's Steksovo estate, were among the sixteen. Yet Melnikov singled out Steksovo village for the special influence it had on all of the Old Believers in the area.[27] Melnikov of course included in his estimate those he called elsewhere "secret Old Believers," who made at least a grudging pretense of being Orthodox even while they practiced the Old Believer rituals.

Yet Melnikov badly underestimated the number of Old Believers in Steksovo village. According to the parish confession register for 1861—just seven years after Melnikov's report—only five of Golitsyn's former serfs (he had sold the estate to Evgraf Solenikov in 1847) in Steksovo parish confessed. The annotations to the confession register noted that 207 parishioners ages seven and above had skipped confession because they were schismatics of varying degrees: "inclined to the schism," "schismatic," "schismatic from birth." Only four others had missed confession because they were away from the village. Steksovo village serfs belonging to the other two major owners were equally schismatic: only 14 of 170 Bibikov serfs ages seven and over, and only 9 of 261 Obolenskii serfs seven and above, confessed.[28] No doubt the Imperial Manifesto on emancipation of February 19, 1861, read to them by their priests during Lent, had emboldened them to declare their emancipation from the Orthodox Church as well.

Sergei Golitsyn and the Orthodox clergy conducted a number of campaigns to force the refractory, heterodox Steksovo serfs into the Orthodox Church and to marry. A failed campaign in 1834 (Old Believers promised to join the church but reneged) was followed by another in 1836, after bailiff Bezborodov reported on January 1 that there were sixty-six unmarried women on the estate between the minimum female marriage age of sixteen and forty-five, and forty-six unmarried men between their legal minimum marriage age of eighteen and forty-two. The Golitsyn office in Moscow promptly, on January 8, ordered that measures be taken then and there to marry young maidens to bachelors, older spinsters to widowers. Bezborodov was to enlist the clergy in this effort, and Sergei Golitsyn personally wrote to the Orthodox priests on the estate asking them to persuade his serfs to marry.[29] On January 22, Bezborodov reported that peasants were marrying as ordered, but many would have married willingly, as marriage peaked during January.[30] The number of peasants actually resisting marriage was in fact much lower than the bailiff's figures suggested. If we take into account the age by which almost all Steksovo serfs married if they were to marry at all—twenty for women, twenty-two to twenty-three for men (as discussed later in this chapter)—perhaps no more than three men and twenty-two women were resisting marriage. Those figures, however, do not include any older single men and women whom the bailiff deemed beyond marital age.

Golitsyn, steward Nikolaev, and the clergy renewed their efforts to press resisting women into marriage in 1839 and 1840. In February 1840, Nikolaev suggested that Golitsyn's willingness to manumit marriageable daughters had only encouraged the schismatics: the manumitees "live in the homes of their relatives and do not wish to marry, by which they multiply the already deep-rooted schism. Presenting this for Your Excellency's judgment, I request Your Excellency's decision whether they should be forced to marry, or removed from the estate."[31] Nikolaev also pointed out that tolerating marriage resistance had economic consequences: fewer serfs in the future. The Moscow office immediately ordered Nikolaev to expel manumitted women.[32] Golitsyn himself instructed Nikolaev "to make every effort to have all maidens without exception given to grooms, who must not be left bachelors after they attain the legal age of 18."[33] While he then went on to reaffirm that fathers could purchase their daughters' manumission for 250 to 500 rubles, he added that they could do so only at the time their daughters turned sixteen (then the legal minimum marriage age for women) and that if they did not do so then, the girls would have to marry Steksovo serfs.

Nikolaev's reports on the 1839–40 campaign suggest the tension it generated on the estate. Outside priests, dispatched by the Nizhnii Novgorod diocese, went from cabin to cabin trying to browbeat peasants into signing pledges to join the church (a tactic later employed at the outset of Stalin's collectivization campaign). Some peasants—including former bailiffs Fedor Groshev and Mikhail Shobalov (who was then the warden of the Steksovo Orthdodox church)—had asked to be allowed to join the local Edinoverie church instead. Nikolaev suspected a ruse and supposed that they intended to shun that church, too, and would likely use the services of runaway priests—that is, wandering priests who had deserted Orthodoxy and moved from place to place administering sacraments to priested Old Believers. Others stubbornly refused to sign agreements to adhere to the Orthodox Church, and one had offered a 100-ruble bribe to be left in peace.[34] For his part and with Golitsyn's approval, Nikolaev sent former bailiffs Mikhail Shobalov and Aleksei Groshev to the Nizhnii Novgorod and Moscow workhouses, respectively, "for sedition and schism." For good measure, he sentenced Shobalov's oldest son to conscription.[35]

In May 1840, Nikolaev summarized the results of his and the priests' efforts to herd Old Believers into the church. During the immediately preceding Lent, 496 Golitsyn men and 477 women had confessed; 89 men had not confessed because they had been working away from the estate (many, surely, had arranged their travel to avoid confession—compare those 89 to the mere 4 who were away from the estate during Lent in 1861); 27 men and 83 women had not confessed because they were under seven or for other reasons.[36] Forcing Old Believers to confess to Orthodox priests was what the 1839–40 campaign had been about, and Nikolaev implied (he did not quite claim) that these figures demonstrated success. Yet if a large majority of Golitsyn's serfs had been bullied into making a show of religious conformity, the campaign did little to reduce female marriage aversion, as we will see shortly.

Golitsyn, at any rate, saw no reason to ease the pressure. In September 1842, he issued an "Instruction" to Aleksandr Shornikov, his new steward. Among Shornikov's duties was the by now customary one of ensuring that serfs marry when they came of age. Golitsyn explicitly linked the need to compel serfs to marry to the presence of Old Believers:

> Take care to marry peasant youths who reach marriage age to brides from the estate; for I know that many peasants out of ignorance and loyalty to the schism, indulging their daughters to lead a depraved life, do not want to give them in marriage. For which reason you must arrange to ward off an evil so harmful to the peasants themselves. Unmarried maidens have in the past separated from their families and lived in cells; and although I have repeatedly instructed that these be destroyed, I make it your obligation to establish whether such cells exist to this day, and should they exist to destroy them immediately.[37]

Golitsyn was not wrong to focus on the women living in cells. While there is scant evidence on how they occupied themselves at Steksovo, cell-dwelling Old Believer spinsters were a fixture in Old Believer communities in many parts of Russia; they played an important role in teaching Old Believer children to read and write (which was simultaneously instruction in the faith), and they sometimes served as community leaders.

Golitsyn obliged Shornikov to act firmly against the Old Belief. The schismatics had promised in 1834, he said, to have nothing more to do with the schism, but they had lied; they continued to christen their children and bury their dead in their own manner. Shornikov was to ensure that Old Believers gave no shelter to their passportless coreligionists and to provide a list of the leading schismatics and their families so that Golitsyn could punish them if they caused trouble.[38] In 1843, Shornikov reported that he had torn down all but eight of the cells. Those he had left standing pending a decision by Golitsyn; Shornikov had provisionally spared them because they were no longer inhabited by Old Believer spinsters. Mikhail Makarov, for example, claimed (falsely) that he had no living relatives and used the cell as his own dwelling, while Ivan Groshev claimed that he now kept cattle in the cell at his homestead.[39]

Despite Golitsyn's expressed determination to force his serfs to marry, his harshest commands were never implemented. In the early 1840s, he himself continued to allow fathers to purchase their daughter's freedom, even past the age of sixteen.[40] Comparison of the 1845 manorial census and the 1850 tax census confirms that serf girls as well as manumitted women continued to refuse to marry. In 1845, there were thirty-five unmarried women in the twenty to forty-nine cohort; nineteen of them were missing from the same cohort, now ages twenty-five to fifty-four, in 1850. One or two of the youngest may have married, and a few had probably died (the tax census did not explain why women had disappeared). Certainly the majority were missing because, not being serfs, they were omitted (as required by the decree on the 1850 census) from the census of estate serfs that year[41]—that is, the single adult women on the estate included roughly equal numbers of manumitted and serf women. Of course, the fact that up to nineteen manumitted women were listed in the 1845 estate household inventory means that the 1840 order to expel manumitted spinsters from the estate had never been carried out. And serf women in their twenties continued to refuse to marry during the 1840s. The 1850 census listed eleven in the twenty-five to twenty-nine cohort and thirteen in the twenty to twenty-four cohort. Serf women who, with the support of their families, refused to yield to repeated efforts by priests and estate administrators to force them into marriage must have been inspired by the example of the manumitted women and by the support of their Old Believer community.

There were so many Old Believers on the estate that they subverted the local clergy. Sometimes—more likely, often—they persuaded or bribed Orthodox priests to administer sacraments in the Old Believer manner. In

1834, the diocesan consistory investigated a report that the Steksovo Orthodox priest Dmitrii Pavlov had performed an Old Believer wedding at the church in Gremiachevo, twenty-eight kilometers away. The groom was the son of Steksovo's current bailiff, the Old Believer Ivan Groshev; the bride was from Gremiachevo. The Gremiachevo priest, Ivan Andreev (author of the denunciation), claimed Pavlov had blessed the couple with the Old Believers' two-fingered sign of the cross, had led the couple clockwise around the lectern as Old Believers did (the Orthodox processed counterclockwise), and had used not the holy water and wine from the Gremiachevo church but wine and water brought by a woman in the groom's party. Furthermore, said Andreev, the three Steksovo men who accompanied the groom had abstained from prayer, so he assumed they were Old Believers. This account was confirmed in whole or part by a large number of those who had attended the wedding. The consistory concluded that Pavlov had in fact conducted an Old Believer marriage service. In addition, it had been discovered in 1833 that many of his Steksovo parishioners actually worshipped at the Pashutina Edinoverie church. The consistory decided to transfer Pavlov to a parish free of schismatics.[42]

Nevertheless, according to the parish register for the Steksovo church, six of the fourteen weddings celebrated in 1839 featured schismatic couples.[43] The wedding ritual employed may or may not have conformed to Orthodox rules, but the priest had clearly ignored the edict—reiterated frequently by government and church officials—that Old Believers could not marry in an Orthodox church unless they converted. Perhaps that was why steward Nikolaev reported to Golitsyn in early 1840 that he had begun to write down in a journal all of the actions of the clergy that encouraged schismatics.[44] In 1851 and 1854, too, a few of the Steksovo weddings were recorded in the parish registers as schismatic, and two of the couples were recorded as Spasovites.[45] No matter the determination of their diocesan superiors to root out the Old Belief, Steksovo priests yielded to strong local pressure to celebrate illicit weddings, just as priests did elsewhere. Steksovo priests must have been well paid to do so.

What sort of Old Believers, then, were those on the Steksovo estate? In 1831, a group of nominally Orthodox peasants from the Golitsyn and contiguous estates petitioned Bishop Afanasii of Nizhnii Novgorod to be allowed to join the Pashutina Edinoverie parish. In the eighteenth century, they wrote, their forebears had been Spasovites; they had not joined the Edinoverie parish because they had not believed that they would actually be permitted to use the old books and old rituals. The petitioners now understood that had been a mistake. They claimed they told their priests every year that they did not attend Orthodox services or confess to Orthodox priests because they were Old Believers. Diocesan officials examined the parish confession registers from the 1820s and found that some of the petitioners were listed as having confessed annually, some intermittently, and that some were reported to have skipped confession because they had forgotten, others because they were schismatics. Two of the petitioners, from the village of Steksovo, had been omitted from the confession registers altogether. The consistory ruled that the petitioners were not confirmed Old Believers but merely weak in the faith and rejected their request.[46] In 1839 and again in 1841, large groups of peasants and townsmen from Steksovo and Pashutina—none belonging to Golitsyn but living alongside his serfs— asked permission to join the Edinoverie church, and most of them said they were Spasovites, too.[47]

Not all of Steksovo's overt and covert Old Believers were Spasovites. In an 1832 petition asking permission to replace their wooden chapel with a stone church, members of the Pashutina Edinoverie parish claimed that they were from "all covenants conjointly."[48] The list of townsmen and peasants seeking to join the Edinoverie church in 1839 had the heading "from various sects," again implying that not all of them were Spasovites.[49] There were indeed priested Old Believers on the estate, as well as members of the priestless Fedoseev covenant. Both bribed priests to administer sacraments, marriage included, in the Old Believer way.[50] Pavel Melnikov reported in 1854 that it was suspected that Steksovo harbored some Wanderers (*stranniki,* Old Believers who shunned all contact with government and church officials).[51] Unfortunately, most of the available documents fail to distinguish priested from priestless, let alone one priestless covenant from another. Although we can be certain that there was a variety of Old Believers on the estate, church documents identify only—and repeatedly—Spasovites by covenant. According to an 1869 description of the Ardatov district, Spasovites predominated among the district's Old Believers.[52] The majority of Steksovo Old Believers were surely Spasovites. It is reasonable to assume that women who refused to marry were disproportionately but perhaps not exclusively Spasovite, but we can also be certain that not all Spasovite young women refused to marry.

The manorial documents offer some evidence about who made the decision not to marry, the young woman or her father (or parents). Those that state that fathers had to be compelled to give their daughters in marriage may seem to imply that fathers controlled marriage, but that phrasing was simply discursive convention: in Russian as in English, fathers "gave" daughters in marriage, even when daughters made their own marital decisions. Sergei Golitsyn, at least, was of the opinion that Steksovo fathers indulged (*poslabliaia docheriam svoim*), or permitted, their daughters not to marry.[53] In his formulation, the young women themselves took the initiative, to which their parents then assented. As discussed below, the residency pattern of unmarried adult women—mostly one to a household—supports this conclusion. And it is a reasonable conjecture that if these young women had the right to choose not to marry, they could also not be compelled to marry someone against their will: if her parents chose an unwanted groom, she might choose not to marry at all.

The manorial documents also throw some light on the anguish that many Old Believers must have experienced when subjected to relentless pressure to conform to Orthodoxy and to marry against their convictions. In late 1840, Ivan Pishchirin—a stubborn Old Believer who was then forty-six years old and widowed, with only his twenty-four-year-old schismatic daughter, Daria, to share the labor—felt compelled to take in a son-in-law. Daria was past twenty, the age by which almost all women on the estate married if they were to marry at all; it must have been Daria's choice (probably with her father's willing assent) not to marry. Yet with the household in need of adult male labor, Daria relented. We may surmise that the decision caused father and daughter great pain, because they were otherwise unwilling to compromise their religious beliefs. In May 1841, Pishchirin fled the estate rather than yield to the pressure of estate administrators and priests to join the Orthodox Church. Shortly thereafter, Daria, who had rejected her husband's pleas that she convert to Orthodoxy, also ran away.[54]

MARRIAGE AVERSION ON THE STEKSOVO ESTATE, 1845

Because the 1795 tax census omits information on the origins of 27 percent of the estate's wives, and nineteenth-century censuses and manorial household inventories provide no information at all on their origins, only the proportion of never-married adult women among the total number of adult women in their villages—including women who had married onto the estate—can be measured with any precision. The proportion of women native to the villages who never married must have been higher, though to an uncertain degree. The propensity to avoid marriage also fluctuated over time. For the sake of consistency, I measure unwillingness to marry among all women twenty-five and over, but this calculation produces a summary of behavior over roughly forty years, not women's inclinations as of the census date. As of 1795 (as I have already pointed out), 14.5 percent of Steksovo estate adult women had never married, but that measurement includes women who came of marriage age before marriage aversion struck Steksovo around 1760. Among women who were ages twenty-five to fifty-four in 1795, 18.5 percent had never married, which more or less reflected the choices women were making as of that date; the rate among women in the twenty-five to twenty-nine cohort was 19 percent.[55] Marriage aversion across the estate rose somewhat—to 17.1 percent by 1814, 17.8 percent by 1834—but this increase was a byproduct of the death of the older women who had married universally and the elevated level of marriage aversion of those who passed through marriage age between 1795 and 1805: 23.3 percent of those women, ages thirty-five to forty-four as of 1814, shunned marriage. In the following ten-year cohort, ages twenty-five to thirty-four in 1814, only 19.6 percent never married.[56] After 1834, women who had avoided marriage between 1795 and 1804 slowly died off, while in the follow-on cohorts, marriage aversion on the estate fluctuated between 10 and 15 percent.[57]

According to the household inventory steward Nikolai Tretiakov compiled in 1845, only 5 of the 213 households resembled the Spasovite households in Kuplia parish that accumulated women because they kept all or most of their women at home. The household of Mikhail Makarov, the same whose cell had been spared in 1843, consisted of Makarov, age sixty-one; his spinster sister-in-law, age fifty-five; and her never-married thirty-seven-year-old daughter. Aleksei Groshev, a widower and one of the leaders of the Steksovo Old Believers, had two married sons, an unmarried daughter of forty-five, and an unmarried granddaughter of twenty-two. (As I will explain, the ceiling age of marriage for women in Steksovo was effectively twenty.) After the Old Believer Nikita Gubanikhin died in 1844, his household consisted of his four minor children and his four unmarried sisters, ages thirty to forty-six. Vasilii Mortukhin, twenty-four, lived with his wife, his spinster sister (age thirty-one), and three unmarried aunts, ages fifty-seven to sixty-eight. Sidor and Sergei Sivov, fifty-nine and forty-nine, respectively, lived with their spinster sisters, ages sixty and thirty-two; Sidor's unmarried daughter, age twenty-five; and Sergei's two married sons.[58]

Many other households held only individual unmarried adult women. For example, Ivan Groshev, who had paid the Steksovo priest to perform an Old Believer wedding service for his son, had one thirty-five-year-old daughter in his household.[59] In all, forty-five unmarried daughters, sisters, nieces, aunts, cousins, and sisters-in-law, all over twenty, were the only single women in their households. Steward Tretiakov explained why three of those forty-five had never married: lame, demented, or blind. The total included three single women living in households in which they apparently had no kin; "taken into the household" was the way Tretiakov described them. The three had joined those households before the 1834 census, and there is no way to know where they came from.

The presence of so many single women in households in which all other adults were married strongly suggests that Sergei Golitsyn was right: the women had themselves chosen not to marry, and their parents had accepted their decisions. That was surely true of Avdotia Shobalova, daughter of Ivan Shobalov of the Old Believer Shobalov clan. In 1845, she was twenty-seven, single, and living in her married brother's household, while in the preceding three years, two of her younger sisters had married.[60] The distribution of women in households in the 1834 and 1850 tax censuses is completely consistent with the 1845 manorial census: in both of those years, too, a few households held multiple single women, while many more held but one.[61] In fact, this pattern was emerging by 1795: in the tax census of that year, forty-six unmarried women ages twenty and above were the only never-married adult women in their households, while twenty-two lived two to a household.[62] Many of the single adult women of 1795, whether living one or two to a household, had older and younger sisters and other female blood relatives who had married. In 1795, in other words, Old Believers on the Steksovo estate imposed neither marriage nor celibacy on their daughters, but apparently let them make their own decisions. Since the distribution of single women among households was similar in the second quarter of the nineteenth century, there is no reason to doubt that women then, too, made their own decisions to marry or not. And in 1861, that was still true: all twenty-one of the never-married Solenikov (formerly Golitsyn) women in Steksovo village ages twenty and over were the only single adults in their households.[63]

Table 7.1 Marital Status on the Golitsyn Steksovo Estate, by Age Cohort, 1845.

Age Cohort	Ever-married males	Never-married males (%)	Ever-married females	Never-married females (%)
0–14	0	167	0	190
15–19	7	53	10	40
20–24	58	3	68	9 (11.7%)
25–29	46	0	50	7 (12.3%)
30–34	43	0	47	8 (14.5%)
35–39	39	1	30	3 (9%)
40–44	35	1	38	3 (7.3%)
45–49	38	1	49	5 (9.3%)
50–54	38	0	30	3 (9.1%)
55–59	20	1	31	7 (18.4%)
60 and over	57	7 (10.9%)	35	15 (30%)
Totals	381	234	388	290
Totals 20 and over	374	14 (3.7%)	378	60 (13.7%)
Totals 25 and over	316	11 (3.4%)	310	51 (14.1%)

Source: GIM OPI, f. 14, d. 2397, ll. 2–45.
Special note: Percentages are irrelevant for ages nineteen and under—both male and female—as well as for males ages twenty to fifty-nine, and these have not been marked as a percentage. For women and men, percentages are irrelevant for "totals," because the totals include many young males and female who hadn't yet reached the local marriage age.

I present the totals for the married and never-married in 1845 at both ages twenty and over and at twenty-five and over; there was no meaningful difference on the Steksovo estate, unlike in crown-appanage villages in Kuplia parish, where the ceiling marriage age for women was twenty-five, or Baki, where the marriage ceiling age had risen to thirty by the 1830s. At least six of the nine unmarried women in the twenty to twenty-four cohort in 1845 remained unmarried five years later, and it is quite possible that none of those nine younger women ever married. The missing three may have married or been manumitted; in either case, they would not have been listed with their natal households in the 1850 census.

Not only do the 1845 household inventory and the 1834 and 1850 census returns suggest that twenty was the effective ceiling age for female marriage at Steksovo, but samples of marriage ages confirm that was so, with very few exceptions. Steward Tretiakov noted the ages of twelve of the seventeen women who married away from the estate between late 1842 and February

1845, when he compiled the household inventory: eleven were sixteen to twenty, one was twenty-two.[64] In 1839, all peasant brides who married at the Steksovo parish church were eighteen to nineteen, peasant grooms between eighteen and twenty (Steksovo priests didn't record age at marriage before the 1830s). In 1851 and 1854, eighteen of the twenty peasant brides were sixteen to twenty, and one was twenty-two; another, a schismatic, was twenty-seven. Daria Pishchirina, also a schismatic exception, married at age twenty-four in 1840, but not because she wanted to. Nineteen of the twenty peasant grooms in 1851 and 1854 were ages eighteen to twenty, while the other was twenty-two.[65]

It seems likely, on the other hand, that men kept marrying up to age twenty-two or twenty-three. Two of the three unmarried twenty- to twenty-four-year-old men in 1845 had married by 1850. Perhaps they were having trouble finding brides as of 1845. Far fewer men than women never married at all: in 1845, only four of the 259 men ages twenty-five to twenty-nine (1.5 percent). The most likely explanation for a very small number of men not marrying would ordinarily be that they were physically or mentally handicapped. However, the household inventory identified four men with disabilities (blind, weakly, weakly, and lame), and they were all married.[66] Ivan Biriukov, thirty-five in 1845, had never married and lived in a household whose only other members were his brother, his brother's wife, and his brother's unmarried twenty-three-year-old daughter.[67] Two unmarried, healthy adults in one household would have been unusual in a village not given to marriage aversion, which suggests that at least Ivan—like a few men in Kuplia parish and on the Baki estate—may have remained a bachelor for religious reasons. Yet for all practical purposes, males on Golitsyn's Steksov estate married universally.

THE HISTORICAL TRAJECTORY OF MARRIAGE AVERSION, 1750s–1860s

To return to a feature of table 7.1 that requires some comment: in 1845, the proportion of women who shunned marriage did not vary greatly in the five-year cohorts from twenty to twenty-four through fifty to fifty-four, while women fifty-five and over, and men sixty and over, were much less likely to have married than younger men and women. This might be thought to be a product of misstatement of ages by the elderly or perhaps a lack of the information needed to determine their marital status definitively; those are common problems in many surviving demographic records. However, while the

1845 household inventory does leave the marital status of some of the oldest men and women uncertain, information in the 1834 tax census and 1814 household inventory provides certainty. The seven unmarried men in the sixty and over cohort of 1845 had never married as of 1834, for instance. As for the never-married women ages fifty-five to fifty-nine and sixty and over, those were the last survivors of the 1795–1804 cohorts, the most marriage-averse on the Steksovo estate. And, as we have seen in Kuplia parish and around Baki, during the rush to adopt an anti-marriage creed, a small but not trivial number of men also rejected marriage. That was a passing phenomenon among men; after 1804, they married almost universally.

The tax census of 1762 identifies Pisarevo as the village in which women first began to shun marriage. Recall that in that year, only 10 of the 292 women ages twenty-five and above on the portion of the Steksovo estate that Sergei Golitsyn would eventually inherit were unmarried; 7 of them lived in Pisarevo, where they accounted for 9.2 percent of the women twenty-five and over.[68] Women in the other section of Pisarevo, descending down a different Golitsyn line, had also begun to resist marriage. Of the 182 women twenty-five and older, 10 (5.2 percent) had never married. Eight of them were ages twenty-five to twenty-nine, and they accounted for 19.5 percent of the 33 women in that cohort. While age-heaping among women in the 1762 census is quite dramatic, the evidence clearly points to marriage resistance emerging in Pisarevo, without much forewarning, in the late 1750s.[69]

The 1795 census allows us to chart the progress of marriage resistance through the estate Sergei Golitsyn later inherited. Of the eighty-one women ages fifty-five and above, only two (2.5 percent) had never married. Of the thirty-three women ages fifty to fifty-four, seven (21 percent) had never married; of those, six were in Steksovo and Pisarevo, while one of the two Pashutina women in that cohort was single. Women in their forties—who had come of marriage age in the 1770s—were marriage-averse in all five villages.[70] According to the 1791 Steksovo parish confession register, women in the small village of Belozerie, then owned by Daria Golitsyna but not part of the estate Sergi Golitsyn inherited, turned marriage-averse only in the 1780s—but then enthusiastically so. As of 1791, every single woman over twenty-nine was married, while four of seven women ages twenty-five to twenty-nine had never married, and five of nine in the twenty to twenty-four cohort had not yet married.[71]

Table 7.2 Proportions of Never-Married Women Twenty-Five and Older on the Golitsyn (from 1847, Solenikov) Steksovo Estate, by Village, 1762–1861.

	1762 tax census	1795 tax census	1814 manorial census	1834 tax census	1845 manorial census	1850 tax census	1861 confession register
Steksovo	1.7%	15.0%	18.0%	22.1%	17.6%	15.4%	16.1%
Pisarevo	9.2%	14.4%	17.7%	19.5%	13.9%	11.0%	
Balakhonikha	2.0%	17.7.%	22.0%	22.4%	18.0%	17.7%	
Pashutina	0.0%	22.6%	21.0%	3.4%	6.5%	8.7%	8.0%
Piatnitskoe	0.0%	7.8%	13.3%	9.3%	7.5%	8.5%	
Entire estate	3.3%	14.5%	17.9%	17.8%	14.1%	12.9%	

Note: The one household in Korobina, 1834–50, is included in the estate totals.
Sources: RGADA, f., 350, op. 2, d. 1264, ch. 2, ll. 1235–3070b.; TsANO, f. 60, op. 239a, d. 163, ll. 297–4000b.; d. 1102, ll. 3630b–476; d. 1606, ll. 317–423; GIM OPI, f. 14, d. 2396; d. 2397; TsANO, f. 570, op. 559a, d. 1502, ll. 100–1050b, 113–140b., 123–280b.

As table 7.2 shows, marriage resistance rose sharply across the entire estate between 1762 and 1795. The propensity to avoid marriage continued to increase up to about 1805 and then declined, but because of the momentum created by the particularly marriage-averse women who turned twenty-five between 1795 and 1804, the proportion of women who had never married rose through 1814 and then declined after 1834. The 1850 census is a problematic source because it excluded manumitted women still living at home; I have conservatively estimated that nine of the nineteen unmarried women ages twenty to forty-nine, listed in 1845 but not in 1850, neither married nor died in the intervening years. The 1861 confession register, which lists (without identifying) manumitees among the parishioners, provides a more accurate measure, but only for the villages of Steksovo and Pashutina.

It may not have been just a coincidence that the refusal of younger women to marry declined shortly after Sergei Golitsyn inherited the estate in 1804. By the 1820s, he had abolished the 10-ruble annual fine on women who refused to marry, and the 250- to 500-ruble price of manumission must have been beyond the means of at least some fathers of reluctant brides. The estate correspondence leaves no doubt that Golitsyn was unrelentingly determined to force young serf women to marry. Nevertheless, variation from one village to another—and in particular the decline in marriage resistance in Pashutina and Piatnitskoe in the early nineteenth century and Pisarevo later—suggests that Golitsyn was not alone responsible. We do not know how Evgraf Solenikov managed the estate after he acquired it in 1847. The level of marriage resistance in Steksovo seems to have stabilized at about the level of 1845. In the fourteen years after Solenikov's purchase, young women continued to join the ranks of the adult unmarried. In 1861, four of the thirty women ages twenty-five to thirty-four in Steksovo village had never married (13.3 percent), while three of the thirteen women (23 percent) ages twenty to twenty-four were still unmarried and at or over what had long been the effective ceiling age for female marriage.[72]

We can be confident that Spasovites predominated in Steksovo and Pashutina. We have no direct evidence on the religious inclinations of the Old Believers in Pisarevo, Balakhonikha, and Piatnitskoe. However, Balakhonikha women's nuptial behavior was indistinguishable from that of Steksovo women, so there is a good chance that there, too, marriage-averse women were predominantly Spasovite. At the very least, Balakhonikha serfs were stubborn. In 1836, fifteen of its thirty-nine households refused point blank Golitsyn's demand that they contribute to a four-ruble, twenty-kopek per capita levy to support the estate's Orthodox parishes.[73] All we can say about marriage resistance at Pisarevo is that it fell considerably after 1834. (With never-married women clustered among the elderly, leftovers from a previous era, as of 1850 only 8.2 percent of women ages twenty-five to fifty-four had never married.) If Pisarevo women's nuptial behavior was rooted in traditional Spasovite beliefs up to 1834 (a hypothesis only), Pisarevo Spasovites may have split between the traditionalists and the pro-marriage Neo-Spasovites (of the Great Rite) after that year. Of course, the statistics are compatible with other hypotheses.

Piatnitskoe, on the other hand, was a consistent outlier, with a rate of marriage resistance topping out at 12.9 percent in 1834 and falling to 7.3 percent in 1850 if we exclude women fifty-five and over from the count. That did not signify any particular inclination to Orthodoxy. In 1854, Pavel Melnikov identified Piatnitskoe as one of the cluster of sixteen parishes along the Ardatov-Arzamas border in which Old Believers made up half the population (and his estimate was probably low, as it was for Steksovo). The Piatnitskoe Old Believers, whatever their covenant, were also obdurate. In 1836, eleven of its forty-two Golitsyn households also defied Sergei Golitsyn's order that they contribute four rubles, twenty kopeks per head to the parish church.[74] Spasovite women in Steksovo village resisted marriage, but most of their Old Believer sisters in Piatnitskoe were the marrying kind.

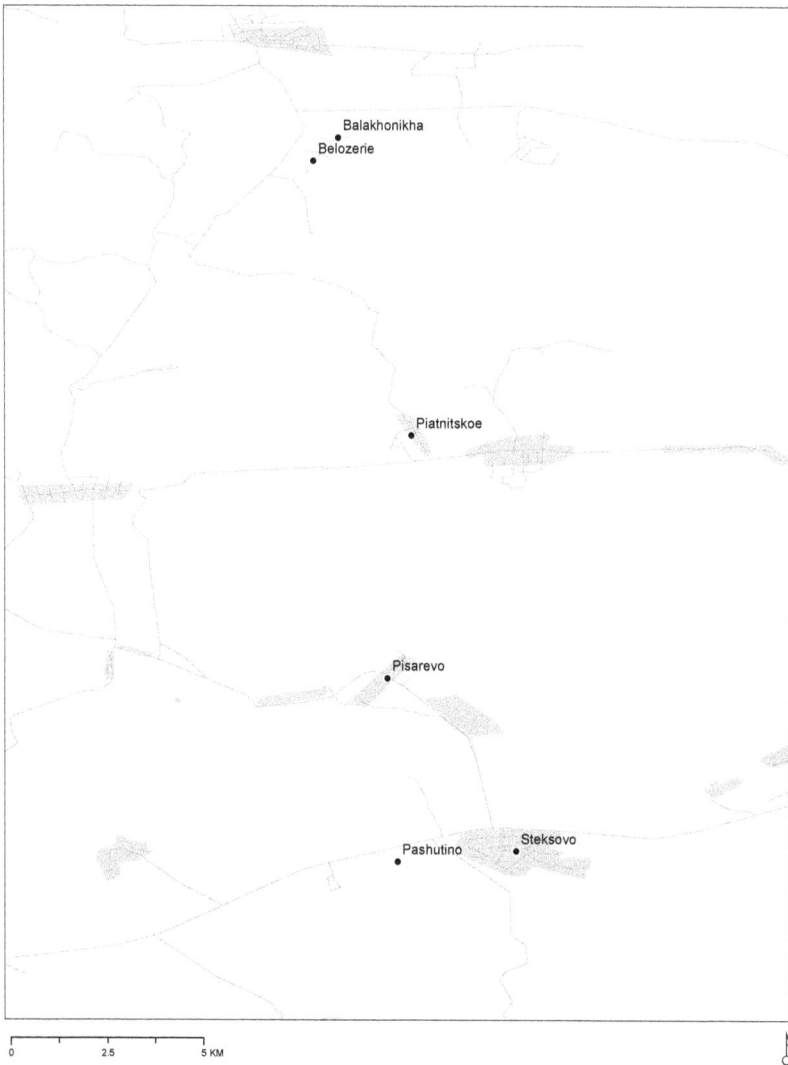

Map 7.1 Sergei Golitsyn's Steksovo Estate and Belozerie. Contains information from OpenStreetMap, which is made available at https://www.openstreetmap.org under the Open Database License (ODbL). Modified by Kelsey Rydland, licensed under CC BY-SA 2.0.

The history of Old Believers and marriage resistance in Pashutina—located only two kilometers from Steksovo village—was quite different but is only partially illuminated by the surviving documents. According to one story, apparently an oral tradition, the village was founded in the middle of the eighteenth century by natives of Steksovo and other villages and took its name from its founder, Pavel.[75] That is unlikely, however, since the portion of Pashutina that was later inherited by Sergei Golitsyn had a total population of 116 men and women in 1762 (no earlier tax census returns for what became the Ardatov district have survived), while the portion of the village that descended through Praskovaia Golitsyna was larger than that.[76] In 1763, all of the women twenty and older in Daria Golitsyna's (and later Sergei's) section were married, and 23 of the 25 wives had been born in the village. That was a larger proportion of native-born wives than elsewhere on the estate. From 60 to 74 percent of wives born in the larger villages of Pisarevo (293 serfs of both sexes in Sergei Golitsyn's future share), Piatnitskoe (160 serfs), and Balakhonikha (215 serfs) were native to those villages, for example. Steksovo, with the largest population at 444 serfs of all ages and both sexes (in Sergei Golitsyn's future share), had the second-largest number of native-born wives at 88 percent, but of course, the larger the village, the easier to find brides close by. The men of Pashutina appear to have brought wives from outside their community only when not a single local woman was available[77]—that is, the choice to marry within the community was deliberate, and the reason almost certainly religious.

Pashutina was a predominantly Old Believer village in the second half of the eighteenth century; it had an unsanctioned Old Believer chapel prior to 1798, the year in which the Nizhnii Novgorod Diocese authorized the establishment of a Edinoverie congregation there.[78] From subsequent petitions in which Old Believers asked to be permitted to join that congregation, we know that many in Pashutina were Spasovites and that many of them initially refused to join the Edinoverie church. A strong Spasovite presence would explain why 24 percent (six of twenty-five) of Pashutina women ages twenty-five to fifty-four were recorded as never married in 1795.[79] Yet after 1795, marriage resistance almost vanished. In 1834, there was a single surviving unmarried adult woman, age forty-eight. In 1845, there was one additional unmarried adult woman, age twenty-one, but she was lame and may have been single for that reason; she remained unmarried in both 1850 and 1861. In 1850, one other adult woman was also unmarried; she was not listed in the census, presumably because she had been manumitted, but was either twenty-three or twenty-seven, depending on whether the 1845 manorial census or the 1861 confession register approximated her age more accurately (I have counted her as twenty-three). Between the early 1800s and 1861, she and the lame woman were the only women born in Pashutina who did not marry.[80] The one known development that might explain the disappearance of marriage aversion in Pashutina was the opening of a legal venue for Old Believer worship, the Edinoverie church. Likely the opportunity for regular practice of the old rituals, including the pre-Nikonian wedding service, persuaded women in the village—including the Spasovites among them—that marriage was godly after all.

DEMOGRAPHIC CONSEQUENCES

Household preferences at Steksovo reduced the demographic risk attendant upon female marriage aversion. Steksovo village couples preferred, although not overwhelmingly, to live in multiple-couple households. Steward Tretia-kov's 1845 household inventory described sixty-nine households with 394 male and female members, for a mean household size of 5.7 individuals. As for Baki, I determine Steksovo household preferences by ignoring the ten remnant (but really existing, not virtual) households that no longer contained married couples in 1845. In the village of Steksovo, only twenty-one of the fifty-nine complete households (36.6 percent) consisted of a single couple (usually with children), while at Baki, fifty-six of the 114 complete households (49.1 percent) consisted of a single couple (usually with children). At Steksovo, twenty households consisted of two married couples, and another eleven had one married couple and widow or widower. At least thirty-one of the fifty-nine complete households (53 percent) were or had recently been two-couple households. There were also seven households with three to five intact married couples. The modal household in Steksovo was the present or formerly two-couple household. At Steksovo, 64 percent of all complete households had, then or recently, two or more married couples; at Baki, that was true of only 51 percent. Death of a husband at Steksovo was thus less likely to leave a household without an adult male. Just as important in preserving viable households was the higher survival rate among adult males at Steksovo. There were only ten widows (8 percent of the 129 women twenty-five and over) in Steksovo village in 1845 as compared to forty-six (21 percent of the 220 women twenty-five and over) in Baki village in 1834.[81]

It turns out, too, that at Steksovo, absence of a married couple did not automatically condemn a household to destitution. Of the ten incomplete (remnant) households in the village in 1845, at least five were, however improbably, viable at least over the short term. The solitary Nikolai Eremeevtsev, age sixty-eight in 1845, had estimated annual earnings of 500 rubles from trade; he had been the only male in the household since his son's conscription in 1831, at age thirty-one. The Gubanikhin household, largest of the ten, had eight members after its head, the widower Nikita Gubanikhin, died in 1844 at age forty-two: Nikita's two sons, ages fourteen and fifteen; two daughters, ages eight and nine; and four never-married sisters, ages thirty to forty-six. According to steward Tretiakov, they earned 1,500 rubles annually from farming and renting out the 270 acres (83.7 hectares) they owned; farming may have contracted after Nikita's death, but rental income surely sustained the family. Fedor Khibarin, seventy-six, and his maiden daughter, fifty-nine, earned 500 rubles annually from commerce. Mavra Gubanikhina, forty-eight, and a sixty-eight-year-old maiden aunt managed to earn 400 rubles per year in trade even after Mavra's husband fled. The Gubanikhin, Khibarin, and Gubanikhina households, with unmarried adult women, were presumptively priestless Old Belivers, likely Spasovites. So, probably, was Nikolai Eremeevtsev—the other Eremeevtsev household in Steksovo included the head's fifty-year-old spinster daughter. The fifty-year-old widower Ivan Shobalov (income 600 rubles from farming and from a mill that he rented) was also probably a Spasovite. Although two of his daughters had married, the oldest was single at twenty-seven and living in her married brother's household. With another son, age nineteen, and two younger daughters, ages seventeen and thirteen, Ivan's household would almost certainly survive his death.

Four of the five poorest households in the remnant group may not have been priestless Old Believers. (The evidence from fragmentary households is necessarily incomplete, but household lists from 1814 and 1834 suggest this was so.) Three had no income at all—Andrei Fedotov, fifteen, and his mother Daria, age sixty; the brothers Semen and Ivan Lapshin, seventeen and nine; and the solitary Natalia Peshanova, thirty-two, whose husband was a fugitive—and held no spinsters. Avdotia Lapshina's husband was also a fugitive, and she cared for two sons, seventeen and nineteen, and two younger children; the family earned 100 rubles by farming and tending livestock. Only the destitute household of Mikhail Oserin (sixty-one), his spinster sister-in-law Anna Egorova (fifty-five), and her spinster daughter (thirty-seven) was likely Spasovite; they did no farming, and Oserin earned only 35 rubles per year as watchman at the estate office. The Oserin household and the three with no income at all can only have survived on charity, but they probably lived in their own cabins.

Those ten households present an apparent paradox. In the village of Steksovo, four of the ten remnant households in 1845 contained spinsters; they accounted for almost one-fifth of the twenty-one households in Steksovo village with unmarried women twenty-five and over. The six crippled households *without* unmarried adult women (none in 1834, either) accounted for just 12.5 percent of the forty-eight households in that group. It is not surprising, in light of the analysis of the demographic fortunes of Baki households, that the presence of unmarried women almost doubled the odds that a Steksovo household would be demographically crippled. Yet among those ten households, three of the four with never-married adult women prospered, while four of the six without spinsters experienced dire poverty or destitution. In the remnant households, spinsters correlated with prosperity rather than penury.

That was no one-time stroke of good fortune true only in or around 1845. Between 1834 and 1845, household survival rates of those with and without spinsters were nearly identical: forty-nine of fifty-six without spinsters in 1834 (87.5 percent) endured through 1845, as did twenty of twenty-two with spinsters (91.1 percent).[82] The 1834 census provides no information on household resources or income, but the economic data in the 1845 household inventory represents recent household economic history as much as the results of a single year's labor. In 1845, of the twenty-one Steksovo village households with unmarried women twenty-five and older, fourteen (67 percent) had earnings of 450 rubles or more. Among the other forty-eight households, only twenty-three (48 percent) earned at least 450 rubles. It was not just among remnant households that spinsters correlated with prosperity—it was true for Steksovo village as a whole. The association between spinsterhood and prosperity may (this is only a hypothesis) have rested on Spasovite communal solidarity.

Between 1814–1816 (the dates of an estate household inventory and of a tax census) and 1834, Steksovo village households with single adult women had a notably better survival rate than those without. In those twenty years, thirteen of the ninety-one Steksovo village households disappeared.

Not one of the thirteen had been burdened by an unmarried adult woman (twenty-five or older) as of 1814. All of the eighteen households with unmarried women of at least twenty-five years recorded in 1814–16 had survived to 1834, while thirteen of the seventy-eight households without single adult women (16.7 percent) disappeared. The principal reason for household expiration was a combination of small size and demographic misfortune. Two households, each with a single adult man, were casualties of war—a husband and a widower were conscripted into the militia to fight the French and never returned. In one household, a widow and her three daughters disappeared, while the sole survivor in the other household, a fourteen-year-old boy, eventually married into a Pisarevo family. Four other households headed by widows in 1814 also disappeared. One of the widows married a Steksovo widower and took her son, age twelve in 1814, into her new husband's household. Another five households, consisting in 1814 of middle-aged couples with young daughters, expired before 1834.[83]

Household extinction would have been greater had at-risk households not brought in reinforcements. Four households with spinsters and two without took in sons-in-law who had become household heads by 1834, while another (without a spinster) adopted a boy who eventually took over. Yet another attempted to perpetuate itself though adoption, but by 1834, the household was doomed: the adoptee had become a solitary fifty-six-year-old widower. Twelve other households (only one of which included a spinster as of 1814–16) had become remnants: they lacked a reproducing couple or any other obvious means to perpetuate themselves. In fact, the household lists leave the impression that in the years just around 1800, a dozen or so married couples either altogether avoided or curtailed reproduction—evidence, though not enough for a hypothesis, that celibate marriage may have been a practice in Steksovo in those years. What is clear is that between 1814 and 1834 households with single adult women were better at staving off collapse than the rest.

For the entire period from 1814 to 1845, three things at Steksovo are clear: there was a relatively slow but steady level of household mortality in Steksovo, the presence of single unmarried adult women had minimal bearing on household destitution and collapse, and—at least for the years 1834 to 1845 and probably earlier as well—households with single adult women were more prosperous than those without. From 1814 to 1834, thirteen of ninety-one households disappeared, as did nine of seventy-eight from 1834 to 1845;

the annual rate of disappearance was just over 0.8 percent annually in the first period and just over 1 percent annually in the second. Measured differently, twenty-two of the original ninety-one households disappeared over twenty-nine years, or 7.8 percent of the original ninety-one households per decade. Of the twenty-two households with spinsters, only two (9.1 percent) collapsed, while twenty of the sixty-nine households (29 percent) without spinsters disappeared. That is just the reverse of the Baki story. Some of the marriage-resistant households had recruited replacement members to prevent demographic collapse, but the larger story is that households with spinsters were on average notably more prosperous than those without.

CONSCRIPTION AND COMPARISON: GOLITSYN STEKSOVO VERSUS OBOLENSKII STEKSOVO

The tax censuses of 1834 and 1850 reveal that on Sergei Golitsyn's Steksovo estate, of the 122 men who turned twenty (the minimum conscription age as of 1831) between 1816 and 1825, 27 (22 percent) were conscripted; in the period from 1826 to 1835, twenty of the 127 men who turned twenty (16 percent) were conscripted; and thirteen of the ninety-two men (14 percent) who turned twenty between 1836 and 1845 were conscripted.[84] Some men from the 1836–45 cohort must also have been conscripted after the 1850 census. Because those tax censuses listed only women alive in 1834 and 1850 and tell us nothing about those who disappeared from estate rolls between 1816 and 1850, we cannot compare the number of men and women who grew into marriage age during those years. The loss of Steksovo males to the army does raise the possibility that conscription may have been one reason why many Steksovo women never married. However, that was no truer at Steksovo in the 1820s to 1840s than among the crown peasants of Kuplia parish or the Lieven's Baki estate in the 1760s to 1790s. That is revealed, more or less directly, by the ages at which men were conscripted and, indirectly, by comparison with the census return from 1850 from the Obolenskii portion of Steksovo village. At Steksovo, as everywhere, conscription debilitated many households and destroyed some but did not materially or perhaps at all reduce the chances for single women to marry.

In the second quarter of the nineteenth century, the majority of the men conscripted nationally were married. That goes against a lingering assumption that in the eighteenth and first half of the nineteenth centuries the majority were single men because they were less critical to household survival than married men. Another assumption is that households with three and more working-age males lost sons to the army first and in the greatest numbers. Those were principles that peasant communities charged with selecting conscripts had worked out, and they were written into the 1831 conscription law. Of course, there were many exceptions, especially on serf estates.[85] Yet data collected by Boris Mironov show that from 1826 to 1830, roughly 40 percent of conscripts were married and from 1831 to 1835, roughly 50 percent were married, while during the decade between 1836 and 1845, around 60 percent were married.[86]

On the Golitsyn estate, the proportion of conscripts married was considerably greater than that. The 1845 Steksovo household inventory identifies six men conscripted in 1843–44. All of them were married; all left behind wives who had been freed when their husbands were conscripted. These Steksovo conscripts were older than the national average. For the period from 1841 to 1846, the national average age was 23.5, while the Steksovo conscripts averaged 28 years (twenty-four, twenty-six, twenty-six, twenty-nine, thirty-one, thirty-two).[87] Their ages explains why they were all married. By age twenty-four, virtually all of the men on the estate were. The tax census of 1850 identifies an additional eight men conscripted from the Steksovo estate between 1840 and 1850 but tells us nothing about their marital status. Two, at eighteen and nineteen, may or may not have been married; the rest ranged from twenty-three to thirty-one (median age twenty-six to twenty-seven) and were likely all married.[88]

The 1834 tax census identifies precisely when Golitsyn and his estate managers began to send predominantly married men into the army: 1831. Between 1816 and 1827, the estate lost only six men through conscription, ages fifteen, sixteen, twenty-one, twenty-three, twenty-four, and thirty-two. (Annual conscription rates nationally during those years ranged from zero to low.) Between 1828 and 1830, fourteen men left the estate for the army, with a median age of twenty-two to twenty-three. Possibly half of those the conscripts from 1816 to 1830 were single. Beginning in 1831, however, average conscript age spiked: the nine conscripts of 1831–33 were from twenty-six to thirty-three years old, with a median age of thirty. The median age of the sixteen conscripts of 1834–39 fell to twenty-three (including two underage boys of sixteen and seventeen—no doubt the two were singled out for punishment).[89] With some exceptions in the mid-1830s, between 1831 and 1850 almost all the men the estate sent to the army were married. My conservative estimate is that 74 percent of all men sent from the Steksovo estate from 1816 to 1850 were marred; my estimate for 1831 to 1850 is 88 percent.

Both the tax censuses and manorial correspondence show that Sergei Golitsyn and his estate administrators were deeply involved in deciding who would be sacrificed to the army, and the choices that they made more or less guaranteed that most of the men conscripted from the Steksovo estate would be married. Golitsyn's 1842 "Instruction" to steward Shornikov mentioned conscription twice, both times as a form of punishment: drunkards who fell behind in their quitrent were to be sent to the army, as were the sons of the estate's elderly forest wardens who were suspected of conniving in the illegal felling of estate timber.[90] And we know from the manorial correspondence that the sons of the most obstinate Old Believers were also singled out for conscription. Steward Tretiakov included no notes in his 1845 household inventory explaining why the six conscripts of 1843–44 had been selected, but in three cases, estate officials had subjected one of two able-bodied male workers in the household to conscription, and in another took the only man under fifty. Conscription had gravely undermined the ability of at least four households to deliver their quitrent and plow their master's fields. On the other hand, the very few single men in their early twenties in 1843–44 had been spared. The same pattern of indifference to household survival can be seen in the tax census information on conscription in the early 1830s, and in part over the rest of that decade. Of course, given the relatively small size of Steksovo households, conscription would inevitably damage many of them.

Golitsyn must have consistently used conscription to rid his estate of troublemaking serfs and probably focused on Old Believers. As of mid-century, it was common practice among the serf-owners of Nizhnii Novgorod province to send Old Believers rather than the Orthodox into the army, in order to compel schismatics to join the church.[91] On the Steksovo estate, Balakhonikha, with one hundred men (from babies to the elderly) in 1834, lost ten men—10 percent—to conscription between 1834 and 1850; the rate for the entire estate was only 4.6 percent. Perhaps that was because the Balakhonikha peasants were particularly stubborn Old Believers. In 1836, fifteen of its thirty-nine households had, after all, defied Golitsyn's demand that they contribute to the levy to support the estate's Orthodox parishes.[92]

The fact that between 1831 and 1850 roughly 90 percent of all conscripts from the Steksovo estate were married means that conscription could have accounted for, at most, only a small portion of the surplus of adult,

Table 7.3 Marital Status in the Obolenskii Portion of Steksovo Village, by Age Cohort, 1850.

Age cohort	Ever married males	Never married males (%)	Ever married females	Never married females (%)
1–14	0	28	0	28
15–19	3	10	7	8
20–24	9	4 (30.7%)	16	2 (11.0%)
25–29	13	1 (7.1%)	4	1 (20.0%)
30–34	7	0	6	0
35–39	9	0	15	1 (6.3%)
40–44	15	0	8	0
45–49	5	0	12	0
50–54	9	0	5	0
55–59	8	0	9	0
60 and over	17	0	16	0
Total	95	43	98	40
Total, 20+	92	5 (5.2%)	91	4 (4.2%)
Total, 25-54	58	1 (1.7%)	50	2 (3.8%)

Note: The total includes four women and two men, all married, who had run away and left behind spouses still living in 1850. The runaways were not counted in the estate population; however, they had earlier been part of the estate's pool of marriageable men and women, so I have included them.

Source: TsANO, f. 60, op.239a, d. 1604, ll. 155–72.

never-married women. Comparison with the Obolenskii share of Steksovo village demonstrates that conscription probably had no impact on the demographic balance at all.

The 1850 tax census for the part of Steksovo village then owned by Sergei Petrovich Obolenskii and his children (276 serfs in fifty-six households) reveals a very different demographic structure than that which obtained in the Golitsyn portion.

Among the Obolenskii serfs, there was a demographic balance among men and women by almost every measure: in total numbers and in totals ever married in the entire population, in total numbers and total ever married at age twenty and over, and in the almost equally low percentages of never-married adult men and women at age twenty and above. The one obvious difference—the shortfall in married women between the ages of twenty-five and fifty-four—was entirely offset by the disproportionately large number of married women in the twenty to twenty-four cohort. The fact that out of a population of 146 men and women twenty-five and older, only one man and two women had never married might indicate that among the Obolenskii serfs all but the most physically and mentally disabled married. In fact, that was so only because the Obolenskies and their estate officials were far more successful than Golitsyn in suppressing female marriage aversion.

It is true that the 1850 tax census did not enumerate manumitted women, but confession registers for 1826 and 1861 did. They show that in 1826, Obolenskii women in Steksovo village refused to marry at about the same rate as Golitsyn women but that by 1861, virtually all women married. In 1826, the twenty-five to fifty-four population numbered seventy-eight men, all but one of them married; eighty-seven women who had married and sixteen who had not; and an additional six *soldatki* (conscripts' wives). Counting *soldatki*, 14.7 percent of the women had never married; not counting *soldatki*, 15.5 percent were single. This figure is about the same as that among Golitsyn estate women in the same age group, again not including *soldatki*, in 1834 (17.8). Adults from seven Obolenskii households had skipped confession in 1826 because they were Old Believers, adults from three households because they were away the estate, and from a further fourteen households because they were "forgetful."[93]

Openly or secretly, Obolenskii serfs were no doubt as universally committed to the Old Belief in 1826 as they were in 1861, when only nine of 261 supposed congregants over the age of six confessed their sins. Nevertheless, by 1861, marriage aversion had been all but eliminated. As of that year, in the twenty-five to fifty-four age group there were sixty-three Obolenskii men (one single) and sixty-eight Obolenskii women (including manumitees), only four of whom (5.9 percent) had never married. One was exactly twenty-five; the others were listed as forty-seven, forty-eight, and fifty-four. Only the twenty-five-year-old was also listed in the 1850 tax census.[94] The others, most likely manumitted in the late 1820s and early 1830s, were survivors from an earlier era, before the Obolenskies had overcome marriage resistance. In suppressing marriage resistance among their Steksovo serfs, they had brought the number of men and women on their estate into balance. That is strong, if indirect, evidence that the demographic imbalance on the Golitsyn estate was due to marriage aversion rather than conscription.

The Obolenskies evidently overcame their female serfs' resistance to marriage by two means. Beginning in the 1830s, as is evident from the

1861 confession register, they stopped selling manumission papers for girls who had no intention to marry. The 1850 census return, which contains no information on Obolenskii women manumitted in earlier years, does note a few changes in the status of men and women down to 1860. A single young woman, Avdotia Ivanovna, was manumitted in 1856, when her father was thirty-six. She was probably of marriageable age, and since she was the only member of her family manumitted and was not living in the parish as of 1861, she was most likely manumitted so she could marry off the estate.[95] Preventing fathers from buying their daughters out of serfdom gradually reduced the number of unmarried free women on the estate and, therefore, the power of their example. Young women who wanted to avoid marriage must have lost confidence that they would be able to do so. But at least initially, the Obolenskies surely resorted to irresistible compulsion of some kind.

Of course, Sergei Golitsyn was also determined to make his Steksovo women marry, and he sent demand after demand that his stewards do so. Yet no matter the level of moral violence he was willing to commit, he lived far away in Moscow and could not force his stewards to follow through. Furthermore, he changed his stewards frequently, every two years or so in the 1830s and 1840s; they must have spent at least half of their tenure learning who was who. And the stewards, in turn, depended on the cooperation of serf bailiffs and elders, almost all of whom must have been Old Believers (because almost all serfs on the estate were). To get his way, Golitsyn would have had to have lived on the estate, not in distant Moscow. Obolenskies, at least some of the time, lived on their Steksovo portion: Princess Aleksandra Andreevna Obolenskaia, age forty-seven, was listed in the 1861 Steksovo confession register along with two house serfs.[96] There were also Obolenskies living about 150 kilometers distant in Nizhnii Novgorod.[97] If Obolenskies lived on or visited the estate even occasionally in the 1830s and 1840s, their estate officials were likely to have enforced orders with a heavy hand. Whatever the means employed, the Obolenskies crushed marriage resistance, while Golitsyn managed, at best, to contain it.

The demographic balance among Obolenskii serfs in 1850 and 1861 also demonstrates that conscription did not necessarily produce a deficit of adult men. Between 1834 and 1850, ten Obolenskii serfs were conscripted into the army (for a conscription rate of 5.5 percent of all men counted in the 1834 census, compared to 3.7 percent in the Golitsyn share of the village and 4.6 percent for the entire Golitsyn estate from 1834 to 1846). Two of the Obolenskii conscripts, ages twenty-eight and thirty-one when they were sent to the army, were married; they left children behind. The census register provides no direct evidence on the marital status of the others. However, we know their ages when conscripted: sixteen, eighteen, twenty-one, twenty-four, twenty-six, twenty-six, twenty-seven, and thirty-one. The five who were twenty-four or older when conscripted were almost certainly married. The sixteen-year-old was too young to marry. The impact on the conscripts' households—some were entirely destroyed—suggests that Obolenskii estate managers used conscription to send troublemakers (no doubt including stiff-necked Old Believers) into the army, whatever the damage to conscript households and apparently in defiance of the law as well, as the sixteen- and eighteen-year-olds were below the legal conscription age.[98]

In sum, conscription seems to have been conducted in the same way on both estates: in the 1830s and 1840s, most men were conscripted past the age at which almost all men on the estates had married, and apparently administrators on both estates used conscription to get rid of undesirables, irrespective of marital status and the impact on households. If there had not been substantial aversion to marriage among Golitsyn's female serfs, the demographic balance among males and females twenty-five and over in 1845 (and 1850 and 1861) should have been as close as it was among Obolenskii serfs in 1850.

The marriage practices of Sergei Golitsyn's Steksovo serfs were representative of only a minority of Russian peasants, but that minority was regionally substantial. It was not, after all, just on Sergei Golitsyn's estate but on all sections of the original Golitsyn estate—his, the Obolenskies', and the Bibikovs'. (Twenty percent of Bibikov serf women twenty-five and over had never married as of 1861.) In other words, serf women resisted marriage across a broad swath of eastern Ardatov district.[99] Resistance endured over many generations: from the 1760s or so to the 1830s on what became the Obolenskii estate, from the 1760s into at least the 1860s on the Golitsyn and Bibikov estates. Women in the small state peasant population at Steksovo were equally likely to avoid marriage.[100] Surely many other of the villages teeming with Old Believers in the Ardatov-Arzamas borderland shared that history.

NOTES

1. TsANO, f. 60, op. 239a, d. 163, ll. 297–4000b.

2. In 1834 and 1845, Golitsyn owned one household in a sixth village, Korobina.

3. Different documents tell different stories about the origins of Golitsyn owner-ship (*Arzamasskie pomestnye*, pp. 421–42; TsANO, f. 177, op. 766, d. 56, l. 10b; d. 133, 1842; TsANO, f. 4, op. 1a, d. 1771). Sergei's brother Aleksandr and, after his death, Aleksandr's two sons were officially co-owners with Sergei, but manorial correspon-dence, tax censuses, and parish confession registers refer to Sergei as sole owner.

4. The 1845 population figures are from a household inventory (GIM OPI, f. 14, d. 2397). In addition, the steward listed six recent conscripts and their wives but did not include them in the population total. He counted four of the ten runaways he listed as part of the population, presumably because they had fled after the 1834 tax census and the estate still had to pay the annual head tax for them. His count included manumit-ted women who continued to live on the estate; in 1834, Golitsyn directed that in the tax census of that year they should be listed in their natal households (ibid., d. 2322, 1840, l. 31), and so the household description of 1845 did the same.

5. Ibid., d. 2397; *Geografichesko-statisticheskii slovar'*, vol. 1, p. 1245; vol. 4, p. 757; Pestov, "Opisanie ardatovskogo," pp. 105–87; *Materialy dlia statistiki*, issue 3, map at the end; Mel'nikov, "Otchet," pp. 43, 63–64, 77, 81–84, 87; Kurmacheva, "Rassloenie," pp. 363–78. Kurmacheva mischaracterizes the steward's estimate of income in 1845 as declared capital.

6. GIM OPI, f. 14, d. 2331, l. 18. In 1843, Steksovo serfs owed arrears of 51,054 rubles for the previous three years and 1,500 rubles for seed that Golitsyn had advanced fol-lowing crop failures in 1840 and 1841 (ibid., ll. 7, 18). The manorial correspondence is peppered with serf requests for temporary forgiveness of quitrent because of hardship and home office demands that the required dues be collected from shirkers. Neverthe-less, my overall impression is that most peasants on the estate were not impoverished. As a case in point, in 1839 the widow Marfa Sivova of Pisarevo was robbed by fellow serfs of 1,000 rubles in paper currency and 59 rubles in coin, a considerable sum for a widow (ibid., d. 2322, ll. 140b–150b).

7. GIM, f. 14, d. 2394; Kurmacheva, "Rassloenie."

8. GIM OPI, f. 14, d. 2397, ll. 2–15.

9. *Kniaz' Sergei Mikhailovich Golitsyn. Vospominaniia; Pis'ma Filareta*, pp. 97–98; Shumikhin, "Marginal s dvoinym dnom (skrytyi kalambur v poslanii Pushkina Prin-cesse Nocturne)," http://www.nasledie-rus/red_port/00900.php. The steward men-tioned the presence of a *gospodskii dom* in 1843 (GIM OPI, f. 14, d. 2331, l. 70b), but this must not have been an actual residence because the 1847–48 land survey does not mention it (Ziuzin and Tiurin, *Steksovo*, p. 38).

10. Following Daria Golitsyna's death, Mikhail Mikhailovich Golitsyn inherited Steksovo. On at least some of his other properties, he imposed marriage by brute force (see chapter 2); he might have continued an established regime of fines but is unlikely to have instituted one himself.

11. GIM OPI, f. 14, d. 2311, l. 8.

12. RGADA, f. 350, op. 2, d. 1264, ch. 2, ll. 1235–88.

13. Ibid., ch. 1, ll. 833–58.

14. GIM OPI, f. 14, d. 2394.

15. TsANO, f. 60, op. 239, d. 163, ll. 297–400ob.

16. GANO no. 3, f. 570, op. 559b, d. 898, no. 10, l. 10; TsANO, f. 570, op. 559a, ll. 449–66. According to Mel'nikov, "Otchet," p. 44, at the time of his 1854 report on Old Believers in Nizhnii Novgorod province, 306 members of the merchant and townsman estates lived in Steksovo village.

17. GIM OPI, f. 14, d. 2311, l. 46–46ob.

18. Ibid., d. 2316, ll. 40b–6; d. 2397, l. 9. The 500-ruble price appears in correspondence with other Golitsyn estates but sometimes with exceptions that do not appear in the Steksovo correspondence (ibid., d. 3106, ll. 11, 26, 46–46ob, 83, 84–84ob, 91).

19. There is no trace of that particular Koloskov household in the 1834 tax census, but it is possible that this family may have been among the sixty-three male serfs (plus dependent women) transferred to a property in Riazan province in 1812 (TsANO, f. 177, op. 766, d. 1842, l. 26). On the other hand, there were many Groshev households, and many Ivan Groshevs, in 1834, but there was no match for the girl Maria of 1823 (TsANO, f. 60, op. 239a, d. 1102, ll. 360b–476).

20. GIM OPI, f. 14, d. 2322, l. 97.

21. Ibid.

22. Ibid., d. 2316, ll. 2–20b, 40b–50b, 22–230b., 26–28, 38.

23. TsANO, f. 60, op. 239a, d. 1102, l. 437.

24. GIM OPI, f. 14, d. 2316, ll. 29–34, 41–42ob.

25. TsANO, f. 570, op. 557, 1824 d. 82, ll. 1–4.

26. Ibid., 1822 d. 40, ll. 1–4. The diocese expressed complete confidence in Petrov. Petrov called the bailiff simply "Kondakov," but the 1834 tax return for Steksovo village listed no Kondakovs.

27. Mel'nikov, "Otchet," pp. 33, 40, 44. On his career as government official, see the 1870 official service record, "Formuliarnyi spisok"; Evtuhov, *Portrait*, pp. 141–45; Usov, "Pavel Ivanovich Mel'nikov," pp. 87–152; Bochenkov, *P. I. Mel'nikov*, pp. 52–68.

28. TsANO, f. 570, op. 559a, d. 1502, ll. 100–107, 123–320b.

29. GIM OPI, f. 14, d. 2322, ll. 18–19, 20–270b. Golitsyn's letters have not survived, but the reply of the Pisarevo priest has; he was willing to help but pointed out that the Old Belief was deeply entrenched (ibid., ll. 40–42).

30. Ibid., ll. 330b–34.

31. Ibid., d. 2322, l. 31.

32. Ibid., l. 330b–34.

33. Ibid., l. 97–990b.

34. Ibid., ll. 14–140b, 30, 54–540b, 770b–790b.

35. Ibid., d. 2331, ll. 70b–8.

36. Ibid., d. 2322, l. 780b.

37. Ibid., d. 2331, ll. 200b–21.

38. Ibid., l. 170b.

39. Ibid., l. 2190b–20.

40. Ibid., d. 2322, l. 870b.; d. 2401, ll. 16–170b.

41. *PSZ*, vtoroe sobranie, vol. 25, p. 23. Manumitted women would have been listed, along with whatever *soldatki* lived in the village, in a separate return that has apparently not survived. For the relevant 1850 Steksovo census (the former Golitsyn portion then owned by Evgraf Solenikov), see TsANO, f. 60, op. 239a, d. 1606, ll. 326–423.

42. TsANO, f. 60, op. 239a, 1834, d. 39.

43. GANO no. 3, f. 570, op. 559b, d. 1086 (no pagination). Only four of the marriages were among Golitsyn serfs: two officially Orthodox, two schismatic.

44. GIM OPI, f. 14, d. 2322, l. 30.

45. GANO no. 3, f. 570, op. 559b, d. 1427, ll. 1310b–340b; d. 1514, no pagination. These are two separate registers from two different Steksovo priests.

46. TsANO, f. 570, op. 557, 1831 d. 27. Because Old Believers routinely bribed priests, confession register data in this case should be considered unreliable. Prior to the official opening of a Edinoverie church in Nizhnii Novgorod in 1798, Old Believers had drawn up a list of conditions that were to be met before they agreed to join. Most of those conditions were not granted, which may be why the schismatics at Pashutina were skeptical (Kaurkin and Pavlova, *Edinoverie*, pp. 75–78).

47. TsANO, f. 570, op. 557, 1839, d. 16; 1841, d. 37.

48. Ibid., 1832, d. 16, ll. 25–26.

49. Ibid., 1839, d. 16, l. 9.

50. "Dnevnye dozornye," pp. 47–48. The information about the priested and Fedoseevites was provided in 1844 by a Ministry of Interior informant posing as a member of the Preobrazhensk Fedoseev community in Moscow. He obtained the information, in turn, from a Fedoseevite from Steksovo.

51. Mel'nikov, "Otchet," pp. 9, 221.

52. Pestov, "Ardatovskii," p. 120.

53. GIM OPI, f. 14, d. 2331, l. 200b.

54. Ibid., ll. 40–410b, 44–450b.

55. TsANO, f. 60, op. 239a, d. 163, ll. 297–4000b.

56. GIM OPI, f. 14, d. 2396.

57. TsANO, f. 60, op. 239a, d. 1102, ll. 3630b–476.

58. Ibid., d. 2397, Steksovo households 51, 32, 58, 66; Pisarevo, household 25.

59. Ibid., Steksovo household 37.

60. Ibid., Steksovo households 25 and 27. Avdotia was still single in 1850.

61. Ibid., d. 1101, ll. 3640b–476 (1834); d. 1606, ll. 326–423 (1850).

62. Ibid., d. 163, ll. 297–4000b.

63. TsANO, f. 570, op. 559a, d. 1502, ll. 100–1050b, 123–280b.

64. GIM OPI, f. 14, d. 2397, Steksovo households 27 (two girls) and 31; Pashutina household 6; Pisarevo households 24, 36, 39; Piatnikskoe households 1, 29, 38; Balakhonikha households 25, 28. Ages were not given for girls marrying away from Steksovo households 4, 8 (two girls), or 21 or Pisarevo household 12. Probably Tretiakov listed

them as having married because they married away. Had they married estate peasants, they would have been listed in other households.

65. GANO no. 3, d. 1086 (no pagination); d. 1427, ll. 990b–101, 1310b–340b. Most of the serfs who married were not Golitsyn's.

66. GIM, f. 14, d. 2397, Piatnitskoe households 12, 19, 32; Balakhonikha household 12.

67. Ibid., Pisarevo household 3.

68. RGADA, f., 350, op. 2, d. 1264, ch. 2, ll. 1235–3070b.

69. Ibid., d. 1264 ch. 1, ll. 832–58.

70. TsANO, f. 60, op. 239a, d. 163, ll. 297–4000b.

71. TsANO, f. 570, op. 559a, d. 409, ll. 441–420b.

72. Ibid., d. 1502, ll. 100–1050b., 123–280b.

73. GIM OPI, f. 14, d. 2321, ll. 222–240b.

74. Ibid.

75. Bazhaev, *Istoricheskie svedeniia*, p. 65.

76. RGADA, f. 350, op. 2, d. 1264, ch. 2, ll. 12880b–93. The census return for the portion belonging in 1762 to Ivan Alekseevich Golitsyn (ibid., ch. 1, ll. 858–690b) is incomplete but lists more than 116 individuals.

77. In 1762, only two Pashutina-born women had married into other villages on the estate.

78. TsANO, f. 570, op. 557, 1832 d. 16, l. 13.

79. The figures apply only to the portion of the village Sergei Mikhailovich inherited.

80. In 1845, there was also an apparently single fifty-eight-year-old woman who had been "taken into a household." She was not listed in Pashutina in the 1834 census and was presumably not native to the village.

81. There were eleven widowers in Steksovo but only seven in Baki.

82. The two households with elderly spinsters that had disappeared by 1845 may have been ghosts as of 1834. In that year, they held no men. The spinsters may actually have been living with neighbors.

83. The 1814 household list identifies seventy-seven households. Three divided immediately thereafter, adding an additional four households to the 1816 count preserved in the 1834 tax census return. In addition, the last ten households in the 1834 return have no antecedents in Steksovo village or estate in 1814. It is possible that they arrived from elsewhere between 1814 and 1816, the requisite notations on those transfers having been made in the missing 1816 tax census (GIM OPI, f. 14, op. 1, d. 2396, ll. 1–250b.; TsANO, f. 60, op. 239a, d. 1102 , ll. 3630b–95).

84. TsANO, f. 60, op. 239a, d. 1102, ll. 3640b–476; d. 1606, ll. 317–423. I have counted conscripts who were under age twenty with the cohort in which they reached that age. Probably some of the wealthier Steksovo serfs purchased exemptions, as permitted by conscription regulations, for 1000 rubles, but I have found no direct evidence of that. According to Mironov, *Blagosostoianie*, p. 303, of all men in European Russia between the ages of eighteen and sixty, conscription claimed 3.1 percent in the 1830s and 3.7

percent in the 1840s. Those statistics do not readily convey the demographic destruction conscription inflicted on any given male cohort.

85. See Wirtschafter, *From Serf*, pp. 3-25; Rediger, *Komplektovanie*, pp. 86–90; Beskrovnyi, *Russkaia armiia i flot v XIX veke*, pp. 69–80; Aleksandrov, *Sel'skaia obshchina*, pp. 242–93.

86. Mironov, *Blagosostoianie*, pp. 222 (the table), 217 (what the figures mean). Pavel Shcherbinin has found that during the first half of the nineteenth century, 63.3 percent of all conscripts in Tambov province were married (Shcherbinin, *Voennyi factor*, p. 92). Hoch, *Serfdom*, p. 152, concludes that "most" of the conscripts from the Gagarin estate at Petrovskoe were married. Bohac, "Mir and Military Draft," p. 653, reports that 60.5 percent of conscripts on the Gagarins' Manuilskoe estate in Tver province, were married between 1820–1855.

87. Mironov, *Blagosostoianie*, p. 222; GIM OPI, f. 14, d. 2397.

88. We do not know how Evgraf Solenikov, who bought the estate in early 1847, handled conscription.

89. TsANO, f. 60, op. 239a, d. 1101 (1834), ll. 3640b–476; d. 1606 (1850), ll. 326–423. On conscription rates nationally, see Beskrovnyi, *Russkaia armiia i flot v XIX veke*, pp. 74–80. On the minimum conscription age, see *PSZ*, series 2, vol. 7, p. 324.

90. GIM OPI, f. 14, d. 2331, ll. 190b–20.

91. Usov, "Pavel Ivanovich Mel'nikov," pp. 89–90, summarizes a memorandum Melnikov submitted to the governor of Nizhnii Novgorod province. Melnikov recommended that the practice be adopted everywhere Old Believers and Orthodox were intermingled; he warned only that measures would have to be taken against Old Believer bribery. Mel'nikov, "Otchet," p. 37, describes the use of conscription by S. S. Sheremetev, once he had taken up permanent residence at his Bogorodskoe estate in 1834, to stamp out the Old Belief: men under thirty-five who repeatedly failed to attend church were sent into the army. The result was that by the early 1850s, only men over thirty-five were open about their heterodox beliefs.

92. GIM OPI, f. 14, d. 2321, ll. 222–240b. The male conscription rate for Golitsyn's portion of Steksovo village was only 3.7 percent, possibly due to the bribe-paying capacities of its relatively wealthy Old Believers or because they had the resources to purchase exemptions.

93. TsANO, f. 570, op. 559a, d. 966, ll. 454–59, households 80–186.

94. Ibid., d. 1502, ll. 1050b–7, 1280b–320b.

95. TsANO, f. 60, op. 239a, d. 1604, l. 158, household 18. She was also an only child. Her father, Ivan Vasilevich Chadaev, was missing from the 1861 register as well. If he had been manumitted, there would have been a note to that effect in the 1850 census return. There is, for example, a note that a man and son, together with their wives, were manumitted in 1860 (ibid., l. 1610b, household 35).

96. TsANO, f. 570, op. 559a, d. 1502, l. 50b.

97. TsANO, f. 177, op. 766, d. 8847. This is the case of never-married Anna Shaposhnikova, a serf from the Obolenskies' Steksovo estate who managed to turn herself into a townswoman. She had help, including from a man who, claiming to be Sergei

Obolenskii, came to the Nizhnii Novgorod district chancellery in 1851 to confirm that he had issued the forged manumission paper that Shaposhnikova had first produced in 1839. The imposter convinced the chancery officials, who at the very least must have thought it plausible that an Obolenskii would turn up in their office.

98. Ibid., households 19, 20, 30, 44, 50, 76, 85, 87, 88.

99. For Bibikov serfs, see TsANO, f. 570, op. 559a., d. 1502, ll. 104–50b.

100. In 1864, in eight state peasant households, there were seven unmarried adult women (TsANO, f. 60, op. 234, 1864 d. 175, ll. 181–85). This listing is a *semeinyi rekrutskii spisok*, a description of the households meant to identify potential conscripts. It provides the same information as a tax census return. Unfortunately, it is the only such Ardatov district list that is extant.

Inconclusion

The *Oxford English Dictionary* quotes a fragment of a sentence written by the nineteenth-century English actress Frances Anne "Fanny" Kemble as an example of usage: "I float comfortably over infinite abysses of inconclusion." Kemble was comfortable with inconclusion, she explained, because she believed that no effort at rational analysis ever produced incontrovertible results; it was better to be guided by instinct and intuition.[1] I do not share Kemble's intellectual nihilism. I am far less comfortable than she with inconclusion, but I am resigned to it. Russian and American historians to whom I have presented pieces of this study over the last few years have asked many good questions that I cannot answer. Some, especially those bearing on the inner lives—the emotions and convictions—of Spasovite and other Russian peasant women who rejected marriage, I have skirted because the sources I know provide no obvious answers. I have offered a few hypotheses; some will think I have pulled up short, others that I have leapt too far. Other questions may in principle have answers, but I do not provide them. My excuse, which is at the same time a claim, is that many of them arise only because of what this study has established, I hope, more or less conclusively.

I begin more conventionally, by pointing out conclusions that are embedded in the preceding chapters but not always insisted on. Here I insist. First and foremost, in refusing to marry in proportions as large as in Kuplia parish and at Baki, Spasovite women inflicted harm on themselves and their households and—so their neighbors believed—on universally marrying households. They rejected the practice of universal marriage that most Russian peasants believed was critical to household and community survival, and so introduced a new field of conflict within Russian peasant society. That conflict was then and later almost entirely unknown outside the villages, except to some serf-owners who were called on to intervene or saw an opportunity to profit from serf women's unconventional behavior. When the Holy Synod and government officials classified Old Believer covenants by the harm they caused or the danger they posed, they assigned Spasovites to the merely "harmful" rather than the "especially harmful" group because Spasovites recognized marriage. With very few exceptions (not even Pavel Melnikov among them), there is little evidence that anyone in a position of religious or secular authority knew what Spasovite marital practices actually were.

Spasovite women's nuptial decisions, clearly supported by the men in their households, violated peasant common sense and socioeconomic interests so completely that only conviction or ideology—that is, religious belief—can explain them. Historians are apt, for very good reason, to search for materialist explanations of peasant behavior. In Spasovite marriage aversion, we confront a case in which faith triumphed over peasant pragmatism, not as a local and temporary aberration, but in a substantial population, spread over many provinces, and lasting for at least a century and a half. In all three of those dimensions, the scale of marriage aversion was actually too large to be reducible to a mere case; it was a consequential part of Russian peasant history at large. I would like to explore in detail the religious thinking that underlay Spasovite marriage practice, but the sources are silent. We cannot say much more than what has come down to us in the lapidary formulations of Kozma Andreev around 1700 and elder Abrosim of the Living Dead in the early 1870s: female marriage aversion was born of the Spasovites' existential despair at living in a world in which God had no interest at all.

Spasovite marriage practices did change over time: male celibacy and cessation of household reproduction seem to have been common only during an early phase of convert zeal, rates of female celibacy crested and then gradually declined; over time, fewer households held more than one unmarried adult woman. Those certainly look like pragmatic adjustments to dangers Spasovites brought on themselves. After a period of truly self-destructive rejection of marriage, most Spasovite communities probably looked for ways to bring their religious beliefs and material interests into reasonable balance. But at least until the appearance of the Neo-Spasovites in the 1830s and 1840s (if Spasovite women's sudden resumption of marriage in Kuplia parish was a harbinger of that new covenant), women's resistance to marriage was the driver of Spasovite social history.

From the time Spasovite doctrine spread from forest sketes to functioning villages, women propelled the covenant toward marriage resistance—or at least that is what the scraps of information on the early history suggest. The covenant was hostile to marriage at its founding, but on that issue, Spasovites differed little from other priestless covenants. It is true that the Spasovite laborers from the Kerzhensk forest who introduced the covenant to the Domodedovo crown peasants south of Moscow in the 1720s brought the original anti-marriage doctrine with them and that at least one of their Domodevovo converts, Iakov Rodionov, thereupon separated from his wife and sent his daughters to the Kerzhenzk sketes to live celibate lives. But in the worldly village communities I have studied in detail, the first few celibates in the early eighteenth century were women, whose example was emulated a generation or so later (and only for a generation) by a few men while more and more women committed themselves to celibacy—even though, at some point in the eighteenth century, the covenant's leaders reversed themselves and accepted marriage celebrated by (heretical) Orthodox priests. Whoever they were, the leaders may possibly have recommended, but certainly did not command, that women not marry. Women of the covenant took the initiative when they adopted celibacy and when they later made it the covenant's consensual, if not invariable, rule. Some women in other Old Believer covenants also chose celibacy, but apparently it was only Spasovites who did so, with few exceptions, on a large scale in locations other than religious centers, out in the world. Resistance to marriage was thus a religiously inspired social movement that was the work of Spasovite women. All of the social and economic consequences I have traced out were the result of the initiative taken by peasant women. Some were surely unintended and unanticipated, but history is a never-ending unwinding of the unforeseen consequences of human actions.

I want to emphasize the peasant component of this history as much as the female component. While historians, and ethnographers outside of Russia, have long since abandoned the view that Russian peasants lived in a self-contained world governed by timeless tradition, we usually locate peasant initiative in resistance or subversion—of oppression of one kind or another, for example—or in opportunism, such as when peasants spotted economic opportunities whose sources lay beyond the village (as at Baki and Steksovo). Peasants, we understand, were not passive. Yet we usually think of peasant initiative as reactive, and for good reason: peasants, whether serfs or not, were subordinate when not oppressed. Whatever the social, economic, or political arena in which they acted, powerful outsiders set the rules. Perhaps that was not so uniformly true as we often think, but that was certainly the way peasants understood, or said they understood, their place in the world.

Spasovite peasant women took the initiative in shunning marriage, but probably they could not have done so, at least in large numbers, had Spasovite men been resolutely opposed. On serf estates, it required the connivance of peasant men—fathers, bailiffs—to protect unwilling brides from marriage or to pay hundreds of rubles to redeem them from serfdom. In crown peasant villages like Sluchkovo, male heads of households had to be willing to support, in some cases, numerous single adult women and also to take in and support elderly women, both relatives and some who in the demographic records seem not to have been related at all. Men played a critical supporting role in women's determination not to marry. Thus, I credit female resistance to marriage to the Spasovite community as a whole. As peasants, women took the initiative and received the support of their men. They acted not against oppression or in response to opportunity but on what was to them a matter of religious faith to overturn long-standing peasant marriage customs. Their actions impinged immediately on neighbors who had no intention of abandoning universal marriage.

Spasovite women who made refusal to marry their community rule also created space for free choice. If most chose not to marry, a few—even in Kuplia parish, where female marriage aversion for a time became a Spasovite universal—chose otherwise. At Baki and Steksovo, I assume but cannot prove, many Spasovite women married. Violating the community rule, they assumed by default the freedom to choose their own husbands. At Baki and surely in many other villages with elevated levels of female marriage aversion, women eloped, with or without their parents' tacit consent. Elopement put choice of spouse in the hands of young men and young women; young women had, at a minimum, a veto. Yet eloping Spasovites were not unique: many other Old Believers, for whom marriage was a sin for which parents could not take responsibility but which they recognized as normal, also resorted to elopement. In this respect, the practice of Spasovite women who married overlapped with custom among some other Old Believer, and Orthodox, peasants.

UNANSWERED QUESTIONS ABOUT HOUSEHOLD AND COMMUNITY

I have left an obvious demographic conundrum dangling: where did wives come from when, as in Kuplia parish and around Baki and probably Steksovo, it was not just one village but a cluster—indeed an entire district—that had to cope with an elevated level of female marriage aversion? The returns from the tax censuses of 1763, 1782, and 1795, where available, provide raw material for an answer. But the answer will certainly be larger than can be found in returns even from a sizeable set of villages linked by marriage, and I have not attempted even that. For Kuplia parish, the onset of a very high rate of marriage aversion between 1763 and 1795 forced the expansion of the search range for brides. Of course: as increasing numbers of women in more and more villages around Kuplia became marriage averse, the local bride deficit grew and could be made good only by searching for willing brides farther and farther from home.

I imagine that expansion to have been both segmented and concentric. When most women born in Sluchkovo and Alëshkovo refused to marry, brides had to be taken from more distant villages, whose young men in turn had to search farther, until the overlapping and expanding search fields finally reached into territory in which most women were willing to marry. But the collective bride deficit in, let us say, all twenty-four appanage peasant villages in the Gorokhovets district—a cumulative total of perhaps four hundred women in 1834—would simply have been exported if four hundred brides had been taken from bordering districts in which men and women were already marrying universally. I imagine, again, that the deficit was dispersed over a very large territory in which, at the outer edge, it finally became imperceptible.

That is only a hypothesis, no doubt simplistic, that might not stand up to the evidence if enough has survived to test it. In the Gorokhovets district, female marriage aversion took root among all categories of peasants and was extraordinarily widespread. There is no reason at all to assume that enough census returns, or confession registers, have survived to permit even the most diligent historian to trace to their final subsidence the centrifugal ripples or, perhaps better, the shock waves set off by large concentrations of women who refused to marry. All we can say for sure is that in the entire section of the Gorokhovets district south of the Kliazma River, bounded to the south and north by uninhabited territory that could provide no brides, the search for brides must have extended far into the connecting territories to east and west by 1800 or earlier. Even if all of the women in those areas wished to marry (an unlikely proposition), the unsatisfied demand for brides pulsing outward from south of the Kliazma must have destabilized the bride markets there, too. The topography of land south of the Kliazma makes it easy at least to imagine the lines of stress. Around Baki, where serfs and crown (later appanage) peasants seem to have intermarried without much encumbrance—but where the search for brides by villagers who lived in the forest away from the east bank of the Vetluga was already hindered by distance, topography, and low population density—the repercussions of the local bride deficit may have been just as far reaching. Since most of the peasants around Steksovo lived on serf estates and we know next to nothing about the obstacles local serf-owners may have placed to movement of women across estate boundaries, we can't even speculate about the larger impact of the bride deficit there.

Close study of female marriage aversion around Kuplia parish, and at Baki and Steksovo, cannot tell us how local bride deficits were made good but does alert us to the larger ramifications of substantial local female marriage aversion. We get a glimpse of a peasant society forced to cope with levels of female refusal to marry that threatened to shred its very fabric—in villages that clung to the tradition of universal marriage just as much as in villages with large numbers of marriage-averse women. That peasant women's refusal to marry caused tension is not at all surprising: peasants who insisted that women who refused to marry threatened their sons' nuptial prospects, and so parental households' well-being, were right. The available sources offer some eloquent testimony to that intra-peasant tension, particularly on the Orlov estates surveyed in chapter 2. Given the stakes, tension must have been great in all bride-deficit districts. Male serfs could appeal to their owners, who sometimes did manage to compel women to marry. Kuplia parish crown peasants were left to their own devices.

Kuplia crown peasants were both perpetrators and victims—allowing, perhaps encouraging, maybe sometimes commanding—their daughters not to marry while simultaneously seeking brides for their sons. We don't know how they made sense of their situation. Were some of the serfs who appealed to Vladimir Orlov and Sergei Golitsyn, or their managers, to compel other households to surrender daughters in marriage, themselves heads of households sheltering women who never married? I can't be certain, but I assume that after a single generation in which a few men, too, avoided marriage, young men in Spasovite households married just as universally as they did in other Old Believer and Orthodox households. Heads of Spasovite households, too, had somehow to overcome the local bride deficit and surely were just as willing as other serfs (and peasants generically) to use any tool that came to hand—their owner's power of compulsion included—to force fellow serfs to cooperate.

I suggested in chapter 3 that peasant households in which marriage and reproduction had ceased had effectively seceded from Russian peasant society. Cessation of marriage expressed their secession: when households ceased to give and receive daughters from others, they severed the biological ties that underlay many of the social linkages that turned households into community. If, as priestless Old Believers, they shunned their Orthodox neighbors, they severed other links. When men, too, ceased to marry, they paid the inevitable price: household extinction.

It is tempting to think, perhaps even likely, that it was precisely that outcome and its consequences, above all end-of-life destitution, that persuaded Spasovites to abandon male celibacy after a single generation and to adopt what became the Spasovite rule: men married, women did not. It is instructive that the sequence at Baki, Kuplia, and Steksovo was the same: a first generation in which some women chose celibacy; a second generation in which female celibacy expanded rapidly and some men chose celibacy, too; a third generation in which female celibacy peaked but men resumed marriage. But if there was a single celibacy sequence, calendar chronology differed. At Baki, a first, priestless foray into male celibacy ended around 1750 (except that males who had already chosen celibacy remained celibate for life); in Kuplia parish, it came to an end in the 1780s. At Baki, a second, Orthodox trial at male celibacy collapsed at the end of the eighteenth century; at Steksovo, male celibacy both peaked and ended around 1800. Each Spasovite community experienced the danger of male celibacy and adjusted nuptial behavior on its own—or so the demographic records suggest.

The dangers posed by female celibacy were not so obvious because they were not so immediate; sons who brought wives in must have seemed to secure the household's future, whether their sisters married or not. Spasovite peasants probably recognized that providing for multiple unmarried women was burdensome; they probably did not understand that even a single unmarried adult woman could pose a threat to household survival.

Yet in one obvious circumstance not uncommon in Russian villages, she did. Outside Spasovite communities, when a household had no surviving sons but did have at least one marriageable daughter, it could bring in a son-in-law as heir and bread winner. Before dying in 1794, Fevronia Afanaseva in Aleshkovo wisely employed a variation on that strategy by adopting a young man to support her three unmarried adult daughters. But that seems to have been unusual. In 1830 in Sluchkovo, Prokofii Vasiliev and Praskovia Fedorovna had no sons but two unmarried daughters, ages thirty-one and forty-two; there could have been no uncertainty, even far in advance, about the household's future. At Steksovo, when Nikita Gubanikhin died in 1844, he left four minor children and four unmarried sisters, ages thirty to forty-six. Not one of the sisters had been willing to marry in the interests of the household; the youngest sister, at least, was still marriageable as the risk to the household became obvious. At Steksovo in 1840, twenty-four-year-old Daria Pishchirina had, apparently very reluctantly, agreed to marry an Orthodox man who moved into her household; however, within a year, her widowed father ran away, and then she did, too. Daria evidently preferred almost certain penury to life as a married woman with an Orthodox husband or maybe even with an Old Believer.

The pragmatic willingness of males to marry contrasts with the stubborn unwillingness of many marriage-averse women to sacrifice religious principle to household survival and raises some questions. Is this yet more evidence that in marriage-averse households daughters were allowed to choose for themselves whether to marry or not? Was the apparent unwillingness of parents (or, as in Gubanikhin's case, household heads) to compel daughters or sisters to marry based on a gendered understanding of worldly and spiritual economies: men had to marry, yes, but women's avoidance of marriage produced a store of righteousness that was credited to the entire household? It does seem to me that refusal to marry even *in extremis*, and an assumption that such a decision was righteous and, at least within the local religious community, brought credit to the household is of a piece with the evidence that young women made their own initial decisions about marriage. Nevertheless, while the demographic evidence from which I infer these possibilities makes those questions reasonable, it does not answer them.

On the other hand, the proportion of households with more than one resident spinster declined over time, which may (or may not) have been a deliberate attempt to avoid the burden and risk multiple spinsters posed. In Steksovo village, for instance, in 1795 (just before the expansion of marriage aversion to around 25 percent in the female cohort that reached age twenty-five in 1805), fourteen households held one unmarried woman twenty-five or over, and four (22 percent) held two. In 1834, sixteen households had solitary spinsters, and six (27 percent) had two or three. In 1845, eighteen households had one, and three (14 percent) had two to four. And in 1861, there were twenty-one spinsters in what had been Sergei Golitsyn's share of the village, all living one to a household.[2] In Baki, the percentage of marriage-resistant households that held multiple spinsters was forty-three in 1812, twenty-one in 1834, and twenty-five in 1858.[3] Because spinsters had chosen not to marry when they were teenagers or young adults, their percentage in the adult population was a lagging indicator, a measure of decisions made a generation or more earlier.

The decline in multi-spinster households may or may not suggest that Spasovites eventually concluded that a single woman who avoided marriage met a household's quota of righteousness, but it certainly prompts another question: if the rule had become one spinster per household in Steksovo, then who in those households decided which daughter would remain single? It is unlikely, after all, that in 1861, in a religious community with a long history of female aversion to marriage, there was one and only one daughter in every one of those twenty-one households who had wished, or been willing, to remain single. Perhaps daughters decided among themselves who felt the greatest attraction to what some must have considered the righteous calling of spinster. Perhaps parents chose the righteous daughter. Or perhaps once one daughter had aged into spinsterhood, parents nudged others toward marriage. Figuring out who made the decision, and on what basis, when only one of several daughters remained single is more difficult than deducing what was going on when most daughters were spinsters but a few chose marriage.

Peasant men and women certainly understood the fateful consequences when both men and women of the household shunned marriage, or deliberately ceased to reproduce, as occurred among the Spasovites of Kuplia parish in the late eighteenth century. If asked about that, they would probably have replied, like elder Abrosim of the Living Dead a century later, "So what?" Why prolong human life in a world abandoned by God and in thrall to the Antichrist? Even after 1800, when Spasovite men of Kuplia parish resumed both universal marriage and reproduction, every single Spasovite woman born in the parish between about 1800 and 1830 (in Sluchkovo, from before 1780 to 1830) avoided marriage. The "men must marry" rule did not prevent the almost complete extinction of Spasovite households in Alëshkovo by 1830–34, or the reduction of most of the Spasovite community in Sluchovo to a clutch of conglomerate, demographically unsustainable households. While the Spasovites probably believed that their commitment to male marriage around 1800 would ensure household survival, they had surely learned that it did not by 1830.

Kuplia parish was the extreme case. Priestless, likely Spasovite, households at Baki experienced considerable extinction (carnage, really) in the late eighteenth century; however, by 1800, male marriage aversion had ended, and aversion among women was about to decline. Yet in the first half of the nineteenth century, Baki village households with one or more unmarried adult women experienced penury and extinction at two (1812) or three (1834–36) times the rate of universally marrying households. Because those households apparently disappeared one by one rather than in a sharp, community-wide crisis, because some universally marrying households also suffered penury and collapse, and because some marriage-averse households prospered, it is not at all certain that Baki Spasovites understood the connection between reduced female nuptiality and their own elevated risk of household extinction. They were probably aware of what was apparently the case—that the disintegration of one fatally weakened, marriage-averse household produced refugees who sought support from, and thereby burdened, other of their households. But unless someone kept tallies, they may not have known that their women's tendency to shun marriage—rather than fate, God's will, or his indifference—was a major source of their adversities.

Yet the heightened demographic stress among the marriage-averse peasants of Baki village was only in part due to their women's nuptial choices. Baki's forest economy produced both wealth and poverty: wealth among those who amassed the capital required to hire laborers who logged and transported wood and other forest products to market, poverty (or the near-poverty of Second Lieutenant Averkiev's third-class households) among those who had little to sell but their labor. The forest economy heightened morbidity and mortality, too, among those who labored in forest and on river and, in consequence, produced many widows. It wasn't the demographic risks inherent in female marriage aversion alone that produced penury and destroyed households at Baki; the way Baki serfs earned a living contributed as well.

At Steksovo, according to the available economic evidence, there were both rich and poor but relatively fewer of the latter than at Baki, and widespread land-ownership insured many demographically crippled (remnant) and otherwise vulnerable households against destitution. The Steksovo economy, too, produced no great numbers of widows. Households with spinsters appear to have been, on average, more prosperous and longer lasting than those without, a fact that the data on Steksovo's economy do not explain. My hypothesis is that Spasovite community solidarity of some sort produced that outcome, but neither the manorial correspondence nor any other source provides information with which to test it. Quite apart from that hypothesis, accumulated household resources, and commercial activity, sustained demographically crippled households long past the point at which they would have expired in Baki. That was part of a virtuous cycle that reduced the outflow of refugees from collapsed households, which in turn spared other households the burden of supporting them.

It is not surprising that households with unmarried women in Kuplia parish and Baki expired more rapidly than others; they were more vulnerable to the demographic risks that altered the balance of household labor and consumption, and the presence of women who would not marry foreclosed one common stratagem—importing a son-in-law—for bringing labor and consumption back into balance. But, again not surprisingly, many other contingencies raised and lowered extinction rates among both marriage-resistant and universally marrying households: household size, household economy, and associated demographic risk factors such as elevated male mortality. These complicate any attempt to assess the contribution of marriage aversion to household collapse.

Historians of the Russian peasantry have paid surprisingly little attention to household expiration. There have been few calculations even at the level of a single village or estate, with the exception of studies of household expiration over less or little more than a generation carried out shortly before and after 1917.[4] There is no body of analysis of household expiration even in typical, more or less universally marrying households over a period longer than a single generation that might provide context for thinking about expiration rates among marriage-resistant households. What was the normal rate of household collapse over a period of twenty or forty or sixty years? Of course, normal must have varied: higher in villages with Baki-type economies, lower in Steksovo-type villages. In any case, there is no scale on which to place the rates at which either marriage-averse or universally marrying households disappeared in Baki and Steksovo.

Two exceptions are Peter Czap's "The Perennial Multiple Family Household, Mishino, Russia, 1782–1858," an analysis of a Riazan province estate owned by the Gagarins, and a study by Rodney Bohac of another Gagarin estate, Manuilskoe, in Tver province.[5] On both estates, households with multiple married couples greatly outnumbered one-couple families, and the Gagarin management deliberately limited household partitions in order to preserve large households. As his title suggests, Czap focused on the ways in which such households reduced demographic and other threats to household survival and managed the centrifugal tensions that naturally arose from within. Toward the end, Czap remarks: "Of all households found in Mishino at the end of the eighteenth century, excluding those later transferred from the estate or moved from one estate village to another, 59 percent persisted continuously on the estate as direct descent groups until 1858."[6]

Not all Mishino households, then, were perennial: 41.0 percent disappeared between 1782 (I assume that was Czap's starting date for this measure) and 1858, or 5.4 percent of the initial total per decade. On the Manuilskoe estate, of the 125 households in 1813 (not counting another 22 that were transferred in 1828), 23 had expired by 1860: 18.0 percent, or 3.8 percent per decade.[7] In Steksovo village, 22 of 91 households disappeared between 1814–16 and 1845—24.0 percent, or 7.8 percent of the initial total per decade—faster than at Mishino or Manuilskoe but perhaps not significantly so. Yet Steksovo households were on average considerably smaller—in 1834, 5.7 members in Steksovo (both village and estate) versus 8.4 at Mishino estate in 1834 and 8.0 at Manuilskoe estate in 1833.[8] If we assume that Mishino's rate of household extinction was about average for large agricultural estates south of the forest line in central Russia, where both serf household heads and managers worked to obstruct household division, might it be the case that at Steksovo, where there was apparently no management effort to maximize household size, the overriding question is how could it be that Steksovo households with spinsters were even more perennial (they disappeared at the rate of 2.9 percent per decade between 1814 and 1845) than Mishino's universally marrying households? The fact that Steksovo's marriage-averse households were significantly more prosperous

than the village's universally marrying households was probably key. I suspect that something about Steksovo's priestless (Spasovite) community
fostered prosperity (perhaps in a way similar to Moscow's much larger and
wealthier Fedoseev community), but there is no actual evidence bearing on
the question.

UNANSWERED QUESTIONS ABOUT GEOGRAPHICAL AND
CHRONOLOGICAL EXTENT

I have focused on Kuplia parish and the Baki and Steksovo estates but have
pointed out, sometimes only in passing, the evidence for startlingly elevated
levels of marriage aversion elsewhere as well. Together, close analysis and sam-
pling support some generalizations. Chapters 3 and 4 provide statistics dem-
onstrating that marriage aversion was remarkably strong among all varieties
of peasants across the entire south-of-the-Kliazma section of the Gorokhovets
district in the second half of the eighteenth and first half of the nineteenth
centuries. A number of serf estates in other Vladimir districts show up as sites
of marriage resistance in chapter 2. Most of the evidence of marriage resistance in Vladimir comes from eastern Vladimir province; probably marriage
aversion was concentrated there. For Nizhnii Novgorod province, as well, we
have the evidence not just from Steksovo and the Arzamas-Ardatov borderland more generally, but also from Iusupov and Sheremetev estates in other
districts. There is no doubt that the province was home to a large number of
marriage-averse women. They may have been found throughout.

Manorial correspondence and demographic statistics deployed in chapter 2 demonstrate that serf women on many estates in many Kostroma province districts resisted marriage. And there is so much more. The 1834 tax
census returns from two small villages on the Lievens' Ilinskoe estate, just
south of Baki, show that in one, all of the 22 women age twenty-five and over
were married, while in the other 6 of 40 (15 percent) had never married.[9]
On a property consisting of two Varnavin district villages, Zdekino and
Cherepanikha, almost evenly divided among Nikolai Iusuopov, Varvara
Golitsyna, and Elizaveta Evreinova, of the 196 women twenty-five and over
in 1834, 43 (22 percent) had never married; in the separate shares, female
marriage aversion ranged from 20 to 24 percent.[10] On the other hand, in
the same year and district, 14 of the 29 women twenty-five and over in the
Iusupov portion of Strelitsy had never married, while in the widow Norova's
portion all twenty-two such women had married.[11]

In 1858, in twelve randomly selected appanage villages in the Varnavin district, female marriage aversion ranged from 0 to 32.3 percent; of the 525 women twenty-five and over in those villages, 62 (11.9 percent) had never married.[12] In the Galich district in 1834, on a Iusuopv estate consisting of six small villages, 8 of 63 women twenty-five and over (11.3 percent) had never married.[13] In the Nerekhta district in 1858, in eight serf villages, female marriage aversion ranged from 0 to 17.4 percent. In the largest of those villages, Mitino, 48 of 346 women twenty-five and over (13.9 percent) had never married; in all six, 70 of 520 women in that age group (11.9 percent) had never married.[14] In 1850, at Count Matvei Dmitriev-Mamonov's Aksenovo estate in the Chukhloma district, northern Kostroma province, 104 of the 549 women twenty-five and above (18.9 percent) had never married. The sex ratio on the estate was further unbalanced by the 157 widows as against only 26 widowers aged twenty and over; widows accounted for fully 24.3 percent of the women who were at least twenty years old.[15] Marriage-aversion was most likely widespread throughout Kostroma province, but not uniformly even in relatively compact areas. In the eighteen villages on the Aksenovo estate, for instance, marriage aversion ranged from 0 to 35.5 percent.

For Iaroslavl province, the evidence of peasant women's widespread refusal to marry is overwhelming. The survey of serf-owners' reactions in chapter 2 covered estates owned by Naryshkins, Orlovs, Glebov-Streshnevs, Sheremetevs, and Iusupovs; some owned multiple marriage-averse estates in the province. I have resisted the impulse, but any one of them might have provided material for yet another case study. And the evidence beyond those estates is, again, overwhelming. I mentioned briefly the monastery-owned village of Zhabino as a likely source of Shcherbatov's opinion that peasant girls wouldn't marry unless their fathers were compelled to give them away. In 1763, 17.0 percent of Zhabino women over twenty-five had never married. In 1782, 15.9 percent of Zhabino women over twenty-five had never married; by 1795, that proportion had fallen to 7.4 percent; a glance at cohorts reveals that it was in the 1770s that almost all young women in the village began to marry.[16] That is interesting and a reminder that sometimes young women collectively changed their minds (and likely their confessional identity).

However, we can't draw conclusions from Zhabino without also considering the fact that in the group of nine state villages of which Zhabino (after secularization in 1763) was a part, women (all ages) outnumbered men by 42.9 percent in 1782 and 63.1 percent in 1795, an almost certain indication that many more women in the area had changed their minds the other way.[17] Those figures summarize tax censuses, which listed all men native to, and paying the head tax in, the villages, whether or not they were present; the huge disproportion had nothing to do with male labor migration. In two groups of state peasants in the same district in 1785, women outnumbered men by 685 to 554 (23.6 percent) in one, 1,717 to 1,456 (17.9 percent) in the other. Those female-to-male ratios were about the same as in the marriage-averse appanage villages in Vladimir's Gorokhovets district in the second quarter of the nineteenth century.[18] In the three state peasant parishes centered on Viatko in the Danilov district in 1810, 20.3 percent of Viatko women twenty-five and above had never married; in the many other villages in those parishes, 15.3 percent had never married. Of the 2,467 parishioners seven and above, 55.9 percent skipped confession because they were forgetful (so said the priests); in one of the parishes, 97.8 percent had forgotten.[19] Spasovites (and other Old Believers) were numerous in the Danilov district in the first half of the nineteenth century.[20]

Even in Iaroslavl province, single adult women did not pile up everywhere. Confession registers from five parishes in the Rostov district reveal that in 1802, among the women twenty-five and over, from 1.4 to 8.1 percent had never married.[21] Women in the first parish displayed no aversion to marriage; in the latter, some did. In 1802, on an estate in the Iaroslavl district owned by the widow Katerina Sofonova, only 6.2 percent of the 225 women twenty-five and over had never married, while on Aleksei Varentsov's neighboring estate, only 5.1 percent of 270 such women hadn't married (but 307 of 619 parishioners from the estate, age seven and above, had not gone to confession, mostly because they were "absent"). Such proportions, while very low by the standards of my case studies, exceed the level of female marital impairment in districts in which marriage was virtually universal; they suggest that some women were deliberately avoiding marriage, but too few to produce serious social repercussions. On Stepan Titov's nearby estate, however, 14.6 percent of the 45 women twenty-five and above had never married.[22] In Ilinskoe parish, Poshekhonie district, in northern Iaroslavl parish, as of 1810 only 4 percent of the women twenty-five and over—all of them serfs in small villages with multiple owners—had never married. On the other hand, on an estate in the same district owned by Anna Orlova-Chesmenskaia, 6 of the 16 women twenty-five and over (37.5 percent) in the estate's five tiny villages never married.[23]

Some properties belonging to Vladimir Orlov's brother Aleksei Orlov (Chesmenskii), and then Aleksei's daughter Anna, merit special comment because the largest group of marriage-averse women there belonged to the priestless Fedoseev covenant. From at least 1790, Aleksei and later Anna received reports from their estates in the Rybinsk district listing unmarried women and others listing Old Believers. Most of the reports have survived only partially, or cover only parts of an estate. We get the best insight into the level of marriage aversion from the surviving portion of the estate's copy of the 1834 tax census for Nikolskoe, covering twenty-five of the forty-two or so villages on the property. Of the 524 women twenty-five and over, 78 (14.9 percent) had never married, about the same rate of marriage aversion as at Steksovo the same year.[24] An 1811 report on the estate's Fedoseevites listed 235 women and 49 men from twenty-eight villages. The men were all over twenty-five, mostly elderly. Of the women, 73 were unmarried, and of those, at least 59 (two names lacked ages) were twenty-five and above.[25] Clearly there were more Old Believers in more villages than that, and probably most of them were Fedoseevites.

It is not surprising that some clusters of Fedoseev peasant women shunned marriage—this was the covenant whose leaders waged the longest and most determined struggle against marriage. However, groups favoring marriage periodically split away, and—so far as the scant evidence I've seen suggests—Fedoseev peasant women elsewhere usually married.[26] Even at Nikolskoe, among Fedoseev women twenty-five and over in 1811, the 148 wives and widows considerably outnumbered the 59 spinsters, albeit many may have married into the covenant.[27] What we learn from Nikolskoe is that at least in some places Fedoseev women contributed significantly to marriage aversion, just as in other places Pomorsk women did. Even for Nikolskoe, the quite incomplete data suggest that non-Fedoseev women—more than likely including Spasovites—also shunned marriage. Nevertheless, Fedoseev women probably comprised the majority of those who rejected marriage in some other villages in the province.

I can say very little either about marriage aversion or Spasovites beyond the four contiguous provinces of Iaroslavl, Kostroma, Vladimir, and Nizhnii Novgorod. There are a few more or less authoritative characterizations of Spasovites elsewhere. One is Pavel Melnikov's observation that Spasovites were to be found in all Volga River provinces, but especially from Nizhnii Novgorod down to Astrakhan, as well as in Penza, Tambov, and Voronezh provinces.[28] As I pointed out in the introduction, Melnikov seems to have been unaware of the large Spasovite presence in eastern Vladimir province. He probably intended his gesture at "Volga provinces" to cover Iaroslavl and Kostroma, but reserving the adverb "especially" for Nizhnii Novgorod and provinces to the south seems to me to misstate the balance. Were Spasovites south of Nizhnii Novgorod proportionately as numerous as in Kostroma province (it is impossible to provide a number, but probably among the multitudes of Kostroma Old Believers, Spasovites held first place), we would need to increase considerably our estimate of the size of the Spasovite covenant (or covenants) both for the middle of the nineteenth and the early twentieth centuries. Nevertheless, as of the 1850s, Melnikov probably knew more about Old Believer numbers and distribution than anyone else in Russia. It is reasonable to assume that Spasovites abounded in the provinces he named.

And indeed there is other information on the Spasovite presence in many of them but, for the most part, not enough to know how numerous they were. According to Pavel Prusskii—who was born into a Fedoseev family in the city of Syzran in Simbirsk province but passed through the Pomorsk covenant before joining the Orthodox Church in 1867 and then became archimandrite of the Edinoverie St. Nicholas monastery in Moscow and wrote extensively about the various Old Believer covenants (in other words, he was an inside informant)—the traditional (underground) Spasovites were strong in Kazan, Simbirsk, Samara, and Saratov provinces. That was, he said, where they were concentrated.[29] He located Spasovite Abjurers (the Neo-Spasovites who had broken with the traditionalists by the 1840s) in Vladimir, Nizhnii Novgorod, and Kostroma provinces.[30] Nikolai Ivanovskii—a specialist on the schism at the Kazan Theological Academy, presumably with access to the Ministry of Interior reports on schismatics deposited there after Nicholas I died—pointed to the special strength of the Great Rite Neo-Spasovites in the Spassk and Tetiushev districts of Kazan province; the creed had arrived from Vladimir province.[31] From Simbirsk and Samara provinces, we have the testimony of a Ministry of Interior official from the early 1850s about the many cell-dwelling Spasovite women.[32] At Vladimir Orlov's Usolie estate in Simbirsk province in the early nineteenth century, many women avoided marriage, probably an indication that they were Spasovites (see chapter 2). Late nineteenth and early twentieth publications by Orthodox missionaries identified Spasovites as among the largest Old Believer covenants in Simbirsk and Saratov provinces.[33]

There are scattered bits of information about Spasovites—both traditional and neo—in other provinces as well. In the middle of the nineteenth century, Pavel Melnikov identified a townsman from Serpukhov, Moscow province (Ignatii Ulianov, age seventy) who spent most the year traveling among the Spasovites in Moscow, Vladimir, Nizhnii Novgorod, Simbirsk, and Samara provinces.[34] A conclave of Neo-Spasovites in 1907 was attended by 175 delegates from thirteen provinces, including (besides provinces already mentioned) Iaroslavl, Riazan, Orenburg, and the Ural territory.[35] The bishop of Tomsk reported in 1897 that Spasovites in his diocese were indifferent to the 1883 law that permitted Old Believers to record births, marriages, and deaths in special registers, because they (traditionalist Spasovites, obviously) married in Orthodox churches.[36] These and other snippets of information about Spasovites add up to almost nothing because small groups of Spasovites most likely could be found in most Russian provinces.

Archives may hold at least qualitative information on Spasovite communities along the middle and lower Volga and elsewhere, but the slim results from my own search in more northerly archives suggests that Spasovites in the south, too, probably deflected attention from themselves, at least up to the 1840s. The Orthodox Church, determined as always to minimize the number of Old Believers of any sort, was a co-conspirator. The Ministry of Interior, after the 1850s, lost interest in producing any realistic assessment of the size of the Old Believer population. On the other hand, the archives can certainly tell us whether there was substantial marriage aversion in the provinces along the central and southern stretches of the Volga and elsewhere that Pavel Melnikov and Archimandrite Pavel identified as home to large numbers of Spasovites. I would take a positive finding to be strong, if indirect, evidence of a Spasovite presence.

Because of the paucity of sources on Spasovites in the second half of the nineteenth century, and because they often fail to distinguish between the Great Rite and Lesser Rite covenants, I cannot even offer a guess as to which of the two was the larger, and that, in turn, obscures the history of Spasovite marriage aversion after the mid-nineteenth century. Great Rite Spasovites confessed their creed openly and were determined to establish a public presence, so the sources create the impression that the Great Rite was ascendant. That may be no more than an artifact of Lesser Rite reserve. The Great Rite, with its emphasis on the Godliness of marriage, and with its own priestless marriage service, can be presumed to have encouraged female nuptiality; the more numerous the Great Rite Spasovites, the more rapidly marriage aversion would have declined. On the other hand, we know that some Lesser Rite communities also adopted a priestless marriage ceremony, while others (*Glukhaia netovshchina*, underground Spasovites) continued to marry in Orthodox churches. That last group may or may not have been more numerous than the less furtive Lesser Rite Spasovites; its women may or may not have sustained the tradition of marriage aversion characteristic of the original Spasovites. On balance, the alterations in marriage practice among both Great and Lesser Rite Spasovites support a hypothesis that Spasovite marriage aversion waned after the middle of the nineteenth century.

Unfortunately, that can only be a hypothesis. The demographic sources I have used for this study all disappear after the early 1860s: the last tax census with household lists was conducted in 1858, serf estate household inventories ended with serfdom in 1861, and parish confession registers from the second half of the 1860s and later were destroyed in the 1920s. Village-level, household-by-household records from the 1897 census were destroyed, lost, or misfiled in the archives.[37]

The published volumes from the 1897 census do provide family status tables by sex and age cohort, but only at the district level. Comparison of the proportion of never-married village women in their sixties (who mostly married between 1857 and 1866) and in their forties (mostly married between 1877 and 1886) shows a decline in spinsterhood from 10.9 to 10.1 percent in the Gorokhovets district (Kuplia parish) and from 7.8 to 6 percent in the Varnavin district (Baki) but a rise from 7.6 to 7.9 percent in the Ardatov district (Steksovo).[38] As of the 1897 census, the numbers and proportions of never-married women in their thirties exceeded the numbers and proportions of never-married women in their forties in all three districts. I assume that appreciable numbers of village women were by then marrying for the first time in their thirties and that by 1907, the number of never-married women in that cohort had fallen slightly below the level in the preceding cohort.[39] The census figures for unmarried women in their forties from the three districts were meaningfully higher than the 4 percent among female villagers in their forties in Russia as a whole.[40] Many individual villages must have exceeded the district averages. But by the end of the nineteenth century, some village women certainly remained single for other than religious reasons.

The district averages from the 1897 census support only the broadest conclusions about nuptial behavior. In the three districts in question, more women never married than the Russian average. The cohort-to-cohort variation in nuptiality provides some clues to historical trends, but we can only guess how much of the intergenerational variation was due to changing religious convictions about marriage. Relying on instinct and intuition, I guess that the figures from 1897 support the hypothesis that, after the mid-nineteenth century, aversion to marriage among Spasovite and other priestless Old Believer women slowly receded.

NOTES

1. The Oxford English Dictionary, 2nd ed. (Oxford: Oxford University Press, 1989), v. 7, p. 813; Frances Anne Kemble, *Records*, pp. 288–89.

2. TsANo, f. 60, op. 239a, d. 163, ll. 2980b–332; d. 1102, ll. 3630b–95; GIM OPI, op. 14, d. 2397, l. 10b–15; TsANO, f. 570, op. 559a, d. 1502, ll. 100–1050b, 123–1280b. The figures for Steksovo in 1795 come from the tax census, which arranged the population by lineage rather than household; nevertheless, I am reasonably confident that I have correctly identified household units. I could not do the same for the 1795 tax census from Baki.

3. LP 47424, ff. 135–46v; GAKO, f. 200, op. 3, d., 462, ll. 6510b–688; ibid., op. 13, d. 30, ll. 4710b–522. For Baki, I have counted unmarried women twenty-five and over, even though the ceiling marriage age rose from twenty-five to thirty between 1812 and 1834. Counting only women thirty and over reduces the proportion of marriage-resistant households to 9 percent in 1834 and 10 percent in 1858.

4. Summarized in Shanin, *Awkward Class*, pp. 81–94 and passim. These studies not only suffered from a foreshortened temporal axis but also grouped household extinction and household merger into separate categories. Mergers were just a version of extinction.

5. Czap, " Perennial Multiple Family"; Rodney Bohac, "Family."

6. Czap, "Perennial Multiple Family," p. 24. Czap recognized that the 1782 and 1795 tax census returns that were among his sources did not divide the population into households; he adopted unspecified rules to break large agglomerations of relatives into households. He probably got them about right. It's not clear that he corrected later census returns for spectral household remnants, but since he also used manorial household registers, he may have.

7. Bohac, "Family," p. 151.

8. Czap, "Perennial Multiple Family," p. 11; Bohac, "Family," p. 178. For Steksovo, see the 1814 and 1845 household inventories and the 1816 and 1834 tax census returns.

9. GAKO, f. 200, op. 3, d. 462, ll. 8330b–36, 8390b–45.

10. RGADA, f. 1290, op. 3, d. 4715, ll. 280b–56; ibid., op. 6, ll. 1–17.

11. Ibid., op. 3, d. 4715, ll. 1–5, 23–27.

12. GAKO, f. 200, op.13, d. 22, ll. 30b–28, 740b–88, 1050b–14, 1230b–30, 2620b–92.

13. RGADA, f. 1290, op. 3, d. 4715, ll. 7–22.

14. GAKO, f. 200, op. 13, d. 399, ll. 50b–23, 16–46, 1140b–23, 271–82, 3460b–540b., 4210b–250b., 427–310b, 445–940b.

15. RGADA, f. 1286, op. 3, d. 255, ll. 360b–580b.

16. GAIaO, f. 100, op. 7, d. 436, ll. 581–95.

17. Ibid. ll. 536–6050b.

18. Ibid., ll. 1–290.

19. GAIaO, f. 230, op. 1, dd. 3905, 3906, 3915.

20. Ibid., d. 12878, ll. 14–47.

21. Ibid., d. 181, ll. 1–220b; d. 182, ll. 1–320b.

22. Ibid., d. 1026, ll. 1–28.

23. Ibid., d. 5128, ll. 523–32; RGADA, f. 1384, op. 1, d. 910, ll. 20b–7.

24. RGADA, f. 1384, op. 1, d. 1373. The even less well-preserved returns are recorded in ibid., dd. 218 (1795), 913 (1816). Lists of unmarried women, 1790 and 1792 are in ibid., dd. 145, 163.

25. Ibid, d. 782. An 1822 summary total of Old Believers in fourteen villages gave 143, covenants not specified, men and women not totaled separately (ibid., d. 1059). Reports from other of Orlova's properties are in ibid., dd. 44, 1060; GAIaO, f. 230, op. 1, d. 3937, ll. 50b–110b.

26. Irina Paert covers the Fedoseev (in her terminology, Theodosian) polemics over marriage briefly in *Old Believers*, pp. 47–48, 153–54, 187–90. In their *Chin oglasheniia*, adopted in 1798, Moscow Fedoseevites recognized, disapprovingly, that their peasant followers generally tried to pass themselves off as Orthodox, accepting Orthodox sacraments and baptizing their children in the church (Popov, *Sbornik*, vol. 1, pp. 96–97). By implication, Fedoseev peasants also married in the church. A compendium of Fedoseev leaders' letters in the early nineteenth century offers considerable information on disputes and local schisms over marriage doctrine in St. Petersburg, Moscow, and elsewhere (RGB OR, f. 98, d. 1044).

27. We know from premortem property distributions made by elderly heads of households at Nikolskoe that at least some spinsters and widows lived in what the documents identify as cells (*kel'i*) (Aleksandrov, *Obychnoe pravo*, pp. 208–13). The surviving lists of Fedoseevite women also identify a few single women and widows living in cells.

28. Mel'nikov, "Schislenie," pp. 388–89, 408.

29. Pavel, *Nikol'skogo edinovercheskogo*, p. 150b; Pavel, "O imenuemoi," p. 29.

30. Pavel, "Kratkie izvestiia," p. 568.

31. Ivanovskii, *Rukovodstvo*, part 1, p. 131; Pyzhikov, *Grani Raskola*, pp. 35–36.

32. Varadinov, *Istoriia Ministerstva*, book 8, p. 543.

33. Summarized in Ershova, *Staroobriadchestvo*, pp. 81–82.

34. Mel'nikov, "Otchet," p. 104.

35. Ageeva, Robson, and Smiljanskaja, "Staroobriadtsy," pp. 107–8.

36. Ivanov, "Metricheskie knigi," p. 114.

37. Litvak, "Perepis' naseleniia," pp. 118–26.

38. *Pervaia vseobshchaia perepis'*, vol. 6, tetrad' 2, p. 12; vol. 18, p. 34; vol. 25, p. 11. For a hyperbolically critical but nevertheless useful analysis of the census, see Kotel'nikov, *Istoriia proizvodstva*. Kotelnikov helped to compile the census results. Also useful is Safonov, "Iz istorii."

39. A rise in the marriage ceiling age accords with Mironov's calculation (Mironov, *Sotsial'naia istoriia*, p. 159), that between 1801 and 1860 and 1909 and 1913, marriages per year among villagers in European Russia dropped from 10.1 to 8.4 per thousand.

40. Tol'ts, "Brachnost'," p. 140.

BIBLIOGRAPHY

ARCHIVAL SOURCES

British Library

 Lieven Papers

Gosudarstvennyi arkhiv Iaroslavskoi oblasti

 f. 100 Iaroslavskaia kazennaia palata
 f. 150 Iaroslavskaia Palata ugolovnogo suda
 f. 230 Iaroslavskaia dukhovnaia konsistoriia

Gosudarstvennyi arkhiv Kostromskoi oblasti

 f. 200 Kostromskaia kazennaia palata
 f. 228 Sidovorskoe votchinnoe pravlenie

Gosudarstvennyi arkiv Nizhegorodskoi oblast, No. 3

 f. 570 Nizhegorodskaia dukhovnaia konsistoriia

Gosudarstvennyi arkhiv Riazanskoi oblasti

 f. 627 Riazanskaia dukhovnaia konsistoriia

Gosudarstvennyi arkhiv Vladimirskoi oblasti

 f. 93 Vladimirskaia palata ugolovnogo suda
 f. 301 Vladimirskaia kazennaia palata
 f. 556 Vladimirskaia dukhovnaia konsistoriia

Gosudarstvennyi Istoricheskii muzei, Otdel pis'mennykh istochnikov

 f. 14 Golitsyny
 f. 17 Lichnyi fond Uvarovykh
 f. 182 Shishkiny
 f. 229 Materialy k istorii zemlevladeniia, krest'ian i dvorian

Iaroslavskii gosudarstvennyi istoriko-arkhitekturnyi muzei

Sobranie rukopisei

Rossiiskaia gosudarstvennaia biblioteka, Otdel rukopisei

f. 17 Barsov
f. 29 Beliaev
f. 98 Egorov
f. 586 Kurakiny

Rossiiskii gosudarstvennyi arkhiv drevnikh aktov

f. 196 Rukopisnoe sobranie F. F. Mazurina
f. 350 Landratskie knigi i revizskie skazki
f. 615 Krepostnye knigi mestnykh uchrezhdenii XVI–XVIII vv.
f. 1187 Troitskii-Gledenskii monastyr'
f. 1200 Novopecherskii-Svenskii monastyr'
f. 1202 Solotchinskii Rozhdestvenskii muzhskoi monastyr'
f. 1239 Dvortsovyi arkhiv
f. 1257 Bezobrazovy
f. 1272 Naryshkiny
f. 1273 Orlovy-Davydovy
f. 1274 Paniny i Bludovy
f. 1277 Samariny
f. 1286 Dmitriev-Mamonovy
f. 1287 Sheremetevy
f. 1288 Shuvalovy
f. 1289 Shcherbatovy
f. 1290 Iusupovy
f. 1365 Buturliny
f. 1384 Orlovy-Chesmenskie
f. 1441 Kirillo-Belozerskii monastyr'
f. 1454 Sidorovskoe votchinnoe pravlenie

Tsentral'nyi arkhiv Nizhegorodskoi oblasti

f. 4 Nizhegorodskoe namestnicheskoe pravlenie
f. 5 Nizhegorodskoe gubernskoe pravlenie
f. 60 Nizhegorodskaia kazennaia palata
f. 177 Nizhegorodskaia gubernskaia palata grazhdanskogo suda
f. 570 Nizhegorodskaia dukhovnaia konsistoriia

Tsentral'nyi istoricheskii arkhiv Moskvy

f. 737 Serpukhovskoe dukhovnoe pravlenie
f. 1614 Semeinyi fond Glebovykh-Streshnevykh

PUBLISHED PRIMARY SOURCES

Akty, otnosiashchiesia do iuridicheskogo byta drevnei Rossii izdany Arkheograficheskoiu Kommissieiu. Vol. 2. St. Petersburg: Arkheograficheskaia kommissiia, 1864.

Akty, sobrannye v bibliotekakh i arkhivakh Roissiiskoi Imperii Arkheograficheskoiu ekspeditsieiu Imperatoskoi Akademii nauk. Vol. 2. St. Petersburg: Tip. II Otdeleniia, 1836.

Akty, sobrannye v bibliotekakh i arkhivakh Rossiiskoi Imperii Arkheograficheskoiu ekspeditsieiu Imperatorskoi Akademii nauk. Vol. 4. St. Petersburg: Tip. II Otdeleniia, 1836.

Akty feodal'nogo zemlevladeniia i khoziaistva. Parts 1–3. Moscow: AN SSSR, 1951–61.

Akty istoricheskie, sobrannye i izdannye Arkheograficheskoiu kommissieiu. Vol. 2. St. Petersburg: Tip. II-go Otdeleniia, 1841.

Akty istoricheskie, sobrannye i izdannye Arkheograicheskoiu kommissieiu. Vol. 5. St. Petersburg: Tip. II-go Otdeleniia, 1842.

Akty khoziaistva Boiarina B. I. Morozova. Part 1. Moscow: AN SSSR, 1940.

Akty sotsial'no-ekonomicheskoi istorii Severo-Vostochnoi Rusi kontsa XIV-nachala XVI v. Vols. 1–3. Moscow: AN SSSR, 1952–64.

Andreev, A. I. "Nakaz votchnnika krest'ianam 1709 g." In *Istoricheskii arkhiv*, vol. 8, pp. 269–77. Moscow: AN SSSR, 1953.

Arkhivnyi material: novootkrytye dokumenty pom'estno-votchinnykh uchrezdenii Moskovskogo gosudarstva XV–XVII stoletii. Moscow: Universitetskaia Tip., 1905.

Arkhiv sela Voshchazhnikova. Moscow: A. V. Vasil'ev, 1901.

Arkhiv stol'nika Andreia Il'icha Bezobrazova. Part 1. Moscow: Pamiatniki istoricheskoi mysli, 2012.

Arnol'di, [L. I.]. "Iz dnevnika Kollezhskogo Assesora Arnol'di po izsledovaniiam raskol'nikov v Kostromskoi gubernii." In *Sbornik pravitel'stvennykh svedenii o raskol'nikakh, sostavlennyi*, issue 2, edited by V. Kel'siev, pp. 18–22. London: Trubner & Co, 1861.

Arzamasskie pomestnye akty (1578–1618 gg.). Moscow: IOIDR, 1915.

Besedy staroobriadetsev Spasova soglasiia, byvshie v Nizhegorodskoi iarmarke, v Kanavine, v d. F. E. Uglanova 17-go avgusta 1907 g. Nizhnii Novgorod: Vsegos. Popechitel'noe bratstvo staroobriadtsev Spasova soglasiia, 1909.

Besedy staroobriadtsa Spasova soglasiia V. A. Voikina s A. A. Antipinym (on zhe Samovarnikov) obshchestva malogo nachala, proiskhodivshie v Nizhegorodskoi iarmarke 16. Avg. 7419 [1911] g. Kovrov: Tip. V. A. Agapova, 1912. Accessed in November 2013. www.starajavera.narod/ru/spasovciVoykin.html.

Brianchaninov, [P. A.]. "Iz dnevnika nadvornogo sovetnika Brianchaninova, po izsledovaniiam raskol'nikov v Kostromskoi gubernii." In *Sbornik pravitel'stvennykh svedenii o raskol'nikakh, sostavlennyi* issue 2, edited by V. Kel'siev, pp. 23–27. London: Trubner & Co, 1861.

Brianchaninov, [P. A.], and [L. I.] Arnol'di. "O raskole v Kostromskoi gubernii." In *Sbornik pravitel'stvennykh svedenii o raskol'nikakh, sostavlennyi*, issue 4, edited by V. Kel'siev, pp. 295–324. London: Trübner & Co, 1862.

"Byvshego bezpopovtsa Grigoria Iakovleva Izveshchenie pravednoe o raskole bezpopovshchiny." *Bratskoe slovo*, nos. 3, 5–9 (1888): pp. 145–73, 317–38, 397–417, 469–490, 649–62, 721–42.

"Cherty iz zhizni kn. E. R. Dashkovoi." *Russkii arkhiv*, nos. 5–6 (1864): pp. 571–86.

Dmitrii, Metropolitan of Rostov and Iaroslavl. *Rozysk o raskol'nicheskoi brynskoi vere, o uchenii ikh, o delakh ikh, i iziavlenie, iako vera ikh neprava, uchenie ikh neprava, uchenie ikh dushevredno, i dela ikh ne bogougodna*. Moscow: Sinodal'naia tip., 1824.

"Dnevnye dozornye zapisi o moskovskikh raskol'nikakh, soobshcheny A. A. Titovym." *Chteniia v Imperatorskom Obshchestve Istorii i Drevnostei Rossiiskikh pri Moskovskom universitete*, no. 2 (1885): pp. 99–224.

Dopolneniia k Aktam istoricheskim, sobrannye i izdannye Arkheograficheskoiu kommissieiu. Vol. 4. St. Petersburg: V tip. Eduarda Pratsa, 1851.

Dovnar-Zapol'skii, M. V. "Materialy dlia istorii votchinnogo upravleniia v Rossii." *Univeritetskie izvestiia*, no. 12 (1903), 1–32; nos. 6–7 (1904), 65–96; nos. 8, 12 (1905), 97–128, 129–146; no. 4 (1906), 161–192; no. 7 (1909), 193–240; no. 11 (1910), 241–288.

Dvortsovye razriady. Vol. 1. St. Petersburg.: Tip. II Otdeleniia, 1850.

Evfrosim. *Otrazitel'noe pisanie o novoizobretennom puti samoubiistvennykh smertei*. St. Petersburg.: Tip. I. N. Skorokhodova, 1895.

Feofilakt (Lopatinskii). *Oblichenie nepravdy raskolnicheskoi, pokazannoi vo otvetakh vygotskikh Pustosviatov*. St. Petersburg: 1745.

Florov, Vasilii. *Oblichenie na raskolnikov [sic]*. Moscow: Tip. E. Lissnera i Iu. Romanova, 1894.

"Formuliarnyi spisok o sluzhbe Sostoiashchego pri Ministerstve Vnutrennikh Del Deistvitel'nogo Statskogo Sovetnika Mel'nikova." *Deistviia Nizhegorodskoi Gubernskoi Uchenoi Arkhivnoi Komissii*. No. 9. Nizhnii Novgorod: 1912: 85–93.

Gurii, ieromonakh. *Skazanie o missionerskikh trudakh Pitirima, arkhiepiskopa nizhegorodskogo*. Moscow: Tip. E. Lissnera i Iu. Romonova, 1889.

Hellie, Richard, ed. and trans. *The Muscovite Law Code (Ulozhenie) of 1649*. Part 1. Irvine, CA: C. Schlacks Jr., 1988.

Iaroslavskaia guberniia. Spiski naselennykh mest po svedeniiu 1859 goda. St. Petersburg: TsSK MVD, 1865.

Indova, E. I. "Instruktsiia kniazia M. M. Shcherbatova prikazchikam ego iaroslavskikh votchin (1758 g. s dobavleniiami k nei po 1762 g.)." *Materialy po istorii sel'skogo khoziaistva i krest'ianstva SSSR*. No. 6. Moscow: Nauka, 1965: 432–69.

Instruktsiia dvoretskomu Ivanu Nemchinovu o upravlenii domu i dereven' i regula ob loshadiakh. St. Petersburg: Tip. V. S. Balasheva, 1881.

"Instruktsiia kniazei Gruzinskikh." *Deistviia Nizhegorodskoi Gubernskoi Uchenoi Arkhivnoi Kommissii*. Vol. 10 (1912): 49–57.

Istoriia o kazanskom tsarstve (Kazanskii letopisets) (Polnoe sobranie russkikh letopisei, t. 19). Moscow: Iazyki russkoi kul'tury, 2000.

"Iz perepiski pomeshchika s krest'ianami vo vtoroi polovine XVIII st." *Trudy Vladimirskoi uchenoi arkhivnoi kommissii*. No. 6. Vladimir: Tipo-Litografiia Gubernskogo Pravleniia, 1904: 1–93.

Izvlechenie iz otcheta po vedomstvu dukhovnkh del Pravoslavnogo ispovedaniia za 1859 god. St. Petersburg: Sinodal'naia tip., 1861.

Izvlechenie iz otcheta po vedomstvu dukhovnykh del Pravoslavnogo ispovedaniia za 1860 god. St. Petersburg: Sinodal'naia tip., 1862.

Izvlechenie iz Vsepodanneishego otcheta Ober-Prokurora Sviateishego Synoda K. Pobedonostseva po vedomstvu Pravoslavnogo ispovedaniia za 1883 god. St. Petersburg: Sinodal'naia tip., 1885.

Karpovich, U. *Khoziaistvennye opyty tridsatletnei praktiki ili nastavlenie dlia upravleniia imeniiami*. St. Petersburg: Tip. I. Vorob'eva, 1837.

Kniga kliuchei i Dolgovaia kniga Iosifo-Volokolamskogo monastyria XVI veka. Moscow: AN SSSR, 1948.

Komissarov, Avvakum. *Vechnaia Pravda*. 1895.

Kostromskaia guberniia. Spisok naselennykh mest po svedeniiam 1870–72 godov. St. Petersburg: Tsentral'nyi statisticheskii komitet Ministerstva Vnutrennykh Del, 1877.

Krest'ianina Ivana Aleksandrova razgovory o vere s nastavnikom Spasova soglasiia, Avvakumom Onisimovym i nastavnikami drugikh soglasii. Moscow: Bratstvo sv. Petra mitr., 1882.

Krest'ianskaia voina pod predvoditel'stvom Stepana Razina. Sbornik dokumentov. Vol. 2, part 1. Moscow: AN SSSR, 1957.

Krest'ianskoe dvizhenie v Rossii v 1826–1849 gg. Sbornik dokumentov. Moscow: Izd-vo sotsial'no- ekonomicheskoi literatury, 1961.

Latkin, V. N., ed. *Proekt novogo ulozheniia, sostavlennyi zakonodatel'noi kommissiei 1754–1766 gg. (Chast' III, "O sostoianiiakh poddannykh voobshche)."* St. Petersburg: Tip. Spb. Odinoichnoi tiur'my, 1893.

Lomonosov, M. V. *Sochineniia.* Moscow: Gos. Izd-vo khudozhestvennoi literatury, 1957.

Materialy dlia istorii Vladimirskoi gubernii. Issue 3. Vladimir: Tipo-litografiia gubernskogo pravleniia, 1904.

Materialy k istorii staroobriadchestva Iuzhnoi Viatki. Po itogam kompleksnykh arkheograficheskikh ekspeditsii MGU imeni M. V. Lomonosova. Sbornik dodumentov. Moscow: MAKS Press, 2012.

Materialy po istorii sel'skogo khoziaistva i kres'tianstva Rossii. Sel'skokhoziastvennye instruktsii (pervaia polovina XVIII v.). Mowcow: AN SSSR, 1984.

Materialy po istorii sel'skogo khoziaistva i krest'ianstva Rossii. Sel'skokhoziaistvennye instruktsii (seredina XVIII v.). Moscow: In-t istorii AN SSSR, 1987.

Materialy Vysochaishe uchrezhdennoi 16 noiabria 1901 g. Kommissii. Part 1. St. Petersburg: 1903.

Mel'nikov, P. I. "Otchet o sovremennom sostoianii raskola v Nizhegorodskoi gubernii, sostavlennyi sostoiashchim pri Ministerstve Vnutrennikh Del Kollezhskom Sovetnikom Mel'nikovym." In *Deistviia Nikzhegorodskoi Gubernskoi Uchenoi Arkhivnoi Komissii,* vol. 9, pp. 3–332. Nizhnii Novgorod, 1910.

———. "Zapiska o russkom raskole." In *Sbornik pravitel'stvennykh svedenii o raskol'nikhakh, sostavlennyi,* issue 1, edited by V. Kel'siev, pp 169–89. London: Trübner & Co., 1860.

———. "Nakaz kupecheskogo obshchestva goroda Gorokhovtsa." *Sbornik Imperatorskogo russkogo istoricheskogo obshchestva,* vol. 107, pp. 176–79. St. Petersburg: 1900.

Nastavlenie pravil'no sostiazat'sia s raskol'nikami, sochinennoe v Riazanskoi Seminarii po predpisaniiu pokoinogo Preosviashchennogo Simona, Episkopa Riazanskogo i Shatskogo. 6th ed. Moscow: Sinodal'naia tip., 1839.

Nizhegorodskaia oblast': topograficheskaia karta. Mowcow: TsEVKF, 2000.

Opisanie aktov sobraniia Grafa A. S. Uvarova. Akty istoricheskie opisannye I. M. Kataevym i A. K. Kabanovym pod redaktsiei professora M. V. Dovnar-Zapol'skogo. Moscow: 1905.

Opisanie arkhiva Aleksandro-Nevskoi lavry za vremia tsarstvovania Imperatora Petra Velikogo. Vols. 1–3. St. Petersburg: Synodal'naia tip., 1903–16.

Opisanie dokumentov i del, khraniashchikhsia v arkhive Sviateishogo pravitel'stvuiushego synoda. Vol. 8. St. Petersburg: Sinodal'naia tip., 1891.

Opisanie dokumentov i del, khraniashchikhsia v arkhive Sviateishogo Synoda. Vol. 10. St. Petersburg: Sinodal'naia tip.ografiia, 1902.

"O rabote mestnykh Razborochnykh komissii." *Biulleten' Tsentrarkhiva RSFSR,* nos. 4/5 (1927): 2–10.

Pamiatniki istorii krest'ian XIV–XIX vv. Moscow: Izd. N. N. Klochkova, 1910.

Perepiska kniazia M. M. Shcherbatova. Moscow: Drevlekhranilishche, 2011.

Pervaia vseobshchaia perepis' naseleniia Rossiiskoi Imperii 1897 g. Obshchii svod po Imperii rezul'tatov razrabotki dannykh pervoi vseobshchei perepisi naseleniia, proizvedennoi 28 ianvaria 1897 goda. St. Petersburg: Tsentral'nyi statisticheskii komitet MVD. Vols. 1 (1905), 6 part 2 (1904), 18 (1903), 25 part 2 (1904).

"Petr Mikhailovich Bestuzhev-Riumin i ego Novgorodskoe pomest'e." *Russkii arkhiv*, no. 1, edited by P. I. Shchukin, pp. 5–42. 1904.

Pis'ma Filareta, mitropolit Moskovskogo k kniaziu Sergeiu Mikhailovichu Golitsynu. Moscow: Universitetskaia tip., 1883.

"Pis'ma kniazia Alesandra Mikhailovicha Golitsyna svoim prikazchikam i burmistram, 1780, 1788, 1792, 1795, 1796, 1798 i 1799 godov." In *Sbornik starinnykh bumag, khraniashchikhsia v Muzee P. I. Shchukina*, part 9, pp. 1–33. Moscow: Tip. A. I. Mamontova, 1901.

Pitirim. *Prashchitsa dukhovnaia Pitirima arkhiepiskopa nizhegorodskogo i Sobornoe deianie na Martina Armianina.* Moscow: Tip. T-va Riabushinskikh, 1915.

Polnoe sobranie postanovlenii i rasporiazhenii po vedomstvu Pravoslavnogo Ispovedaniia Rossiiskoi Imperii. Vol. 6. St. Petersburg: Sinodal'naia tip., 1889.

Polnoe sobranie postanovlenii i rasporiazhenii po vedomstvu Pravoslavnago Ispovedaniia Rossiiskoi Imperii, Tsarstvovanie Gosudaryni Imperatritsy Ekateriny Vtoroi. Vol. 1. St. Petersburg: Sinodatl'naia tip., 1910.

Polnoe sobranie postanovlenii i rasporiazhenii po vedomstvu Pravoslavnogo Ispovedaniia Rossiiskoi Imperii [Seriia 4] Tsarstvovanie Gosudaria Imperatora Pavla Pervogo 6 noiabria 1796 g.-11 marta 1801 god. Petrograd: Tip. 1-oi Trudovoi Arteli, 1915.

Polnoe sobranie postanovlenii i rasporiazhenii po vedomstvu Pravoslavnogo Ispovedaniia Rossiiskoi Imperii. [Seriia 5] Tsarstvovanie Gosudaria Imperatora Nikolaia I. Vol. 1. Petrograd: Tip. 1-oi Petr. Trudovoi Arteli, 1915.

Polnoe sobranie russkikh letopisei. Vol. 14. Moscow: Iazyki russkoi kul'tury, 2000.

Polnoe sobranie zakonov Rossiiskoi Imperii. 45 vols. St. Petersburg: Gosudarstvennaia Tip., 1830.

Polnoe sobranie zakonov Rossiiskoi Imperii. Sobranie vtoroe. 55 vols. St. Petersburg: Gosudarstvennaia Tipographiia, 1830–1884.

Polushin, N. A. "Vypiski iz pamiatnoi knigi A. F. Polushina." *Russkii arkhiv*, no. 6 (1898): 177–205.

Popov, Nikolai, ed. *Materialy dlia istorii bespopvshchinskikh soglasii v Moskve, Feodosievtsev Preobrazhenskogo kladbishcha i Pomorskogo Moninskogo soglasiia.* Vols. 1–2. Moscow: IOIDR, 1870.

———. *Sbornik dlia istorii staroobriadchestva.* Vols. 1–2. Moscow: Universitetskaia tip., 1864–66.

Pososhkov, I. T. *Zerkalo ochevidnoe (Redaktsiia polnaia).* Vols. 1–2. Kazan': Imperatorskii Universitet, 1898–1905.

"Povelenie, podpisannoe grafinoi Irinoi Vorontsovoi, 27 iiulia 1796 goda." In *Sbornik starinnykh bumag, khraniashchikhsia v Muzee P. I. Shchukina*, p. 144. Moscow: Tip. A. I. Mamontova, 1900.

"Prikaz iaroslavskogo pomeshchika Karnovicha." *Osmnadtsatyi vek. Istoricheskii sbornik*, no. 2 (1869): 365–68.

"Prikaz pomeshchika A. M. Cheremisinova, Kovrovskoi votchiny, derevni Elokhova, staroste Egoru Vasil'evu i vsemu miru." In *Arkhiv istoricheskikh i prakticheskikh svedenii, otnosiashchikhsia do Rossii*, vol. 3, edited by Nikolai Kalachev, pp. 15–30. St. Petersburg: 1862.

"Rasporiazheniia Grafa Arakcheeva." *Novgorodskii sbornik,* no. 4 (1865): 271–79.

Razriadnaia kniga 1475–1598 gg. Moscow: Nauka, 1966.

Riazradnaia kniga 1559–1636 gg. Moscow: AN SSSR, 1975.

Rudakov, S. V. "'Drugopriemnoe postrizhenie.' K rodosloviiu Spasova soglasiia (Bol'shogo nachala)." In *Staroobriadchestvo: istoriia, kul'tura, sovremennost'. Materialy,* vol. 2, edited by V. I. Osipov, pp. 172–78. Moscow: Muzei istorii i kul'tury staroobriadchestva, 2005.

Rumiantseva, V. S., compiler. *Narodnoe antitserkovnoe dvizhenie v Rossii XVII veka. Dokumenty prikaza tainykh del o raskol'nikakh 1665–1667 gg.* Moscow: AN SSSR, 1986.

Russkaia istoricheskaia biblioteka izdavaemaia Arkheografichskoiu kommissieiu. Vol. 5, *Akty Iverskogo Sviatoozerskogo monastyria (1582–1706).* St. Petersburg: Arkheograficheskaia kommissiia, 1878.

Russkie krest'iane. Zhizn'. Byt. Nravy. Materialy "Etnograficheskogo biuro" kniazia V. N. Tenisheva. Vol. 2, *Iaroslavskaia guberniia.* Part 1, *Poshekhonskii uezd.* St. Petersburg: Rossiiskii etnograficheskii muzei, 2006.

Sbornik pravitel'stvennykh svedenii o raskol'nikakh, sostavlennyi V. Kel'sievym. Issue 4. London: Trübner & Co., 1862.

Sbornik starinnykh bumag, khraniashchikhsia v Muzee P. I. Shchukina. Part 3. Moscow: Izd. P. I. Shchukina, 1897.

Sbornik starinnykh bumag, khraniashchikhsia v Muzee P. I. Shchukina. Part 7. Moscow: Tip. A. I. Mamontova, 1900.

"'Se az pozhaloval esmi . . . v pomest'ie. Zhalovannaia gramota Ivana III 1482 goda." *Istoricheskii arkhiv,* no. 5 (1993): pp. 187–89.

Shcherbatov, M. M. *Izbrannye trudy.* Moscow: ROSSPEN, 2010.

———. *On the Corruption of Morals in Russia.* Cambridge: Cambridge University Press, 1969.

———. *Sochineniia kniazia M. M. Shcherbatova.* Vol. 2. St. Petersburg: Tip. M. Akinfieva i I. Leont'eva, 1898.

Shumakov, A. A. *Obzor gramot "Kollegii ekonomii."* Vol. 2, *Teksty i obzor belozerskikh aktov (1395–1758 gg.).* Moscow: IOIDR, 1900.

———. *Obzor "Gramot Kollegii Ekonomii."* Vol. 4, *Kostroma "s tovarishchi" i Pereslavl'-Zalesskii.* Moscow: Sinodal'naia tip., 1917.

Sipitsyn, Ivan. ["Introduction"]. In *Sbornik pravitel'stvennykh svedenii o raskol'nikakh, sostavlennyi,* issue 4, edited by V. Kel'siev, pp. 1–53. London: Trubner & Co, 1862.

———. "O raskole v Iaroslavskoi gubernii." In *Sbornik pravitel'stvennykh svedenii o raskol'nikakh, sostavlennyi,* issue 4, edited by V. Kel'siev, pp. 59–187. London: Trübner & Co., 1862.

Skitskoe pokaianie. [1909].

Sobranie postanovlenii po chasti raskola. 2nd ed. St. Petersburg: MVD, 1875.

Sobranie postanovlenii po chasti raskola, sostoiavshikhsia po vedomstvu Sv. Synodu. Book 2. St. Petersburg: MVD, 1860.

Staraia Vologda XII–nachalo XX v. Sbornik dokumentov i materialov. Vologda: Gosudarstvennyi arkhiv Vologodskoi oblasti, 2004.

Statisticheskie svedeniia o staroobriadtsakh (k 1 Ianvaria 1912 g.). Moscow: Departament Dukhovnykh Del Ministerstva Vnutrennikh Del, 1912.

Titov, A. A., ed. *Rukopisi slavianskie i russkie prinadlezhashchie Deistvitel'nomu Chlenu Imperatorskogo Russkogo Arkeologicheskogo Obshchestva I. A. Vakhrameevu.* Sergiev Posad: Tip. A. I. Snegirevoi, 1892.

Tulupov, T. S. *Istoriko-dogmaticheskii ocherk o proiskhozhdenii staroobriadcheskogo Spasskogo ili Netovskogo soglasiia.* Samara: 1915.

———. *Put' zhizni. Sobranie sochinenii.* Samara: Ofort, 2008.

Ustiugov, N. V. "Instruktsiia votchinnomu prikazchiku 1-I chetverty XVII v." In *Istoricheskii arkhiv*, vol. 4, pp. 150–83. Moscow: AN SSSR, 1949.

SECONDARY SOURCES

Ageeva, E. A., N. A. Kobiak, T. A. Kruglova, E. B., and E. B. Smilianskaia. *Rukopisi Verkhokam'ia XV–XX vv. Iz sobraniia Nauchnoi biblioteki Moskovskogo universiteta imeni M. V. Lomonosova.* Moscow: Tsimeliia, 1994.

Ageeva, E. A., R. R. Robson, and E. B. Smiljanskaja. "Staroobriadtsy spasovtsy: Puti narodnogo bogosloviia i formy samosokhraneniia traditsionnykh obshchestv v Rossii XX stoletiia." *Revue des études slaves* 69, nos. 1–2 (1997): 101–17

Aleksandrov, V. A. *Obychnoe pravo krepostnoi derevni Rossii XVIII-nachalo XIX v.* Moscow: Nauka, 1984.

———. *Sel'skaia obshchina v Rossii (XVII-nachalo XIX v.).* Moscow: Nauka, 1976.

A. N. "O Bezhetskom uezde i Teblishanakh." *Moskvitianin*, no. 16 (1853): 195–96.

Andreev, N. I. *Gorokhovetskaia istoricheskaia khronika.* Vladimir: Tranzit-Iks, 2008.

———. *Kotel'shchiki: gorokhovetskie otkhodniki.* Vladimir: Tranzit, 2010.

Anisimov, E. V. *Five Empresses. Court Life in Eighteenth-Century Russia.* Westport, CT: Praeger, 2004.

———. *Rossiia v seredine XVIII veka. Bor'ba za nasledie Petra.* Moscow: Mysl', 1986.

Ankudinov, A. I. "Gorokhovetskii uezd—tsentr Staroobriadchestva Vladimirskoi gubernii v 17- nach. XX v." In *Staroobriadchestvo: istoriia, kul'tura, sovremennost'. Materialy*, vol. 1, edited by V. I. Osipov, N. V. Zinovkina, E. I. Sokolova, and A. V. Osipova, pp. 266–68. Moscow: Tsentr istorii i kul'tury staroobriadchestva, 2014.

Antonov, A. V., "Iz istorii Troitskoi Varnavinoi pustini." *Russkii diplomatarii*, issue 6 (2000): 148–54.

Antonov, D.N., and I. A. Antonova. "Istochniki genealogicheskikh rekonstruktsii krest'ianskikh semei (na premire Iasnoi Poliane)." In *Istochniki po istorii russkoi usadebnoi kul'tury*, edited by Istominam E. G. and M. A. Poliakov, pp. 46–56. Iasnaia Poliana–Moscow: Muzei-usad'ba L. N. Tolstogo "Iasnaia Poliana," 1997.

Antonova, Katherine Pickering. *An Ordinary Marriage. The World of a Gentry Family in Provincial Russia.* New York: Oxford University Press, 2013.

Arakcheev, V. A. "Sobornoe ulozhenie 9 marta 1607 g." In *Rossiiskoe gosudarstvo v XIV–XVII vv. Sbornik statei, posviashchennyi 75-letiiu so dnia rozhdeniia Iu. G. Alekseeva*, edited by A. P. Pavlov, pp. 98–114. Saint Petersburg: Dmitrii Bulanin, 2002.

Ardatovskii krai: proshloe i nastoiashchee. Nizhnii Novgorod: Nizhpoligraf, 2000.

Arkhangel'skii, S. I. "Simbileiskaia votchina Vl. Gr. Orlova (1790–1800 gg.)." *Nizhegorodskii kraevedcheskii sbornik*, no. 2 (1929): 166–92.

A-v, E. "Nechto o bezpopovskikh sektakh, izvestnykh pod nazvaniem: pokreshchevantsy, netovtsy i otritsantsy." *Bratskoe slovo*, no. 1 (1884): 31–37.

Baldin, M. A. *Varnavinskaia starina. Ocherki istorii Povetluzh'ia.* Varnavin–Nizhnii Novgorod: 1993.

Bazhaev, Aleksandr. *Istoricheskie svedeniia o seleniiakh ardatovskogo raiona. Zagadki pokhoda Ivana Groznogo. Onomastika ardatovskogo raiona.* Ardatov-Arzamas: AGPI, 2004.

Begunov, Iu. K., and A. M. Panchenko. "Arkheograficheskaia ekspeditsiia sektora drevnerusskoi literature v Gor'kovskom oblast.'" In *Trudy Otdela drevnerusskoi literatury Instituta russkoi literatury*, vol. 15, pp. 387–97. Moscow-Leningrad: AN SSSR, 1958.

Berenskii, P. *Arkhmandrit o. Pavel (Prusskii) i ego protivoraskol'nich'ia deiatel'nost'*. Kiev: Tip. I. I. Chokolova, 1899.

Beskrovnyi, L. G. *Russkaia armiia i flot v XVIII veke (Ocherki)*. Moscow: Voennoe izdatel'stvo, 1958.

———. *Russkaia armiia i flot v XIX veke*. Moscow: Nauka, 1973.

Bochenkov, V. V. *P. I. Mel'nikov (Andrei Pecherskii): mirovozzrenie, tvorchestvo, Staroobriadchestvo*. Rzhev: Margarit, 2008.

Bogdanovich, P. F. *Istoricheskoe izvestie o raskol'nikakh*. St. Petersburg: 1787.

Bohac, Rodney. "Family, Property, and Socioeconomic Mobility: Russian Peasants on Manuilskoe Estate, 1810–1861." PhD diss., University of Illinois, 1982.

———. "The Mir and the Military Draft." *Slavic Review* 47, no. 4 (Winter 1988): pp. 652–66.

Borisoglebskii, Ia. "Svadebnye obriady v Gorokhovetskom uezde." *Vladimirskie gubernskie vedomosti*, no. 1 (1854). Republished in *Semeinye obriady Vladimirskoi derevni*, part 2, edited by Vladimir Dmitriev, pp. 92–94. Vladimir: Vladimirskii oblastnoi tsentr narodnogo tvorchestva, 2006.

Borisov, V. "Pomeshchich'e khoziaistvo. Tsena liudei v kontse XVII veka." *Chteniia v Imperatorskom Obeshchestve Istorii i Drevnosti Rossiiskikh*. 1898, Book 4, Smes': 22–24.

Borodkin, A. V. "Istoriia staroobriadchestva Verkhnevolzh'ia XVII–nachala XVIII vv." In *Staroobriadtsy Verkhnevolzh'ia: proshloe, nastoiashchee, budushchee*, edited by I. V. Pozdeeva, pp. 31–46. Kostroma: 2005.

Breshchinskii, D. I. "Zhitie Korniliia Vygovskogo Pakhomievskoi redaktsii (teksty)." In *Drevnerusskaia knizhnost' po materialam Pushkinskogo Doma*, edited by A. M. Panchenko, pp. 65–107. Leningrad: Nauka, 1985.

Bulygin, I. A. *Monastyrskie krest'iane Rossii v pervoi chetverti XVIII veka*. Moscow: Nauka, 1977.

Bushen, A., ed. *Statisticheskie tablitsy Rossiiskoi Imperii, izdavaemye, po rasporiazhenii Ministra Vnutrennykh Del, Tsentral'nym Statiticheskim Komitetom*. Part 2, *Nalichnoe naselenie imperii za 1858 god*. St. Petersburg: Tip. K. Vul'fa, 1863.

Bushnell, Dzhon. "Bor'ba za nevestu. Krest'ianskie svad'by v Riazanskom uezde 1690-kh gg." *Russkii sbornik*. No. 2. Moscow: Modest Kolerov, 2006): 81–98.

———. "Proiskhozhdenie Spasova soglasiia." In *Staroobriadchestvo: istoriia, kul'tura, sovremennost'. Materialy*, vol. 1., edited by V. I. Osipov, N. V. Zinovkina, E. I. Sokolova, and A. V. Osipova, pp. 420–35. Moscow: Tsentr istorii i kul'tury staroobriadchestva, 2014.

Bushnell, John. "Did Serf Owners Control Serf Marriage? Orlov Serfs and Their Neighbors, 1773–1861." *Slavic Review* 52, no. 3 (August 1993): pp. 419–45.

Byt velikorusskikh krest'ian-zemlepashtsev: opisanie materialov Ėtnograficheskogo biuro kniazia V. N. Tenisheva: na primere Vladimirskoi gubernii. St. Petersburg: Izd-vo Evropeiskogo doma, 2003.

Chaev, N. S. *Bulavinskoe vosstanie (1707–1708 gg.)*. Moscow: Izd-vo Vsesoiuznogo Ob-va politkatorzhan i ssyl'no-poselentsev, 1934.

Crummey, Robert O. *The Old Believers and the World of the Antichrist*. Madison: University of Wisconsin Press, 1970.

———. *Old Believers in a Changing World*. Dekalb: Northern Illinois University Press, 2011.

Czap, Peter. "The Perennial Multiple Family Household, Mishino, Russia, 1782–1858." *Journal of Family History* 7, no. 1 (Spring 1982): 5–26.

Daniel, Wallace. "Conflict between Economic Vision and Economic Reality: The Case of M. M. Shcherbatov." *Slavonic and East European Review* 67, no. 1 (January 1989): 42–67.

Dennison, Tracy. *The Institutional Framework of Russian Serfdom*. Cambridge: Cambridge University Press, 2011.

Dimitriev, V. D. "Vosstanie iasachnykh liudei Srednego Povolzh'ia i Priural'ia 1615–1616 Godov." In *Voprosy drevnei i srednevekovoi istorii Chuvashii*, edited by V. A. Prokhorov, V. F. Kakhovskii, and N. E. Egorov, pp. 109–19. Cheboksary: Nauchno-issledovatel'skoi institute iazyka, literatury, istorii i ekonomiki pri Sovete Ministrov Chuvashskoi ASSR, 1980.

Dmitrieva, Z. V. "Ustavnye gramoty Kirillo-Belozerskogo monastyria XVI–XVII vv." In *Rossiiskoe gosudarstvo v XIV-XVII vv. Sbornik statei, posviashchennyi 75-letiiu so dnia rozhdeniia Iu. G. Alekseeva*, edited by A. P. Pavlov, pp. 261–69. St. Petersburg: Dmitrii Bulanin, 2002.

Dobroklonskii, A. P. "Solotchinskii monastyr', e go slugi i krest'iane v XVII veke." *Chteniia v Imperatorskom Obshchestvom istorii i drevnostei rossiiskikh*, no. 1 (1881): 1–130.

Dobrotvorskii, N. "Krest'ianskie iuridicheskie obychai v vostochnoi chasti Vladimirskoi Gubernii." *Iuridicheskii vestnik* 28, nos. 6–7 (1888): 322–49.

Dubenskii, N. I. *Vladimirskaia guberniia v sel'skokhoziaistvennom otnoshenii*. Saint-Petersburg: Ministerstvo gosudarstvenykh imushchestv, 1851.

Efimenko, P. S. *Obychai i verovaniia krest'ian Arkhangel'skoi gubernii*. Moscow: OGI, 2009.

Engelstein, Laura. *Castration and the Heavenly Kingdom: A Russian Folktale*. Ithaca, NY: Cornell University Press, 1999.

Ermolaev, I. I. *Srednee Povolzh'e vo vtoroi polovine XVI–XVII vv. (upravlenie Kazanskim kraem)*. Kazan': Kazanskii un-t, 1982.

Ershova, O. P. *Staroobriadchestvo i vlast'*. Moscow: Unikum-tsentr, 1999.

Esipov, G. *Raskol'nich'i dela XVIII stoletiia, izvlechennye iz del Preobrazhenskogo prikaza i Tainoi rozysknykh del kantseliarii*. Vol. 1. St. Petersburg: D. E. Kozhanchikov, 1861.

Evtuhov, Catherine. *Portrait of a Russian Province: Economy, Society, and Civilization in Nineteenth-Century Nizhnii Novgorod*. Pittsburgh: University of Pittsburgh Press, 2011.

Fedosov, I. A. *Iz istorii russkoi obshchestvennoi mysli. M. M. Shcherbatov*. Moscow: MGU, 1967.

Freeze, Gregory. *The Russian Levites: Parish Clergy in the Eighteenth Century*. Cambridge, MA: Harvard University Press, 1977.

Garelin, Ia. P. *Gorod Ivanovo-Voznesensk, ili byvshee selo Ivanovo i Voznesenskii posad*. Part 1. Shuia: Tip. Ia. I. Borisoglebskogo, 1884.

Geografichesko-statisticheskii slovar' Rossiiskoi Imperii. 4 vols. St. Petersburg: Tip. V. Bezobrazova i Komp., 1863–85.

Gnevkovskaia, E. V. *Masterstvo romanista P. I. Mel'nikova—Andreia Pecherskogo*. Nizhnii Novgorod: Nizhegorodskii gosudarstvennyi universitet, 2003.

Gnevushev, A. M. *Novgorodskii dvortsovyi prikaz v XVII veke (Kratkii ocherk deiatel'nosti prikaza i dokumenty)*. Moscow: Russkaia pechatnaia, 1911.

Gorchakov, M. I. *O zemel'nykh vladeniiakh Vserossiiskikh mitropolitov, patriarkhov i Sv. Sinoda, 988–1738 gg.* St. Petersburg: Tip. A Transhelia, 1871.

Gorlanov, L. R. "Udel'nye krest'iane Rossii 1797–1865 gg." Doktorskaia dissertatsiia, Vladimirskii gos. Ped. in-t, 1988.

———. *Udel'nye krest'iane Rossii 1797–1865 gg.* Smolensk: Smolenskii gos. ped. in-t, 1986.

Got'e, Iu. V. *Zamoskovnyi krai v XVII veke. Opyt issledovaniia po istorii ekonomicheskogo byta Moskovskoi Rusi.* Moscow: Sotsekgiz, 1937.

Gritsevskaia, I. M. "Istoriia i sovremennost' seiminskogo staroobriadchestva." In *Mir staroobraidchestva: istoriia i sovremennost'*, issue 5, edited by V. I. Osipov, N. V. Zinovkina, E. I. Sokolova, and A. V. Osipova, pp. 243–61. Moscow: MGU, 1999.

Gromyko, M. M. *Traditsionnye normy povedeniiai i formy obshcheniia russkikh krest'ian XIX v.* Moscow: Nauka, 1986.

Hajnal, John. "Age at Marriage and Proportion Marrying." *Population Studies* 7 no. 2 (November 1953): 111–36.

Hellie, Richard. *The Economy and Material Culture of Russia, 1600–1725.* Chicago: University of Chicago Press, 1999.

———. *Enserfment and Military Change in Muscovy.* Chicago: University of Chicago Press, 1971.

Hoch, Steven. *Serfdom and Social Control in Russia: Petrovskoe, a Village in Tambov.* Chicago: University of Chicago Press, 1986.

Hyde, H. Montgomery. *Princess Lieven.* Boston: Little, Brown and Company, 1938.

Iukhimenko, E. M. *Pomorskoe staroverie v Moskve i khram v Tokmakovom pereulke.* Moscow: VINITI, 2008.

Iukht, A. I. *Russkie den'gi ot Petra Velikogo do Aleksandra I.* Moscow: Finansy i statistika, 1994.

Ivanov, K. Iu. "Metricheskie knigi staroobriadtsev Tomskoi gubernii (1906–1931 gg.) kak istoricheskii istochnik." In *Staroobriadchestvo: istoriia i sovremennost', mestnye traditsii, russkie i zarubezhnye sviazi. Materialy III Mezhdurnarodnoi nauchno-prakticheskoi konferentsii 26-28 iiunia 2001 g., g. Ulan-Ude*, edited by R. P. Matveeva, pp. 113–17. Ulan-Ude: Izd-vo BNTs SO RAN, 2001.

Ivanov, V. I. *Drugoi Iusupov (Kniaz' N. B. Iusupov i ego vladeniia na rubezhe XVIII–XIX stoletii). Istoricheskii ocherk.* Moscow: Grifon, 2012.

Ivanovskii, N[ikolai]. "Iz staroobriadcheskogo mira." *Pravoslavnyi sobesednik*, November 1883: 323–54.

———. *Rukovodstvo po istorii i oblicheniiu staroobriadcheskogo raskola.* Part 1, *Istoriia raskola.* Kazan': Imperatorskii un-t, 1887.

Ivina, L. I. *Vnutrennee osvoenie zemel' Rossii v XVI v.* Leningrad: Nauka, 1985.

J. Siebmachers grosses und allgemeines Wappenbuch. Bd. 3, Abt. 11. Nürnberg: Bauer & Raspe, 1898.

Kabuzan, V. M. *Narodonaselenie Rossii v XVIII–pervoi poloviny XIX v. (Po materialam revizii).* Moscow: AN SSSR, 1963.

Kafengauz, B. B. *I. T. Pososhkov: zhizn' i deiatel'nost'.* Moscow-Leningrad: AN SSSR, 1950.

Kahan, Arcadius. *The Plow, the Hammer and the Knout: An Economic History of Eighteenth-Century Russia.* Chicago: University of Chicago Press, 1985.

Kaizer, D. "Vozrast pri brake i raznitsa v vozraste suprugov v gorodakh Rossii v nachale XVIII v." In *Sosloviia i gosudarstvennaia vlast' v Rossii. XV-seredina XIX w.*, edited by N. V. Karlov, pp. 225–36. Moscow: MFTI, 1994.

Kapustina, G. V. "Zapisnye knigi Moskovskoi krepostnoi kontory kak istoricheskii istochnik." *Problemy istochnikovedeniia*, Issue 7. Moscow: Nauka, 1958: 216–73.

Kataev, Ivan Matveevich. *Na beregakh Volgi. Istoriia Usol'skoi votchiny Grafov Orlovykh.* Cheliabinsk: Cheliabgiz, 1948.

Kaurkin, R. V., and O. A. Pavlova. *Edinoverie v Rossii. Ot zarozhdeniia ideia do nachala XX veka.* St. Petersburg: Aleteiia, 2011.

Kemble, Frances Anne. *Records of Later Life.* Vol. 3. London: Richard Bentley and Son, 1882.

Khval'kovskii, A. V., and E. M. Iukhimenko. "Pomorskoe staroverie v Moskve." In *Staroobradchestvo v Rossii (XVII–XX vv.)*, edited by E. M. Iukhimenko, 314–43. Moscow: Iazyki russkoi kul'tury, 1999.

Kititsyn, P. "Iz proshlogo. Tserkov' vo imia Rozhdestva Presviatyia Bogoroditsy, v s. Semenove, Varnavinskogo uezda, Kostromskoi gubernii." *Drevniaia i novaia Rossiia*, no. 2 (1879): 351–52.

———. "Staroobriadcheskie skity v Varnavinskom uezde Kostromskoi gubernii." *Drevniaia i novaia Rossiia*, no. 1 (1879): 174–75.

Klochkova, E. S. "Put' samoopredeleniia nizhegorodskoi spasovshchiny kontsa XIX—nachala XX v.: samokresty." In *Mir staroobriadchestva. Istoriia, sovremennost'*, issue 5, edited by I. V. Pozdeeva, pp. 217–42. Moscow: MGU, 1999.

Kniaz' Sergei Mikhailovich Golitsyn. Vospominaniia o piatidesiatiletnei sluzhbe ego v zvanii Pochetnogo opekuna i predsedatel'stvuiushego v Moskovskom Opekunskom sovete. Moscow: Tip. V. Got'e. 1859.

Kogan, E. S. "Volneniia krest'ian penzenskoi votchiny A. B. Kurakina vo vremia dvizheniia Pugacheva." *Istoricheskie zapiski*, no. 37 (1951): 104–24.

Kondrashova, L. I. "Maloizvestnye pomeshchich'i nakazy upraviteliam XVIII veka." In *Trudy Moskovskogo Gosudarstvennogo Istoriko-Arkhivnogo Instituta*, vol. 10, pp. 222–38. Moscow: MGIAI, 1957.

Korbin, V. B. *Vlast' i sobstvennost' v srednevekovoi Rossii (XV–XVI vv.)*. Moscow: Mysl', 1985.

Kordatov, A. "Samokrutka." In *Nizhegorodskii sbornik*, vol. 3, edited by A. I. Gatsiskii, pp. 139–50. Nizhnii Novgorod: Nizhegorodskii gubernskii statisticheskii komitet, 1870.

Kotel'nikov, A. *Istoriia proizvodstva i razrabotki vseobshchei perepisi naseleniia 28-go ianvaria 1897 god*. St. Petersburg: Nasha zhizn', 1909.

Krzhivoblotskii, Ia. *Materialy po geografii i statistiki Rossii, sobrannye ofitserami General'nogo Shtaba. Kostromskaia guberniia*. St. Petersburg: Tip. N. Tivlena i ko., 1861.

Kupletskii, M. "Beglye krest'iane na votchinnykh zemliakh Kazhirskoi pustini vo vremia i posle Petra Velkogo (Po rukopisam tserkovnoi biblioteke s. Kazhirova)." *Strannik*, no. 6 (1881): 171–91; no. 7 (1881): 339–56.

Kurmacheva, M. D. "Rassloenie krest'ian v ardatovskikh votchinakh Golitsynykh v kontse XVIII-seredine XIX v." In *Ezhegodnik po agrarnoi istorii vostochnoi Evropy*, edited by V. K. Iatsunskii, 363–78. Riga, 1963.

Latkin, V. N. *Zakonodatel'nye komissii v Rossii v XVIII stoletii*. Vol. 1. St. Petersburg: L. F. Panteleev, 1897.

Lebedev, V. *Bulavinskoe vosstanie (1707–1708)*. Moscow: Prosveshchenie, 1967.

———. "Krest'ianskoe dvizhenie v metropolii v gody Bulavinskogo vosstaniia." In *Krest'ianskie i natsional'nye dvizheniia nakanune obrazovaniia Rossiiskoi Imperii. Bulavinskoe vosstanie (1707–1708 gg.)*, edited by I. I. Kirievskii, 60–67. Moscow: Izd-vo Vsesoiuznogo ob-va polikatorzhan i ssyl'no-poselentsev, 1935.

Lentin, Antony. "A la recherche du Prince méconnu: M. M. Shcherbatov (1733–1790) and his critical reception across two centuries." *Canadian-American Slavic Studies* 28, no. 4 (Winter 1994): 361–98.

Leskov, N. "Blagoslovennyi brak." *Istoricheskii vestnik*, June 1885: 499–515.

Levin, Eve. *Sex and Society in the World of the Orthodox Slavs, 900–1700*. Ithaca, NY: Cornell University Press, 1989.

Litvak, K. V. "Perepis' naseleniia 1897 goda o krest'ianstve Rossii (Istochnikovedcheskii aspekt)." *Istoriia SSSR*, no. 1 (1990): 118–26.

Liubavskii, M. K. *Obrazovanie osnovnoi gosudarstvennoi territorii velikorusskoi narodnosti. Zaselenie i ob "edinenie Tsentra.* Leningrad: AN SSSR, 1929.

Liubopytnyi, Pavel. "Istoricheskii slovar'starovercheskoi tserkvi." *Chteniia v Imperatorskom Obshchestve istorii i drevnostei rossiiskikh*, no. 1 (1863): 67–176.

———. "Katalog ili Biblioteka starovercheskoi tserkvi." *Chteniia v Imperatorskom Obshchestve istorii i drevnostei rossiiskikh*, no. 1 (1863): 1–66.

Mainov, Vladimir. *Poezdka v Obonezh'e i Korelu.* St. Petersburg: Tip. V. Demakova, 1874.

———. "Skopcheskii eresiarkh Kondratii Selivanov (ssylka ego v Spaso-Evfimiev monastyr'." *Istoricheskii vestnik*, no. 4 (1880): 755–78.

———. "Zhivye pokoiniki." *Istoricheskii vestnik*, no. 12 (1881): 747–72.

Makarii (Bulgakov), archimandrite. *Istorii nizhegorodskoi ierarkhii, soderzhashchaia v sebe skazanie o nizhegorodskikh ierarkhakh s 1672 po 1850 goda.* St. Petersburg: N. G. Ovsiannikov, 1857.

———. *Istoriia russkogo raskola, izvestnogo pod imenem Staroobriadstva.* St. Petersburg: Tip. Koroleva i komp., 1855.

Mal'tsev, A. I. "Maloizvestnyi istochnik po istorii staroobriadtsev spasova soglassia." In *Staroobriadchestvo: istoriia i sovremennost', mestnye traditsii, russkie i zarubezhnye sviazi*, edited by R. P. Matveeva, pp. 307–9. Ulan-Ude: BNTs SO RAN, 2001.

———. *Staroobriadcheskie bespopovskie soglasiia v XVIII-nachale XIX v.* Novosibirsk: Sova, 2006.

———. *Starovery-stranniki v XVIII-pervoi polovine XIX v.* Novosibirsk: Nauka, 1996.

Malygin, I. P. "Materialy po osmotru zimovok na lesnykh promyslakh v Vetluzhskom uezde." *Vrachebnyi sanitarnyi obzor Kostromskoi gubernii*, no. 3 (1907): 105–15.

Man'kov, A. G. *Razvitie krepostnogo prava v Rossii vo vtoroi polovine XVII veka.* Moscow-Leningrad: AN SSSR, 1962.

Marsden, Thomas. *The Crisis of Religious Toleration in Imperial Russia. Bibikov's System for the Old Believers, 1841–1855.* Oxford: Oxford University Press, 2015.

Materialy dlia statistiki Rossii, sobiraemye po vedomstvu gosudarstvennykh imushchestv. Issue 3. St. Petersburg: 1861.

Mel'nikov, P. I. "Pis'ma o raskole." In *Sobranie sochinenii*, vol. 8, edited by P. I. Mel'nikov, pp. 3–62. Moscow: Pravda, 1976.

———. "Schislenie raskol'nikov." In *Polnoe sobranie sochinenii*, 2nd ed., edited by P. I. Mel'nikov, pp. 384–409. St. Petersburg: A. F. Marks, 1909.

———. *V lesakh.* Moscow: Khudozhestvennaia literatura, 1956.

Melton, Edgar. "Household Economies and Communal Conflicts on a Russian Serf Estate, 1800–1817." *Journal of Social History*, Spring 1993: 559–85.

Michels, Georg B. *At War with the Church: Religious Dissent in Seventeenth-Century Russia.* Stanford, CA: Stanford University Press, 1999.

Mironov, Boris. *Blagosostoianie naseleniia i revoliutsii v Imperskoi Rossii: XVIII-nachalo XX Veka.* Moscow: Novyi Khronograf, 2010.

———. "Consequences of the Price Revolution in Eighteenth-Century Russia." *Economic History Review* 49, no. 3 (1992): 457–78.

———. "Ispovednyi i metricheskii uchet v imperskoi Rossii." In *Materialy tserkovno-prikhodskogo ucheta naseleniia kak istoriko-demograficheskii istochnik: sbornik statei*, 8–47. Barnaul: Izd-vo Altaiskogo gosudarstvennogo universiteta, 2007.

————. "'Revoloiutsiia tsen' v Rossii v XVIII v." *Voprosy istorii*, no. 11 (1971): 49–61.

————. *Sotsial'naia istoriia Rossii perioda imperii (XVIII-nachalo XX v.). Genzis lichnosti, demokraticheskoi sem'i, grazhdanskogo obshchestva i pravovogo gosudarstva.* 2nd ed. Vols. 1–2. St. Petersburg: Dmitrii Bulanin, 2000.

————. "Traditsionnoe demograficheskoe povedenie krest'ian v XIX-nachale XX v." In *Brachnost', rozhdaemost', smertnost' v Rossii i v SSSR: sbonik statei,* edited by A. G. Vishnevskii, pp. 83–104. Moscow: Statistika, 1977.

Moon, David. *The Russian Peasantry 1699–1930: The World the Peasants Made.* London: Longman, 1999.

Morokhin, Aleksei. *Arkhiepiskop Nizhegorodskii i Alatyrskii Pitirim. Tserkovnyi deiatel' epokhi Peremen.* Nizhnii Novgorod: Knigi, 2009.

Morokhin, Nikolai. *Po reke Vetluge.* Nizhnii Novgorod: Litera, 2012.

Mukhina, Z. Z. "Starye devy v russkoi krest'ianskoi srede (vtoraia polovina XIX-nachalo XX v." *Zhenshchina v rossiiskom obshchestve,* no. 4 (2013): 50–57.

Murtaeva, Iu. V. "Staroobriadtsy Spasova soglasiia Kovrovskogo uezda (seredina XIX v.–1917 g.). In *Provintsial'nyi gorod v istorii Rossii: XX Rozhdestvenskii sbornik,* pp. 113–17. Shuia: PoliTsentr, 2013.

Nagradov, I. S. *Raskolot' "raskol": Gosudarstvennaia konfessional'naia politika i ee vliianie na razvitie staroobriadchestva vo II chetverti XIX–I chetverti XX vv. (na materialakh Kostromskoi i Iaroslavskoi gubernii).* Kostroma: Kostromizdat, 2013.

————. "Urenskii miatezhnyi dukh: dva vosstaniia kostromskikh krest'ian-staroobriadtsev." In *Staroobriadchestvo: istoriia, kul'tura, sovremennost'. Materialy,* vol. 1, edited by V. I. Osipov, pp. 207–15. Moscow: Tsentr istorii i kul'tury staroobriadchestva, 2011.

Nasonov, A. N. "Iz istorii krepostnoi votchiny XIX veka v Rossii." *Izvestiia AN SSS,* ser. 6, nos. 7–8 (1926): 499–526.

————. "Khoziaistvo krupnoi votiny nakanune osvobozhdeniia krest'ian v Rossii." *Izvestiia AN SSSR. Otdelenie gumanitarnykh nauk,* ser. 7, nos. 4–7 (1928): 343–74.

Neelov, N. N. "Sledstvennaia kommissiia o zloupotrebleniiakh Penzenskoi voevody Zhukova (1752–1756 gg.)." *ChOIDR,* no. 1 (1888): 1–40.

Nil'skii, I. *Semeinaia zhizn' v russkom raskole. Istoricheskii ocherk raskol'nicheskogo ucheniia o brake.* Vols. 1–2. St. Petersburg: Tip. Departamenta udelov, 1869.

Novosel'skii, A. A. *Votchinik i ego khoziaistvo v XVII veke.* Moscow-Leningrad: Gos. Izd-vo, 1929.

"O merakh, predpriniatykh v 50-60 godakh nastoiashchego stoletiia dlia oslableniia raskola v Nizhegorodskoi eparkhh." *Nizhergorodskie eparkhal'nye vedomosti,* no. 1 (1896), Chast' neofitsial'naia: 22–38; no. 2 (1896): 70–83; no. 3 (1896): 110–29; no. 4 (1896): 155–68; no. 5 (1896): 217–26.

Orlov-Davydov, Vladimir. *Biograficheskii ocherk grafa Vladimira Grigor'evicha Orlova.* St. Petersburg: Tip. Imperatorskoi Akademii nauk, 1878.

Owen, Thomas C. "A Standard Ruble of Account for Russian Business History, 1769–1914: A Note." *Journal of Economic History* 49, no. 3 (1989): 699–706.

Paert, Irina. *Old Believers, Religious Dissent and Gender in Russia, 1760–1850.* Manchester: Manchester University Press, 2003.

————. "Regulating Old Believer Marriage: Ritual, Legality, and Conversion in Nicholas I's Russia." *Slavic Review* 63, no. 3 (Autumn 2004): 555–76.

————. "'Two or Twenty Million?' The Languages of Official Statistics and Religious Dissent in Imperial Russia." *Ab Imperio* 7, no. 3 (2006): 75–98.

Pamiatnaia kniga dlia Kostromskoi eparkhii. Kostroma: Gubernskaia tip., 1868.

Pavel, arkhimandrit. "Kratkie izvestiia o sushchestvuiushchikh v raskole sektakh." *Bratskoe slovo*, no. 9 (1885): 555–76.

———. *Nikol'skogo edinovercheskogo monastyria inoka Pavla, izvestnym po imenem Prusskom, Vospominaniia i besedy so glagolemom staroobriadchestve*. Moscow: Izdanie N. M. Alasina, 1868.

———. "O imenuemoi glukhoi netovshchine, ili Spasovom soglasie." In *Sobranie sochinenii Nikol'skogo edinovercheskogo monastyria nastoiaelia Arkhimandrita Pavla*, 4th ed., pp. 29–33. Moscow: Synodal'naia Tip., 1883.

———. "Razgovor o vere s imenuemymi po Spasovu soglasiiu, ili Otritsantsami." In *Sobranie sochinenii Nikol'skogo edinovercheskogo monastyria nastoiaelia Arkhimandrita Pavla*, 4th ed., pp. 34–36. Moscow: Synodal'naia Tip., 1883.

Pestov, M.P. "Opisanie ardatovskogo uezda nizhegorodskoi gubernii." In *Nizhegorodskii sbornik*, vol. 2, pp. 105–87. Nizhnii Novgorod: Tip. Nizhegorodskogo Gubernskogo Pravleniia, 1869.

Petrikeev, D. I. *Krupnoe krepostnoe khoziaistvo XVII v. Po materialam votchiny boiarina B. I. Morozova*. Leningrad: Nauka, 1967.

Petrovskaia, I. F. "Nakazy votchinnym prikazchikam pervoi chetverty XVIII veka." In *Istoricheskii arkhiv*, vol. 8, pp. 221–68. Moscow: AN SSSR, 1953.

Petrushevskii, A. F. *Generalisimus Kniaz' Suvorov*. Vol. 1. St. Petersburg: Tip. M. M. Stasulevicha, 1884.

Platonov, S. F. *Ocherki po istorii smuty v Moskovskom Gosudarstve XVI–XVII vv*. 3rd ed. St. Petersburg: Ia. Bashmakov, 1910.

Pochinskaia, I. V. "O bytovanii rodoslovnii Filippovskogo soglasiia na Viatke." In *Obshchestvennaia mysl' i traditsii russkoi dukhovnoi kul'tury v istoricheskikh i literaturnykh pamiatnikakh XVI-XX vv*, edited by E. K. Romodanovskaia, pp. 424–30. Novosibirsk: SO RAN, 2005.

Pod"iapol'skaia, E. P. *Vosstanie Bulavina*. Moscow: AN SSSR, 1962.

"Pokhishchenie nevest." *Nizhegorodskie gubernskie vedomosti*, no. 14 (April 5, 1845).

Polushkin, L. P. *Briat'ia Orlovy*. Moscow: TERRA-Kniznyi klub, 2003.

Posokha, I. E. "Svadevnyi obriad." In *Taditsionnaia kul'tura Gorokhovetskogo kraia. Ekspeditsionnye, arkhivnye, analiticheskie materialy*, vol. 1, edited by V. E. Dobrovol'skaia and A. S. Kargin, pp. 133–54. Moscow: Gos. Respublikanskii tsentr russkogo fol'klor, 2004.

Preobrazhenskii, A. "Neizvestnyi avtograf sibirskogo letopistsa Savvy Esipova." *Sovetskie arkhivy*, no. 2 (1983): pp. 63–65.

"Prisoedinenie iz raskola chrez kreshcheniia i novoe soglasie v raskole 'nekreshchenykh'." *Tserkovnye vedomosti*, no. 32 (1891): pp. 1082–83.

Prokof'eva, L. S. *Krest'ianskaia obshchina v Rossii vo vtoroi polovine XVII–pervoi polovine XIX v. (na materialakh votchin Sheremetevykh)*. Leningrad: Nauka, 1981.

Prokof'eva, N. V., and I. S. Nagradov. "Istoriia staroobriadchestva v Verkhnem Povolzh'e v seredine XVIII–nachale XX vekov." In *Staroobriadtsy Verkhnevolzh'ia: proshloe, nastoiashchee, budushchee*, edited by I. V. Pozdeeva, pp. 47–136. Kostroma: 2005.

Pushkareva, N. L. *Chastnaia zhizn' russkoi zhenshchiny: nevesta, zhena, liubovnitsa (X-nachalo XIX v.)*. Moscow: Ladomir, 1997.

Pyzhikov, A. V. *Grani russkogo raskola. Zametki o nashei istorii ot XVII veka do 1917 goda*. Moscow: Drevlekhranilishche, 2013.

Rediger, A. *Komplektovanie i ustroistvo vooruzhennoi sily*. 3rd ed. St. Petersburg: Voennaia tip., 1900.

Riazanovskii, F. A. *Krest'iane Galichskoi votchiny Mesherinovykh v XVII–pervoi polovine XVIII Veka*. Galich: Izd-vo Galichskogo otd-niia Kostromskogo nauch. ob-va, 1927.

Rogers, Douglas. *The Old Faith and the Russian Land: A Historical Ethnography of Ethics in the Urals*. Ithaca, NY: Cornell University Press, 2009.

Rubinshtein, N. L. *Sel'skoe khoziaistvo Rossii vo vtoroi polovine XVIII v. (istoriko-ekonomicheskii ocherk)*. Moscow: Gos. Izdat-vo politicheskoi literatury, 1957.

Rumiantseva, V. S. *Narodnoe antitserkovnoe dvizhenie v Rossii v XVII veke*. Moscow: Nauka, 1986.

Russkie vedomosti, no. 25, January 31, 1875.

Russkii biograficheskii slovar'. 25 volumes. St. Petersburg: various publishers, 1896–1913.

Rybkin, I. *Generalissimus Suvorov. Zhizn' ego v svoikh votchinakh i khoziaistvennaia deiatel'nost'*. Moscow: Patriot, 1993.

Ryzhkov, Vladimir. "Domostroitel'stvo' i politika: Mesto predstavlenii o pravil'nom ustroistve sel'skogo pomest'ia v sisteme obshchestvenno-politicheskikh vzgliadov M. M. Shcherbatova i N. M. Karamzina." In *Dvorianstvo, vlast' i obshchestvo v provintsial'noi Rossii XVIII veka*, edited by O. E. Glagoleva, and I. Shirle, pp. 327–74. Moscow: Novoe Literaturnoe Obozrenie, 2012.

Safonov, A. A. "Iz istorii podgotovki Pervoi vseobshchei perepisi naseleniia Rossiiskoi Imperii 1897 g." *Dokument. Arkhiv. Istoriia. Sovremennost'*. no. 1 (2001): 211–31.

Semevskii, V. I. *Krest'iane v tsarstvovanie Imperatritsy Ekateriny II*. 2nd ed. Vols. 1–2. St. Petersburg: Tip. M. M. Stasiulevicha, 1903.

———. "Sel'skii sviashchennik vo vtoroi polovine XVIII veka." *Russkaia starina*, August 1877: 501–38.

Shanin, Teodor. *The Awkward Class: Political Sociology of Peasantry in a Developing Society. Russia 1910–1925*. Oxford: Clarendon Press, 1972.

Shchepetov, K. N. *Krepostnoe pravo v votchinakh Sheremetevykh*. Moscow: Izd. Dvortsa-muzeia, 1947.

———. "Sel'skoe khoziaistvo v votchine Iosifo-Volokolamskogo monastyria v kontse XVI veka." *Istoricheskie zapiski*, no. 18 (1946): 92–147.

Shcherbinin, P. P. *Voennyi factor v povsednevnoi zhizni russkoi zhenshchiny v XVIII-nachale XX v*. Tambov: Tambovskii gosudarstvennyi universitet, 2004.

Shul'gin, V. S. "'Kapitonovshchina' i ee mesto v raskole XVII v." *Istoriia SSSR*, no. 4 (1969): 130–39.

Shumikhin, Sergei. "Marginal s dvoinym dnom (skrytyi kalambur v poslanii Pushkina Princesse Nocturne)." *Nashe Nasledie*. Accessed September 2013. http://www.nasledie-rus/red_port/00900.php.

Sivkov, K. V. *Ocherki po istorii krepostnogo khoziaistva i krest'ianskogo dvizheniia v pervoi polovine XIX veka*. Moscow: Izd-vo AN SSSR, 1951.

Slovar' geograficheskii Rossiiskogo gosudarstva, part 2. Moscow: Universitetskaia tip., 1804.

Smilianskaia, E. B. *Dvorianskoe gnezdo serediny XVIII veka. Timofei Tekut'ev i ego "Instruktsiia o domashnikh poriadkakh."* Moscow: Nauka, 1998.

Smirnov, P. S. *Istoriia russkogo raskola staroobriadstva*. 2nd ed. St. Petersburg: Tip. Glavnogo Upravleniia Udelov, 1895.

———. "Proiskhozhdenie samoistrebleniia v russkom raskole." *Khristianskoe chtenie*, nos. 5–6 (1895): 617–35.

———. *Sporyi i razdeleniia v russkom raskole v pervoi chetverti XVIII veke.* St. Petersburg: Tip. M. Meruksheva, 1909.

———. *Vnutrennie voprosy v raskole v XVII veke.* St. Petersburg: Pechatnia S. P. Iakovleva, 1898.

Smith, Alison K. "Sustenance and the Household Economy in Two Kostroma Serf Villages, 1836–1852." *Russian History/Histoire Russe* 35, nos. 1–2 (Spring–Summer 2008): 165–79.

Sokolovskaia, M. L. "Krest'ianskii mir kak osnova formirovaniia vygovskogo obshchezhitel'stva." In *Staroobiaidchestvo v Rossii*, edited by E. M. Iukhimenko, pp. 269–79. Moscow: Iazyki russkoi kul'tury, 1999.

Solov'ev, S. M. *Istoriia Rossii s drevneishikh vremen.* 15 vols. Moscow: Izd-vo Sotsial'no-ekonomicheskoi literatury, 1959–66.

Sretenskii, L. V. "Pomeshchich'ia instruktsiia vtoroi poloviny XVIII veka." *Kraevedcheskie zapiski [Gosudarstvennogo Iaroslavsko-Rostovskogo istoriko-arkhitekturnogo i khudozhestvennogo muzeia-zapovednika]*, no 4 (1960): 197–211.

Staritsyn, A. N. "Starovercheskie poseleniia Kargopol'ia kontsa XVII–nachale XVIII v." In *Istoriko-kul'turnyi landshaft Severo-Zapada*, edited by V. E. Grusman and E. N. Kalshchikov, pp. 160–67. St. Petersburg.: Evropeisksii Dom, 2011.

Staroobriadchestvo. Litsa, sobytiia, predmety i simvoly: Opyt entsiklopedicheskogo slovaria. Moscow: Tserkov', 1996.

Strel'bitskii, I. *Istoriia russkogo raskola, izvestnogo pod imenem staroobriadchestva.* 3rd ed. Odessa: Tip. E. I. Fesenko, 1898.

Taseva, Galina. "Organizatsiia upravleniia krupnoi pomeshchich'ei votchiny i votchinnyi rezhim v kontse XVIII–pervoi polovine XIX vv. Po materialam votchinnogo arkhiva (instruktsiia m ulozheniiu Orlovykh-Davydovykh)." *Godishnik na Sofiiskiia universitet "Kliment Okhridski"* 76 (1973): 305–32.

Tatishchev, V. N. *Izbrannye proizvedeniia.* Leningrad: Nauka, 1979.

Thompson, E. P. "The Moral Economy of the English Crowd in the Eighteenth Century," *Past and Present* 50 (Feb. 1971), pp. 76–136.

———. "The Moral Economy Reviewed," in E. P. Thompson, *Customs in Common* (Pontypool: Merlin Press, 1991), pp. 259–351.

Tikhonov, Iu. A. "Dogovor (Kontrakt) 1740 goda M. G. Golovina s vybornymi krest'ianami ob upravlenii imi imeniem v sele Kimry s derevniami." *Otechestvennaia istoriia*, no. 3 (2003): 146–51.

———. *Dvorianskaia usad'ba i krest'ianskii dvor v Rossii XVII–XVIII vv.: sosushchestvovanie i protivosostoianie.* Moscow–St. Petersburg: Letnii sad, 2005.

Titov, A. A. *Kurakovshchina. Istoriko-etnograficheskii ocherk.* Iaroslavl': Tip. Gubernskogo Pravleniia, 1886.

———. *S. Voshchazhnikovo i voshchazhnikovskaia votchina v starnnom Zapurskom stanu Rostovskogo uezda.* Iaroslavl': Tipolit. Gub. zemsk. upravy, 1903.

Tol'ts, M. "Brachnost' naseleniia Rossii v kontse XIX-nachale XX v." In *Brachnost', rozhdaemost', smertnost' v Rossii i v SSSR: sbornik statei*, edited by A. G. Vishnevskii, pp. 138–53. Moscow: Statistika, 1977.

Topograficheskie izvestiia sluzhashchiia dlia polnogo geograficheskogo opisaniia Rossiiskoi Imperii. Vol. 1, part 2, *Moskovskoi gubernii. Pereslavskaia Zaleskogo, Volodimirskaia, Suzdal'skaia, Iur'evskaia Pol'skogo, Pereslavskaia Riazanskogo provintsii i chast' Kaluzhskoi provintsii.* St. Petersburg: Imperatorskaia Akdademiia Nauk, 1772.

Tsvetkov, M. A. "Geografiia vnutrennikh lesnykh rynkov v Evropeiskoi Rossii vo vtoroi polovine XIX–nachale XX v." In *Istoricheskaia geografiia*, edited by V. K. Iatsunskii, pp. 91–109. Moscow: Gos. Izd-vo geograficheskoi literatury, 1960.

Tul'tseva, L. A. "Chernichki." *Nauka i zhizn'*, no. 11 (1970): 80–82.

Usov, P. "Pavel Ivanovich Mel'nikov, ego zhizn' i literaturnnaia deiatel'nost'." In *Pol'noe sobranie sochinenii P. I. Mel'nikova (Andreia Pecherskogo)*, vol. 1, pp. 1–152. St. Petersburg–Moscow: M. O. Vol'f, 1897.

Varadinov, N. *Istoriia Ministerstva Vnutrennikh Del*. Book 8, dopolnitel'naia, *Istoriia rasporiazhenii po raskolu*. St. Petersburg: Tip. Vtorogo Otdeleniia, 1863.

Veselovskii, K. "Svadebnye obriady v Mordvinovskoi volosti Gorokhovetskogo uezda." *Trudy Vladimirskogo gubernskogo statisticheskogo komiteta*, no. 3 (1864): 17–40.

Vishniakov, A. "Novozheny i brakobortsy. (Ocherki istorii raskol'nich'ego braka)." *Nevskii sbornik*. Vol. 1. St. Petersburg: 1867.

Vozdvizhenskii, Tikhon. *Istoricheskoe obozrenie Riazanskoi ierarkhii*. Moscow: Tip. S. Selivanovskogo, 1820.

"Vtoraia poezdka missionera-sleptsa Alekseia Egorovicha Shashina po raskol'nicheskym seleniiam Kostromskoi eparkhii." *Kostromskie eparkhial'nyie vedomosti*, no. 24 (1894): pp. 557–58.

Waldron, Peter. "Religious Reform after 1905: Old Believers and the Orthodox Church." *Oxford Slavonic Papers* 20 (n.s.) (1987): 110–39.

Wirtschafter, Elise Kimerling. *From Serf to Russian Soldier*. Princeton, NJ: Princeton University Press, 1990.

Worobec, Christine. *Peasant Russia. Family and Community in the Post-Emancipation Period*. Princeton, NJ: Princeton University Press, 1991.

Zabelin, I. E. "Bol'shoi boiarin v svoem votchnnom khoziaistve (XVII vek)." *Vestnik Evropy*, no. 1 (1871): 5–49; no. 2 (1871): 465–514.

Zaozerskaia, E. I. "Pomeshchik Zhukov i ego khoziaistvo." In *Dvorianstvo i krepostnoi stroi Rossii XVI-XVIII vv*, edited by A. A. Novosel'skii and N. I. Pavlenko, pp. 213–26. Moscow: Nauka, 1975.

Zarubin, P. "Zametki o Varnavinskom uezde." *Russkii vestnik*, October 1856: 392–422.

Zenkovsky, Sergey. *Russkoe staroobriadchestvo. Dukhovnye dvizheniia semnadtsatogo veka*. München: Wilhelm Fink Verlag, 1970.

Zhuravlev, A. I. *Polnoe istoricheskoe izvestie o drevnikh strigol'nikakh i novykh raskol'nikakh, tak nazyvaemykh staroobriadstakh*. Moscow: Tip. F. K. Ioganson, 1890.

Zimin, V.I., and A. S. Spirin. *Poslovitsy i pogovorki russkogo naroda. Ob"iasnitel'nyi slovar'*. Moscow: Siuita, 1996.

Ziuzin, V., I. Tiurin. *Steksovo: svedeniia iz istorii sela*. Arzamas: Arzamaskomplektavtomatika, 1999.

Zvezdin, A. I. "K 50 letiiu ob"iavleniia manifesta 19 fevralia 1861 goda v Nizhegorodskoi gubernii." *Deistviia Nikzhegorodskoi Gubernskoi Uchenoi Arkhivnoi Komissii* 10 (1912): 61–70.

INDEX

John Bushnell is Professor of History
at Northwestern University.

www.ingramcontent.com/pod-product-compliance
Lightning Source LLC
Chambersburg PA
CBHW030835300326
41935CB00036B/112